Underdevelopment
and Social Movements
in Atlantic Canada

Underdevelopment and Social Movements in Atlantic Canada

Edited by
Robert J. Brym
and
R. James Sacouman

New Hogtown Press
Toronto

Canadian Cataloguing in Publication Data

Main entry under title:

Underdevelopment and social movements in Atlantic Canada

ISBN 0-919940-13-7 bd.   ISBN 0-919940-14-5 pa.

1. Social movements - Atlantic Provinces -Addresses,
essays, lectures.* 2. Atlantic Provinces - Economic
conditions - Addresses, essays, lectures.* 3.
Atlantic Provinces - Social conditions - Addresses,
essays, lectures.* I. Brym, Robert J., 1951- II. Sacouman, R. James, 1948-

HN110.A8U54   301.24'2'09715   C79-094752-8

Typeset by Missy Powell and Gus Richardson; tables by Shirley Tillotson and other members of the Workers' Union of Dumont Press Graphix, Kitchener, Ontario. The production collective of New Hogtown Press would like to thank the Workers' Union of Dumont Press Graphix for their patience, good humour, and generosity in the face of our many requests.

New Hogtown Press receives financial assistance from the Ontario Arts Council.

Contents

The Region

Nova Scotia

Newfoundland

Acknowledgements

The contributors to this volume are deeply indebted to the members of the production collective at New Hogtown Press—especially to our editors at the press—Missy Powell and Gus Richardson—for the firm and able assistance needed to bring this project to fruition.

Acknowledgement is made to the editors of the *Canadian Journal of Sociology* for permission to reprint R. James Sacouman, 'The differing origins, organisation, and impact of Maritime and Prairie co-operative movements to 1940,' and Robert J. Brym and Barbara Neis, 'Regional factors in the formation of the Fishermen's Protective Union of Newfoundland;' to the editors of *Labour/Le Travailleur* for permission to reprint David Frank and Nolan Reilly, 'The emergence of the socialist movement in the Maritimes, 1899-1916;' to the editors of *Acadiensis* for permission to reprint a revised version of R. James Sacouman, 'Underdevelopment and the structural origins of Antigonish Movement co-operatives in eastern Nova Scotia.' Figure 10-3 is taken from a poster from the national tour of the stage play *What's That Got To Do with the Price of Fish?* reprinted by permission of the Mummers Troupe of Newfoundland

Introduction

Robert J. Brym and R. James Sacouman

This collection of essays deals with some of the organised responses of wage labourers and petty primary producers in twentieth century Atlantic Canada to the underdevelopment of their region. Many will no doubt regard the topic as trivial, our treatment of it controversial. Trivial because it is frequently assumed—and, as we seek to demonstrate, wrongly so—that social movements in Atlantic Canada have been virtually nonexistent in the course of this century. Controversial, because the authors of these essays take for granted a proposition that is far from widely accepted: fundamentally, underdevelopment in Atlantic Canada is a result neither of the natural or human resource deficiencies of the region, nor of the unfair treatment accorded the easternmost provinces by the more powerful central and western ones, but of capitalist development itself.

The key word in the preceding sentence is 'fundamentally,' for accepted explanations of Atlantic regional underdevelopment *do* contain elements of truth. It is just that they do not allow us to approach the whole truth. Undeniably, fish stocks off Newfoundland and coal reserves under the ocean floor off Cape Breton are now depleted; some potential business leaders have been lost to the area in their search for better opportunities elsewhere; and federal policy has on the whole served to undermine the productive capacity of the region. But are these *causes* of underdevelopment, as we are often told, or *consequences* of some more basic set of socio-economic processes? There is, we suggest, good reason to endorse the latter interpretation.

Those who speak of the region's 'unfortunate lack of natural resources'[1] as the chief cause of its failure to industrialise overlook some critically important facts. In the first couple of decades after Confederation the Maritimes contained a disproportionately high concentration of the new Dominion's productive capacity, and its manufacturing establishments were growing more quickly than those elsewhere in the country. In 1885 less than 20% of Canada's population lived in Nova Scotia, New Brunswick, and Prince Edward Island, but these provinces contained eight of the country's twenty-three cotton mills, three of five sugar refineries, two of seven rope factories, one of three glass works, six of twelve rolling mills, and both steel mills. Nova Scotian industrial output increased 15% more than Ontario's or Quebec's between 1880 and 1890; Saint John, New Brunswick's, 27% more than Hamilton, Ontario's. It was widely believed that Nova Scotia would become the industrial heartland of the country, and given its vast reserves of coal and iron, this belief was hardly chimerical.[2] Newfoundland, meanwhile, could boast of having ready access to the richest fishing grounds in the world and of being the world's largest exporter of salt cod;[3] later it was to discover reserves of iron and sources of hydro-electric power sufficient to supply a modern, industrialised country with a population numbering in the tens of millions. Neither Newfoundland nor the Maritimes were, then, lacking in the resources necessary for industrial advance. However, they did decline or, more accurately, plummet into economic stagnation, and now they do lack some natural resources that were formerly in good supply. Why? Because Atlantic Canada was underdeveloped—we use the word here as a verb, not an adjective—in the course of this century.

Did underdevelopment occur as a result of Atlantic Canadians' lack of talent to use their resources efficiently? Was the region deficient in what some contemporary social scientists refer to as 'entrepreneurial skill'?[4] Hardly. Much of the vibrant economy that existed in 1890 was controlled by local businessmen, and even if such names as Kenny, Gibson, Stairs, and Fraser have long been forgotten, those of Aitken and Irving, Cunard and McCain, Crosbie and Stirling, have not: there are, even today, many highly successful businessmen in the region. This does not of course detract much from the apparent *overall* tendency for potential entrepreneurs to leave the east coast, but we would do well to remember what introductory demography textbooks teach us in this regard: migration is a reaction to lack of opportunity, not a reason for it.[5] Our search for an explanation cannot then end here.

'The history of Canada since Confederation—the outcome of a commercio-political conspiracy—has been a history of heartless robbery of both the people of the Maritimes and of the Prairie Sections of Canada by the politically and financially stronger central Provinces.' Thus wrote E. A. Partridge, Prairie populist, in 1925. The argument that 'heartless robbery' by the central provinces is the basic reason for Atlantic regional underdevelopment did not, however, expire with Partridge; although its tone has frequently been tempered by academic propriety, it may even be said to have experienced something of a revival in the past decade or so.

Now, there can be little doubt that, overall, federal policy *has* helped sap the lifeblood out of the Atlantic region's economy. For example, in the early years of Confederation, freight rates in the Maritimes were kept well below those of central and western Canada by the main regional carrier, the Inter-colonial, and this greatly aided local exporters who could ship their goods to more populous centres very cheaply indeed. However, when the regulation of freight rates was eventually centralised nationally, the Board of Railway Commissioners, bowing to western pressure, boosted the Maritime rates to such a degree that the competitive advantage of local exporters was undercut. This was directly, if only partly, responsible for the decline of Maritime manufacturing industry in the twentieth century.[6] Nor, to provide a less obvious illustration, have those federal policies apparently aimed at *correcting* 'regional imbalances' had a very different net effect. Thus, the Department of Regional Economic Expansion (DREE) has provided corporations with billions of dollars in direct and indirect incentives to set up shop in Atlantic Canada. But most of these industries are not locally controlled, so that capital drain from the region has thereby been enhanced; many are capital-intensive operations and therefore create relatively few jobs; most continue operations only to the degree that incentives continue to be offered, wage levels remain comparatively low, and workers stay relatively unorganised. For these reasons, it may be said without fear of exaggeration that DREE programmes have benefitted mainly the *owners* of industry and have actually *institutionalised* the conditions of Atlantic regional underdevelopment.[7]

These and other examples might tell us a good deal about *how* Atlantic regional underdevelopment has occurred. But, beyond some rather primitive analytical statements (e.g., people are generally motivated by self-interest so that those with more power will, in their search for gain, generally come to ill-use the less powerful), they provide us with few insights into the question of *why* it has happened. Stated otherwise, a fully adequate explanation of regional underdevelopment ought to tell us why capitalist dynamics distribute power in certain, irregular patterns; we have to know whence power derives and how it is produced before we can analyse the consequences of its uneven distribution.

It is our opinion that Marxist theory provides us with a penetrating analysis of this question—an analysis which, in cursory form, might be presented as follows: Under capitalism, power is distributed fundamentally in accordance with the relationship of persons to society's means of production. Those who control productive resources have more power than those who are compelled to sell their labour on the market for wages. This is evident, first and foremost, in the capacity of the controllers to appropriate that portion of value added in the production process not needed to cover the costs of raw materials, depreciation, and workers' subsistence. This 'surplus value,' embodied in the commodities produced by workers, is transformed into profit if and when the commodities are sold. Entrepreneurs who make profits and reinvest them in technological improvements that increase the efficiency, and therefore the profitability, of their enterprises, survive and prosper; entrepreneurs who fail to do so so are driven out of business by their more efficient competitors. In this manner, control over markets, and over society's productive apparatus, becomes increasingly concentrated in the hands of a small class of businessmen.

None of this would present much of a problem for members of this small class were it not for the fact that they face a growing *disincentive* to reinvest profits. Since technological improvements increase the profitability of enterprises, investment in labour tends to decline over time in relation to investment in capital equipment. But since potential profits ultimately derive from the labour power expended in production, potential profits must also decline over time. There is, in short, a tendency for the capitalist machine to grind to a halt because of the tendency of the rate of profit to fall.

It is significant, however, that certain countertendencies can buoy up the rate of profit, thus enabling capitalism to endure and expand. Wages may be decreased, labour hours extended, or, more commonly, new markets, sources of cheap labour, and sources of cheap raw materials may be discovered or created. These last-named items are precisely those provided by underdeveloped regions. The economies of underdeveloped regions depend upon the mere extraction of cheap natural resources and their subsequent export for further processing. They contain vast pools of surplus labour, maintained at subsistence levels, to be utilised, like any other commodity, as an export material when needed in times of economic expansion. They provide a ready market for the manufactured goods produced in more developed regions. Capitalism may well cause control over productive resources to become increasingly concentrated; but at the short end of the stick it creates underdevelopment in order to prevent the rate of profit from falling and thus to ensure capitalist growth.

It follows that class conflict will be much more variegated and complex in underdeveloped regions than in developed ones. In developed regions, the relationship between labour and capital defines the principal locus of class conflict. This relationship also exists in underdeveloped regions, but it is augmented by two other types of class relations which tend not to be present in developed regions. First, because underdeveloped regions specialise in the extraction of raw materials, they provide an arena for the appropriation of surplus value by large capitalists from semi-proletarianised petty primary producers. Second, as part of the production and reproduction of surplus labour pools within the region, capitalist underdevelopment maintains a significant proportion of primary producers in a nonmarket or subsistence form of production. The interrelationships between, and flux within, this variety of classes and class segments—on the one hand, large capitalists; on the other hand, wage labourers, semi-proletarianised petty primary producers, and independent, subsistence-level petty primary producers—is the principal basis for explaining lower-class social movements in Atlantic Canada. Capitalist underdevelopment not only results from capitalist development; it also produces complex variations in class structure that help explain the spatial and temporal distribution of lower class social movements in underdeveloped regions.

In Atlantic Canada, participants in some of these movements have sought to achieve political office, while participants in other (notably co-operative) movements have not found it necessary to seek formal political power in order to achieve their goals. Because many collective reactions to the underdevelopment of the region have not been formally political, and, even more important, because of sheer ignorance concerning the politics of the region, it has widely been assumed, especially by central Canadian scholars, that Atlantic Canadians are inherently conservative creatures, basically satisfied with their way of life. There is, however, much less truth in this argument than we are frequently led to believe. Atlantic Canadians *have* engaged in a wide variety of both formally political and nonpolitical movements to improve their lot; and if formally political attempts at improvement have not been as successful as in, say, the Canadian west, this is due less to any inherent conservatism than it is to the fact that the character of regional underdevelopment has, at least until recently, distributed political resources so unevenly as to militate against widespread success.

This is, at least, one synthesis that may reasonably be derived from the following essays; which is to say that, although no one author has developed this argument in its entirety, specific aspects of it are elaborated upon and given concrete grounding in each of the contributions to this volume. As the section headings and chapter titles suggest, we first seek to provide the reader with an understanding of the impact that capitalist underdevelopment has had on the class structure of Atlantic Canada, and of the resultant inter- and intra-regional variations in the growth of lower-class social movements. This is followed by a series of more specific case studies of Nova Scotia and Newfoundland.

We fully recognise that this collection displays a number of serious shortcomings. Little is said here specifically about New Brunswick, and next to nothing about Prince Edward Island. Industrial workers are given far less attention than petty primary producers, and the role of the state—in facilitating capital accumulation, controlling discontent and blocking its eruption, etc.—is too much ignored. Many of the essays ignore, or seriously play down, work done by women.

Nonetheless, if this volume is received in the spirit in which it was written—as a *first* step toward constructing a Marxist analysis of Atlantic Canada—we shall feel reasonably satisfied with our efforts. All the more so if this book begins to provide an informed, theoretical basis for practical political activity in the region.

NOTES

1. George Rawlyk, 'The Maritimes and the Canadian community,' *Regionalism in the Canadian community, 1867-1967*, ed. Mason Wade (Toronto, 1971), 100-116.
2. T. W. Acheson, 'The National Policy and the industrialization of the Maritimes, 1880-1910,' *Acadiensis*, I (1972), 3-4, 6.
3. David Alexander, 'Development and dependence in Newfoundland, 1880-1970,' *Acadiensis*, IV (1974), 14.
4. R. E. George, *A leader and a laggard: manufacturing industry in Nova Scotia, Quebec, and Ontario* (Toronto, 1970).
5. W. E. Kalbach and W. W. McVey, *The demographic bases of Canadian society* (Toronto, 1971), 82; cf. J. W. Grant, 'Population shifts in the Maritime provinces,' *Dalhousie Review*, XVII (1937-38), 282-94.
6. E. R. Forbes, 'Misguided symmetry: the destruction of regional transportation

policy for the Maritimes,' *Canada and the burden of unity*, ed. D. J. Bercuson (Toronto, 1977), 60-86.

7. Ralph Matthews, 'Canadian regional development strategy: a dependency theory perspective,' *Plan Canada*, XVII (1977), 131-44.

THE REGION

1 The Capitalist Underdevelopment of Atlantic Canada

Henry Veltmeyer

Few problems of Canadian society have resisted explanation or solution for as long as the relative underdevelopment and poverty of the Atlantic region. Reflected in chronically high levels of unemployment and net out-migration, a weak manufacturing sector, and substantially lower personal incomes per person—as compared to Canada as a whole—this problem once again is being pushed to the forefront of theoretical debate and political action by the latest crisis of capitalism in Canada.

Over the years, a number of economic and sociological theories of this regional underdevelopment have been advanced. Some have stressed factors internal to the region, such as failure of entrepreneurship or lack of achievement orientation.[1] Others point to historical conditions of institutional or political factors.[2] Still others see Atlantic Canada's relationship to central Canada as part of a global process of industrialisation based on 'forces of spatial concentration and diffusion.'[3] Finally, there are those theories that link underdevelopment to geographic factors and variable conditions of capital formation such as natural resources, labour quality and supply, and access to markets.[4] One such theory, in particular, has had a major impact on studies in the Canadian context: staple theory. According to this theory, development (in the form of 'multiplier-effects') is tied (in the form of 'backward linkages') to the production and export of staples based on a region's natural resources. Underdevelopment, as a corollary, is based on a failure to exploit a region's resources within limits established by geographic and technological factors.[5]

There is no need to dwell on the sad fate shared by these theories. As observed in a recent study by the Economic Council of Canada not one of them has ever provided anything but a very partial explanation of regional underdevelopment. 'No single economic theory,' the authors of this study conclude, 'can explain regional disparities.'[6] What the authors fail to establish, however, is the basis of this theoretical failure. And for good reason: they share the same misplaced assumptions about the conditions that produce underdevelopment. Shifting loosely among five of the identified theories, the authors examine the variable relations of a given system of economic conditions, and measure the effect of each isolated factor, without at any point coming close to an understanding of the underlying structure of underdevelopment. Ignoring Marx's theory of capitalist development (the one general theory that even raises questions about this structure), the authors of the Economic Council study, like their many predecessors and counterparts, adopt an approach that prevents them from linking the social and economic conditions of underdevelopment to the underlying structures that produced—and continues to reproduce—them.

It is in response to this problem of *structural underdevelopment* that there has emerged a more promising line of inquiry based on a 'dependency theory'[7] of peripheral capitalist development.[8] On the assumption, with a loose reference to Marx, that development and underdevelopment are reciprocal conditions of the same process of capital accumulation, the theory takes various forms but can be reduced to two central propositions: (1) The development of underdevelopment: Capitalist development on the periphery is based on a hyper-exploitation of labour, a massive capital drain that blocks the production of surplus value, distorts the structure of production, limits the internal market, and generates the chronic unemployment and marginality of a surplus population.[9] (2) Dependent capitalist development: Capitalism on the periphery accelerates the production of relative surplus value, and expands the forces of production and their corresponding relations; and, if it generates unemployment and poverty under some conditions (contraction), it absorbs labour power under others (expansion), producing an effect similar to capitalism at the centre, where unemployment and absorption, poverty and wealth, coexist.[10]

These two propositions are not mutually exclusive. Both define underdevelopment as a historical product of conditions created by the workings of capitalism on the periphery. With a loose reference to Marx's general theory of capitalist development, both propositions are based on a metropolis-hinterland model of an international and, by extension, inter-regional system. Unlike staple theory, which is also based on this model, both strains of dependency theory emphasise that the structure of this metropolis-hinterland relationship is maintained by mechanisms of exploitation.[11] Where the difference lies is in the assumption on the one hand of a progressive underdevelopment and of a dependent uneven development on the other.

Can this metropolis-hinterland model be applied to the structure of central Canada's relationship to the Atlantic region? If so, which form of dependency applies: the *development of underdevelopment* or *uneven combined development*? What are the structural and historical conditions of this dependence?

Raising these questions forces us to come to terms with a conceptual ambiguity deeply rooted in dependency theory. On the one hand, its ultimate centre of reference is a Marxist theory of capitalist development based on principles of a class analysis. On the other hand, its metropolis-hinterland model forms the framework of a regional analysis based not on productive class relations but on relations of exchange. In its revision of Marx's general theory of capitalist development, its central focus has shifted from mechanisms of surplus extraction to those of surplus transfer—on the assumption that the same principles apply; and that on the international level, whatever the mix of productive relations, the main form of exploitation is based not so much on ownership of the means of production as on monopoly control over market relationships.[12]

This is where dependency theory becomes problematic. It escapes the limitations of staple theory based on geographic and technological factors of resource extraction by directing analysis towards the process of capital accumulation based on the production of surplus value. But an emphasis on exchange relations formed in the sphere of circulation leads dependency theory to play down or even ignore fundamental class relations formed in the sphere of production. To a large extent this misplaced emphasis originates with the assumption that a class analysis has no spatial dimension—that a regional analysis is necessarily based on exchange relationships. A more valid approach, however, would be to connect the class and regional conditions of peripheral capitalism: to show how the exploitative relation of wage labour is reproduced in the regional structure of production and exchange, and to analyse the political implications of this process. This is the challenge for a Marxist theory of dependence taken up at different levels by the other authors in this collection of essays.

The necessary groundwork for such an analysis in the case of Atlantic Canada is still being laid, and what follows is but a preliminary application of a line of research suggested by Marx's theory of capitalist development. On this basis, the development of the capitalist system is conceived of as being shaped by the attempts of capitalists to counteract the system's inherent tendency towards a declining rate of profit.[13] Given this tendency, the process of capital accumulation creates the following class and regional conditions of an uneven polarised development:

more capitalists or larger capitalists at this pole, more wage-workers at that.... The mass of social wealth ... thrusts itself into old branches of production, whose market suddenly expands, or into newly formed branches ... [an industrial cycle that depends] upon the constant transformation of a part of the labouring population into unemployed or half-employed hands.... The greater the social wealth, the functioning capital ... the greater is the industrial reserve army ... the mass of a consolidated surplus-population [subject to] ... the dead weight of pauperism.[14]

What this signifies for a regional analysis, is that the expanded reproduction of capital at one pole (the centre) both requires and creates on the other (the periphery) conditions for a mass of 'free' labour held in reserve but available for purchase. In effect, what this suggests, and what I will argue, is that underdevelopment in Atlantic Canada can best be understood in terms of Marx's concept of an 'industrial reserve army'—as a lever of capital accumulation.

CAPITAL AND CLASS IN ATLANTIC CANADA

The social relation that defines the working class under capitalism is the exchange of labour power for a wage. When the purchase and sale of labour power was introduced, at the time of European settlement of the Atlantic colonies, the historically significant form of productive relationship was independent commodity production, in which there was no direct economic exploitation because the bulk of labour was provided by the real owner or family members and thus not exchanged against capital. As shown by Antler[15] in the case of Newfoundland, the conditions of these productive relations were quite variable and historically specific. From the very first, the development of large-scale agriculture and other forms of independent commodity production were limited by the property relations of commercial capital.[16] Nevertheless, the capitalist relation of wage labour, at first coexistent with other forms of productive relationship, very soon penetrated and ultimately came to dominate the larger structure so formed. Surface indications of this complex process are given in available statistics on the history of self-employment. In the early nineteenth century, perhaps four-fifths of the population was self-employed. By 1881 this had declined to about one-third and by 1951 to less than one-fifth; by 1977 only seven per cent of the labour force was classified as self-employed.[17] Even without any reference to the changing class conditions of this self-employment or any further analysis, it is clear that the labour process has been largely shaped by forces produced in the accumulation of capital.

Some of the other studies in this collection of essays have begun to ask questions about the historical conditions of this process, but they are too complex for us to treat at this point. The structural requirements of these conditions, however, can be gauged by changes in the regional distribution of productive activities and in the occupational categories of the structure so formed. With some rough approximations concerning the class conditions of this regional structure of production and occupation, we can analyse the process of capital accumulation in terms of official data, which are not generally amenable to class analysis.[18]

First of all, the expanded reproduction of capital has brought about a massive increase in the size of the urban proletariat, the regional distribution and occupational categories of which are given in Tables 1-1 and 1-2.[19]

Second, the *proletarianisation* of an ever larger proportion of the population, both at the centre and on the periphery of the capitalist system, has affected above all production relations in the agricultural sector of primary production. At the turn of this century, this sector formed the basis for nearly 40% of the active labour force in Canada, while by 1971, at a much higher level of capitalist development, it had fallen below 4%.[20] In the case of the Atlantic region, the concentration and centralisation of capital in agriculture, together with its destruction of independent commodity production, has brought about a drastic decrease in the number of occupied farms and the level of farm employment. From 1931 to 1961, when capital investment in farming increased by almost 450%, the farm labour force declined by almost 50%; and from 1965 to 1971 it declined a further 43%.[21] In relation to an overall growth in the labour force, the various sectors of primary production declined drastically from 43.4% in 1921 to 8.4% in 1971 (see Table 1-2). Evidently, the accumulation of capital in primary production has produced a mass of surplus labour, a vast pool of dispossessed workers subject to the dictates of industrial capital.

TABLE 1-1

POPULATION OF CANADA AND PROVINCES,
PERCENTAGE DISTRIBUTION

	REGIONAL DISTRIBUTION					PERCENTAGE URBAN				
	1851	1881	1921	1951	1971	1851	1881	1921	1951	1971
Newfoundland	—	—	—	2.6	2.4	—	—	—	43.3	57.2
P.E.I.	2.6	2.5	1.0	1.7	0.5	—	10.5	18.8	25.1	38.3
New Brunswick	8.0	7.4	4.4	3.7	2.9	14.0	17.6	35.2	42.8	56.9
Nova Scotia	11.4	10.2	6.0	4.6	3.7	7.5	14.7	44.8	54.5	56.7
Quebec	26.5	31.4	26.9	29.0	28.0	14.9	23.8	51.8	66.8	80.6
Ontario	39.1	44.6	33.4	32.8	35.7	14.0	27.1	58.8	72.5	82.4
Western provinces	2.2	2.5	28.2	26.4	26.6					
Canada	100.0	100.0	100.0	100.0	100.0	13.1	23.3	47.4	62.4	76.6

SOURCE: L.O. Stone, *Migration in Canada* (Ottawa, 1969), L.O. Stone and A.J. Siggner, eds., *The population of Canada* (New York, 1974).

NOTE: Western provinces, excluded in this study, embrace British Columbia and the Prairies — Saskatchewan, Alberta, and Manitoba.

The dependence of this mass of 'free' workers on the movement of capital can be traced out in the large regional redistribution of economic activity that followed Confederation.[22] As reflected in the specific case of manufacturing, which became increasingly concentrated in central Canada and appreciably declined in the Atlantic region, this process had little to do with market factors such as economies of scale, productivity, location, capital flow, etc.[23] Rather, it was closely tied to the consolidation of externally owned capital in the industrial and financial sectors of the Maritime economy. In the late 1880s and early 1890s, and then again in the early twentieth century, industry after industry and bank after bank, largely based on local capital, fell to this consolidation.[24] In fact, by 1914 the Maritimes had become a branch-plant economy with most of its capital controlled from Montreal or Toronto.

The effects of this consolidation were dramatic. Between 1917 and 1921 production and employment in Maritime manufacturing industry fell by nearly 40%.[25] As the consolidated corporations began to close their Maritime branches and to concentrate their production facilities in central Canada, numerous other Maritime plants were forced into bankruptcy by the ruinous freight rates applied by the Canadian National Railway.[26] As a result, by 1926

TABLE 1-2

OCCUPATIONAL STRUCTURE OF THE LABOUR FORCE,
1881-1971 PERCENTAGE DISTRIBUTION

	Atlantic	Ontario	Quebec	Prairies	B.C.	Canada
Primary						
1881	56.8	49.4	49.5	65.2*	44.4	51.3
1921	43.4	28.2	30.9	55.2	29.4	36.6
1951	27.1	13.1	17.2	37.3	13.7	19.8
1971	8.4	5.4	5.2	19.5	7.3	8.3
Manufacturing						
1881	18.2	26.8	25.1	16.4	27.8	24.3
1921	17.4	26.4	26.9	7.1	19.3	20.8
1951	20.1	29.8	29.4	13.6	24.0	25.1
1971	15.0	27.4	26.2	10.1	17.8	22.2
Construction						
1881	4.2	4.8	4.4	5.1	5.5	4.5
1921	5.4	6.7	6.5	3.2	8.0	5.8
1951	5.9	6.4	6.8	4.8	6.8	6.2
1971	7.5	5.8	5.3	6.2	7.0	6.0
Transportation						
1881	4.9	2.2	2.6	1.4	5.5	2.9
1921	7.7	8.1	7.1	7.2	11.2	7.8
1951	10.9	9.4	9.3	8.8	11.9	9.5
1971	10.4	7.5	8.7	9.7	10.5	8.8
Trade						
1881	5.6	5.1	5.3	4.1	5.5	5.3
1921	8.2	10.7	9.9	8.3	11.2	9.4
1951	9.3	10.7	9.3	10.1	11.9	10.1
1971	19.8	16.4	15.9	17.2	19.2	16.9
Services						
1881	9.1	11.5	13.0	7.6	11.1	11.6
1921	16.9	19.9	17.9	19.3	20.8	19.2
1951	26.1	30.6	27.9	10.1	11.9	28.2
1971	38.8	37.4	37.8	37.2	38.1	37.6

SOURCE: See note 19.

NOTE: Statistics for 1881 and 1921 are based on the age group of 10 and over. Statistics for 1921 and 1951 are for the age group 14 and over. For 1971, statistics are based on the age group 15 and over.

* Only Manitoba for this year.

eight of the leading industrial towns and cities along the Intercolonial provided 45% fewer jobs in manufacturing than they had at the beginning of the decade.

　　Under such conditions, surplus labour released from agriculture clearly was not absorbed by industry in the region. Forced to migrate for productive

TABLE 1-3

PERSONS EMPLOYED IN MANUFACTURING IN
SELECTED MARITIME CITIES AND TOWNS,
1920 AND 1926

	1920	1926
Amherst	2,267	735
Dartmouth	1,581	946
Halifax	7,171	3,287
New.Glasgow	2,610	611
Sydney	2,929	2,053
Truro	1,080	778
Moncton	3,061	2,133
Saint John	4,630	3,394

Source: *Canada Year Book,* 1922-23, 438, and 1929, 453-54.

employment, at least 300,000 Maritimers abandoned the region over the first three decades of the twentieth century. A similar flight occurred from Newfoundland. It is significant that nearly half of this emigration (which, it has been estimated, involved half of the region's most productive workers), occurred between 1921 and 1931.[27] Existing data on the direction of this movement show that the volume of internal movement was much larger than external migration and, although for several decades a considerable portion of the region's migrants went to the northeastern United States, the most consistent pattern was that of a westward movement out of the Atlantic region.[28] The connection between this movement and capital formation in central Canada is demonstrated by Buckley.[29] In response to similar conditions, the massive exodus of people out of the region in the following decades continued apace, assuming alarming proportions in the 1960s. By a conservative estimate, more than 150,000 persons (almost two-thirds of whom were between the ages of 15 and 34) left the region between 1961 and 1969, as compared with an increase of 113,000 in the number of employed persons.[30] The various studies that have been conducted suggest that the major provincial recipient of the endemic out-migration from the Maritime region has been Ontario (see Table 1-4). In a period (1956-61) for which data on internal and external migration are broken down, Ontario received 46.9% of emigrants from Newfoundland and Nova Scotia, 42.2% of those from New Brunswick, and 40.7% of those from P. E. I.[31]

Not all workers, however, have chased capital into the expanding industries of central Canada. Instead, many have been sought out and yoked by capital in local industries based on resource extraction.[32] The consequent expansion of staple production, together with the noted decline of basic consumer-good industries, has produced a long-term dependence: capital shifts in and out of staple production in response to world-market fluctuations,

TABLE 1-4

NET MIGRATION RATIOS,
CANADA AND PROVINCES, 1921-61

	1921-31	1931-41	1941-51	1951-61	1956-61	
Nfld.	—	—	—	- 6.7	0.3	- 3.7
P.E.I.	-10.2	- 3.3	-12.4	-10.8	- 8.1	- 2.9
N.S.	-12.0	1.5	- 6.4	- 4.9	- 1.6	- 3.2
N.B.	- 9.3	- 2.3	- 8.6	- 6.6	- 3.9	- 2.8
Quebec	0.6	- 0.1	- 0.3	4.4	2.3	2.2
Ontario	4.9	2.1	7.3	12.6	7.5	5.3
Canada	2.4	- 0.9	1.3	7.0	4.1	3.0

SOURCE: Kari Levitt, *Input-output study of the Atlantic provinces* (Ottawa, 1975) 74-76.

NOTE: Net migration ratio is 100 (net migration/population at beginning of decade).

with corresponding effects on the mass of labour employed. A most dramatic instance of this development was the long-term slump in the production of regional staples (coal, lumber, pulp, and fish), whose prices in 1930 had dropped to 1913 levels.[33] The capitalist development of these staples is more generally reflected in the long-term decline of employment in industries based on their production (Table 1-9), while short-term variations in this decline reflect the notorious instability of the international market in staples.[34]

Paralleling this dependence on the export sector is the even heavier dependence of regional industry on imports. This is especially the case for manufactured goods in which every product sector except fish, beverages, pulp and paper, printing and publishing, has an import content well over 50%.[35] With a continuous rise in the value and variety of imports of manufactured goods from central Canada, the Atlantic region's trade gap (import surplus) has increased from $476.3 million in 1960 and $623 million in 1965 to well over one billion dollars in 1977.[36] With an import ratio of 54.3% on industrial capital formation in the region, it has been estimated that even the considerable transfer payments of the federal government take as much capital out of the region as they put into it. The limited benefits derived from the region's staple economy in the form of capital expansion or wages are largely spent on central Canadian products, most of which are purchased at a considerable premium over comparable American goods. As an economic hinterland of the central Canadian metropolis, the Atlantic region cannot afford the price of national unity.

There is an even more significant dimension to the concentration of industrial capital in central Canada: it is to a large degree foreign-controlled, and as such, an adjunct of US capital (see Table 1-5). The significance of this foreign ownership is that the subsidiaries of US-based corporations are concentrated in the most rapidly growing, capital-intensive, high wage and profitable industries, which are highly centralised by region. In fact, 83% of

TABLE 1-5

CONTROL OF MAJOR CANADIAN INDUSTRIES
BY FOREIGN CAPITAL,
PERCENTAGE SHARE OF TOTAL, 1974

	Firms	Assets	Profits
Manufacturing	10.8	57	62.7
Gas and Oil	4.8	99	99.2
Transportation equipment	16.3	80	89.4
Machinery	19.9	68	73.7
Chemicals	31.3	78	89.0
Paper and Allied	21.2	44	46.9
Food	8.7	49	59.5
Wholesale Trade	2.7	25	24.3
Services	1.3	25	44.4

SOURCE: My calculations based on CALURA, *Report for 1974, Part One —Corporations*(Ottawa, 1974), 42-77.

NOTE: Based on Foreign ownership of 50% or more.

American-controlled manufacturing plants are estimated to be within 400 miles of Toronto.[37] What makes this so important is that if US-based capital had the same industrial distribution as Canadian capital, it would mean an estimated 20% more manufacturing employment in the Atlantic region.

The degree to which capital has been centralised and concentrated is indirectly reflected in the regional distribution of wage levels and its associated income structure. Throughout the twentieth century and since at least the time of Confederation, wage levels and per capita income in the Atlantic region have lagged far behind levels in the other provinces, especially Ontario, which has averaged a per capita income level well above one and a half times that of the Atlantic region.[38] Although this disparity is not quite as startling when the size and impact of the capitalist labour market are taken into account, average earner income in the region in the post-World War II period has suffered a steady decline relative to the rest of Canada (see Table 1-6). As shown by Table 1-7, available data on comparative wage rates indicate that most of the income disparity can be accounted for by a greater preponderance of low-wage industries (fish products, pulp and paper, food and beverages, trade and services) in the Atlantic region, as well as by a sizeable wage differential in each industry. Despite a dramatic increase in income earners as a proportion of the total population (see Table 1-8), the Atlantic region has received a much lower proportion of new income generated by productive employment (invested capital) than the other provinces. Although this disparity of income reflects the effects of age-selective migration, a different industrial structure, lower labour participation rates, higher unemployment rates, and lower wage levels, it can in one way or another be

TABLE 1-6

PROVINCIAL AVERAGE EARNED INCOME AS A
PERCENTAGE OF NATIONAL AVERAGE, 1946-71

	1946	1951	1956	1961	1966	1971
Nfld.	—	93	81	82	78	79
P.E.I.	90	79	78	76	69	67
N.S.	91	85	84	84	81	83
N.B.	89	83	83	79	80	78
Quebec	97	98	97	98	99	97
Ontario	104	105	106	106	106	108
Canada	100	100	100	100	100	100

SOURCE: Department of National Revenue, *Taxation Statistics,* Table A or I, appropriate years;
calculations by Leo Johnson, *Poverty in Wealth*

traced back to the concentration and centralisation of capital.

THE STRUCTURE OF UNDERDEVELOPMENT

This mass of concentrated and centralised capital is but one side of a complex
process. On the other side is an accessible supply of cheap, exploitable labour
needed for capitalist development at the centre.[39] As reflected in both its
structure of production (limited absorption) and out-migration, some of the
conditions for this labour reserve have long existed in Atlantic Canada, where
traditional communities based on independent commodity production are
broken down by forces beyond their control.

These conditions form the basis of a complex class system with quite
distinct, structurally determined regional variations. At the centre (the golden
triangle between Sarnia, Toronto, Montreal, and Ottawa), a concentration of
productive forces brings about the formation of a sizeable class of wage
labourers, an industrial proletariat that draws on migration from overseas
and rural areas as well as the Atlantic provinces. On the periphery (Atlantic
Canada), the class system is more clearly formed by conditions of surplus
labour that produce a severely restricted industrial proletariat, a dramatic
emigration of workers, an expanding mass of unproductive workers, and,
most notably, a growing concentration of unemployed and partially
employed persons, subject to the requirements of capital accumulation at the
centre.[40]

The economic basis of this class system and its associated social conditions
are found in the region's structure of underdeveloped primary production.
In the typical case of Nova Scotia, this structure of underdevelopment is
concentrated in agriculture, forestry, and fish production, and, on a subreg-
ional level (Cape Breton), in coal and primary steel production. In the latter
primary sector, which is the basis of well-established social relations between
capitalist and working classes, production is characterised by the concentra-

TABLE 1-7

AVERAGE WEEKLY SALARIES/WAGES
BY INDUSTRY, 1971-1976

Industry	CANADA		NOVA SCOTIA		Nova Scotia average as a percentage of Canadian average.	
	1971	1976	1971	1976	1971	1976
Construction	193	326	148	254	77	78
Mining	175	331	133	240	76	77
Transportation/ Communications	158	254	140	219	89	86
Manufacturing	144	236	114	206	79	87
iron & steel	179	276	146	225	82	82
durable goods	156	252	127	217	81	86
non-durable	133	220	106	199	80	90
food & beverages	124	218	88	167	71	77
fish products	79	—	90	153	114	—
Finance/Insurance	131	211	116	183	89	87
Trade	110	173	94	144	85	83
Service	99	168	70	121	71	77
Industrial Composite	139	223	112	188	81	84

SOURCE: My calculations from data in Nova Scotia Department of Labour, *Selected labour statistics,* 1972, Table 15; and 1976, Tables 4-5.

TABLE 1-8

INCOME EARNERS AS A PERCENTAGE OF TOTAL POPULATION
BY PROVINCE, 1946-71

	1946	1951	1956	1961	1966	1971
Nfld.	—	12.7	20.7	20.6	26.8	30.9
P.E.I.	9.1	13.2	14.0	17.1	26.5	35.2
N.S.	21.5	22.6	24.1	25.9	32.1	38.8
N.B.	18.5	20.9	24.3	24.9	31.1	38.3
Quebec	20.9	24.3	27.6	28.9	34.4	40.1
Ontario	31.4	36.6	38.5	38.3	44.1	49.0
Canada	25.7	29.3	32.2	32.7	38.6	44.2

SOURCE: Leo Johnson, *Poverty in Wealth* (Toronto, 1974) Table XVIII, p. 18. Calculations from *Taxation Statistics* and *Census,* appropriate years.

tion of external capital and centralisation of secondary manufacturing out-side the region. The monopolistic structure of this concentration and centrali-sation has not only shaped productive relations and major conditions of work in the region (up to 20% of Nova Scotians have been wholly or in part dependent on the coal and steel industry), but has formed the basis of a massive reserve of unemployed, mobile labour.[41]

As for agriculture, the Atlantic provinces have become increasingly sub-ject to capital in the form of vertically integrated corporations such as McCain's and the Weston group, but have maintained a significant small-scale nonmarket (subsistence) form of production, the basis of petit-bourgeois social relations. In 1940 53.1% of all farms in Nova Scotia were subsistence farms or combinations of subsistence; and, when combined with part-time farms, over three-quarters of all farms in eastern Nova Scotia were noncom-mercial operations. As recently as 1965, one-third of all farms in Nova Scotia and New Brunswick yielded less than $50 of saleable output, and were thus classified as subsistence.[42] These subsistence farms clearly function as a source of reserve labour. However, a much greater reserve is found in the rural dispossessed (those forced off their farms) who, it is estimated, make up one-third of the population in the Maritimes.[43] The disproportionate size of this class is reflected in the statistics on rural nonfarm population. In 1971 in the Atlantic region, it constituted 40.3% of the total as opposed to 17.3% for the rest of Canada.[44]

Other equally important structures of underdevelopment are found in the primary and secondary sectors of forest and fish production, whose industries have formed the basis of both capitalist and petit-bourgeois rela-tions. Prior to World War II, inshore fishermen and small woodlot workers predominated, but increasingly these 'independents'—who are often forced to combine fishing and lumbering with subsistence or part-time farming, or, like their wives, to sell their labour cheaply off-season to fish plants or pulp and paper mills—are dependent on conditions of exchange (input industry, processing, and marketing) controlled by large, vertically integrated corpora-tions that themselves buy labour.[45] Under monopoly conditions, the price that the 'independent' inshore fishermen and woodlot workers receive for their products amounts to a wage, and in effect, despite their ownership of limited means of production, these 'independents' must be counted among the pro-letariat.

THE INDUSTRIAL RESERVE ARMY

How is this structure of underdevelopment, reproduced with variations in each Atlantic province and other peripheral regions, to be understood? Although Marx's theory of capitalist development has to be adapted to the specific historical conditions that apply in Atlantic Canada, the structure of these conditions can best be analysed in terms of Marx's concept of an 'indust-rial reserve army,' a relative surplus population that is both required for, and a product of, capital accumulation. After Marx, we can distinguish three forms of reserve labour: the *floating*, the *latent*, and the *stagnant*.[46]

TABLE 1-9

THE LABOUR MARKET IN ATLANTIC CANADA, PERCENTAGE DISTRIBUTION BY SECTOR, 1881-1977

	THE LABOUR FORCE BY SECTOR					EMPLOYMENT RATIO
	1881	1921	1951	1971	1977	1977
Primary	56.8	43.4	17.1	8.4	7.4	80
Manufacturing	18.2	17.4	20.1	15.0	13.4	77
Construction	4.2	5.4	5.9	7.5	7.3	61
Transportation	4.9	7.7	10.9	10.4	11.1	75
Trade	5.6	8.2	9.3	19.8	19.3	87
Service	9.1	16.9	26.1	38.8	40.2	91

SOURCE: For 1881-1971 see note 19. For 1977, Statistics Canada, *The labour force*, Tables 16-18.

NOTE: Employment ratio is the difference between number of individuals distributed by sector actually employed and registered in the labour force.

Floating relative surplus labour forms with the alternate expansion and contraction of production which throws some workers out, and then draws them back into, production. Found in both the industrial system and in the export sector of primary production, this form of surplus population is presently maintained by the system of unemployment insurance which supports workers in their forced movement within a capitalist labour market. As reflected in Table 1-9, this market exists for the most part in the rapidly expanding service sector of unproductive labour as well as in several restricted sectors of productive labour (transportation, resource-based manufacturing, export-oriented primary production). Although unemployment also affects middle-class occupations such as professional services, the system of unemployment insurance clearly functions to support the working class in its role as a floating reserve '[to be] thrust ... frantically into old branches of production, whose market suddenly expands, or into newly formed branches ... the need for which grows out of the development of the old ones.'[47]

This movement of workers from job to job is reflected in partial statistics on the duration of unemployment and in the proportion of unemployed workers actually laid off in a given year. As for the former, 17.6% of those unemployed in the Atlantic region in February 1977 had been unemployed for four weeks or less; 33% for five to thirteen weeks; and 48% for more than thirteen weeks; on the average from 13.5 to 18.2 weeks.[48] Excluding those who had not worked for five years or had never worked at all, 24% of the unemployed had been laid off.[49]

Latent relative surplus labour is formed by the process of primary accumulation, the conditions of which contract the economic basis of self-subsistent, simple commodity, or other precapitalist forms of production (farming, inshore fishing, artisanry, etc.). By definiton this form of reserve labour is forced back into self-subsistent or independent commodity production, where, with the support of unemployment insurance, its labour power is held in reserve without the capitalist having to bear the full cost of its reproduction.

The rural sectors of primary production, however, are not the only sources of a latent reserve. As analysed by Braverman[50] with respect to US capital, domestic production of female labour is an increasingly important source of a latent reserve army of workers. As Table 1-10 establishes, all of the regional increase in labour force participation over the last several decades is accounted for by women, who now constitute 39.2% of the labour force.

TABLE 1-10

LABOUR FORCE PARTICIPATION RATES
IN THE ATLANTIC REGION,
BY SEX, PERCENTAGES, 1953-73

	Male	Female	Total
1953	76.4	17.9	46.9
1958	74.6	19.9	47.7
1962	72.4	23.7	47.8
1968	68.1	28.5	48.2
1973	69.0	32.3	50.5

SOURCE: Statistics Canada, *The labour force,* March 1974, vol. 30, Tables 32 and 38.

The economic function and class position of this female labour is made clear by an examination of its distribution within the capitalist labour market. With respect to the data given for 1977 in Table 1-9, 61.7% of the largest and most rapidly (if not only) expanding sector (services) comprises female labour, 49% of which is found in this sector. Seventy per cent of female labour is found in either the trade or service sectors, and is highly concentrated (64.4%) in the sales and clerical subsectors of service occupations, which house by far the worst paid and least organised stratum of the working class. That female labour is not only cheap but also readily accessible is indicated by the high level of registered unemployment (14%) and ratio of part-time to full-time employment (26%) in these typically female occupations.[51] In the typical case of Nova Scotia, 76% of all women who had registered their unemployment in 1973 were concentrated in clerical, sales, and service occupations.[52] In terms of its cheapness, availability, and marginality, with respect to the capitalist labour market, women constitute a vital part of an expanding industrial reserve army.[53]

The *stagnant* form of surplus population is formed by workers in marginal, very irregular employment, and another stratum, lower still, of individuals unable to sell their labour at any price—the 'hospital ... and the dead

TABLE 1-11

RATES OF LABOUR FORCE PARTICIPATION AND UNEMPLOYMENT, PROVINCES RELATIVE TO CANADA

	LABOUR FORCE PARTICIPATION RATE			UNEMPLOYMENT RATE		
	1950-59	1960-69	1970-72	1950-59	1960-69	1970-72
Atlantic	88.4	87.5	85.6	175.5	167.1	135.4
Quebec	100.4	98.0	97.3	130.5	134.0	131.2
Ontario	104.8	104.5	104.1	73.8	71.3	76.8
Canada	100.0	100.0	100.0	100.0	100.0	100.0
Canada (actual rate)	53.5	54.6	56.1	4.2	5.1	6.2

SOURCE: Statistics Canada, *The labour force,* monthly, various years.

weight of the industrial reserve army.'[54] This form of surplus population, which 'furnishes to capital an inexhaustible reservoir of disposable labour-power,' creates the economic and social foundation of the class structure, formed with variations in each of the four Atlantic provinces. Employment conditions in this structure with regard to mass, type, and wage levels, cannot be separated from conditions of unemployment reproduced by the same structure. This stagnant form of surplus population surfaces not only in welfare roles but more generally in various indicators of widespread sub-employment, such as a low labour force participation rate and the number of taxable returns, which government sources themselves clearly associate with underemployment: 'if ... low, there is a lot of low wage or part-time employ-ment; if ... high, there is little underemployment.'[55] There are at present no adequate measures of this subemployment, only indications such as the low rate of taxable returns (68% of the total), low labour force participation rates, high rates of part-time/seasonal employment (17-22%), and widespread rural poverty reflected in statistics on income and subsistence/part-time farms and marginal fishermen. Without regard to the massive data on the working poor, the combination of chronic high unemployment and low participation (Table 1-11) in Atlantic Canada points to a staggering number of individuals and families that are neither absorbed nor expelled, but increasingly 'hospitalised' by the process of capital accumulation.

CONCLUSION

The development of capital and class in Canada as elsewhere has been very uneven. Over the years since Confederation, the Atlantic region has been seriously underdeveloped by forces that have reproduced in the region the conditions of an industrial reserve army. The force of these conditions has not only resulted in structural poverty but has formed the regional basis of social and political conflict. Now, with unemployment in the region reaching further and further into the ranks of males 25 and over (up 23.2% from June 1976 to June 1977), the 'winter of our discontent' is upon us; this was the conclusion drawn by the Atlantic Provinces Economic Council, a private research organisation set up by local capitalist enterprise, in a statement concerning the unemployed in November 1977. 'Such people,' APEC went on to warn, 'are likely to be more politically active ... and are more likely to be organised into unions or capable of organising into protest groups.'[56]

The social links between the broad structural context of capitalist underdevelopment, and the social movements it has generated are explored in the articles that follow.

NOTES

1. Ray George, *A leader and a laggard: manufacturing industry in Nova Scotia, Quebec, and Ontario* (Toronto, 1970).

2. Ernest Forbes, 'Misguided symmetry: the destruction of regional transportation policy for the Maritimes,' *Canada and the burden of unity*, ed. D. J. Bercuson (Toronto, 1977).

3. Michael Ray, *Canadian urban trends* (Toronto, 1976).

4. Economic Council of Canada, *Living together* (Toronto, 1977).

5. Mel Watkins, 'A staple theory of economic growth,' *Approaches to Canadian economic history*, ed. W. T. Easterbrook and M. H. Watkins (Toronto, 1967).

6. Economic Council, *Living together*, 23.

7. The dominant Latin American tradition of this theory is reviewed in Ronald Chilcote, 'A critical synthesis of the dependency literature,' *Latin American perspectives*, I (1974). The questions of political economy raised by this 'dependency theory' are increasingly taken up by a network of Canadian scholars, as reflected in the work of the Toronto-based Latin American Working Group and in 'A user's guide to Canadian political economy' (Toronto, September 1977), compiled by D. Drache and W. Clement.

8. See especially A. G. Frank, *Capitalism and underdevelopment in Latin America* (New York, 1967); Samir Amin, *Accumulation on a world scale* (New York, 1974) and *Unequal development* (New York, 1976); Theotonio Dos Santos, 'El neuvo caracter de la dependencia,' *Pensamiento critico*, XL (1970); F. H. Cardoso, 'Dependency and development in Latin America,' *New Left Review*, no 74 (1972).

9. Frank, *Capitalism and underdevelopment*; Amin, *Accumulation* and *Unequal development*. This form of dependency theory ('the development of underdevelopment') is most clearly represented by A. G. Frank in *Capitalism and underdevelopment*. For a strict application of Frank's thesis see Bruce Archibald, 'The development of underdevelopment in the Atlantic provinces' (unpub. MA thesis, Dalhousie University, 1971).

10. F. H. Cardoso, *Dependencia y desarrollo en America Latina* (Mexico, 1969) and 'Dependency and development in Latin America.'

11. This is the main point of difference between dependency theory and staple theory, which, like sociological theories of modernisation, views the metropolis-hinterland structure as a useful framework for resource development based on mechanisms of diffusion. On mechanisms of diffusion as a condition of development (modernisation), see R. Chilcote and I. Edelstein, *Latin America* (Cambridge, Mass., 1974), introduction.

12. This tendency is at the heart of dependency theory's ambiguous relationship to Marxism. On this, see Veltmeyer, 'Dependency and underdevelopment: some questions

and problems,' *Canadian Journal of Political and Social Theory*, II (1978). For a more general critique of dependency theory's misplaced emphasis on market relations and of its neglect of productive class relations, see Geoffrey Kay, *Development and underdevelopment: a Marxist analysis* (New York, 1975).

13. This whole question of a declining rate of profit as a law of capitalist development is still in dispute, but as I argue elsewhere, the proposition of such a long-term tendency is the theoretical basis of a dependency analysis of structural underdevelopment. See Veltmeyer, 'Dependency and underdevelopment.'

14. Karl Marx, *Capital* (3v., New York, 1967), I, 613, 632-33, 644.

15. Steven Antler, 'The capitalist underdevelopment of nineteenth-century Newfoundland,' in this volume.

16. Gerald Sider, *Mumming in outport Newfoundland* (Toronto, 1978).

17. Canada, *Census*, 1871-1951; Statistics Canada, *The labour force* (Ottawa, 1977), v. 33.

18. For a preliminary application of such data to categories of class analysis see Veltmeyer, 'The working class in Halifax: notes towards its further study,' *Scottish Journal of Sociology*, III (1979).

19. The official census makes a twofold classification of the labour force: an *industrial* classification that shows the number of workers in each industry distributed by occupation; and an *occupational* classification that shows the number of workers in each occuptional group distributed by the industries in which they pursue their occupations. For better comparability over time, Table 1-2 is based on the industrial classification. Source: calculated from Canada, *Census, 1880-81*, v. 11, Table XIV; *Census, 1921*, v. 4, Table 2; *Census, 1951*, v. 4, Table 4; Statistics Canada, *The labour force*, cat. 71-001 (Ottawa, 1973).

20. Noah Meltz, *Manpower in Canada, 1931-1961* (Ottawa, 1969), Table A1.

21. *Rural Canada in transition*, ed. M.-A. Tremblay and Walter Anderson (Ottawa, 1968), 29-31; and Atlantic Provinces Economic Council, *Atlantic Canada today* (Halifax/ Fredericton, 1977), 57.

22. Kenneth Buckley, *Capital formation in Canada, 1896-1930* (Toronto, 1974).

23. Cf. George, *A leader and a laggard*.

24. T. W. Acheson, 'The Maritimes and "Empire" Canada,' *Canada and the burden of unity*, ed. D. J. Bercuson (Toronto, 1977), 20-27.

25. *Canada Year Book*, 1929, 401 and 1931, 466-509. That this concentration of manufacturing in central Canada has deepened over time can be seen by a comparison of population statistics and manufacturing statistics. In 1971, the Atlantic region had 9.5% of the population, but only 4.6% of the employees and 3.5% of the value added in manufacturing. A similar relationship holds for the Prairie provinces excluded from this study. In comparison, Ontario had 35.7% of the population but accounted for 49.1% of manufacturing employees and 54.1% of value added. Together Quebec and Ontario accounted for somewhat more than half the national population but more than 80% of employees and value added in manufacturing; Statistics Canada, *Manufacturing industries of Canada* (Ottawa, 1974), catalogue no 31-204/206. As indicated below, this concentration of manufacturing in central Canada is closely connected to the operation of US capital in Canada.

26. Cf. Forbes, 'Misguided symmetry.'

27. *Historical statistics of Canada*, ed. M. C. Urquhart and K. A. H. Buckley (Toronto, 1965), 22.

28. Nathan Keyfitz, 'The growth of Canadian population,' *Population Studies*, IV (1950); I. B. Anderson, *Internal migration in Canada, 1921-1961* (Ottawa, 1966); L. O. Stone, *Migration in Canada* (Ottawa, 1969); George, *A leader and a laggard*.

29. Buckley, *Capital formation*, 64-73.

30. Kari Levitt, *Input-output study of the Atlantic provinces* (2 v., Ottawa, 1975), II, 16.

31. Stone, *Migration in Canada*, 34-39.

32. This expansion of staples development became more pronounced throughout the interwar period when the output of goods produced for the domestic market continued its steady downslide; the processing of the staples—lumber, pulp, and fish—rapidly became an even more important element in the region's manufacturing sector, rising from about 32% of all manufactures in 1911 to 38% in 1951; Canada, *Census, 1891*, v. III, 178-83, 190-91; *Canada Year Book*, 1952, 689-90, 697. By 1965, 75% of the region's exports, mainly destined for foreign markets, were resource-based; Levitt, *Input-output study*, II, 68.

33. Atlantic Provinces Economic Council, *Atlantic Canada today*, 25.

34. The instability of this market as well as a tendency to a long-term deterioration in the terms of trade is well established, although not with reference to the theory of unequal exchange that could be applied to it. With exports sustaining 34.7% of employment and 32.5% of income in the region (see Levitt, *Input-output study*, II,46), market instability and deteriorating terms of trade are likely to have some of the impact that they do in many third-world countries. This is particularly the case for Nova Scotian primary steel and coal, on which a majority of people in the subpeninsula of Cape Breton have been directly or indirectly dependent.

35. Levitt, *Input-output study*, II,74-76.

36. *Ibid.*, Tables 2.4A-D.

37. Michael Ray, 'The spatial structure of regional development and cultural differences,' paper presented before the Regional Science Association annual meeting, 8 November 1968.

38. A study by the Economic Council of Canada, *Second annual report* (Ottawa, 1965) established that average income levels in the Maritime provinces have always been well below the national average as of 1926. A more recent study by Alan Green traced this disparity back to at least 1890; Alan Green, 'Regional aspects of Canada's economic growth, 1890-1929,' *Canadian Journal of Economics and Political Science*, XXXIII (1967).

39. This is not to say that it is essential that the surplus labour needed for the expansion of industrial capital at the centre has to be drawn from the Atlantic region. This surplus is drawn from all over. The process of primitive accumulation has created conditions for this reserve army on an international scale as well as on central Canada's own doorstep. The point is, however, that the conditions for such a reserve (cheap, exploitable, expendable) have been created in Atlantic Canada by the operation of capital controlled from central Canada.

40. No systematic study of these conditions is as yet available. Working notes towards such a study can be found in Veltmeyer, 'The working class in Halifax.'

41. D. A. Frank, 'The Cape Breton coal industry and the rise and fall of the British Empire Steel Corporation,' *Acadiensis*, VII (1977).

42. Canada, *Census, 1941*, VII, 197; Levitt, *Input-output study*, I, 40-44.

43. *Rural Canada in transition*, ed. Tremblay and Anderson, 12.

44. Atlantic Provinces Economic Council, *Atlantic Canada today*, 57.

45. L. G. Barrett, 'Development and underdevelopment and the rise of trade unions in the fishing industry in Nova Scotia, 1900-1950' (unpub. MA thesis, Dalhousie University, 1976).

46. Marx, *Capital*, I, 640ff.

47. *Ibid.*, 632.

48. Statistics Canada, *The labour force*, February 1977, T25.

49. *Ibid.*, T28.

50. Harry Braverman, *Labor and monopoly capital* (New York, 1974).

51. Statistics Canada, *The labour force*, February 1977, T10; March 1974, T5-2.

52. Nova Scotia, Department of Development, *Selected labour statistics for Nova Scotia*, February 1974, 4.

53. Cf. esp. Patricia Connelly, *Last hired, first fired* (Toronto, 1979).

54. Marx, *Capital*, I, 64.

55. Nova Scotia, Department of Development, *Selected labour statistics*, November 1974, I.

56. *Halifax Mail Star*, 22 November 1977.

2 The Differing Origins, Organisation, and Impact of Maritime and Prairie Co-Operative Movements to 1940

R. James Sacouman

INTRODUCTION

In both the Maritime and Prairie regions of Canada, primary producers were especially active in social movement organisation during the last decades of the nineteenth and the first half of the twentieth century. On the east coast, collective attempts by primary producers to alter their material and social conditions tended to occur in waves of co-operative organisation,[1] or of militant unionism.[2] The few primary-producer-based political movements that did arise in the Maritimes during this period were distinguished by their failure to gain broad electoral support.[3] On the prairies, of course, *the* primary producer movement, the grain growers' co-operative movement, was the basis for subsequent populist political organisations.

Understanding the social origins of Prairie political movements has been one of the most important concerns of Canadian social scientists and historians.[4] Most treatments of Prairie political protest during the early twentieth century stress the metropolitan domination of a single-staple/single-class grain-growing frontier made up of independent commodity producers. For example, in his analysis of the CCF in Saskatchewan, Lipset has referred to the marginalisation of a whole province given its 'one-class social structure' *vis-à-vis* a one-class east of 'bankers, middlemen, and big business.'[5] More recently, structural studies of Prairie agrarian radicalism have maintianed this emphasis while adding to its class analytic component.[6]

Even the most cursory knowledge of Maritime history indicates the inapplicability of the frontier single-staple/single-class argument to the region's political economy. By the late nineteenth century, it is clearly stretching the point to consider the Maritimes as a frontier region.[7] In most places agricultural production has not been commodity or market production, let alone dependent on a single staple. Fish production has also varied by type, species, and market; and woodswork has most often been an adjunct to other forms of primary production. More important, primary production has not exhibited a single-class structure of independent producers. The main forms of primary production in the Maritimes have always exhibited *multiple* class relationships—relationships that have differed between, and often within, the farming, fishing, forestry, and coal and raw steel producing sectors of the economy.

Scholarly inattention to the wealth and diversity of nonpolitical east coast social movements of primary producers during the late nineteenth and early twentieth centuries has encouraged the acceptance of the Prairies-derived argument as applicable to all Canadian movements of petty primary producers. Furthermore, the important comparative work that has been done[8] has maintained a focus on interregional *political* movements and has, therefore, not been forced to come directly to grips with the question of alternative class bases for organised primary producer action.[9]

Comparing the class bases of a variety of Maritime co-operative movements with the structural roots of Prairie co-operative protest movements provides an excellent opportunity to re-examine the single-staple/single-class thesis, sincle formal co-operation preceded third-party political protest on both the Prairies and the east coast; yet this did not result in third-party support on the east coast. It will be argued that the single-staple/single-class explanation is deficient because it fails to account for the origins of a variety of Maritime co-operative movements. Yet the core of the explanation—the view of co-operative movements as collective responses to the onslaught of capitalist development—is sound.[10] A re-interpretation of the co-operative responses of primary producers to capitalist development across Canada is necessary because of the widespread growth of various tactical programmes of co-operation during the period considered, each supposedly based on the social-material situation of the producers involved. I will argue that a more encompassing and more incisive explanation of the class roots, organisation, and impact of primary-producer-based co-operative movements in the Maritimes and the Prairies entails a Marxist examination of the differing forms of the capitalist underdevelopment of primary production in the two regions.

The framework employed in this analysis begins with Marx's working assumption that social movements within any region in modern times are part of *the* social movement, viz. capitalist development and its consequent class struggles.[11] Capitalist development is, in this view, necessarily and increasingly uneven as capitalism becomes further concentrated and centralised, creating pools of relative surplus labour as a consequence.[12] The short end of uneven capitalist underdevelopment—regional underdevelopment—is characterised by the following set of interrelated features: (1) dependence within the region on primary production, the products of which are often exported to the capital centres for further processing; (2) the creation and maintenance of large pools of surplus labour power, to be utilised, like any other commodity, as export material when demanded; and (3) the export of surplus value to the capital centres.[13]

While the third of the interrelated factors most immediately conditions the *distribution* of regional inequalities,[14] the first two factors produce the third.[15] If the production of marketable items for private gain, of exchange-values or commodities is the fundamental locus of capitalist development,[16] the production of marketable raw materials and semiprocessed goods (i.e., primary products) tends to be the *more restricted* locus of capitalist underdevelopment. If the social relationship of working-class exploitation through capitalist production is basic to an understanding of class conflict under the capitalist mode of production in general, social relationships of production tend to be *more variegated* in regions of capitalist underdevelopment. Primary producers in underdeveloped regions are distributed and maintained not only in (and often not mainly) capitalist/working-class relationships of exploitation, but also in capitalist/petty-producer social relations based on the appropriation—by large capital—of the surplus of petty commodity producer domestic units.[17] Indeed, as an integral part of the production and reproduction of surplus-labour pools within the region, capitalist development maintains a significant percentage of petty primary producers in a 'precapitalist,' noncommodity or subsistence domestic mode of production.[18]

Precisely because capitalist development is uneven, capitalist underdevelopment is also uneven in terms of differing modes and social relationships of primary production in the underdevelped regions. This last point, a point that is often missed, is the central theoretical foundation of the following analysis. The analysis compares the results of research on the grain growers' co-operatives in the Prairies with the author's research on three Nova Scotian co-operative movements. Varying co-operative responses in the Prairies and Maritimes are linked to structural variations in the capitalist underdevelopment of primary production and to variations in the degree of integration and subordination to a national economy and national policy between types of primary production.[19]

CAPITALIST UNDERDEVELOPMENT, INDEPENDENT COMMODITY PRODUCTION, AND THE PRAIRIE CO-OPERATIVE WAY

In the Prairies, both the predominant settlement patterns and the predominant mode of production from the 1880s on were the result of the spread of central Canadian commercial, industrial, and finance capitalism west across the plains. A variety of 'nation-building' policies were developed to obtain central Canadian domination of the economy. This was accomplished, in large part, through the creation and subordination of a vast region of independent commodity production.[20] Capitalist regional underdevelopment of this new land took the form of the controlled creation and subordination of an *unusually monolithic and truncated mode of petty commodity production*, commercial grain growing.[21] This mode of production provided the principal structural basis for the particular programmatic path and the unique impact of the Prairie co-operative movement.

Capitalist regional underdevelopment has been characterised by primary production dependence, surplus-labour production and reproduction, and the export of surplus value. In most of the Prairie west over the period considered, underdevelopment took the highly restricted form of wheat monoculture for export by domestic producer units who were indirectly exploited by commercial, industrial, and finance capital through mechanisms of unequal exchange. This process of capitalist regional underdevelopment is most often referred to as 'the National Policy,' the key planks of which, with respect to the Prairie west, were open settlement policies, a highly subsidised national transportation network, and protective tariffs on many consumer and producer goods.[22]

The crushing of a north-south prairie political economy with the defeat of the Riel rebellions,[23] allowed for extensive settlement by commodity producers who could be locked into an east-west national economy. The human geography of Prairie settlement was reshaped by federal land grants, and the location of the main and branch lines of the Canadian Pacific Railway monopoly, of other land companies, and of grain elevators.[24] The CPR's transportation monopoly and the land and elevator companies' effective commercial monopoly in Prairie communities tended to control not only the settlement process but also much of the everyday social existence of the agrarian pioneers.[25]

Successful underdevelopment of the Prairies entailed as well the creation of a large captive market, an 'internal colony,' for producer and consumer goods manufactured in central Canada.[26] The tariff wall protecting existing eastern (mostly central Canadian) industry from American competition permitted the capture of the Prairie west.[27] The wheat boom of 1896-1913 ensured a rapidly growing market in the prairies and locked many prairie agrarians into monocultural export dependence.[28]

Closely related to this process of underdevelopment through single staple dependence was the creation via state immigration and settlement policies of a mass of independent producers organised in household units. Settlement policies of free and cheap land gave immigrants the possibility of beginning or maintaining a domestic mode of production by owning and working their land, the principal means of production during the period considered. At the same time that the spread of capitalist/working-class relations of production was eliminating 'precapitalist' petty production in some developing areas of the capitalist world, commercial, industrial, and finance capital in Canada was creating and maintaining, until the Depression of the 1930s, a relative haven for a surplus population engaged in 'precapitalist' petty production. However, the form of petty production produced and reproduced was specialised, a form that provided a cash basis for surplus appropriation by big capital of the independent labour of this newly created population: independent (domestic) *commodity* production. The wheat boom provided the link between capitalist underdevelopment through single-staple dependence and capitalist underdevelopment through the production and reproduction of a surplus population via the domestic mode of commodity production.

Because wheat growing by Prairie petty producers tended to be done by household units on owner-operated farms with few hired hands,[29] and because this mode of production tended to be organised around the fulfillment of household needs,[30] direct exploitation of non-owning workers was mitigated, though by no means eliminated.[31] However, in the broader context of capitalist development, mechanisms of unequal exchange, as *distinct* from capitalist/working-class exploitation at the point of production, were utilised to appropriate value that was surplus to the production and reproduction of these producers' means of subsistence and mode of commodity production. Underdevelopment in terms of surplus appropriation was therefore indirect, not derived from the process of production itself but from the costs of inputs and the prices of outputs of production:[32]

Prairie farmers sold their crop as individual small unit producers on a ... world market. The agricultural producer owned and controlled nothing but his farm and whatever farm machinery he was able to afford (many farmers would insist that the bank really owned their means of production). Eastern finance capital controlled every other step in the financing, storage, transportation, processing, and marketing of the farmer's product.[33]

In the context of capitalist underdevelopment through the production and reproduction of a subordinated, monolithic, single-staple/single-class regional economy, Prairie wheat growers directed their co-operative attack against big capital's surplus appropriation through unequal exchange. Caught in a cost-price squeeze defined by land alienation to the CPR and land companies, protective tariffs, and monolithic transportation and marketing mechanisms, all in the context of a world wheat trade system, Prairie farmers established co-operative business ventures keyed to freeing the free market wherever possible.

Grain growers' co-operative business enterprises grew out of prior experience gained in the failure of fraternal, educational, and protest movements to achieve a better deal through formal political alterations to the system of unequal exchange.[34] Before 1900, organisations such as the Manitoba and Northwest Farmers' Union and the Patrons of Industry,[35] had attempted to combat rising production costs and falling wheat prices primarily by securing antimonopolistic legislative regulations.[36] With the wheat boom and its associated increasing staple dependence and rising wheat prices (until 1909), growers began focusing their main organisational efforts on co-operative marketing in order to receive a larger portion of the increasing value of their staple product.[37] Conceivably, without changing their staple dependence and mode of production, grain growers could receive a better return on their investment and labour by cutting the costs of inputs, or by receiving a better price for their output by lowering marketing margins.[38] Grain-handling and marketing co-operatives represented an attempt to cut out or at least compete effectively with grain-company middlemen and thereby secure better returns. Marketing co-operation became the main programme because (1) it attacked locally controllable aspects of the monopolistic system of unequal exchange; (2) it did not require the tariff changes necessary to cut production costs quickly; and (3) it could nelp secure single-staple dependence and independent commodity production while attacking collectively, in a capitalistic, business-like, joint-stock manner, unfair marketing margins.[39]

Beginning with the successful formation of grain growers' associations in

1901 and culminating in 1917 with the formation of a region-wide joint-stock company, the United Grain Growers Limited, wheat growers attempted to combat the North West Grain Dealers Association's marketing monopoly by collectively competing with it. This struggle led directly to the successful fight for contract co-operative wheat pools in the 1920s (and the unsuccessful fight for the 100 per cent pool):

Under the pool system of non-profit operation and direct selling, the farmer is receiving in effect the competitive world price, less the actual costs of handling, transportation and selling. The advantage to producers lies not only in the direct return of that portion of marketing margins which constitutes the middleman's profit, but also in further reduction of marketing costs through the potential economies of large-scale, centralized selling.[40]

Cutting marketing margins for better returns was the central aim of the Prairie co-operative movement. Its organisational success was enormous, based as it was on a precise and monolithic structure of capitalist underdevelopment.

Intertwined with this co-operative marketing thrust was, of course, a reviving formal political attack against the non-locally controllable aspects of unequal distribution such as the protective tariff.[41] In formal third-party politics, as in formal co-operation, unequal distribution was the rallying point; in this case, unequal distribution was perceived to be corrigible by altering the rules of the game of capitalist development. In the absence of an attack on capitalist underdevelopment and the consequent single-staple mode of primary commodity production, both the Prairie co-operative path and its third parties have failed to solve for many Prairie farmers their 'persistent inability to transform their productive organization in response to evolving conditions of production which continually threaten to undermine their viability.'[42]

CAPITALIST UNDERDEVELOPMENT, VARYING MODES OF PRIMARY PRODUCTION, AND THREE NOVA SCOTIAN PATHS ON THE MARITIME THIRD ROAD

While central Canadian capital encouraged the underdevelopment of the west, it extended its nation-building hegemony over the Maritimes through a process of industrial and financial consolidation. Competitive indigenous manufacturing industries were absorbed by relatively more concentrated and centralised central Canadian capital pools and were often shut or run down—a process that was abetted by the national transportation policy.[43] An active indigenous banking system was completely absorbed and altered; small or noncompetitive indigenous industries such as the fisheries were starved of capital.[44] Along with this de-industrialisation of the Maritimes and consequent production and reproduction of a huge surplus population, the building of a consolidated national economy with division of labour between (and within) regions encouraged the expansion of selected primary industries, notably coal and steel, to take advantage of the Maritime region's vast resources and surplus-labour pools.[45] At the same time, other 'precapitalist' modes of primary production, notably subsistence farming and inshore fishing, were left alone or further subordinated.

In this process of capitalist underdevelopment, the region became dependent on a *wide variety* of primary production activities arranged in a variety of modes of primary production which exhibited radically different relations of production and therefore different mechanisms of surplus appropriation.

A. Coal miners' co-operative stores, 1861-1913, and the growth of capitalist/working-class relations of primary production

The main features of the capitalist underdevelopment of the Nova Scotian coal industry prior to WW 1 were (1) battles between primarily external capital centres for control over the coal fields; (2) the growing dominance of central Canadian finance capital; (3) rapid growth in coal production abetted by favourable tariffs; and (4) dependence on central Canadian markets for coal and raw steel exports.[46]

Large-scale coal mining in Nova Scotia began under the royal monopoly control of British capital when, in 1827, the General Mining Association (GMA) opened its first mine at Stellarton in Pictou County. To work it, the GMA 'brought out from England a considerable number of Miners, Colliers, Engineers and Mechanics, and a large quantity of machinery tools, implements, etc., of various descriptions.'[47] Over the first twenty years of its Nova Scotian existence, the GMA took control of all the coal mines in Nova Scotia that were or had been in operation prior to the granting of royal monopoly in 1826.[48]

In the years 1857 and 1858, in the face of sustained protest over the royal monopoly, the Nova Scotian and British governments agreed to terminate the GMA's lease to all mineral rights in the colony with the exception of operating properties in Cape Breton, Cumberland, and Pictou counties, which were leased until 1866. In return the GMA received reduced coal royalty rates.[49] Termination of this absolute monopoly and the beginning of reciprocity with the USA led to a spate of new mining operations.[50] By 1865 there were fourteen mines operating on Cape Breton Island, 'and the New Mines [centred in the Sydney-Glace Bay-Port Morien district of Cape Breton County] were raising considerably more coal than the Association's Island collieries.'[51] In 1866 there were 3,043 coal miners employed in Nova Scotia; during this period coal accounted for 30% of the value of Nova Scotia's exports, and 80% of all coal produced went to the United States.[52]

Rapid expansion of coal mining in Cape Breton County during the 1860s included an influx of American capital seeking to feed the American east coast's demand for gas, prompted by delays in extending American railways and in opening new mines due to the civil war.[53] In Cape Breton, the Glace Bay Mining Company and Little Glace Bay Mining Company (both of which involved Halifax interests as well), the Caledonia, the International Coal and Railway of New York, and the Blockhouse Mining companies were all dominated by American capitalists.[54] This domination deepened Cape Breton's dependence on the American market. Virtually all of the International's coal was destined to supply the New York Gas Works, while virtually all of the Blockhouse's coal went to similar American markets.[55]

Incursion of British capital, though more limited in size than its American counterpart, occurred during this period in both Cape Breton and Pictou counties. In 1871 the Glasgow and Cape Breton Coal Company of London began operations at Reserve Mines; later it reorganised into the Sydney and Louisbourg Coal and Railway Company, again of London.[56] In 1872 the GMA sold Albion Mines to another British operator, Sir George Elliott, through his Halifax Company. The Halifax Company was 'a subsidiary of a vast industrial-mining complex' which included mining interests in England, Wales, and Scotland; heavy industry and manufacturing; construction of European and trans-Atlantic cables; and of the Royal Alexandria Docks in Egypt; and the financing of Egyptian and Sudanese loans.[57] In 1886 Elliott sold his Pictou properties to the Acadia Coal Company.

The Acadia Coal Company had been formed as a joint-stock company in New York on 1 May 1865 and began its operations in Pictou County at Westville. Its first directors, all financial potentates, included General Marshall Lefferts, Cambridge Livingstone, Edward S. Sanford, Cyrus Field, all of New York, and Hugh Andrew Allen of Montreal.[58] In 1873, Hugh Andrew Allan (president of Allan Steamship Lines, Merchants Bank, Montreal Telegraph, and fourteen other companies, promoter and director of the Halifax and East Railway, confidant of John A. MacDonald, and a major loser in the Pacific Railway scandal) also bankrolled and became president of the Vale Coal, Iron and Manufacturing Company which operated at Thorburn in Pictou County. After Hugh Allan's death the Vale merged with Acadia, concomitant with Acadia's takeover of the Halifax Company.[59] Hugh Andrew Allan's son, Hugh Montague Allan, became president of the reorganised Acadia Coal Company and remained in this position until 1923. By 1907, a Belgian financial bloc centred around the Banque d'Outremer had acquired control of Acadia, selling out to Nova Scotia Steel and Coal in 1919.[60] By the time of Confedera-tion, Montreal-centred capital had also entered Nova Scotia in the form of the Intercolonial Coal Company, backed by the Drummond-Redpath and Molson groups of Montreal (the bank and the city) with the intention of supplying Montreal and the CPR with 'a source of coal near, and in friendly territory.'[61] The Intercolonial carried on operations in Pictou County at Westville until 1953, though production peaked in 1910.

Every company discussed thus far exhibited a common structure. All companies were joint-stock ventures, externally owned and controlled (whether American, British, or Montreal-based), and organised for the pur-pose of gleaning profits primarily through the export of the raw material from the region in order to fuel other areas and industries usually within the owners' domains. None of these companies developed any substantial coal-fired industries in Nova Scotia.

National tariff policies helped ensure a rapid growth in coal extraction, heightened dependence on the central Canadian industrial market, and intra-regional dependence on the Sydney steel plant:

The division of labour between regions established the coal industry in Nova Scotia as an important—but vulnerable—source of industrial energy in Canada.... By the eve of the First World War, Nova Scotia supplied 54 per cent of Canada's coal production—but 57 per cent of the coal consumed in Canada was imported from the United States.... In 1913 the steel plant at Sydney consumed 1,362,000 tons of coal, more than half the total coal sales in Nova Scotia.[62]

These tariff policies also abetted a Montreal-centred finance capital consolidation movement of the Nova Scotian coal fields that had begun in Pictou County in the 1860s, was joined by Toronto-centred finance capital in Cape Breton in the 1900s, and that virtually absorbed the industry by WW I.[63]

Completion of the railway to central Canada in the 1870s was followed by mergers dominated by Montreal interests in the mainland coalfields in 1884 (Cumberland Railway and Coal Co.) and 1886 (Acadia Coal Co.). Plagued by the insecurities of seasonal operations, distant markets and inadequate capital, the Cape Breton coal operators also turned to mergers.... The creation of Dominion Coal [in 1893] marked the integration of the coal industry in Cape Breton into a metropolitan network of financial control.... The establishment of the merger also marked the triumph of the strategy of exporting the province's coal resources in large volume.[64]

A further merger in 1910 of Dominion Coal, Dominion Iron and Steel, and the Cumberland Railway and Coal Company, locked the newly created Dominion Steel Corporation into a vast central Canadian finance capital network centred in Montreal around the Bank of Montreal and in Toronto around the Bank of Commerce.[65]

Externally centred monopolistic control and gradual central Canadianisation, in terms of both control and principal market, created and sustained a lack of coal-fired secondary industry in the coal-producing area. A wide array of single-industry-dependent coal towns in northern and eastern Nova Scotia were created in the process. Capitalist/working-class relations and the resultant class conflict dominated the workplace and indeed the whole community. A miner's contract bound him not only to the company mine but also to company housing and the company store; concomitantly, the petite bourgeoisie or merchants in the coal towns were permanently underdeveloped.[66]

Drawing upon organisational traditions that they had carried with them from Britain, coal miners reacted to this virtually complete corporate dominance over their lives by linking a craft unionisation struggle at the workplace to a struggle against the company store in the community. Between 1861 and 1907 every major pit was organised into the craft union, the Provincial Workmen's Association, and a co-operative store was formed in every major coal town.[67] With the post-WW I decline of the coal industry, the failure of farmer-labour third-party politics, and the consequent upsurge of militant industrial unionism and socialism in the 1920s,[68] the miners' co-operative store movement lost its link with organised workplace struggles, regaining it in the 1930s with the assumption of moderate union leadership and the consequent founding of the CCF in Nova Scotia in 1938.[69]

B. Fruit marketing co-operatives in the Annapolis Valley, 1905-1928, and the underdevelopment of independent commodity production.

Capitalist underdevelopment of the Annapolis Valley subregion of Nova Scotia produced, during the same period as the decisive underdevelopment of the west, a structure of underdevelopment remarkably similar to the Prairie west: single-staple dependence, truncated petty commodity production, and surplus appropriation through cost-price merchandising mechanisms. However, while much of the structure produced was entirely similar to that of the west, the history of the capitalist underdevelopment of the Annapolis Valley demonstrates a crucial difference between the two regions—the *lack* of integration and subordination of the valley apple industry into a central-Canadian-controlled national economy. These major structural similarities provided the principal basis for the rapid growth of marketing co-operatives in the valley during the same period as in the west. This one key difference conditioned the lack of any even moderately strong linkage between apple-marketing co-operatives and populist political formation.

From the 1860s onward, with the rise of modern rail and steamship transportation, mixed farming in the valley became increasingly dependent on a single primary product, the culinary apple, and a single export market, Britain.[70] By the early 1900s, the valley apple industry was 'the most highly specialised and prosperous agricultural industry in Nova Scotia;' represented 'the largest movement of apples from [any] single producing district to an overseas market;' and was the most geographically delimited form of agriculture in Nova Scotia.[71] Apple production grew enormously, though cyclically, in the early twentieth century; by the 1920s more than 60% of the apples produced in Nova Scotia were exported to Great Britain while Great Britain received more than 80% of its apple imports from Nova Scotia—over 90% of which were from the valley.[72]

As in Prairie grain growing, valley apple farming was overwhelmingly carried out through the domestic mode of production, though, as in the west, seasonal hiring of harvesters (in this case, pickers) did provide a mechanism of direct exploitation by the petty producers.[73] Mechanisms of surplus appropriation through unequal exchange were developed in a structurally similar fashion to those in the west. A single rail system (the Dominion Atlantic Railway, for the most part) led to a single major port (Halifax) and a British-dominated shipping cartel (that included Canadian and American shipping concerns); collective agreements among British commission houses and high insurance and mortgage rates further ensured that apple growers would be kept at about the level necessary to produce their means of subsistence and reproduce their mode of production.[74]

As growers did in the west, valley growers focused their grievances on mishandled and rapacious marketing mechanisms of unequal exchange in a period of expanding production.[75] Valley marketing co-operatives, similar to the businesslike, joint-stock variety of the Prairie grain growers, burgeoned in the pre-WW I period, leading to the formation of the United Fruit Companies of Nova Scotia in 1912 and its controversial, unsteady growth thereafter.

TABLE 2-1

NOVA SCOTIA APPLE MARKETS
BY PERCENTAGES, 1921-22 AND 1923-24

Major Markets	1921-22	1923-24
Great Britain	66.0	69.2
Liverpool	18.5	16.0
London	16.8	22.7
Manchester	15.4	21.3
Glasgow	9.4	5.1
Hull	3.1	2.4
Cardiff and Bristol	2.8	1.7
U.S.A.	5.8	—
Newfoundland	0.8	0.7
West Indies	0.3	0.2
Maritime Provinces (including apples for evaporators, cider mills and vinegar plants)	15.2	20.8
Unaccounted for	11.9	9.1
TOTAL	100.0	100.0

SOURCE: C.C. Colby, "The apple industry of the Annapolis-Cornwallis Valley," *Economic Geography*, II (1926), 338.

In a context of heightening single-staple dependence and subordinated petty commodity production, the view became generally held that 'the crux of the success of this apple industry lies in selling apples in large bulk and of medium quality at a low price in the British markets.'[76] Marketing co-operatives were formed to do a better marketing job at lower margins, thus increasing dependence on the British market while obtaining better returns on capital and labour invested, in the short run.[77] Heightened dependence on the British market proved disastrous to a majority of specialised valley apple growers when the British market collapsed absolutely during WW II and after, causing a severe structural transformation in both the industry and the valley.[78]

Concurrent with the formation of co-operative grain storage and marketing companies by single-staple-dependent wheat farmers in western Canada, apple growers in the valley were uniting for the same goals and for substantially the same reason: commercial dependence upon a single staple and upon externally controlled monopolistic storage and transportation facilities. Within Nova Scotia, valley farmers were the most specialised and dependent of all farmer segments despite being the most prosperous. Therefore, they were the most oriented to co-operative marketing action. Like western wheat farmers they formed marketing co-operatives not to attack capitalist underdevelopment through staple dependence and petty commodity production *per se*, but to profit from its growth by making redundant some of the storage middlemen and by increasing marketing efficiency through petty-producer-based mutual aid. Like Prairie co-operatives, valley co-operative fruit companies have, over the longer term, grown to typify the best of co-operative capitalism,[79] thereby often exhibiting the most oppressive of capitalist/working-class relations of production in their fruit-processing and producer-goods plants.[80]

Despite the presence of a few valley fruit growers in the Nova Scotian section of the United Farmers movement, what minimal electoral success the United Farmers of Nova Scotia did attain in the early 1920s, and what few consumer- and producer-goods co-operative stores they did establish between 1917 and 1924, did not occur in the Annapolis Valley.[81] Valley fruit growers have maintained their conservative (both small and large 'c') political culture and their co-operative integrity *despite* the many structural similarities between valley apple and Prairie grain growing. The lack of linkage between valley and Prairie political movements has indeed been an immediate consequence of the inability of western-dominated populist movements to appreciate Maritime agrarian concerns.[82] But this failure has itself been rooted in the key difference between the capitalist underdevelopment of the Prairies and the capitalist underdevelopment of the Annapolis Valley: the lack of the integration and subordination of the valley apple industry by central Canadian capital.

Capitalist underdevelopment of the Annapolis Valley was characterised by the growth of single-staple dependence on the British market and by the subordination of petty commodity production through marketing mechanisms most often dominated by British interests. There was no real integration of the apple industry into the national economy; there was no national policy with respect to underdeveloping the apple industry. Since the apple industry remained largely outside the national economy and national policy, there was no need for third-party populist political formations. Alterations in provincial regulations were obtained through the agency of the two existing parties, and proved sufficient to expand apple production; to increase staple dependence; to facilitate co-operative marketing; and to provide relative prosperity even through the Depression of the 1930s.[83]

C. Antigonish Movement co-operatives in eastern Nova Scotia, 1928-40, and varying modes of direct and indirect capitalist underdevelopment.

The amazingly diverse structure of the capitalist underdevelopment of eastern Nova Scotia[84] and its implications for Antigonish Movement co-operative formation in the period 1928 to 1940, have been amply recorded in my previous work.[85] Here it will suffice to review and *rework* my argument in the context of this comparative analysis.

i) Capitalist underdevelopment of the coal and steel industry and the success of the Antigonish Movement.

Capitalist underdevelopment of the coal and steel industry in eastern Nova Scotia during the 1920s and 1930s featured even greater capital concentration (to the point of monopoly), increased central Canadian centralisation, heightened exploitation of the working class, and further deindustrialistion of the industry in Nova Scotia.[86] Initially the working class responded to these developments with intensely militant class conflict through long and bitter strikes.[87] The smashing of these strikes by the state in the mid 1920s, and the isolation of the socialist leadership by the state, cleared the way for support among coal miners of a truncated 'middle road' response to capitalist underdevelopment—a response not of militant class struggle at the workplace and in the community but a response of bettering the condition of the worker-as-consumer through revitalised co-operative stores, credit unions, and co-operative housing projects. This was the Antigonish Way of the 1930s in the industrial areas. With the destruction of militant unionism as the main path, the movement swept the coal and steel towns and was highly successful in helping redirect working-class struggle during the 1930s and 1940s.

ii) Direct capitalist underdevelopment of the inshore fisheries and the success of the Antigonish Way.

Capitalist underdevelopment of the small-boat inshore fisheries of eastern Nova Scotia was (and is) highly complex. Like the underdevelopment of Prairie grain growing and valley fruit farming, the inshore fisheries were export dependent, the inshore fishermen's mode of petty commodity production was increasingly subordinated to the exigencies of increasingly concentrated fish companies, and the surplus value of inshore fishermen's labour was appropriated through cost-price mechanisms of unequal exchange. Like the Annapolis Valley and unlike the Prairies, capitalist underdevelopment was not integrated into the national economy and national policy. Unlike the valley and the Prairies, the cost-price squeeze was so unequal that returns were often insufficient to produce even the means of subsistence for fishermen and their families, let alone reproduce and expand the mode of petty production.[88] This situation forced members of the household unit to engage, when and where possible, in subsistence farming, woodswork, roadwork, fish-plant and other industrial labour—in the process engaging in a variety of modes and relationships of production.

Differences between the capitalist underdevelopment of the inshore fisheries in eastern Nova Scotia and Prairie and valley petty commodity production were not merely matters of degree but, more importantly, of kind. Surplus appropriation by increasingly concentrated and externally centralised fisheries capital occurred not just in the area of high costs of production (especially bait and gear) and low prices for the catch. The same merchant who sold the means of production (and of subsistence) high and bought the commodity low was himself increasingly dependent upon or actually integrated into the fish companies that directly competed with inshore fisheries *at the point of production* through ownership of the hated, but vastly more efficient, trawlers. Actual production of about half the catch in the region and control over much of the remainder allowed the integrated fish companies to treat eastern Nova Scotian inshore fishermen *as if* they were workers, treating their labour power—paid through mechanisms of unequal exchange—as a cost of the companies' integrated production and thus lowering that cost below the means of subsistence as their labour power became increasingly redundant to capitalist development through capitalist/working-class relations.[89]

While never brought into the social organisation of capitalist/working-class relations of exploitation, eastern Nova Scotia small-boat fishermen were nevertheless exploited at the point of production through capitalist/petty-producer relations of *production* within which the formal legal owners of the means of production were so subordinated to capitalist production that their independent labour became labour power from the point of view of the companies—a mere cost of production that could be lowered more safely than the labour power of socially concentrated trawler workers. This process I have termed direct underdevelopment.[90] Primary production dependence, the production and reproduction of a surplus population, *and* surplus appropriation throughout the productive labour process, even when accomplished by controlling mechanisms of unequal distribution, is direct underdevelopment.[91]

The coal and steel industries and the inshore fisheries shared the same structural problem—direct capitalist underdevelopment—despite the real differences between the social organisation and culture of capitalist/working-class relations of production in the coal and steel industry and capitalist/petty-producer relations of production in the inshore fisheries. The Antigonish Movement was highly successful in co-operatively organising the fishing villages of eastern Nova Scotia into consumer, marketing, and *producer* co-operatives precisely because it did present a third road between big capitalism, the underdeveloper, and working-class struggle—a struggle that the remnants of their 'precapitalist' mode of petty production did not immediately underpin. In the fishing villages of eastern Nova Scotia, the movement's third road represented an attempt not to link with working-class struggles at the point of production but to 'regain for the little people a stake in society'—to reclaim some independence on the consumer, marketing, and producer fronts by attacking the mechanisms of unequal exchange that were destroying their petty mode of production.

Despite the impressive growth in co-operative lobster canneries and the like, the Antigonish Movement in the fishing villages failed to alter the structure of direct capitalist underdevelopment. By 1940 many of the co-operatives had ceased business; big capital simply paid higher prices for produce until the undercapitalised co-operatives failed.

iii) Indirect capitalist underdevelopment and the failure of the Antigonish Movement in the agricultural areas of eastern Nova Scotia.

Agricultural production in eastern Nova Scotia was, during the entire period considered, principally subsistence (noncommodity) oriented or part-time, or both. In order to obtain some cash, members of the household unit were, like inshore fishermen and their families, forced to engage in other forms of petty production that were at least partially commodity oriented (fishing, woodlot cutting)[92] or in forms of wage labour. The farming areas of eastern Nova Scotia have, in the main, not participated in the national economy through commodity production precisely because these areas were (and are) necessary as a holding place for surplus-population production and reproduction—a holding area for the export of labour power to industrialised areas when needed and a relatively secure place of return during capitalist crises.[93]

Given the subsistence or part-time (or both) nature of most agricultural production in the subregion, surplus appropriation in agriculture through mechanisms of unequal exchange was much less common than in Prairie or valley petty commodity production; capitalist underdevelopment was much more indirect. This relative lack of participation in capitalistic underdevelopment, even indirectly through mechanisms of unequal exchange, explains the relative failure of the Antigonish Movement to form co-operative marketing agencies and co-operative stores in the farming areas.[94] Even those that were incorporated tended to fall apart quickly. The lack of direct underdevelopment and the relatively low degree of indirect underdevelpment explains this failure.[95]

CONCLUSIONS AND IMPLICATIONS

Prairie grain and Annapolis Valley apple production were similarly *indirectly* underdeveloped through mechanisms of unequal exchange involving capitalist/petty-producer relations of distribution in a context of increasing single-staple dependence; in both regions co-operative marketing associations mushroomed. Prairie primary producer protest included a formal political component while valley co-operation did not, largely because of a crucial difference in both the integration of primary production into a national economy and the policy of regional underdevelopment. One other case of indirect underdevelopment was considered: subsistence/part-time agricultural production in eastern Nova Scotia. In this instance, capitalist underdevelopment was so indirect and so little a part of the national market economy that eastern Nova Scotia agricultural production remained (and remains) a cheap and a safe (i.e., unorganised) holding ground for surplus-labour production and reproduction.

Two cases of the *direct* capitalist underdevelopment of primary production in the Maritimes have been examined: the coal and steel industry and the inshore fisheries of eastern Nova Scotia. In the first case, externally controlled staple dependence and capitalist/working-class relations of exploitation combined to support the coincident craft unionising and co-operative store drive by coal miners prior to WW I and the Antigonish Movement 'revitalisation' of the consumer aspects of this struggle following the destruction of the strike movement in industrial Cape Breton during the 1920s.[96] Direct capitalist underdevelopment of the inshore fisheries through externally controlled staple dependence and capitalist/petty-producer relations of *production* supported the widespread acceptance of Antigonish Movement consumer, marketing, and producer co-operatives during the 1930s in eastern Nova Scotia. Unlike the movement's programme in the coal and steel towns, the full range of co-operation (including producer co-operatives) was encouraged and organised. Unlike the valley and Prairie cases, direct underdevelopment conditioned the acceptance of the movement's third road—an acceptance that was aided by the failure of the socialist leadership in industrial Cape Breton to forge strong links with the directly underdeveloped inshore fisheries areas.[97] Like the valley and unlike the Prairie case, the inshore fisheries stood outside the national economy and thus a formal political response was neither necessary nor forthcoming.[98]

This analysis and its focus on variegated processes and structures of capitalist underdevelopment should provoke considerable rethinking on the part of students of Canadian society and, more particularly, of Canadian social movements. It is true that as long as one examines only the formal, political activities of primary producers during the period considered, the Maritimes do indeed look as bleak as a salt-cod shingle *vis-à-vis* Prairie protest; but this view is deficient. An analysis of variations on the theme of capitalist underdevelopment facilitates not only the recognition but also the explanation of the incidence, direction, and impact of a wide variety of both political and nonpolitical social movements in a manner that is more adequate (i.e., more encompassing and incisive) than the western-based single-staple/single-class model. Presumably, the underdevelopment argument will work for the understanding of other nonco-operative paths on the third road. Certainly the argument requires that political decentralists[99] incorporate a position on capitalist development/ underdevelopment *per se*. Finally, the argument provides a nonpopulist, structural basis for the critical linking of directly underdeveloped petty producers and their struggles to the general framework of capitalist/working-class conflict.

NOTES

An earlier draft of this paper was presented before both the third Atlantic Canada Studies Conference (University of New Brunswick, April 1978) and the meetings of the Canadian Sociology and Anthropology Association (University of Western Ontario, June 1978). I greatly appreciate the detailed comments on this earlier draft that were made by Bob Brym, David Frank, Colin Howell, Dan MacInnes, Sheva Medjuck, and Del Muise.

1. J. T. Croteau, *Cradled in the waves: the story of a people's co-operative achievement in economic betterment on Prince Edward Island, Canada* (Toronto, 1951); Monique Gauvin-Chouinard et al., 'Vue d'ensemble sur le mouvement cooperatif acadien,' *L'Acayen*, III (1976), 10-34; R. J. Sacouman, 'Underdevelopment and the structural origins of Antigonish Movement co-operatives in eastern Nova Scotia,' chapter 2 in this volume; R. J. Sacouman, 'Co-operative community development among Nova Scotian primary producers, 1861-1940: a critical review of three cases,' *Issues in regional/urban development of Atlantic Canada*, ed. N. B. Ridler (Saint John, 1978), 11-26; L. R. Ward, *Nova Scotia: the land of co-operation* (New York, 1942).

2. L. G. Barrett, 'Development and underdevelopment, and the rise of trade unionism in the fishing industry of Nova Scotia, 1900-1950' (unpub. MA thesis, Dalhousie University, 1976); David Frank, 'Class conflict in the coal industry: Cape Breton 1922,' *Essays in Canadian working class history*, ed. G. S. Kealey and P. Warrian (Toronto, 1976).

3. E.g., A. A. Mackenzie, 'The rise and fall of the Farmer-Labour Party in Nova Scotia' (unpub. MA thesis, Dalhousie University, 1969).

4. E.g., J. A. Irving, *The Social Credit movement in Alberta* (Toronto, 1959); S. M. Lipset, *Agrarian Socialism* (Berkeley, 1971); C. B. Macpherson, *Democracy in Alberta* (Toronto, 1953); W. L. Morton, *The Progressive Party in Canada* (Toronto, 1950).

5. Lipset, *Agrarian socialism*, 39-56.

6. E.g., J. F. Conway, 'From petitions to politics: the agitation for redress of Prairie agrarian grievances 1830-1930,' a paper presented before the Canadian Sociology and Anthropology Association (Fredericton, 1977); J. N. McCrorie, 'Change and paradox in agrarian social movements: the case of Saskatchewan,' *Canadian society: pluralism, change and conflict*, ed. R. J. Ossenberg (Scarborough, 1971), 36-51; P. R. Sinclair, 'Class structure and populist protest: the case of western Canada,' *Canadian Journal of Sociology*, I (1975), 1-17.

7. See, for example, D. Campbell and R. A. MacLean, *Beyond the Atlantic roar: a study of the Nova Scotia Scots* (Toronto, 1974).

8. R. J. Brym, 'Regional social structure and agrarian radicalism in Canada: the cases of Alberta, Saskatchewan, and New Brunswick,' *Canadian Review of Sociology and Anthropology*, XV (1978); E. R. Forbes, 'Never the twain did meet: Prairie-Maritime relations, 1910-1927,' a paper presented before the Canadian Historical Association (Fredericton, 1977). For a comparison of a producer-based social movement in Newfoundland, with the western agrarian movement, see G. Panting, 'The Fishermen's Protective Union of Newfoundland and the farmers' organizations in western Canada,' CHA, *Report*, 1963, 141-51.

9. Brym, *ibid.*, has clearly presented the structural similarities between independent commodity production in the potato-growing Saint John River valley of New Brunswick and the wheat-growing west and has demonstrated the positive significance of those similarities as a support base for the United Farmers movement. What remains is to document the *positive* significance of other forms of primary production in the Maritimes for the formation of 'nonpolitical' social movements.

10. J. A. Banks, *The sociology of social movements* (London, 1972); R. Hann, *Farmers confront industrialism: some historical perspectives on Canadian agrarian political movements* (Toronto, 1973).

11. K. Marx, *Capital* (3 v., New York, 1967), III; *Grundisse: foundations of the critique of political economy* (London, 1973); *The revolutions of 1848* (London, 1973); *Surveys from exile* (London, 1973); *Capital* (London, 1976), I.

12. Marx, *Capital*, I. Besides Marx's argument, see the recent restatement of the necessity of capital concentration and centralisation, and therefore uneven development, given 'the tendency for the rate of profit to fall,' in H. Veltmeyer, 'Dependency and underdevelopment: some questions and problems,' *Canadian Journal of Political and Social Theory*, II (1978), 55-71.

13. P. A. Baran, *The political economy of growth* (4th ed., New York, 1967); E. Mandel, *Capitalism and regional disparities* (Toronto, 1973).

14. S. Amin, *Unequal development* (New York, 1976).

15. See, for example, Veltmeyer, 'Dependency and underdevelopment,' and chapter 1 of this volume.

16. Marx, *Capital*, I, first section.

17. B. Bernier, 'The penetration of capitalism in Quebec agriculture,' *Canadian Review of Sociology and Anthropology*, XIII (1976), 422-34; M. J. Hedley, 'Independent commodity production and the dynamics of tradition,' *Canadian Review of Sociology and Anthropology*, XIII (1976), 413-21; 'Transformation of the domestic mode of production,' a paper presented before the Canadian Sociology and Anthropology Association (Fredericton, 1977).

18. Sacouman, 'Underdevelopment,' and 'The underdevelopment of primary produc-

tion dependent rural communities in Maritime Canada,' a paper presented before the Ninth World Congress of Sociology, held under the auspices of the International Sociological Association (Uppsala University, 1978).

19. The preceding three paragraphs introduce my version of 'revisiting' the staples approach to political economy. See, for example, M. Watkins, 'The staple theory revisited,' *Journal of Canadian Studies*, XII (1977), 83-95.

20. V. C. Fowke, *The National Policy and the wheat economy* (Toronto, 1957); 'The myth of the self-sufficient Canadian pioneer,' Royal Society of Canada, *Transactions*, LVI (1962), pt. 3, 23-27. See also P. Phillips, 'The hinterland perspective: the political economy of Vernon C. Fowke,' *Canadian Journal of Political and Social Theory*, II (1978), 73-96.

21. In this analysis, ranching and mining, both of which were centred in southwestern Alberta, are ignored in order to focus on the predominant form of primary production in the rest of the region, grain growing. For a comparison of ranching and farming, see J. W. Bennett, *Northern plainsmen: adaptive strategy and agrarian life* (Chicago, 1969). For an analysis of the implications for populist political support of the differing social organisation of ranching and grain growing in the prairies, see Brym, 'Regional social structure.' For a description of the radical thrust of southwestern Alberta miners, see A. R. McCormack, *Reformers, rebels, and revolutionaries: the western Canadian radical movement, 1899-1919* (Toronto, 1977).

22. See, for example, V. C. Fowke, *Canadian agricultural policy: the historic pattern* (Toronto, 1946), and *The National Policy*.

23. G. F. G. Stanley, *The birth of western Canada: a history of the Riel rebellions* (Toronto, 1963), and, more clearly, J. F. Conway, 'The place of the prairie west in Confederation,' a paper presented before the Canadian Sociology and Anthropology Association (Fredericton, 1977).

24. A. S. Morton, *History of prairie settlement* (Toronto, 1938).

25. C. A. Dawson and E. R. Younge, *Pioneering in the prairie provinces: the social side of the settlement process* (Toronto, 1940).

26. Macpherson, *Democracy in Alberta*.

27. See, for example, W. A. Mackintosh, *Economic problems of the prairie provinces* (Toronto, 1935), and *The economic background of dominion-provincial relations* (Toronto, 1964), 29-34.

28. Mackintosh, *Economic problems*. See also *The Rowell-Sirois report: book one*, ed. D. V. Smiley (Toronto, 1963). The wheat boom of 1896-1913 was global in impact due to a restructuring of the world wheat economy, rising wheat prices, and generally falling transportation costs: D. B. Grigg, *The agricultural systems of the world* (Cambridge, 1974). As well as these factors, regional conditions of free and cheap land intensified the boom in the west: Mackintosh, *Economic problems*. Between 1900 and 1920 the wheat area in Canada expanded from 1.6 to 7.3 million hectares: Grigg, *Agricultural systems*, 262. For data on wheat production, wheat and flour exports, and prairie population growth, see Mackintosh, *Economic problems*, 14, 15, and 281. For discusssions of the impact of the wheat boom on increased central Canadian manufacturing, see Conway, 'From petitions to politics,' 25ff., and *Rowell-Sirois*, 107.

29. Sinclair, 'Class structure and populist protest,' tables 2 and 3.

30. Hedley, 'Transformation,' 2.

31. Of course, hired hands were directly exploited. And since legal ownership and actual control of farm commodity production rested with the male head of the household, farm women and children can be viewed as having been exploited. While this point needs a great deal more research, it is unquestionable that working conditions of all household members, but especially of women and children, became increasingly oppres-

sive with post-WW II farm mechanisation and the onslaught of corporate farming;*ibid.*

32. Fowke, 'The myth;' Hedley, 'Independent commodity production,' 416, and 'Transformation.' On this general point, see also McCrorie, 'Change and paradox,' and J. W. Warnock, 'The farm crisis,' *Essays on the left*, ed. L. Lapierre et al. (Toronto, 1971).

33. B. Jeffcott, 'Co-operative capitalism: arc co-ops really different?' *Next Year Country*, V (1978), 24.

34. H. S. Patton, *Grain growers' co-operation in western Canada* (Cambridge, Mass., 1928), chapter 3.

35. Morton, *History of prairie settlement*, 93-116; Patton, *Grain growers' co-operation*; P. F. Sharp, *The agrarian revolt in western Canada: a survey showing American parallels* (Minneapolis, 1948); L. A. Wood, *A history of farmers' movements in Canada: the origins and development of agrarian protest, 1872-1924* (Toronto, 1975), 11-146.

36. Patton. *Grain growers' co-operation*. Conway, 'From petitions to politics,' has provided the most concise and apposite review of these organisations to date.

37. Sharp, *The agrarian revolt*, 29. A subsidiary development to the growth of marketing co-operation was the growth of producer and consumer goods co-operatives to lower the costs of production and the means of subsistence. See J. F. C. Wright, *Prairie progress: consumer co-operation in Saskatchewan* (Saskatoon, 1956).

38. Patton, *Grain growers' co-operation*, 399.

39. The detailed story of the rapid rise of grain growers' marketing co-operation has been told often and will not be repeated here. See H. Boyd, *New breaking: an outline of co-operation among the farmers of western Canada* (Toronto, 1938); R. D. Colquette, *The first fifty years: a history of United Grain Growers Limited* (Winnipeg, 1957); Fowke, *The National Policy*, 85ff.; Patton, *Grain growers' co-operation*, 30ff.; Sharp, *The agrarian revolt*, 32-53; Wood, *A history of farmers' movements in Canada*, 157-222, 314-27.

40. Patton, *Grain growers' co-operation*, 399.

41. See Conway, 'From petitions to politics,' 48ff.

42. Hedley, 'Transformation,' 1. See also L. A. Johnson, 'The development of class in Canada in the twentieth century,' *Capitalism and the national question in Canada*, ed. G. Teeple (Toronto, 1972).

43. T. W. Acheson, 'The National Policy and the industrialisation of the Maritimes,' *Acadiensis*, I (1972), 3-28; 'The Maritimes and "Empire Canada,"' *Canada and the burden of unity*, ed. D. J. Bercuson (Toronto, 1977), 87-114; E. R. Forbes, 'Misguided symmetry: the destruction of regional transportation policy for the Maritimes,' *Canada and the burden of unity*, Bercuson, 60-86; N. Reilly, 'The origins of the Amherst general strike, 1890-1919,' a paper presented before the Canadian Historical Association (Fredericton, 1977).

44. Acheson, 'The National Policy;' T. Naylor, *A history of Canadian business* (2v., Toronto, 1975); J. T. Sears, *Institutional financing of small business in Nova Scotia* (Toronto, 1972).

45. D. Frank, 'The Cape Breton coal industry and the rise and fall of the British Empire Steel Corporation,' *Acadiensis*, VII (1977), 5.

46. *Ibid.*, 5-13; R. J. Sacouman, 'Social origins of Antigonish Movement co-operative associations in eastern Nova Scotia' (unpub. PhD thesis, University of Toronto, 1976), 93-109.

47. Cited in J. M. Cameron, *The Pictonian colliers* (Kentville, N. S., 1974), 22.

48. *Ibid.*, 21-33.

49. B.D. Tennyson, 'Economic nationalism and Confederation: a case study in Cape Breton,' *Acadiensis*, II (1972), 40; Cameron, *The Pictonian colliers*, 30.

50. C. O. MacDonald, *The coal and iron industries of Nova Scotia* (Halifax, 1909), 21-37.

51. Tennyson, 'Economic nationalism and Confederation,' 40.

52. *Ibid.*

53. Saunders, 'The Maritime provinces and the reciprocity treaty,' *Dalhousie Review*, XIV (1934), 366-77.

54. MacDonald, *The coal and iron industries*, 21-27.

55. *Ibid.*, 26; Tennyson, 'Economic nationalism and Confederation,' 42n.

56. MacDonald, *The coal and iron industries*, 34.

57. Cameron, *The Pictonian colliers*, 83.

58. *Ibid.*, 48.

59. *Ibid.*, 71-73.

60. *Ibid.*, 54-55.

61. Cited in *ibid.*, 34.

62. Frank, 'The Cape Breton coal industry,' 9-10.

63. By 1913 the single major exception to this rule was the indigenously controlled Nova Scotia Steel and Coal Company: Acheson, 'The National Policy;' J. M. Cameron, *Industrial history of the New Glasgow district* (New Glasgow, N. S., 1964). But even this exception was closely linked to central Canadian finance capital: Frank, 'The Cape Breton coal industry,' 13.

64. Frank, 'The Cape Breton coal industry,' 10-11. In examining the debilitating effects of the entrance of Montreal capital into Maritime manufacturing, Acheson has contrasted Montreal-based consolidations of Maritime manufacturing, which 'aimed to restrict output and limit expansion,' with Montreal takeovers of Maritime coal fields, which 'were designed to control and expand the output of this fuel source, partially in an effort to free the Canadian Pacific Railways from dependence upon the strike-prone American coal industry.' While a more secure, strike-free source of fuel was undoubtedly a major reason for coal field takeovers, Acheson tends to overstate the positive effects of Montreal control over Nova Scotian coal production. He rates as positive the mere expansion of coal extraction for Montreal industry without accounting for the underdeveloping effects of a failure to utilise within the region an irreplaceable resource for the development of local manufacturing. See Acheson, 'The National Policy,' 15-16.

65. *Ibid.*, 12; G. Piédalue, 'Les groupes financiers au Canada, 1900-1930: étude préliminaire,' *Revue d'Histoire de l'Amérique Française*, XXX (1976), 3-34; Sacouman, 'Social origins,' 103-105.

66. I am indebted to Del Muise, an historian of industrial Cape Breton, for emphasising this point.

· 67. For a detailed description of the incidence, socio-cultural underpinnings, programme, and impact of the coal miners' co-op stores, see Sacouman, 'Co-operative community development,'.

68. Frank, 'Class conflict in the coal industry;" Mackenzie, 'The rise and fall of the Farmer-Labour Party.'

69. P. MacEwan, *Miners and steelworkers: labour in Cape Breton* (Toronto, 1976).

70. Indeed, given these two factors, the valley apple industry became dependent on specialised types of culinary apples, those tasty to the British palate.

71. C. C. Colby, 'An analysis of the apple industry of the Annapolis-Cornwallis Valley,' *Economic Geography*, I (1925), 173-75.

72. *Ibid.*, 173, and 'The apple industry of the Annapolis-Cornwallis Valley: part II,' *Economic Geography*, II (1926), 337.

73. B. A. Campbell, 'Changes in farm organization and practices in the Annapolis Valley of Nova Scotia from 1929-32 to 1939-41,' *Economic Annalist*, II (1942), 24-27; N. Morse, 'An economic history of the apple industry of the Annapolis Valley, Nova Scotia' (unpub. PhD thesis, University of Toronto, 1952).

74. Nova Scotia, Royal Commission on the Apple Industry, *Report* 1930; R. J. Sacouman, 'Dependence and co-operation: the Annapolis Valley co-operative movement to WW II,' *Maritime regional studies: the Annapolis Valley*, ed. the Maritime Research Group (Windsor, N. S., forthcoming).

75. W. V. Longley, *Some economic aspects of the apple industry in Nova Scotia* (Halifax, 1932), 35.

76. Colby, 'An analysis of the apple industry,' 195.

77. This dependence situation also underpinned a variety of individual entrepreneurial responses to high marketing margins. A major example of such a response was George A. Chase's establishment of Port Williams as a competitive port to Halifax. See Sacouman, 'Dependence and co-operation.'

78. H. A. Blackmer, 'Agricultural transformation in a regional system: the Annapolis Valley, Nova Scotia' (unpub. PhD thesis, Stanford University, 1976); also A. D. Ells, 'The Nova Scotia fruit industry' (unpub. MA thesis, Acadia University, 1965); A. Lewis, 'An apple-less valley?: processes and change in the apple industry of King's County, Nova Scotia, 1940-1974' (unpub. BA honours thesis, Acadia University, 1974); Morse, 'An economic history of the apple industry.'

79. Jeffcott, 'Co-operative capitalism.'

80. For a more detailed description of the valley marketing co-operative path, see Sacouman, 'Dependence and co-operation.'

81. Forbes, 'Never the twain did meet,' 6-10; Mackenzie, 'The rise and fall of the Farmer-Labour Party.'

82. Forbes, 'Never the twain did meet,' 6-10.

83. In his commentary on an earlier draft, Colin Howell, an historian of Maritime political agitation, has noted that 'the only exception [to this point] would be the valley's support for repeal in the 1880s—but that at a time when markets were shrinking.' Bob Brym has argued to me that the widespread, though admittedly short-lived, success of the United Farmers of New Brunswick in the potato counties may well represent a falsifying case of my argument regarding the strong linkage between lack of integration in an underdeveloping national economy and the likelihood of a political response: see Brym, 'Regional social structure.' This would indeed be so if staple dependence on an external, nonnational market (the USA) was in fact increasing during WW I and the immediate post-WW I period; my initial reading of rather crude census data indicates that this was not the case and that decline in external staple dependence did combine with threatened and real changes in national transportation policy to condition a political response: see Forbes, 'Misguided symmetry.'

84. Eastern Nova Scotia is coterminus with the Roman Catholic Diocese of Antigonish and consists in the three easternmost counties of mainland Nova Scotia (Pictou, Antigonish, and Guysborough) and Cape Breton Island.

85. Sacouman, 'Social origins of Antigonish Movement;' and 'Underdevelopment.'

86. Frank, 'The Cape Breton coal industry,' 14ff.; Sacouman, 'Social origins of the Antigonish Movement,' 106-111.

87. See esp. Frank, 'The Cape Breton coal industry.'

88. Sacouman, 'Underdevelopment,' 80-81.The extreme degree of unequal exchange wrought by fish merchants and,later, by integrated fish companies has led some analysts, notably S. Antler, 'Colonial exploitation' and E. Antler,'Maritime mode of production' to argue for the objectively proletarian character of the inshore fisheries. It seems to me that this argument is overstated because it does not adequately confront important social organisational differences between the mode of production of the inshore fisheries on the east coast during the period considered and the modern capitalist mode of production that concentrates and organises in one place a mass of machinery and of labour

power. Indeed, S. Antler (in this volume) has since altered his interpretation to focus on capitalist/petty-producer relations of surplus appropriation. Direct underdevelopment, as discussed in this subsection of the text, is suggested as leading to a more apposite understanding of the actual process of subordination and surplus value appropriation than the view of the inshore fisheries as having been a mode of production exhibiting capitalist/working-class relations. For an analysis of the Fishermen's Protective Union of Newfoundland that uses a somewhat similar notion of direct capitalist underdevelopment, see chapter 9.

89. E. Antler, 'Colonial exploitation;' Barrett,'Development and underdevelopment.'

90. Sacouman, 'Underdevelopment.'

91. The current onslaught of corporate farming in both the Annapolis Valley and the Prairie west is rapidly bringing these areas into the realm of direct capitalist underdevelopment. See Blackmer, 'Agricultural transformation;' Hedley, 'Transformation;' and Warnock, 'The farm crisis.'

92. Indeed, in many shore areas of eastern Nova Scotia petty producers are still unsure of their own occupation—one day defining themselves as farmers, the next fishermen, the next woodlot owners.

93. Sacouman, 'Underdevelopment,' 74-44; J. F. Graham, *Fiscal adjustment and economic development: a case study of Nova Scotia* (Toronto, 1963), 22; Veltmeyer, 'The underdevelopment of Atlantic Canada.'

94. Sacouman, 'Underdevelopment,' 83.

95. Coal and steel, fishing, and farming areas accounted for over 90 per cent of the census subdivisions of eastern Nova Scotia during the period considered. See Sacouman, 'Social origins of Antigonish Movement,' esp. tables 5, 10, 15, 21, and 23.

96. F. J. Mifflen, 'The Antigonish Movement: a revitalization movement in eastern Nova Scotia' (unpub. PhD thesis, Boston College, 1974).

97. See chapter 4.

98. Of course, my argument awaits more extensive comparative support.

99. As in, for example, *Canada and the burden of unity*, Bercuson

3   Political Conservatism in Atlantic Canada

Robert J. Brym

The Liberal and Progressive Conservative parties dominate the political environment [of New Brunswick] without fear of challenge or stimulation by third parties....The electorate seems satisfied with this arrangement. If there were a felt need in the province for a more progressive or ideological mode of politics, then presumably viable alternatives to the two traditional parties would have arisen.[1]

A presumption like the above—that electors in New Brunswick or, for that matter, in any liberal-democratic political system, get, if not what they deserve, then at least what they want—lies at the basis of most political theorising in contemporary North America. It supports the argument that ours is a society composed of various sections (class, regional, ethnic, religious, etc.); that these sections freely compete in the political marketplace to have their interests best served; that conflicting demands are balanced and reconciled through compromise and concession; and therefore that in the long run all sectional interests are woven into the fabric of public policy.

However, as a number of sociologists and political scientists have recently sought to establish, the assumption that mass demands are equitably translated into government action is not without its problems. In a review of North American research that bears upon this issue, John Shiry notes that most citizens are typically not active and informed participants in the political process, so that only a minority make demands that have implications for public policy in the first place.[2] Second, it has been shown that 'such political factors as level of party competition, level of voter turnout, degree of malapportionment, and party in office ... [are] *not* predictive of the levels of expenditure across a wide range of policy areas:' precisely the opposite of what one would expect if mass demands mattered much in deciding public policy.[3] On the basis of these and other findings Shiry concludes that 'citizen attitudes, and the structures through which they are expressed, either do not have the influence on policy outcomes which they are thought to have, or they have an impact which is independent of any political intentions by the public expressing them.'[4]

Rick Ogmundson reaches much the same conclusion in his analysis of why, as has frequently been noted, the class issue is relatively unimportant in Canadian politics—indeed, less important than in almost all other Western political systems.[5] Use of a semantic differential scale on a random sample of electors revealed the existence of a wide discrepancy between actual class images of parties (i.e., perceptions of party policies on class issues) and ideal class images of parties (i.e., desired party policies on class issues). Canadian political parties are generally viewed as 'too middle class,' even by members of the middle class themselves, but especially by working-class people. This, combined with the survey finding that the extent of working- and lower-class identification in Canada appears to be as high as that in France, Italy, and other European countries,[6] amounts to a pretty devastating empirical critique of the view that, if lower-class voters in New Brunswick or elsewhere do not establish or vote for third parties, then this can be attributed exclusively to their own preferences.

Consider also in this connection the following direct evidence concerning Atlantic Canadians' political preferences. The results of two large surveys conducted in 1965 and 1968, at a time of relative *prosperity*, clearly reveal that voters in Atlantic Canada are the most politically disaffected and cynical citizens in the country. On the whole, they tended more than voters in other regions to believe that there is widespread government corruption and wastage of tax money; that members of government can be trusted to do what is right only some of the time; that quite a few members of government do not know what they are doing; and that at least some government officials pay more attention to large rather than small interests.[7] They overwhelmingly felt that they could do nothing to have the federal government change a proposed bill they considered wrong or unfair; that they have no say in what government does; that the government does not care what people like them think; and that persons elected to Parliament soon lose touch with the people.[8] These and other researches[9] indicate the existence of widespread grievances in Atlantic Canada against government: the commonly held opinion that Atlantic Canadians are more or less satisfied with the way in which they are ruled, or are at least more satisfied than other Canadians who have aligned themselves with third parties, is obviously contradicted by these findings.

It may be altogether more accurate to claim that they have little alternative to traditional party choices. What Maurice Pinard wrote about the lower classes in Quebec (this was before the rise of the Parti québécois) applies with equal force to Atlantic Canada: 'What has characterised the Quebec political scene is the failure of the elites even to develop leftist organisations and parties....The lower classes often supported conservative organisations or parties, but only because they were not presented with strong alternatives more consonant with their interests and sentiments.'[10] Pinard (along with Ogmundson and Shiry) thus suggests that we consider substantially revising the logic of much political theory. In liberal democracies, public policy, and the direction and level of party support, may be more the result of ruling-

class interest than of lower-class desire. As Michael Mann has demonstrated
for the USA and Britain, lower classes may accept ongoing political arrangements only pragmatically: not by internalising the moral expectations of the
ruling class and viewing their own inferior position as legitimate, but merely
by complying because no realistic alternatives are perceived.[11] He might well
have added that realistic alternatives tend not to be created when a ruling
class has enough power to prevent their emergence.

It should be apparent that what is fundamentally at stake here is an
adequate conception of the relationship between social classes and political
parties—one that will allow us to explain the texture of political life in given
settings. The view that parties are merely mechanical expressions of class (or
other group) interests is, I submit, overly simplistic.[12] The dialectical view that
parties, in addition to expressing their members' class interests can, under
certain specifiable conditions, prevent the expression of *other* classes' interests,
more reasonably captures the manner in which political systems operate. As
Antonio Gramsci wrote: 'In fact, if it is true that parties are only the nomen-
clature for classes, it is also true that parties are not simply a mechanical and
passive expression of those classes, but react energetically upon them in order
to develop, solidify and universalise them.'[13]

Central to an understanding of how many and what types of parties
compete in a given setting is an appreciation of the relative *power* of classes
within that setting. The power of a class may be defined as its structurally
determined capacity to decide issues, to determine which issues are to be
considered contentious, to suppress manifest conflict, and to prevent latent
conflict from emerging.[14] The structural determinants of power are (in
ascending order of importance) the class's relative size, its level of social
organisation, and its control over material and other resources.[15] It may be
suggested that, the more *closely* ranked antagonistic classes are in terms of
their relative power, the more likely it is that opposed political parties will
reflect the interests of these classes. On the other hand, the greater the *discrepancy* between the power positions of antagonistic classes, the more likely it is
that opposed political parties will reflect the interests only of the *dominant*
class: the interests of subordinate classes will in the latter case tend not to be
represented at all since the dominant class has the capacity to universalise its
interests through the party system as well as other institutions;[16] party conflict, rather than being a manifestation of conflict between opposed classes,
will in essence be merely a conflict betweens the 'ins' and the 'outs' of the same
class.[17]

Below I shall suggest that the Atlantic Canadian situation closely resembles the second case. Third parties representative of the interests of petty
primary producers or of workers (or of both) have tended not to emerge
because these classes are relatively powerless. And their powerlessness is, I
hope to show, largely explicable in terms of the character of underdevelopment in the region.

Not that third parties have failed entirely to surface in Atlantic Canada.
In the 1910s and 1920s fishermen, farmers, lumbermen, miners, and steel-

workers were particularly successful in mobilising politically, and I shall seek to demonstrate that these exceptions to the general rule occurred due to a shift in the distribution of power between classes—a shift occasioned partly by the emergence of different patterns of underdevelopment.

POLITICS AND CLASS STRUCTURE IN ATLANTIC CANADA

In Atlantic Canada political life has typically been fueled by a steady flow of material inducements from members of the ruling class to political leaders to electors. Partly as a simple matter of exchange, electors deliver votes to the traditional parties with numbing regularity and political leaders enact legislation which, at least in the long run, tends to favour the common interests of the whole ruling class.[18]

Even today, a substantial portion of these exchanges falls under the rubric of corrupt pratice.[19] Vote-buying, for example, is one of the most widespread and effective means of soliciting support for one's party or encouraging supporters of the other party not to show up at the polling station on election day. J. B. McNair, long-time Liberal premier of New Brunswick, privately estimated in 1931 that as much as half the electorate in some constituencies could be bought, and there is no reason to believe that exchanging pints of rum or envelopes containing $2 bills for votes was at the time any less common in the other provinces of Atlantic Canada.[20] Nor should one assume that vote-buying is a thing of the past, given the 1975 statement by no less an authority than Premier Gerald Regan of Nova Scotia that the practice still exists.[21] So do minor forms of election-day patronage. In New Brunswick, parties paid up to $25 a day in the 1950s to scrutineers and to drivers who transported voters to the polls; it may be taken for granted that such persons readily exchanged their votes for these payments.[22] Party representatives can and do also promise jobs—constructing roads, clearing snow, inspecting buildings, etc.—in exchange for support. And once it forms the government, a party has the added capacity to engage in 'pork-barrelling:' providing entire constituencies, especially those in which support for the incumbent party is low, with special inducements to vote correctly: new roads, schools, bridges, and the like.

A portion of the material resources available to political leaders is of course used to purchase normative means (generally regarded as noncorrupt) of influencing voters. The use of public relations agencies, campaign literature, radio, and, more recently, television advertising is so obviously widespread and growing that it need hardly be documented. The extent to which their use influences voting behaviour has been called into question from time to time, but contemporary research confirms that these expenses do pay off on election day.[23]

Where does the money used for advertising, minor patronage, and vote-buying come from? Although Atlantic Canada is and always has been a net importer of party contributions (most of the large party contributors have their head offices on St James Street in Montreal and Bay Street in Toronto),[24] local companies and branch operations are also faithful suppliers of funds to both provincial and federal levels of the traditional parties. Distilleries and breweries, firms holding or expecting government construction or supply contracts, pulp and paper concerns, mining and oil interests, banks and insurance companies rank among the most important. Money is frequently given without *very* specific expectations regarding a *quid pro quo*,[25] but, as one New Brunswick industrialist put it, 'we naturally expect the government to treat us right after we did our part to put them in.'[26] Some contributors are motivated by rather deeper concerns, supplying funds because they 'wish to preserve the two old parties and are suspicious of ... radical groups that might advocate some interference with their operations.'[27] However, regardless of whether such anxieties prompt many entrepreneurs to make party contributions, it may safely be concluded that traditional parties, because they are amply financed by owners of the means of production, have access to sufficient material resources to exercise a considerable degree of control over voting patterns.

Control over voters by a party machine is greatest where the short-run benefits offered by the machine represent a relatively large percentage of per capita income: the larger the percentage, the greater the control. As Steven Wolinetz writes in his discussion of Liberal Party organisation in Joey Smallwood's Newfoundland, a

machine-ready electorate is likely to exist when large numbers of individuals with marginal socio-economic status gain the franchise or when voters, by dint of local economic conditions, or, more likely, processes of social and economic change, become dependent on the government for the jobs, favors, or local improvements which it can offer. The large numbers of unschooled immigrants who once crowded North American cities are one example of a machine-ready electorate. Voters living in depressed economies or areas in which the government is the principal source of jobs and benefits are another.[28]

Stated otherwise, persons relatively deficient in resources that can be used to further their own political ends are prone to being induced to favour others' political ends when provided with resources by others. This condition obviously obtains more in economically depressed Newfoundland, Nova Scotia, New Brunswick, and Prince Edward Island than in other Canadian provinces.

It is not only in terms of resource control that there exists an enormous power imbalance between ruling class and lower classes. The same holds true for a second determinant of power—the level of social organisation characteristic of these two broad groupings: on the one hand, a smoothly functioning party machine, its levers and pulleys well greased by entrepreneurial largesse; on the other hand, citizens whose economic conditions render them for the most part socially atomised and therefore incapable of collective action.

The notion that collective action is greatly facilitated by the existence of strong ties among potential partisans of a social movement, and greatly hindered by the existence of weak ties, goes back at least as far as Marx and Engels' discussion, in the *Manifesto of the Communist Party*, of how the growing concentration of workers in industrial establishments permits workers increasingly to recognise their common class situation, communicate their shared sentiments, and organise collective means of defending and furthering their interests.[29] Scores of studies have subsequently confirmed the existence of a high, positive correlation between level of social solidarity and propensity to engage in collective action.[30] But the high level of capital investment necessary for the creation of a solidary, concentrated work force is precisely what an underdeveloped region lacks. Indeed, insofar as one of the chief functions of underdeveloped regions is to provide developed regions with a cheap labour supply ready for export when industrial expansion occurs, there are relatively few jobs in large *or* small industrial establishments in underdeveloped regions. Newfoundland had a real unemployment rate of about 34 per cent in 1978,[31] and, one would judge, this figure has never fallen below 20 per cent or so in any province of Atlantic Canada over the past half century or more.[32]

Moreover, petty primary production has not created many solidary groupings of farmers, fishermen, and lumbermen in Atlantic Canada. Why this is the case can be readily understood if we distinguish among three ideal-typical forms of capitalist underdevelopment: indirect/subsistence, indirect/commercial, and direct.[33] *Indirect/subsistence* capitalist underdevelopment refers to the maintenance of surplus pools of independent petty primary producers engaged mainly in subsistence (i.e., nonmarket) production. *Indirect/commercial* capitalist underdevelopment refers to the investment of capital—by both petty producers (in means of production) and large capitalists (in the realms of transportation, marketing, and supply)—for purposes of extracting cheap raw materials from underdeveloped regions and surplus value from the direct producers. Appropriaton of surplus occurs mainly through mechanisms of unequal exchange: means of production are sold high, the commodity produced is sold low. The unit of production is typically the household, and its greater efficiency as compared to large-scale capital-intensive operations involving capitalist/wage-labour relations, derives partly from the fact that the costs of its reproduction are borne to some degree by the direct producer and his family, members of which may be engaged in part-time subsistence production or in wage labour.[34] The latter process is accelerated to the extent that terms of exchange become more unequal, and when the proportion of wage labour performed by family members increases, we may speak of the partial breakup of the household productive unit and the semi-proletarianisation of its members.

Proletarianisation of *non*-wage-labouring producers in the household unit may occur when terms of exchange become more unequal or when large capitalists begin to compete with the petty producer at the point of production owing to, for example, the development of expensive technological improvements which enable large capitalists to exceed the efficiencies of the household unit. In either case the petty producer faces increasing indebtedness and therefore the loss of control over his means of production. To the extent that proletarianisation proceeds apace it is possible to speak of a third, *direct* form of capitalist underdevelopment, which involves investment of capital at the point of production for purposes of extracting raw materials from underdeveloped regions and extracting surplus value through control of the means of production. In its extreme form, direct capitalist underdevelopment involves the creation of relatively concentrated pockets of wage labourers.

Now, it is of considerable importance to note that, historically, many, if not most, petty primary producers in Atlantic Canada have tended to be affected chiefly by indirect/subsistence capitalist underdevelopment. In New Brunswick, to cite only one example, 54% of farms in 1940 were subsistence operations, compared to about 15% in heavily commercialised Saskatchewan and Alberta.[35] These figures increase to 67% for New Brunswick and 18% for Saskatchewan and Alberta if we lump together part-time and subsistence operations. This fact is significant because commercialised operations tend to draw petty producers together socially, while noncommercialised operations tend to set them apart. Thus, farmers or fishermen who sell their goods on the market will, especially if they produce only one or a few basic commodities, be affected more or less visibly and uniformly by fluctuations in the market prices for these commodities. They will have to come into contact with middlemen—merchants, bankers, salespeople—whom they tend readily to identify as their common exploiters. And they will face similar marketing and production problems, which often lead to the formation of co-operative organisations.[36] In contrast, subsistence producers have little if any need to co-operate in marketing and producing their goods. They have little or no contact with a readily identifiable set of exploiters. They are not affected very much if at all by the boom and bust cycles typical of many foodstuff prices. They are, in a word, not involved in a system of production that generates solidarity among them, and, like so many primary producers in Atlantic Canada, have no basis for organisation and therefore power. Illustrative of the problem is the fact that by the early 1920s the co-operative movement in the Maritimes was by and large 'in a dormant state.'[37] By 1939 there were only 32 shareholders and members of farmers' co-operative business organisations per 1,000 rural residents over the age of fourteen in New Brunswick, compared to 326 in Alberta and 789 in Saskatchewan.[38]

Those petty primary producers who do experience indirect/commercial capitalist underdevelopment, or even those who are faced with competition by large capitalists at the point of production and are 'so subordinated to capitalist production that their independent labour becomes labour power from the point of view of' large capitalist enterprises,[39] experience fewer, but still substantial, organisational problems. As we shall see, it is from among those who are exploited through direct and indirect/commercial forms of capitalist underdevelopment that partisans of third parties have typically been recruited; this does not, however, mean their political mobilisation is always easy. Rick Williams, in commenting upon the difficulties that Nova Scotia fishermen face in this regard, underscores the continuing existence of the political culture of the independent commodity producer, a culture which seems to survive long after any real independence has been lost. The majority of professional fishermen are employees of the companies because they fish on contract or because they are fishing merely for the bank, the company credit office or the Fisheries Loan Board. Fishermen know they are not businessmen....But given the opportunity, they will still act out the role of the self-sufficient and heroic figure [who] single-handedly wrests a living from the deeps. This consciousness is clearly changing, but still it is a major barrier to effective collective action and solidarity.[40]

This persistent individualistic ideology, based upon historical memory and the mere ownership of boat and gear, is reinforced by another, related factor. Because fishing is an unevenly underdeveloped industry there is a high level of competition among fishermen who use different technologies (gill nets, long-liners, etc.) for fishing on the same grounds, thus adding further to the social atomisation of the work force.[41]

Finally, it deserves to be noted that widespread subsistence production and the low level of industrialisation in Atlantic Canada have not only generated few political resources for, and a low level of social organisation of, potential partisans of a third party, but are also responsible for the existence of a relatively small recruitment base. If, to continue with the illustration used above, 67% of New Brunswick farms were subsistence or part-time operations four decades ago—a full 49% more that Saskatchewan and Alberta—it may there be added that the manufacturing sector of New Brunswick's economy employed only 29% of the labour force at that time, compared to 45% in Ontario.[42] There is of course no reason why lower level white-collar employees, who constitute a proportion of Atlantic Canada's work force close to the national average, should not, insofar as they are dependent wage labourers, become bound up with the working-class movement. The activities of such groups as nurses in Nova Scotia and New Brunswick demonstrate that this is already happening.[43] But this is a very recent development; historically, white-collar employees in Atlantic Canada (as elsewhere) have constituted a relatively small group and have apparently tended to think of themselves as members of the middle class so that, on balance, the potential recruitment base for third parties has indeed been small when compared with, for example, Saskatchewan or Ontario.

EXCEPTIONAL DECADES: THE 1910s AND 1920s

From the foregoing analysis one may conclude that in terms of all three determinants of power—size, organisation, and resource control—the potential partisans of a third party have been in a most disadvantageous position in Atlantic Canada. This structural reality, not alleged satisfaction with the *status quo* or any ideological aversion to radical politics, explains well the political conservatism of the region. It follows, however, that historical shifts in the distribution of power between potential partisans and authorities ought to have been accompanied by disturbances in the otherwise calm waters of regional politics. In order to ascertain the validity of this argument let us

TABLE 3-1

SELECTED STATISTICS ON NEW BRUNSWICK
AGRICULTURE AND UFNB VOTE

| | Mortgage Debt per farm, 1930 | Income from sale of farm products per farm, 1921 | POTATO ACREAGE | | Percentage UFNB vote 1920 |
			1910	1921	
Victoria and Carleton counties	$524	$1,949	8,785	21,584	61
Thirteen other counties	$157	$1,250	31,648	41,185	14

SOURCES: *Canadian Annual Review, 1920*, 717; *Canadian parliamentary guide, 1921*, 415-16; Chapman, 'Henry Harvey Stuart,' 100; Canada, *Census, 1921*, V, 96-98, 176-82; *Census, 1931*, VIII, 154-55, 159-61; New Brunswick, Royal Commission on the New Brunswick potato industry, *Report*, 1962, 39; Hyson, 'Factors which prevent the electoral success of "third parties" in the Maritime provinces' (unpub. MA thesis, McGill University, 1972), 201-4.

NOTES: (a) This is a revised version of Table II in Brym, 'Regional social structure,' *CRSA*, reprinted with permission. (b) Because of new information in Chapman, *ibid.*, regarding the third party vote in Northumberland County, the percentage UNFB vote outside Victoria and Carleton has been changed from eleven, in the original version, to fourteen. (c) Data on mortgage debt were not collected by the government in 1921. (d) The constituencies of Saint John City and Moncton City have been omitted since they are urban constituencies. (e) For four constituencies one can state only the probable affiliation of third party candidates, and in deciding these affiliations I have followed the judgement of Hyson, ibid., 203-4: all the King's, Queen's, and Restigouche third-party vote, and half that in Sunbury, have been categorized as UNFB.

examine in some detail the emergence in the 1910s and 1920s of third parties in New Brunswick and, in passing, Nova Scotia and Newfoundland.

In the 1920 New Brunswick provincial election, third parties reached the high point of their development in that province. The United Farmers of New Brunswick won 9 seats, Labour 2, Farmer-Labour 1, Independent (pro-Liberal) 1, Conservatives 11, and Liberals 24.[44] It is significant that support for third-party candidates was unevenly distributed. Five of the successful UFNB candidates represented the neighbouring counties of Victoria and Carleton, and we must therefore first focus our attention on these two ridings.

In an often quoted passage in the *Eighteenth Brumaire of Louis Bonaparte* Karl Marx explained the conservatism of the mid nineteenth-century French peasantry by likening the small, isolated peasant holdings of that country to so many potatoes in a sack.[45] Just as a sack of potatoes is formed by a 'simple addition of homologous magnitudes,' so that there is no interconnection between the potatoes, the French peasantry's mode of production 'isolates them from one another instead of bringing them into mutual intercourse.' Ironically, it was precisely the potato that bound farmers in Carleton and Victoria counties together and so distinguished them from most farmers in New

Brunswick. According to one geographer,[46] the 'most extensive and easily cultivatable soils of the entire Atlantic region' are to be found in these two counties and, especially after World War I, the export of upper Saint John River valley potatoes to the United States and (after 1922) Cuban markets became a major provincial industry and the biggest money earner of all agricultural sectors.[47] Carleton and Victoria were in the 1920s the two biggest potato producing counties in New Brunswick and two of the three fastest growing, which is why average income from the sale of farm products was greater in these counties than anywhere else in the province (see Table 3-1); and why, in 1920, 10 of the 21 United Farmers' Co-Operative Company stores in New Brunswick were located there.[48]

From the beginning of the modern potato industry in New Brunswick a few large buyers, such as McCain's and Hatfield's, were responsible for the indirect/commercial underdevelopment of Carleton and Victoria counties by virtue of their holding prices down, forcing competitors out of business, and gaining greater market control: already in the 1920s allegations of price fixing by combines were being investigated and confirmed.[49] That farmers in the area were in consequence more indebted than farmers elsewhere in the province (which *in the present context* signifies that they were losing control over their means of production, i.e., becoming more proletarianised) is evident from Table 3-1.[50] Indirect/commercial capitalist underdevelopment of the potato industry thus created a semi-proletarianised segment of the New Brunswick farming population. Its level of socio-economic organisation was sufficiently high to bear closer comparison with the Prairie situation than with that typical of the Atlantic region. It was therefore with relative ease that T. W. Caldwell and other outstanding leaders of the UFNB could politically mobilise farmers in Carleton and Victoria in the 1920s.

Before examining other New Brunswick counties where third-party candidates were successful in 1920 it must be noted that, for early twentieth-century Newfoundland and Nova Scotia, one discerns a similar relationship between indirect/commercial or direct underdevelopment, on the one hand, and the strength of third parties on the other. The Fishermen's Protective Union of Newfoundland, which was the second largest party in the colony in 1919 in terms of popular vote, received the overwhelming bulk of its support from fishermen, sealers, and lumbermen along the northeast coast of the island. The Labrador fishery, sealing, and the pulp and paper industry were all concentrated there, and all witnessed the infusion of large-scale capital and the creation of a relatively solidary, albeit seasonal, wage-labouring class at the time of the FPU's growth. In the rest of the island indirect/subsistence underdevelopment was more widespread and the FPU made little headway.[51] In the 1920 Nova Scotia provincial election, farmer and labour candidates won 11 seats (compared to the Conservatives' 3 and the Liberals' 29), and, again, one notes an uneven distribution of support for third-party candidates.[52] As Table 3-2 shows, the successful UFNS candidates came from constituencies where both income from the sale of farm products and indebtedness were relatively high, while constituencies where UFNS candidates were either

unsuccessful or did not run displayed less commercialisation and proletarianisation of farmers.[53] Nor is there any secret as to why the four successful labour candidates came from Cape Breton and Cumberland counties:
these counties experienced a high level of direct underdevelopment. The coal
and steel industries there had been expanding rapidly up to the end of World
War I, and the concentration of control over these industries by Boston,
Toronto, Montreal, and London financiers was paralleled by the creation of a
tightly knit, concentrated class of workers:

The flow of life in the coal mining communities of Cape Breton promoted a spirit of
interdependence and cohesion among the population. United in 'the largest industrial
community in Canada,' dependent on a single employer, facing common hardships and
enjoying common recreations, the coal communities 'had what was a togetherness, and
one's trouble was the other, one's joy was the other. They were a very close knit
people.'[54]

None of this, however, should be taken to imply that forms of underdevelopment alone can fully explain the distribution of support for third parties

TABLE 3-2

SELECTED STATISTICS ON NOVA SCOTIA
AGRICULTURE AND UFNS VOTE

	Mortgage debt per farm, 1931	Income from Sale of farm products per farm, 1921	Successful UFNS candidates
Antigonish, Colchester, Cumberland, Hants, and Cape Breton Counties	$141	$1,277	7
Twelve other Counties	$63	$802	0

SOURCES: Canada, *Census, 1921*, V, 93-95; *Census, 1931*, VIII, 84-85, 89-91; Hyson, 'Factors
which prevent the electoral success of "third parties" in the Maritime provinces' (unpub. MA thesis,
McGill University, 1972), 205-9; Rawlyk, 'The Farmer-Labour movement,' *Essays on the left*, 34.

NOTES: (a) The constituency of Richmond/Cape Breton West has been matched with the census
division of Richmond county. In all other cases census divisions and constituncy boundaries correspond. (b) For reasons specified in note 53, *infra*, Kings county has not been included in this table.

in early twentieth-century Atlantic Canada. To return to the New Brunswick
case, there were sectors of primary production other than potato farming in
Victoria and Carleton counties that experienced indirect/commercial
underdevelopment—the dairy industry in King's County and woodcutting
operations in Gloucester, York, Westmorland, and Northumberland counties
being among the more important—albeit none to the same degree as the
potato-growing districts.[55] In these other areas it was *possible* to mobilise primary producers for third-party politics, but, given their lower level of indirect/
commercial underdevelopment and socio-economic organisation, it was

necessary for the movement leadership to expend greater organising effort than in Carleton and Victoria.

This leadership was however forthcoming only in a few counties, notably Westmorland and Northumberland, where a total of three UFNB candidates were elected in the 1920 provincial election. Woodsmen, small woodlot operators, lumber mill workers, and farmers engaged in part-time forestry production on or off their farms apparently played a major role in the UFNB in these ridings.[56] It will therefore prove worthwhile to devote a few words to the forestry industry, which had dominated New Brunswick since early in the nineteenth century when Britain was denied access to Baltic and American lumber.

Although a part-time wage-labouring force was created at the inception of the forestry industry, the 'widespread introduction of contracting or job-bing by the expanding lumber companies [in the 1880s] allowed the exploitation of part-time, subsistence farmers in areas remote from the companies' main camps.'[57] This process was extended still further when large pulp and paper companies subsequently began exporting their products from New Brunswick. As was the case with potato farmers in Victoria and Carleton, indirect/commercial underdevelopment allowed large capitalists to exploit small woodlot operators and farmers who contracted to supply wood to the companies. 'Wages' were paid (in the form of legally contracted payments for supplies of wood). The companies kept these payments at or below subsistence levels, and were able to do this because part of the woodsman's means of subsistence was produced without pay on the farm in the off-season; yet woodsmen still retained legal title to their property.

Woodsmen in Westmorland and Northumberland counties had a political advantage over those in other parts of the province in that they had access to the leadership skills of such men as Thomas Parker, former magistrate and county councillor, Henry Harvey Stuart, newspaperman and educator, P. D. Ayer, publisher of the *Eastern Labor News*, and others. Parker and Stuart, by playing on the grievances of woodsmen against the trusts and combines involved in forestry, instigated the formation of the Northumberland People's Union in 1918, an organisation of farmers, woodsworkers, and longshoremen which provided 'the nucleus for and much of the stimulus to the successful campaign of Farmer-Labour candidates in Northumberland County in the provincial election of 1920.'[58] Stuart was also instrumental in the creation in 1919 of the first important industrial union in the area, the 1,600-member Miramichi Longshoremen's Union. He urged not just the economic, but also the political union of the longshoremen, and when in 1919 he moved to a suburb of Moncton in Westmorland County (Moncton was the railway centre of the Maritimes and had a concentration of workers rivaled in New Brunswick only by Saint John) he was able to drive his point home. As a delegate to the New Brunswick Federation of Labour and as one of the founders of the Westmorland, Northumberland, and Moncton Independent Labour parties, Stuart was anxious to effect a union of farmers and workers. In spite of the distrust between the two groups,[59] Westmorland and Northumberland counties were the only ridings in the province where they joined forces. The results of these organisational and educational efforts were impressive. In the 1920 election labour candidates ran only where Stuart had been active.[60] In Moncton city 23% of the popular vote went to labour, in Westmorland County 12%, and in Northumberland County, where two labour candidates were elected, 32%. In addition, two UFNB candidates with 30% of the popular vote were elected in Northumberland and one UFNB candidate with 37% of the vote was elected in Westmorland.[61]

But even if, as has been argued above, the distribution of support for UFNB and labour candidates can be adequately explained as a function of the social-organisational consequences of direct and indirect/commercial under-development, and aggressive political leadership,[62] a full explanation of the emergence of third parties must take into account the relatively *disorganised* state of the traditional political parties in the years following World War I. That is to say, certain types of underdevelopment and effective leadership may have provided some lower-class people in New Brunswick with the organisational basis for challenging the hegemony of the old parties, but this challenge might well have failed entirely had the old parties not been in such a state of disarray.

At the national level, the conscription crisis of 1917 had precipitated a split in the Liberal Party between those for and those against compulsory military service, the latter being concentrated particularly in Quebec. Many Liberals had joined forces with the Conservatives to form the Union govern-ment, thus leaving the Liberal Party in a weakened state. Liberals in the Maritimes were divided over the conscription issue and there were a number of significant desertions from the party—including one in the federal riding of Victoria-Carleton, where 'traditional party ties had suffered maximum disruption from the entry of the local Liberal champion, "Fighting" Frank Carvell, into the Union Government.'[63] The Liberal Party thus failed to con-test the 1921 federal by-election in Victoria-Carleton, and this was an impor-tant factor in the victory of T. W. Caldwell, president of the UFNB and the only federal third-party candidate ever elected in New Brunswick history, for the national Progressive Party.[64] But, perhaps even more important, the con-scription crisis had damaged the old party system *per se*: the very existence of the Union government testified eloquently to the partial destruction of old party ties.

Provincially, the Liberals were rather more united, but the Conservatives suffered from internal discord and scandal.[65] Some Conservatives wanted their party to become the champion of farmers and other disaffected ele-ments in the province, and when the 1919 party convention refused such a move, some defectors ran as independents or joined third parties. Moreover, the reputation of Conservative leader James Murray was greatly impaired when evidence of corruption in the department of agriculture during Mur-ray's tenure in that office surfaced in the legislature. Only a couple of weeks before election day a new leader had to be chosen—too late to allow the

Conservatives to run an effective campaign. They did not even bother to field candidates in five of the province's seventeen ridings.

Similar problems existed in Newfoundland and Nova Scotia at the time of the rise of the FPU and the Farmer-Labour coalition. In the 1920 election in Nova Scotia the farmers faced opponents from only one of the old parties in four of the eighteen ridings, while in Newfoundland the FPU ran against only one of the old parties in three of the eighteen ridings. J. M. Beck refers to Nova Scotia in the early 1920s as a 'political vacuum:' the Liberals had atrophied after 38 uninterrupted years in office and the Conservatives, 'suffering from the bad image of the Unionist adminstration in Ottawa had fallen into disarray.'[66] In Newfoundland, too, the political scene was hardly propitious from the point of view of those inured to the *status quo* since the Liberals, long in power, 'had been thrown into a state of disarray by their defeat in 1909 [by the People's Party] and had not been quick to recover; indeed ... they were greatly handicapped by the uncertain state of their leader's health.'[67]

CONCLUSION

In sum, the relative success of third parties in New Brunswick and in other parts of Atlantic Canada in the 1910s and 1920s can be attributed to a shift in the distribution of power between lower-class partisans and traditional authorities. The old parties were momentarily disorganised so that their grip on the electorate was loosened; those members of the lower classes who had experienced direct or indirect/commercial underdevelopment and who had access to able leadership were sufficiently organised to assert their political independence. Conversely, the subsequent decline of third parties can be attributed to the restoration of the old distribution of power. Rural depopulation robbed petty primary producers of much of their power base, and hopes that the size of this base could be augmented through affliation with Prairie protest movements were dashed when the westerners proved to be insensitive to the Maritimers' interests.[68] The Depression further exacerbated the social disorganisation of petty primary producers (by encouraging the decline of commercial farming, fishing, and forestry) and of wage labourers (by causing unemployment to reach previously unheard-of proportions). The old parties, having weathered their post-World War I crises, reasserted their control over the electorate through a combination of minor policy shifts, co-optation, and the reconstruction of worn party machines.

On 23 June 1933 a new phase of Atlantic Canadian third-party history began when the New Brunswick CCF held its first convention in Moncton.[69] In 1938 a Nova Scotia section of the CCF was formed.[70] The focus of political protest thereby shifted somewhat away from petty primary producers and toward urban workers. When in the mid 1940s the CCF made major advances throughout the country, voters in Atlantic Canada, too, moved left; workers in Saint John, Moncton, Cape Breton, and other industrial centres were largely responsible for the party's gains.[71] But overall, the gains registered were well below the national average, thus confirming that the perennial problem of Atlantic Canadian third parties had scarcely disappeared.

When direct and indirect/commercial underdevelopment occur where ruling classes are weak and disorganised, as in much of the Third World, political protest is usually widespread and often takes on revolutionary dimensions.[72] But when direct and indirect/commercial underdevelopment occur where ruling classes are relatively strong and organised, as in the provinces of Atlantic Canada, political protest is usually muted and infrequent— and all the more so if indirect/subsistence underdevelopment socially disorganises large numbers of potential partisans. Little has changed in Atlantic Canada over the past several decades to alter this basic set of facts,[73] and no *substantial* changes in the texture of the region's political life can be expected until it does.[74] To be sure, there is a great deal more organising work that can be done given the existing distribution of power. The recent organisation of the Maritime Fishermen's Union and the Newfoundland Fishermen, Food, and Allied Workers are important steps that may have—and, with the election of an NDP candidate in a 1978 Newfoundland federal by-election, already have had—some political repercussions.[75] The same may be true for some white-collar unions. With an unemployment rate among university graduates as bad as, if not worse than, the regional average, and with the expected worsening of this picture until at least the mid 1980s,[76] there exists, moreover, a large recruitment base for organisers. None of this, however, changes the fundamental fact that, *overall*, as at least two surveys have demonstrated,[77] the citizens of Atlantic Canada know well that they have little political power. Indeed, they manifest by far the lowest sense of what political scientists call 'political efficacy' of any group of Canadians. 'The Little Man,' Alden Nowlan quotes his Nova Scotian father as saying, 'had better learn to keep his mouth shut and his arse low.'[78] The social bases of this entirely rational assessment of capabilities, and not, as is frequently claimed, any stubborn clinging to tradition or any illusory sense of satisfaction with one's lot, are largely responsible for the long history of political conservatism in Atlantic Canada.[79]

NOTES

This paper was presented before the meetings of the Atlantic Association of Sociologists and Anthropologists (Halifax, 1979). In part, it represents an attempt to overcome some of the cruder points of interpretation in my earlier work. For critical comments on an earlier draft I am greatly indebted to Jim Sacouman, David Frank, Doug Campbell, Lorne Tepperman, and Jack Wayne, whose wise counsel I have not, however, always heeded.

1. P. J. Fitzpatrick, 'New Brunswick: the politics of pragmatism,' *Canadian provincial politics: the party systems of the ten provinces*, ed. Martin Robin (Scarborough, 1978), 120-21.

2. John Shiry, 'Mass values and system outputs: a critique of an assumption of socialization theory,' *Foundations of political culture: political socialization in Canada*, ed. J. H. Pammett and M. S. Whittington (Toronto, 1976), 36-58.

3. *Ibid.*, 41; emphasis in the original.

4. *Ibid.*, 43.

5. Rick Ogmundson, 'Mass-elite linkages and class issues in Canada,' *Canadian Review of Sociology and Anthropology*, XIII (1976), 1-12.

6. James Rinehart and I. O. Okraku, 'A study of class consciousness,' *Canadian Review of Sociology and Anthropology*, XI (1974), 197-213.

7. M. A. Schwartz, *Politics and territory: the sociology of regional persistence in Canada* (Montreal and London, 1974), 209.

8. Richard Simeon and David Elkins, 'Regional political cultures in Canada,' *Canadian Journal of Political Science*, VII (l974), 404-408.

9. A July 1978 Gallup poll asked a sample of Canadians: Who will be the biggest threat to Canada in the coming years—big government, big business, or big labour? Respondents in all regions aside from Quebec chose big government, but a much higher proportion of those living in Atlantic Canada did so. Only Atlantic Canadians saw big business as the second biggest threat (all others saw big labour in this position). And only Atlantic Canadians saw big labour as the least threatening force: 'Labor tied with government as "greatest threat",' *Daily Gleaner* (Fredericton), 16 August 1978, 4. A 1970 study of Cape Breton Caucasian and Indian school children showed that, already at an early age, Cape Breton children are not very supportive of the Canadian state, and become less so as they grow older: S. H. Ullman, 'The socialization of orientation toward Canada: A study of Cape Breton whites and Indians,' *Foundations of political culture*, Pammett and Whittington, 265-87.

10. Maurice Pinard, 'Working class politics: an interpretation of the Quebec case,' *Social stratification: Canada*, ed. J. E. Curtis and W. G. Scott (Scarborough, 1973), 268.

11. Michael Mann, 'The social cohesion of liberal democracy,' *American Sociological Review*, XXXV (1970), 423-39.

12. I have restricted my remarks to classes because they are the most consequential groups in the contexts analysed here: precisely because the class system is organised as described below, other group affliations—notably ethnic and religious—have traditionally been the major bases of political cleavage in Atlantic Canada.

13. Antonio Gramsci, 'State and civil society,' *Selections from the prison notebooks*, ed. Q. Hoare and G. Smith (London, 1972), 222.

14. Stephen Lukes, *Power: a radical view* (London, 1974).

15. Robert Bierstedt, 'An analysis of social power,' *Power and progress: essays on sociological theory* (New York, 1974), 220-41; R. J. Brym, 'Review essay: *Power and progress*,' *Scottish Journal of Sociology*, II (1977), 115-19; Anthony Oberschall, *Social conflict and social movements* (Englewood Cliffs, N. J., 1973), 246ff.

16. Cf. Robert MacIver's statement in his *The web of government* (rev. ed., New York, 1965), 92, that 'the party system takes the sting out of the class system.' The following analysis is restricted to the party system although other institutions—trade unions, schools, the mass media—are probably more important political control mechanisms in areas economically more developed than Atlantic Canada.

17. This approaches the situation in some single-party systems, where 'elections buttress the regime ... by prompting the population to show that the *illegitimacy* of its "democratic" practice has been accepted and that no action to undermine it will be forthcoming:' Victor Zaslavsky and R. J. Brym, 'The functions of elections in the USSR,' *Soviet Studies*, XXX (1978), 371.

18. Note, however, that the argument that political leaders tend to favour the common interests of the whole ruling class assumes a certain degree of *autonomy* of political leaders and, more generally, of the state, from the ruling class: cf. Ralph Miliband, 'Poulantzas and the capitalist state,' *New Left Review*, no 82 (1973), 85, fn.4. That is to say, material exchanges and other linkages between state personnel and members of the ruling class *may* not be very widespread, and there can be and frequently are

conflicts among political leaders, among members of the ruling class, and between these two groups: see, e.g., Richard Wilbur, 'New Brunswick power struggle: K. C. Irving vs. Louis Robichaud,' *Canadian Dimension*, VI (1969), nos 3-4, 11-15. Nevertheless, the state in capitalist society generally facilitates capitalist development.

19. Judging from the available literature, such practices appear also to have characterised politics in Quebec and in rural areas west of the Ottawa River, although the paucity of material on corruption in urban Ontario and the west may be due at least in part to a 'subtlety of corruption styles' in the latter areas: K. M. Gibbons, 'The political culture of corruption in Canada,' *Political corruption in Canada: cases, causes and cures*, ed. K. M. Gibbons and D. C. Rowat (Toronto, 1976), 242.

20. Reginald Whitaker, *The government party: organizing and financing the Liberal Party of Canada, 1930-58* (Toronto, 1977), 387. Cf. J. M. Beck, 'Nova Scotia: tradition and conservatism,' *Canadian provincial politics*, Robin, 177-78.

21. Alden Nowlan, 'Passing the time with Gerry Regan,' *Maclean's*, LXXXVIII (1975), no 5, 64.

22. H. G. Thorburn, *Politics in New Brunswick* (Toronto, 1961), 136-37.

23. See esp. K. S. Palda, 'Does advertising influence votes? An analysis of the 1966 and 1970 Quebec elections,' *Canadian Journal of Political Science*, VI (1973), 638-53.

24. Thorburn, *Politics in NB*, 113; Whitaker, *The government party*, 54, 74, and *passim*.

25. Although bribery, graft, influence peddling, corrupt campaign financing, and especially large-scale patronage are far from unknown, as is partly evident from the following remark of one New Brunswick MLA in the mid 1960s: 'Doing away with the patronage system ... wouldn't that be doing away with the democratic system?' Quoted in Fitzpatrick, 'New Brunswick: politics of pragmatism,' 129.

26. Quoted in Thorburn, *Politics in NB*, 113.

27. *Ibid.*, 112.

28. Steven Wolinetz, 'Party organization in Newfoundland: the Liberal Party under Smallwood,' a paper presented before the Canadian Political Science Association (Edmonton, 1975), 23-24; cf. Peter Neary, 'Democracy in Newfoundland: a comment,' *Journal of Canadian Studies*, IV (1969), 42; George Perlin, 'Patronage and paternalism: politics in Newfoundland,' *Social space. Canadian perspectives*, ed. D. I. Davies and Kathleen Herman (Toronto, 1971), 190-96.

29. Karl Marx and Frederick Engels, 'The manifesto of the Communist Party,' *The Marx-Engels reader*, ed. Robert Tucker (New York, 1972), 331-62.

30. R. J. Brym, *The Jewish intelligentsia and Russian Marxism: a sociological study of intellectual radicalism and ideological divergence* (London, 1978); 'Regional social structure and agrarian radicalism in Canada: Alberta, Saskatchewan and New Brunswick,' *Canadian Review of Sociology and Anthropology*, XV (1978), 339-51; *Intellectuals and politics* (London, 1979); see also chapter 9 in this book. The view that *strong* ties *within* a sector of a network facilitate communication flow must be distinguished from the convincing argument in Mark Granovetter, 'The strength of weak ties,' *American Journal of Sociology*, LXXVIII (1973), 1360-80, that *weak* ties *between* sectors of a network have the same effect.

31. Newfoundland and Labrador Federation of Labour, People's Commission on Unemployment in Newfoundland and Labrador, *Now that we've burned our boats* (St John's, 1978), 48.

32. The official unemployment rate is calculated as the percentage of those *actively* looking for work who are not working; the real unemployment rate is calculated as the percentage of those who *can* work who are not working; which is to say that it includes those who have given up hope of finding employment and so do not bother to search for it. As a rough rule of thumb, the real unemployment rate is about two to two-

and-a-half times higher than the official rate.

33. Sacouman distinguishes between direct and indirect underdevelopment in terms of whether appropriation takes place, respectively, through control over the means of production or through mechanisms of unequal exchange: see chapters 2 and 5 in this volume, and also 'The underdevelopment of primary production dependent rural communities in Maritime Canada,' a paper presented before the ninth World Congress of Sociology (Uppsala, 1978);. Elsewhere the same terms are used to indicate whether capital investment in a given area is, respectively, high or low: Brym, 'Regional social structure;' chapter 9 of this book. The present discussion, by distinguishing three forms of underdevelopment, synthesises both sets of concerns—with the location of appropriation mechanisms and with the level of capital investment.

34. Harriet Friedman, 'World market, state, and family farm: social bases of household production in the era of wage labor,' *Comparative Studies in Society and History*, XX (1978), 545-86; M. J. Hedley, 'Independent commodity production and the dynamics of tradition,' *Canadian Review of Sociology and Anthropology*, XIII (1976), 413-21.

35. Canada, *Census, 1941*, VIII, pt 1, 351; pt 2, 1335, 1495.

36. Chanoch Jacobsen, 'Who joins farm organizations?' *Journal of Cooperative Extension*, VII (1969), 225-32; S. M. Lipset, *Agrarian socialism: the Cooperative Commonwealth Federation in Saskatchewan* (Berkeley, 1968).

37. L. A. Wood, *A history of farmers' movements in Canada: the origins and development of agrarian protest, 1872-1924* (Toronto, 1975), 304.

38. Canada, *Census, 1941*, VII, 296-320; A. E. Richards, 'Farmers' cooperative business organizations in Canada, 1938-39,' *Economic Annalist*, X (1940), no 1, 38. Population data are from the 1941 census, cooperative membership data for the year 1939. The latter do not include several types of cooperative organisations, so that the actual differences among the provinces are probably even greater than the figures suggest.

39. See chapter 2 in this volume.

40. Rick Williams, 'Fish ... or cut bait!' *This Magazine*, XI (1977), no 3, 5.

41. *Ibid.*

42. Canada, *Census, 1941*, VII, 663, 665. This includes persons involved in supplying electricity, gas, water, and those involved in construction, transportation, communication, and mining.

43. Cf. Robert Laxer, *Canada's unions* (Toronto, 1976); James Rinehart, *The tyranny of work* (Don Mills, 1975).

44. J. K. Chapman, 'Henry Harvey Stuart (1873-1952): New Brunswick reformer,' *Acadiensis*, V (1976), 100. Reports concerning the results of the 1920 election vary, but Chapman's appears to be based on the most exhaustive research.

45. Karl Marx, 'The eighteenth Brumaire of Louis Bonaparte,' *Marx-Engels reader*, Tucker, 515. This paragraph is reprinted in slightly revised form from my 'Regional social structure' with permission.

46. Ian Brookes, 'The physical geography of the Maritime provinces,' *Studies in Canadian geography: the Atlantic provinces*, ed. A. Macpherson (Toronto, 1972), 31.

47. Canada, Depart of Labour, Investigation into alleged combine limiting competition in the marketing of New Brunswick potatoes, *Interim Report*, 1925, 7; N. H. Morse, 'Agriculture in the Maritime provinces,' *Dalhousie Review*, XXXIX (1959-60), 476ff.; F. A. Blanchard, 'A statistical study of the agricultural problems of the province of New Brunswick' (unpub. MA thesis, Cornell University, 1938), 14, 50.

48. A. M. Trueman, 'New Brunswick and the 1921 federal election' (unpub. MA thesis, University of New Brunswick, 1975), 68, notes that there were also six stores in York, two in Westmorland, and one each in Charlotte, King's, and Restigouche.

49. Canada, Dept of Labour, Investigation into alleged combine, *Interim report*, 73.

50. This is not to suggest that indebtedness is the same thing as proletarianisation. It is, rather, an index of proletarianisation in situations where persons are losing control over their means of production. This was clearly the case in Victoria and Carleton counties: in the area around Bath, New Brunswick, for example, about 10% of farm families abandoned their farms in the first half of the 1920s after going into debt incurred as a consequence of a cost/price squeeze: *ibid*, 8.

51. See chapter 9.

52. J. M. Beck, 'Nova Scotia,' *Canadian provincial politics*, Robin, 195.

53. The only major exception to this pattern was King's County, the centre of the Nova Scotia apple industry and the most commercialised and indebted sector of Nova Scotia agriculture. Sacouman in chapter 2 of this volume attributes the failure of the UFNS in King's to the apple industry's not being integrated in the national economy and not being much affected by the National Policy. But I find this to be unsatisfactory as a general explanation. For while it is true that much of the political animus of prairie farmers derived from these factors, the radicalism of New Brunswick potato farmers did not: potato production in New Brunswick was, as noted in the text above, integrated into American and Cuban, not Canadian, markets. The failure of the UFNS in King's is better explained by the following facts: (a) Marketing of potatoes in New Brunswick was totally controlled by shippers and this situation was, as noted by one official in the department of agriculture, 'entirely unlike [that of] the apple growers:' Canada, Dept of Labour, Investigation into alleged combine, *Interim report*, 6. As Anthony Mackenzie remarks, 'collective action by the apple producers in Nova Scotia had brought about a very substantial reduction in shipping rates; in addition, they had persuaded the Dominion Government to build a plant for processing the Valley apple crop, when access to their British markets was disrupted in 1914:' 'The rise and fall of the Farmer-Labour Party in Nova Scotia' (unpub. MA thesis, Dalhousie University, 1969), 13. In other words, well before the emergence of the UFNS, collective action on the part of apple farmers had resulted in important concessions being won; there was probably, as a consequence, little perceived need for entry into third-party politics in 1920. (b) There was a moderately strong association between success of UFNS candidates and proximity to industrial towns; labour support was in some cases a key factor in determining the outcome of a farmer's candidacy: *ibid.*, 100-102. King's County did not, however, contain an industrial town. (This second factor was, incidentally, probably a principal reason for the failure of the Antigonish movement to spread into southwestern Nova Scotia a decade later.) If King's were included in Table 3-2, income from sale of farm products where UFNS candidates were either unsuccessful or did not run would be $905 per farm, and mortgage debt would be $136. Thus, predicted socio-economic differences between counties where the UFNS was relatively successful and those where is was not would still obtain, but they would be smaller.

54. David Frank, 'Class conflict in the coal industry: Cape Breton, 1922,' *Essays in Canadian working class history*, ed. G. S. Kealey and Peter Warrian (Toronto, 1976), 165.

55. Canada, *Census, 1921*, V, 96-98; D. F. Putnam, 'Distribution of agriculture in New Brunswick,' *Public Affairs*, III (1939), no 1, 8-11.

56. Chapman, 'Henry Harvey Stuart,' 95ff.; A. T. Doyle, *Front benches and back rooms: a story of corruption, muckraking, raw partisanship and intrigue in New Brunswick* (Toronto, 1976), 187.

57. Sacouman, 'The underdevelopment of primary production dependent communities,' 17.

58. Chapman, 'Henry Harvey Stuart,' 96.

59. Farmers considered industrial workers to be partly responsible for the high cost of manufactured goods, while workers considered farmers to be capitalists partly responsi-

ble for the high cost of food.

60. In Saint John, with its 6,000 trade unionists (according to union sources), an Independent Labour Party was formed early in 1920, but, in spite of its decision to field candidates in the upcoming provincial election, this aim was not realised: C. A. Woodward, *The history of New Brunswick provincial election campaigns and platforms, 1866-1974* (Toronto, 1976), 46. Was this due to a lack of leadership in Saint John? The situation there may well have been analogous to that in Halifax, where the labour loss in 1920 was partly due to the fact that a number of labour leaders left town to seek employment elsewhere because of the long strike in the Halifax shipyards: Mackenzie, 'Rise and fall of the Farmer-Labour Party,' 103.

61. *Canadian annual review, 1920*, 717; *Canadian parliamentary guide, 1921*, 415-16; Chapman, 'Henry Harvey Stuart,' 100; R. V. S. Hyson, 'Factors which prevent the electoral success of "third parties" in the Maritime provinces' (unpub. MA thesis, McGill University, 1972), 201-204.

62. I have not been able to discover in which constituency the one successful Farmer-Labour candidate mentioned in Chapman, 'Henry Harvey Stuart,' 100, was elected. As far as the election of S. D. Guptill for the UFNB in Charlotte is concerned, it should be noted that 'the electorate apparently voted for the Conservative-Farmer coalition as a ticket' so that Guptill's election 'was not a reliable indicator of the United Farmer strength:' Trueman, *NB and the 1921 federal election*, 218.

63. W. L. Morton, *The Progressive Party in Canada* (Toronto, 1950), 51; E. R. Forbes, 'Never the twain did meet: Prairie-Maritime relations, 1910-1927,' *Canadian Historical Review*, LIX (1978), 25.

64. Morton, *The Progressive Party*, 83.

65. Doyle, *Front benches*, 191ff.; Woodward, *History of NB provincial election campaigns*, 46-47.

66. Cf. G. A. Rawlyk, 'The Maritimes and the Canadian community,' *Regionalism in the Canadian community, 1867-1967*, ed. Mason Wade (Toronto, 1969), 113.

67. S. J. R. Noel, *Politics in Newfoundland* (Toronto, 1971), 96. An examination of the social organisation of the church would add to our understanding of the distribution, level, and duration of support for third parties. The FPU was successful only where clerical authority was divided among several denominations, thus allowing the union to play one off against another. Where the Roman Catholic Church predominated, on the other hand, clerical leaders were able to suppress involvement in the FPU: see chapter 9. Similarly, the 'considerable influence of the church, especially the Roman Catholic Church ... [encouraged] the final disintergration of the farmer-labour movement' in Nova Scotia: G. A. Rawlyk, 'The farmer-labour movement and the failure of socialism in Nova Scotia,' *Essays on the left*, ed. L. LaPierre et al. (Toronto, 1971), 36.

68. Forbes, 'Never the twain did meet.'

69. 'New Brunswick section of CCF organized,' *Pilot* (Moncton), I (1933), no 9, 1.

70. W. G. Godfrey, 'The CCF in Ottawa, Ontario, and the Maritimes,' *Acadiensis*, III (1974), no 2, 101.

71. *Ibid.*; Thorburn, *Politics in NB*, 102.

72. John Kautsky, 'An essay in the politics of development,' *Political change in underdeveloped countries: nationalism and communism* (New York, 1962), 3-119.

73. I do not regard the progressive breakup of the subsistence family unit through the taking on by family members of part-time jobs for wages as being politically significant, for such persons are still extremely atomised socially, as recent field work in northern New Brunswick clearly reveals: S. D. Clark, *The new urban poor* (Toronto, 1978), 47-48, 51. Full-time wage labourers thrown out of work usually suffer from the same problem. The recent development of capital-intensive farming operations involving capitalist/

wage-labour relations in the New Brunswick potato industry may have some radicalising effect, but the number of persons employed by these enterprises is relatively small: Kim McClaren, 'Hold the gravy! The plight of the potato farmers,' *This Magazine*, XI (1977), no 3, 7-9. Lower level white-collar workers, fishermen, and industrial workers—not part-time wage labourers, farmers, and the unemployed—will probably provide the major support bases for third parties in the future, and the single factor that would do more than anything else to speed the advance of such a party is increased industrialisation.

74. For a provocative discussion of the relationship between capitalist development and the development of the party system in Canada, see John Wilson, 'The Canadian political cultures: towards a redefinition of the nature of the Canadian political system,' *Canadian Journal of Political Science*, VII (1974), 438-83.

75. Earle McCurdy, 'The Fishermen's Union in Newfoundland,' *Canadian Dimension*, XIII (1978), no 3, 28-29; Rick Williams, 'Nova Scotia: "Fish at my price or don't fish,"' *Canadian Dimension*, XIII (1978), no 2, 29-33. In the New Brunswick election of 23 October 1978, the NDP doubled its popular vote (to 6.1% of the total) and the Parti acadien quadrupled its vote (to 4%): Bonny Pond, 'New Brunswick's third force,' *Canadian Dimension*, XIII (1979), no 5, 22-13. In the Nova Scotia election of 19 September 1978, the NDP increased its popular vote from 13% to 14.9%, and gained one seat for a total of four: David Frank, 'Nova Scotia 1978: the Godfather, Santa Claus and the Tweedle NDP,' *Canadian Dimension*, XIII (1979), no 5, 8-11. In the 1979 election the NDP popular vote was almost as high in Atlantic Canada as it was in Ontario (about 20%); in Newfoundland it was half again as high.

76. Canada, Statistics Canada, M. von Zur-Muehlen, 'The new "crisis" of Canadian universities' (unpub. MS, 1977).

77. Schwartz, *Politics and territory*, 277; Simeon and Elkins, 'Regional political cultures,' 404-5.

78. Nowlan, 'Passing the time with Gerry Regan,' 64.

79. For a recent historiographic critique of the traditional stereotypes, see E. R. Forbes, 'In search of a post-Confederation Maritime historiography, 1900-1967,' *Acadiensis*, VIII (1978), no 1, 107-14.

4   The Emergence of the Socialist Movement in the Maritimes, 1899-1916

David Frank and Nolan Reilly

A standing theme in the writing of Canadian history has been the innate 'conservatism' of the people of the Maritimes. Historian Ernest Forbes has recently shown the weaknesses of this 'Maritime stereotype' as an interpretation of the Maritime experience. Several studies of social and political movements in the region have also questioned the adequacy of this approach to regional history. As J. K. Chapman has noted in an account of one Maritime radical's career, the Maritimes 'shared in the collectivist responses to industrialization and unbridled capitalism which appeared in Great Britain and North America in the closing decades of the nineteenth century.' Businessmen and politicians raised the standard of Maritime rights. The churches began to turn their attention to social action. Small producers established farmers' and fishermen's co-operatives. Trade-union membership increased and workers engaged in militant strikes. In the early 1920s radical politics also enjoyed success. The established political parties were often compelled to respond flexibly, though incompletely, to these new concerns and pressures in regional politics. It is also important to note that the region's diverse economic structure and pervasive economic difficulties created enormous obstacles to the establishment of a more successful radical tradition in the Maritimes. But it is clear that conservatism is not an adequate explanation of regional history.[1]

The emergence of a small but vigorous socialist movement in the Maritimes in the early twentieth century casts further doubt on the Maritime stereotype. At a time when the region included about thirteen per cent of the Canadian population, Maritimers made up about ten per cent of the membership of the Socialist Party of Canada. The circulation of *Cotton's Weekly*, the Canadian socialist newspaper, ranged from 7.7 to 15.6% of the national circulation. At its peak in 1910, the Socialist Party of Canada had fifteen locals in the Maritimes and claimed about 300 members. By 1913 *Cotton's* boasted a circulation of more than 2,400 copies in the Maritimes and Newfoundland.[2] The strength of the socialist movement in the Maritimes in this period was no less than in central Canada and bore many resemblances to the stronger radical movement in western Canada. Although the historiography of Canadian radicalism has been dominated by accounts of western movements, a full picture requires attention to the history of socialism in the other regions of the country.[3]

Our purpose in this paper is to trace the emergence of a socialist movement in the Maritimes in the years 1899-1916 and to describe the scope, activities, and importance of the movement. We will introduce several key individuals and communities, and explore the socialists' approach to a number of economic, social, and political issues. Reference to a variety of local situations within the region will, we hope, provoke further research in these areas.[4] The history of the early socialist movement in the Maritimes sheds some new light on the response of Maritimers to industrial capitalism, and also helps to establish a basis for studying the development of Canadian socialism as a whole.

During the 1890s the new era of industrial capitalism awakened intellectual concern among various Maritimers. In Halifax, novelist Marshall Saunders described urban social problems. At the University of New Brunswick political economist John Davidson lectured on contemporary labour problems. Politicians pondered the labour policies of Gladstonian Liberalism, and clergymen explored the principles of the social gospel. In the press and in public lectures and discussions, the social reform ideas of Henry George and Edward Bellamy attracted attention.[5]

This pattern of middle-class concern produced at least one organisation that, though not avowedly socialist, provided a forum for the discussion of socialist ideas and had 'many members who are out and out socialists.' In Saint John in May 1901 a Fabian League was formed 'for the discussion of Sociological questions' and the 'propagation of all ideas that tend to lighten the toil, promote the welfare and elevate the social and moral conditions of the people.'[6] The leading spirit among the Fabians was W. F. Hatheway, a wholesale grocer and former president of the Board of Trade. In his poetry and essays Hatheway praised 'the nobility of labor' and deplored contemporary extremes of wealth and poverty. In 1903 he stood as a Conservative-Labor candidate for the provincial house.[7] In co-operation with the Saint John labour council, the Fabians sponsored an investigation of New Brunswick industrial conditions. League members inspected sawmills, cotton mills, and factories, and reported their findings at public meetings. As a result, a provincial royal commission prepared a factory bill, which was enacted in 1905. To one contemporary observer, the Factory Act was 'perfectly harmless from the employers' standpoint.' In late 1905 the Fabians adjourned their meetings indefinitely.[8]

The formation of the first distinctly socialist organisation in the region was the result of a turn towards the Marxist socialism of Daniel DeLeon's Socialist Labor Party. In 1898 various Halifax reformers participated in the creation of the United Labor Party. One of the members, stenographer A. M. Muirhead, corresponded with the New York headquarters of the Socialist Labor Party,[9] and in February 1899 the Halifax group resolved to form a section of the SLP. 'The change was made not without loss,' reported Muirhead, 'for the "Girondist" element was strong.' But he was pleased to note that the new local formed 'one of the termini of the Socialist girdle round the northern half of the continent.'[10] The Halifax group published a monthly newspaper, the *Cause of Labor*, and carried their message to open-air meetings in the city's parks and streets, where they spoke on 'Questions of vital interest to Workingmen.'[11] The party's most popular spokesman was a young law student, Adolph F. Landry. The son of an Amherst railway worker, Landry had gone to work as a boy in the Springhill coal mines. He survived the disastrous 1891 explosion and subsequently worked as a carpenter before coming to Halifax.[12] By 1903, however, the Halifax socialists were in disarray; according to H. H. Stuart, the Halifax SLP 'unfortunately split over the ST&LA question, and finally broke up.'[13]

In industrial Cape Breton the emergence of the socialist movement was closely linked to the growth of the coal industry and the experiences of the trade-union movement. At the end of the 1890s the industrial boom in Cape Breton attracted thousands of immigrants, both from within the region and from beyond. Immigrant coal miners from Scotland and Belgium had been familiar with socialist ideas in their homelands. Native Cape Bretoners like Alex McKinnon and Alex and Hugh McMullin, who had lived and worked in western Canada and in the United States, returned home imbued with socialist ideas. In 1900 two members of the Halifax Socialist Labor Party, D. N. Brodie and Fred Lighter, settled in Glace Bay.[14] The year 1904 brought two important setbacks for the local labour movement. The first major strike undertaken by the Provincial Workmen's Association was badly defeated during the summer by Dominion Iron and Steel with the aid of federal troops and militia. An Independent Labor Party, advocating a minimum wage and public ownership of mines, railways, and other natural monopolies, nominated Stephen B. MacNeil, a PWA leader, to run in the federal election in November 1904. The local socialists actively supported the campaign. MacNeil did poorly in the election, as did a second labour candidate in a provincial by-election in December.[15] In the wake of these disappointments, a Socialist Club was formed at Glace Bay on 22 November 1904 and a similar club at Sydney Mines in 1905. The socialists participated in public debates with local clergymen and gained influence within the PWA. P. F. Lawson, editor of the *Provincial Workman*, was converted to the socialist cause and shared the socialists' enthusiasm for the newly formed Industrial Workers of the World. Forced to resign his position, Lawson moved to Chicago to work for the IWW.[16]

Organised socialism also took root in New Brunswick during this period. In July 1902 Martin Butler and Henry Harvey Stuart collaborated in the formation of the Fredericton Socialist League which became branch 67 of the Canadian Socialist League. Martin Butler's road to socialism began in the Maine and New Brunswick woods. As a youth he lost his arm in a mill accident and supported himself as an itinerant pedlar. A self-described 'poet, printer, peddler, patriot, workman, editor,' Butler established a monthly newspaper in Fredericton in 1890, which continued to publish until 1915.[17] *Butler's Journal* staunchly advocated republicanism and egalitarianism, defended 'The Rights of Labor,' and celebrated 'the honest, large-hearted working men and farmers of New Brunswick.'[18] Butler's populism was also accompanied by an interest in Bellamyite and Christian-socialist ideas.[19] In 1898 Butler published the Socialist Labor Party's Declaration of Principles, 'to which we give our unhesitating and unqualified approval.' Without abandoning his repub-licanism, Butler now gave equal importance to Canadian independence and social and economic reform. 'We have not lost sight of the principles of national independence, which we have advocated for so long,' he assured his readers, 'but consider that the principles of economic administration should take prece-dence.' 'Monarchy is but a modification of Despotism, as is Republicanism an off-shoot of Monarchy,' Butler explained. 'Only in Socialism can be found true freedom and social and economic equality for all.'[20]

A frequent contributor to the journal and an important influence on Butler was H. H. Stuart.[21] A printer in his youth, Stuart had become a teacher in 1894. Active as a Sunday School teacher and temperance advocate, Stuart was a strong Presbyterian until he withdrew in 1899 to become a lay preacher in the Methodist church. In 1897 and 1898 he was a reader of socialist newspap-ers like the *Appeal to Reason*. In a letter to the *Citizen and Country* in 1899 he signed himself 'a New Brunswick teacher who teaches and preaches socialism.' A few months later he was dismissed from his post at Fredericton Junction for 'circulating the *Weekly People*, placing socialist books in the Sunday School Library, and talking socialism in public places.'[22] He soon secured another teaching post and was a founding member of the New Brunswick Teachers' Union in 1902. In *Butler's Journal* Stuart reviewed the progress of the interna-tional socialist movement and informed readers in 1899 that socialism stood for public ownership of mines, railways, utilities, insurance companies, and for 'cooperation in manufacturing and commercial life,' direct legislation, univer-sal peace, and the abolition of poverty. 'In fact,' he concluded, 'socialism in its true sense is nothing more or less than Christianity applied.'[23]

The establishment of the Fredericton Socialist League in 1902 affords an opportunity to analyse briefly the ideological positions adopted at this stage by Butler, Stuart, and their supporters. In an extensive declaration of principles, the Fredericton group appeared to depart from the Christian socialism and reformist principles of the 1890s and to stress the doctrine of class struggle which was to be associated with the Socialist Party of Canada after 1904. The declaration contained no appeals to 'Christianity applied' as a justification for a socialist programme. In place of the limited public-ownership programme espoused earlier by Stuart, the league announced that it 'stands squarely for the public ownership of all the means of production, distribution and exchange.' A sharp distinction was drawn between 'Government' and 'public' ownership, with a warning against 'such public ownership movements as are an attempt of the capitalist class to secure governmental control of public utilities for the purpose of obtaining greater security in the exploitation of other industries and not for the amelioration of the condition of the working class.' While socialists were pledged to support trade unions, the declaration added that 'the workers can most effectively act as a class in their struggle against the collective power of capitalism by united action at the polls.' A large obstacle facing the workers, however, was the fact that 'the capitalists largely control the newspapers, colleges, churches and political parties, and use them to advance their own interests.' Here then was a prime role for the socialists to play: 'We desire to educate the people to become conscious of their interests and to refuse to fight the battles of the capitalists.' The ultimate aim was described as 'the overthrow of capitalism and the establishment of the Co-operative Commonwealth.'[24] As president of the Fredericton Socialist League, Stuart carefully distinguished his group from the Socialist Labor Party, whose views on trade unionism he disapproved of, and the Saint John Fabian League, which he considered 'scarcely Socialist.' In 1904 Stuart travelled to Cape Breton to participate in the campaign to elect an ILP candidate to the House of Commons. Never numerous, the Fredericton socialists actively pursued their eductional work, 'each year finding the soil of the Province more receptive and encouraging.'[25]

The establishment of the Socialist Party of Canada in January 1905 was the product of a merger between the Canadian Socialist League and the Socialist Party of British Columbia. The new party adopted a programme of uncompromising class struggle. The party platform described an 'irrepressible conflict' between capitalist and worker which was rapidly culminating in 'a struggle for possession of the reins of government.' The party platform specified no immediate demands, but called on workers to unite under the party banner in order to achieve three goals:

1. The transformation, as rapidly as possible, of capitalist property in the means of wealth production (natural resources, factories, mills, railroads, etc.) into the collective property of the working class.

2. The democratic organization and management of industry by the workers.

3. The establishment, as speedily as possible, of production for use instead of production for profit.[26]

The party regarded its 'impossiblist' position as the most revolutionary in the world and refused to join the Second International on the grounds that it was a reformist body.[27]

The Socialist Party of Canada soon achieved ascendancy within the socialist movement in Canada. In the Maritimes the party supplied a rallying point for socialists in the region. Members of the Fredericton Socialist League welcomed the formation of the SPC, adopted the party platform, and in April 1905 formed Fredericton Local No 1 of New Brunswick.[28] In August 1907, with the help of Stuart, the Cape Breton socialists received a charter as Local Cape Breton and brought 31 new members into the party.[29] In February 1908 a second New Brunswick local, with 40 charter members, was formed among the CPR workers at McAdam Junction.[30] A third New Brunswick local was formed in 1908 in rural Albert County. Here the inspiration was Roscoe Fillmore, whose road to socialism was a reminder that one of the concomitants of rural depopulation and emigration in the Maritimes was the contact young labourers established with labour and socialist movements they encountered while travelling in search of work. Born in 1887, Fillmore went to Portland, Maine, as a youth and worked at casual jobs and in a locomotive repair shop. One evening in 1903 he heard a socialist speaker on a streetcorner, and on his return to Albert County soon afterwards he was a convinced socialist. A voracious reader, Fillmore confirmed his socialism through extensive reading and on trips to Portland, Rochester, Alberta, and British Columbia. In western Canada he worked on the harvests and on railway construction and met a number of militant unionists and socialists. On his return to Albert County early in 1908 he organised a party local and soon became the region's most active socialist agitator.[31]

The year 1909 was a time of rapid growth for the socialist movement in the Maritimes. Early in 1909 there were five locals in existence; by the end of the year there were fifteen.[32] In New Brunswick new locals were formed in Saint John, Newcastle, and Moncton; in Nova Scotia locals were established at Amherst, Halifax, New Glasgow, and Springhill; in Cape Breton locals were organised at Sydney, Sydney Mines, Dominion No 6, and a large branch in Dominion. In April 1909 the Dominion executive appointed Wilfrid Gribble to conduct an organising tour in the Maritimes. A British-born carpenter and exserviceman, Gribble was an active Toronto party leader with a flair for propagandistic verse. The tour was financed partly by the party executive, but mainly from contributions to a special fund established by Fillmore.[33] Gribble arrived on 5 May, planning to spend two months in the region, but remained until 24 October. At the end of his tour, he reported: 'I have been and still am surprised at the ripeness of the field for Socialist propaganda in the Maritimes, especially in Nova Scotia' and added that 'if the same amount of public propaganda that was put in Ontario had been put in Nova Scotia, the results would have been immeasurably more; this I have not the slightest hesitation in saying.'[34] The Maritime locals also sponsored a tour by W. D. 'Big Bill' Haywood of the IWW in November and December. The massive coal miners' strike in the summer of 1909, which lasted for 10 months in Cape Breton and 21 months in Cumberland County, provided a host of illustrations for socialist propagandists. In 1910, on Gribble's recommendation, a Maritime provinces executive committee was established at Glace Bay. In November 1913, at the insistence of Saint John members, separate provincial executives were established for Nova Scotia and New Brunswick.[35] The institutional evolution of the movement in the region may be followed in detail in Table 4-1.

A significant measure of the growth of socialist influence in the region is provided by the circulation figures for *Cotton's Weekly*. The 'live propaganda paper' founded at Cowansville, Quebec, by W. U. Cotton in December 1908, was modeled on Julius Wayland's immensely successful *Appeal to Reason*. Always more popular than the official party organ, the *Western Clarion*, *Cotton's* reported a national circulation of 31,000 copies in 1913.[36] Atlantic Canada consistently accounted for a substantial part of the *Cotton's* readership. Detailed circulation figures are given in Tables 4-2 and 4-3. For a sample issue in each of six years, from 1909 to 1914, readers in Atlantic Canada accounted for 15.6, 13.0, 9.8, 7.7, 8.9, and 7.8 per cent of the paper's national circulation. In

TABLE 4-1   SOCIALIST ORGANISATIONS IN THE MARITIMES, 1899-1916

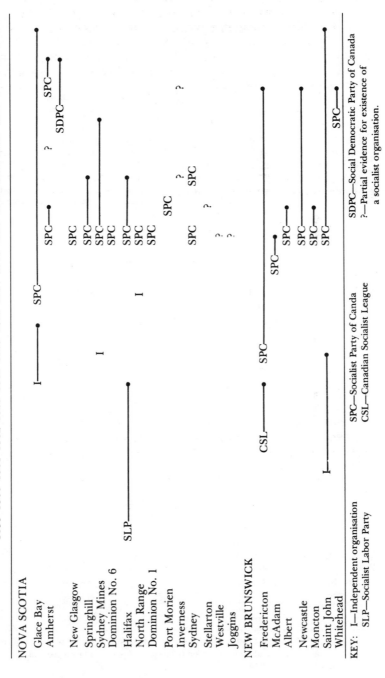

KEY: I—Independent organisation
SLP—Socialist Labor Party

SPC—Socialist Party of Canda
CSL—Canadian Socialist League

SDPC—Social Democratic Party of Canada
?—Partial evidence for existence of
a socialist organisation.

TABLE 4-2

COTTON'S WEEKLY CIRCULATION
IN ATLANTIC CANADA, 1909-1914

Date of Issue	Canada	ATLANTIC REGION					Atlantic Circulation as a percentage of total circulation
		Total	N.S.	N.B.	PEI	Nfld.	
23 December 1909	5,014	786	514	286	4	?	15.6
1 December 1910	10,383	1,352	1,147	171	13	21	13.0
7 September 1911	11,962	1,172	927	225	6	15	9.8
24 October 1912	26,274	2,025	1,382	430	27	186	7.7
9 October 1913	27,556	2,439	1.683	420	71	265	8.9
12 March 1914	19,619	1,546	1,156	230	47	113	7.8

TABLE 4-3

COTTON'S WEEKLY CIRCULATION
24 October 1912, BY FEDERAL CONSTITUENCY

Nova Scotia		New Brunswick		Prince Edward Island	
Annapolis	30	Carleton	0	Kings	9
Antigonish	10	Charlotte	7	Prince	6
Cape Breton North Victoria	43	Gloucester	0	Queens	7
Cape Breton South	346	Kent	17		
Colchester	43	Kings and Albert	40		
Cumberland	350	Northumberland	6		
Digby	6	Restigouche	2		
Guysborough	14	Saint John City	158		
Halifax	270	Saint John City and County	208		
Hants	24	Sunbury, Queens	12		
Inverness	188	Victoria	14		
Kings	10	Westmoreland	83		
Lunenburg	28	York	19		
Picton	48				
Richmond	16				
Shelburne and Queens	6				
Yarmouth	16				

SOURCES FOR TABLES 4-2 and 4-3: Each issue of *Cotton's* contained a report of circulation figures for the previous issue. The table was compiled from these reports, and from a detailed breakdown in the issue of 7 November 1912.

December 1910 *Cotton's* had more than 1,300 subscribers in the region. Of these more than 1,100 were in Nova Scotia, principally in Cumberland County (553), Cape Breton and Victoria counties (334), Halifax (99), and Pictou (43).[37] The newspaper had little success on Prince Edward Island, where circulation never exceeded 100 copies. The socialists found greater response in New-foundland, where there were 265 subscribers in 1913 and where the socialists enjoyed an episodic organisational presence. By late 1912 copies of *Cotton's* were being mailed weekly into all but two federal constituencies in the Maritimes. Nevertheless, the urban and industrial centres of Cape Breton, Cumberland, Inverness, Halifax, and Saint John accounted for about three-quarters of the subscribers. Readership reached a peak of more than 2,400 copies in October 1913.

The socialists encountered some vexatious obstacles in their efforts to build a radical movement in the region. The soil of Albert County proved inhospitable. Upon its formation, the party local was denounced by the clergy and the meeting place was stoned. Clarence V. Hoar wrote that the members felt 'shunned as if they were poisonous reptiles, and ... were thought capable of such outrages as bomb-throwing or throat-cutting.' A clerk at the Bank of New Brunswick, Hoar was compelled to resign his job and move to Portland, where he remained an active socialist.[38] Fillmore himself made frequent forays into Moncton, where party supporters included William Mushkat, a Moncton mer-chant and Russsian *émigré* of 1905, and his daughter Sophie Mushkat, later active in the Alberta SPC. On one occasion Fillmore's street meeting was disrupted and the socialists took the offender to court; the next night the police broke up the meeting, but the pugnacious Fillmore was able to intimidate the police chief into allowing meetings to continue.[39] There were similar difficul-ties in Nova Scotia. In Pictou County Gribble had no trouble in attracting attentive crowds at his open-air meetings in New Glasgow and Westville. In Stellarton, however, he faced competition. His streetcorner speeches were surveyed by 'a bunch of bosses standing at the opposite corner' to take note of his audience and his oratory was interrupted by the arrival of the Salvation Army 'who showed their Christian spirit by starting a meeting close by, thump-ing the drum and howling something like "Oh, you must wear a collar and a tie. Or you won't go to heaven when you die." '[40] In Halifax Gribble spoke nightly at the Grand Parade, but the members found their efforts 'slow, uphill work.'[41]

The socialists did achieve some influence in the public press. In Moncton an influential recruit to the socialist cause was Bruce MacDougall, editor of the fiercely independent weekly, *Free Speech*. Stuart contributed many articles on labour and socialism and the paper published the SPC platform, complete with membership application. In June 1909 the *Clarion* announced that the radical paper 'has come out flat-footed for Socialism.' When the editor published an attack on Saint John's mayor, police magistrate, and other leading citizens in September 1909, he was swiftly convicted of libel and *Free Speech* was sus-pended.[42] By contrast, Stuart himself enjoyed greater success in Newcastle. In January 1907 he took up an appointment as editor of the *Union Advocate*, a local weekly. His first editorial, 'Socialism in Canada,' announced the end of the two-party system. In subsequent issues he attacked railways and corporations and advocated public ownership, reported sympathetically on the growth of the New Brunswick teachers' union and the local labour movement, and described developments in international labour and socialist activities. In local affairs, Stuart advocated a single tax on unimproved land and opposed subsidising industries, proposing instead a system of joint ownership in exchange for concessions to industries. He ceased to edit the *Advocate* in 1910 and returned to teaching. Elected to the town council in Newcastle in 1911, Stuart was returned each year, except for 1914 and 1917, until 1919. Stuart continued to write for many newspapers, including the *Eastern Labor News*, and made frequent public speeches. Although he advocated a variety of reforms, ranging from the abolition of the Senate to free textbooks in the schools, he remained a member of the SPC and helped sustain the small Newcastle local which, except for a lapse in part of the period 1912-13, remained in existence as late as 1916.[43]

The SPC's strongest New Brunswick unit was in Saint John, where the local formed in 1909 was still thriving in 1913 with 30 paid-up members. The local held weekly meetings and maintained a hall. Three of the leading members were British immigrant workers: Alec Taylor, J. W. Eastwood, and F. O. Hyatt. Fillmore had known Hyatt in the west where they 'raised a bit of a row with the unemployed of Calgary.'[44] In November 1909 Fillmore earned his first night in jail in Saint John. When Haywood arrived in town, Fillmore accompanied him to King's Square where the Salvation Army was holding forth that evening:

Said Haywood, 'Why don't we hold a meeting?' Said I, 'As soon as these people are through.' As the Army marched away I shouted 'Fellow Workers' and the meeting was on but not for long. In five minutes all traffic on King Street was jammed where it enters the Square.

The police ordered Fillmore to end the meeting and when he refused he was whisked off to jail.[45] This was not the last trouble with the Saint John authorities. When the socialists attempted to run a candidate in the 1911 federal election on a free-speech platform, they were prevented from filing their nomination papers.[46] Free-speech fights continued in Saint John during the summer of 1912, when the police chief continued to issue orders to disperse outdoor socialist meetings. In June 1913 the *Eastern Labor News* complained that the labour paper was banned from the Saint John public library.[47]

The Saint John socialists achieved some influence in the local labour movement, but not without some soul-searching on their part. When the local was first formed, Colin McKay noted that 'some of the comrades made the mistake of sneering at the trade unions ... and this blunder has not been wholly forgotten yet. At any rate the trade unionists have held aloof.' However, McKay himself helped revive the Saint John Trades and Labour Council in 1910 and Hyatt subsequently became a delegate to the council and was elected its secretary; when the New Brunswick Federation of Labour was formed in 1913, Hyatt was a member of the executive. 'My own impression,' wrote McKay, 'is that he has done more to make converts to Socialism by his connection with the trade union movement than by any of his speeches in the Socialist Hall.'[48]

The socialists enjoyed mixed success in the region. They established a presence in most of the urban and industrial districts in the region but generally failed to reach the fishing, farming, and lumbering population of the Maritimes. A few exceptions to this pattern may be noted. Locals were established among farmers in the Saint John Valley (Whitehead Local) and in the Annapolis Valley (North Range), and Stuart enjoyed considerable personal influence in the Newcastle district. And in the prewar period the SPC was much less successful in industrialised Pictou County than in other industrial communities, although there was a pronounced degree of radicalism in that county in the 1920s. However, it was in the coal-mining and factory towns of Cumberland County, and in the coal and steel communities of Cape Breton, that the socialists enjoyed their greatest influence. To analyse the socialist movement in these areas we turn to two brief case studies.

In Cumberland County the socialists played an influential role. In December 1908 Amherst socialists were corresponding with party headquarters and a local was formed with ten members in January 1909. Three months later recording secretary Albert Collins, a local labourer, boasted that the unit had almost 40 members. 'It is really surprising to find so many people who have for years been nursing the principles of socialism within their thinking chambers,' wrote Collins to the *Clarion*.[49] Gribble spent seven days in Amherst during his tour that summer, addressing thirteen meetings; in his report to *Cotton's* he singled out the careful preparations made by the Amherst members for his meetings.[50] Roscoe Fillmore also found ready audiences in the factory town. On 1 July 1909 he took over the bandstand at the town's Dominion Day celebrations and lectured the crowd on socialism for about twenty minutes; when the concert began, Fillmore led an audience of about 100 people to a hall for a socialist meeting.[51]

An analysis of Amherst socialist supporters shows the close links between the socialists and the local labour movement, in which they occupied key leadership positions. In 1903 Dan McDonald and George McLeod organised the tailor shops and helped build the town's first trades and labour council. Also active in the labour council and their international union were moulders John McLeod, Tom Godfrey, John Logan, and James Duxberry. Blacksmith Zabred McLeod, carpenters John Ball and William McInnis, and fellow socialist Clarence Babcock took the lead in organising workers in the large Rhodes-Curry Company works. Among the almost 30 socialists identified in Amherst, the majority were skilled workers: carpenters and tailors led the way with solid representation from shoemakers, millmen, masons, and machinists. Although information on women's participation in the socialist movement is scarce, in 1915, a Mrs Zora Richardson was corresponding with the *Clarion* on behalf of the Amherst SPC. She may have been the owner of a boarding house that sheltered itinerant socialists and was used as union headquarters during the 1919 general strike. Mrs Logan and Mrs Godfrey, who together with their husbands had emigrated from Scotland, were also known for their strong socialist ideas.

A similar situation prevailed in Springhill among the Cumberland County coal miners. Socialist agitators were well received on their visits to Cumberland. Gribble found Springhill 'simply grand' and added: 'I think Springhill must have broken the record in number of names on charter application.'[52] A month later in Joggins, Fillmore held a successful meeting in the UMW Hall, and with the help of the local UMW secretary, Walter A. Grice, formed another party local.[53] *Cotton's Weekly* quickly achieved a large circulation in Cumberland County and carried extensive reports on the progress of the miners' strike, submitted by local socialists. Among the leading socialists in Springhill were Seaman Terris and William Watkins, both popular UMW leaders; Terris later ran for the House of Assembly on a socialist ticket and Watkins, secretary of the Springhill UMW local, later became president of District 26. Perhaps the most flamboyant radical was Jules Lavenne, a Belgian coal miner and socialist, who was a strong booster of *Cotton's* and other socialist literature and the organiser of the Socialist Young Guard among the miners' children.[54] On one occasion during the 1909 strike Lavenne entered the compound where immigrant strikebreakers were housed and on a Sunday morning, riding a white horse and carrying a red flag, he led them through the town to join the strikers.[55] Fillmore later recalled that many German and Belgian miners, recognising socialist songs sung by the strikers, came out in support of the strike; he noted many of the German coal miners had been members of the German Social Democratic Party.[56]

The socialists had an important impact on the development of working-class political activity in Cumberland. In 1908 Amherst unionists and Springhill coal miners discussed and planned the formation of a local labour party.[57] The Cumberland Labor Party was formally launched on 1 May 1909. The founding convention adopted a statement of principles which was based on the Trades and Labour Congress platform, but prefaced by a declaration in favour of the collectivisation of all the means of production, distribution, and exchange. Two candidates were named to stand for election to the provincial legislature.[58] The candidates were Seaman Terris, the Springhill miners' leader, and Adolph Landry, the former Halifax SLP spokesman. (After leaving Halifax, Landry worked in the Amherst and Moncton area as a representative of the International Correspondence Schools and appeared frequently at labour and socialist meetings, sharing the platform with Keir Hardie in Moncton in 1908 and Wilfrid Gribble in Amherst in 1909.)[59] Upon formation of the Cumberland Labor Party, both Stuart and Fillmore appealed to the new organisation to join the SPC, urging them to become 'class conscious workers' and 'up to date workingmen by throwing away your immediate demands and adopting the platform of the Socialist Party of Canada.'[60] Shortly afterwards the party members voted by a two-to-one margin to endorse the platform and principles of the SPC.[61] An unexpected provincial by-election in November 1909 occupied the Cumberland party's attention. Landry was chosen to run and after a vigorous campaign he polled 1,250 votes, mainly in Amherst and Springhill.[62] In June 1910 the party met in convention at Maccan and dissolved in favour of the SPC. Those who were not already members of the SPC signed applications. The meeting then reconvened under Fillmore's chairmanship as a socialist convention and nominated Landry and Terris to run in the next provincial general election.[63] The Maritime executive made the candidacy of Terris and Landry conditional on Landry's membership in the SPC; Landry apparently did not become a member, however, and a dispute followed over the 'ideological purity' of Landry and Lavenne, his most important supporter in the party. The result was the expulsion of Lavenne and the party's failure to contest either the provincial or federal elections in 1911.[64]

The Springhill local apparently collapsed after the defeat of the 21-month strike in 1911. The Amherst local survived; although it lapsed in 1913, it was soon reorganised and active in 1914 and 1915. Amherst also provided the only local of the Social Democratic Party of Canada in the region. It was formed in Amherst by T. H. Dorion in late 1913 and continued to exist in 1914 and 1915.[65]

The Cumberland radicals also had an impact on local politics. In the 1910 elections the Cumberland Labor Party successfully ran three labour candidates in Springhill and two in Amherst. The labour candidate for mayor in Amherst was narrowly defeated, but in 1911 he became the first mayor to break the reign of the town's business elite in that office. In the 1914 town elections a socialist ticket was sponsored by the SDPC members. Three members ran for council seats and machinist Leon Knowlton was the candidate for mayor. During the campaign some three to four thousand copies of the SDPC platform were distributed. Another manifesto, written by the Amherst socialists, was addressed 'To the Wealth Producers of the Town of Amherst.' 'As tomorrow is election day,' the document proclaimed, 'you will be called upon to vote for the suppression or continuance of the system that makes the rich richer and the poor poorer.... Our present social system puts profits ahead of human life and while it exists the Golden Rule is impracticable. We are not making a personal canvass for votes. We are leaving it to the discretion of the workers themselves to vote for their emancipation.' Knowlton obtained 361 votes the next day, more than 25% of the ballots cast.[66]

In industrial Cape Breton the socialist movement had become well established prior to 1909. In 1908 one 'Rover Jim' was overjoyed on his first night in Glace Bay to discover 'an enormous Socialist meeting' of 1,200 people.[67] H. H. Stuart, concerned that the ILP units might challenge the SPC in the Maritimes following the endorsement of political action by the Trades and Labour Congress, was confident that such efforts would fail in Cape Breton, 'for the Cape Breton comrades are able to much more than hold their own in debate.'[68] On his arrival in Cape Breton in 1909 Gribble was likewise impressed by 'a whole crowd of stalwarts ... some of them exceptionally well posted.' At an open-air meeting in Sydney Mines the audience forced him to speak 'till my voice squeaked and still they wanted more, so we had a song, the Red Flag;' by dark he had gained 25 membership applications. Sydney Mines, Gribble predicted, would become the Nanaimo of the east. 'Comrades should know,' he reported, 'that results have been obtained long since in Cape Breton that are being manifested now. These recruits we are getting are no sudden conversions, but men and women who have been merely waiting for the assembly to be sounded.'[69]

As in Amherst, the socialists were predominantly working class and enjoyed close links with the local labour movement. In a group of 25 prominent SPC members in industrial Cape Breton, at least 12 were coal miners; other occupations included steelworkers and printers, a baker, and a tailor. Three party members, Wilberforce McLeod and Alex and Hugh McMullin, were officials in local co-operative societies; the first two were also active in the formation of the Co-operative Union of Canada. Four party members were prominent trade union leaders: J. B. McLachlan and J. D. McLennan were executive officers of District 26 of the United Mine Workers of America, Alf Brenchley was secretary of a UMW local, and steelworker H. C. Gregory was secretary of the Sydney Trades and Labor Council.

Gribble arrived in Cape Breton in the midst of the turmoil preceding the strike for recognition of the UMW. A strong proponent of the official SPC position on the ineffectuality of trade unions, Gribble greeted the arrival of UMW president T. L. Lewis with loud sneers. According to Gribble, 'Lewis talked "Brother Capital and Brother Labour," "fair profits," "rightful division of the products," "conciliation" and a lot of other rot.' Gribble's attitude no doubt troubled prominent socialist trade unionists like McLachlan and McLennan. More suited to the situation was Jimmy Simpson, the Toronto trade union leader and party member, who arrived on the scene to write sympathetic reports on the strike for the Toronto press. Gribble and Simpson represented opposite tendencies within the SPC on the party's 'impossiblism.' The two socialist spokesmen clashed briefly at one public meeting in Glace Bay before Gribble, with the consent of the local members, agreed to continue his organising tour elsewhere in the region. 'The majority of the miners are in a state of fatuous confidence as to their success,' wrote Gribble unperturbed, 'and are just now unfitted to some extent for listening to the real thing. It will not be long before many of them will be disillusioned however and then will be the chance of Maritime comrades to see that the only hope of the workers is again expounded to them.' During the remainder of his tour Gribble predicted defeat for the coal miners and, according to the *Eastern Labor News*, 'accused the trade unions of being no use to the working class, because they stood for the present system of industry.'[70]

Socialist agitation continued unabated through the long strike period. The course of events featured strikebreaking, evictions, armed confrontations, arrests, and blacklists. 'It has been a grand time for socialist propaganda,' wrote McLachlan in the *International Socialist Review*. 'The local comrades have taken advantage while the miners were in a mood to think and have spread the literature of socialism amongst them, where, hitherto stoic conservativeism [sic] reigned, it is now fast becoming red.' McLachlan also noted that the socialists were particularly effective in gaining the support of non-English-speaking workers for the UMW. Visiting a group of imported strikebreakers, he found the workers were unimpressed when the interpreter introduced him as an officer of the UMW. 'He then said, I was a member of the Glace Bay socialist local. That did the trick, in a moment they were round me shaking my hand and the grins gave place to beaming faces.'[71] At the invitation of the socialists, Big Bill Haywood toured the Cape Breton district in early December. The famous Wobbly addressed crowded audiences in local theatres in Sydney Mines, Sydney, and Glace Bay, and smaller meetings at Dominion and Dominion No 6. His topic was 'The Class Struggle' and according to the report filed by the Cape Breton socialists 'he told the workers that they must achieve their own emancipation. They need not look for some kindly savior to do it for them.' He also 'gave a very different idea of unionism from that held down there in the past—that of making the union an industrial school in which the workers study and develop themselves in such a manner that when the Socialist Party has achieved political emancipation, the industrial union would be prepared to efficiently and economically man and administer the means of production. His picture of the coal miners under an industrial democracy brought forth the hearty and spontaneous cheers of the workers.'[72]

In October 1909 a convention of the five Cape Breton locals resolved to contest the next provincial election on the issue of 'the present system of exploitation.' The convention declared that 'the present industrial system is based on the exploitation of the worker, the working class being under the necessity of selling its labor power for what maintains a bare existence' and concluded that 'this condition can only be remedied by the abolition of the present wage system under which all production is carried on for the profit of the capitalist class.' The resolution also noted that 'all other political parties under whatever name known stand for the maintenance of the present system of exploitation.'[73] In May 1910 the socialists again confirmed their uncompromising hostility towards other political parties and selected their candidate. Born on a Cape Breton farm, Alex McKinnon went to work at ten years of age on the death of his father, and entered the mines at 14. Through night-school study he earned a certificate qualifying him as a mine manager. An admirer of Eugene Debs, he learned his socialism under the influence of the Socialist Party of America and in Chicago attended the party's Ruskin University. Returning to Cape Breton, he was town engineer for Glace Bay from 1906 to 1918. A founder of the Socialist Club in 1904, McKinnon was an effective speaker with a talent for 'making puzzling things plain.'[74]

The provincial election finally took place in June 1911. McKinnon claimed the honour of being the first socialist candidate for any legislature east of Saskatchewan. An election manifesto attacked the capitalist system and called for 'collective and social ownership of all the means of life by the working class.' 'What do we mean by a "revolution"?' the manifesto continued. 'We mean that the proletariat must become the politically dominant class and use this power to take over the ownership and control of all capitalist industries.' Comrade McKinnon was running on 'the only vital and real issue before the workers of this country as well as the world, viz.: "Socialism versus Capitalism." '[75] McKinnon polled a total of 713 votes, mostly in the mining towns where there were SPC locals. In the dual constituency McKinnon's vote amounted to 11.4% of the total polled by Tory John C. Douglas, the leading candidate.[76] This showing was no better than Stephen B. MacNeil's vote as a labour candidate in 1904, but the socialists once more raised 'that $200 to pay the fine' and conducted similar 'clear-cut revolutionary propaganda' in the September federal election. On this occasion McKinnon received only 223 votes, though in a close contest this was sufficient to result in a margin of defeat for the sitting Tory member.[77] In both elections McKinnon had faced Liberal and Tory candidates with some prominence as supporters of working-class causes: as mayor of Glace Bay Douglas had opposed the use of troops in the 1909 strike; J. W. Maddin and Douglas had both appeared as solictors on behalf of the UMW; colliery doctor A. S. Kendall had supported the consideration of compulsory recognition of trade unions. In light of these candidacies, and the radical character of the socialist campaign, the socialist votes in 1911 must be regarded as class-conscious ballots. The electoral results indicated the existence of a strong core of socialist supporters, but they also revealed that the party system in Cape Breton responded resourcefully to working-class militancy.

Following the 1911 campaigns, the Cape Breton socialists remained active. In April 1912, for instance, the Glace Bay local boasted 59 members and in the next four months recruited 42 new members and sold more than $200 worth of socialist literature. Among the most popular items were issues of the *International Socialist Review*, *Coming Nation*, *Western Clarion*, *New York Call*, *Progressive Woman*, and the various books and pamphlets published by Charles H. Kerr. *Cotton's Weekly* continued to circulate in the hundreds and one coal miner recalled that as a boy he read *Cotton's* to his father. The party local continued to hold public meetings and weekly educational classes, and maintained rooms on the main street in Glace Bay, where a huge portrait of Karl Marx stared down from the wall.[78]

The socialists in the Maritimes, as elsewhere in Canada, shared many of the customs of the world-wide movement from which they drew inspiration. They celebrated the first of May and the anniversary of the Paris Commune, signed their correspondence 'Yours in Revolt' and, on public occasions, wore red neckties. They made no important contributions to the development of Marxist theory in Canada, but in this they were little different from most North American socialists, whose commitment and zeal habitually found expression in tireless activism. The primary immediate goal of the socialist movement was the making of socialists; the precise strategy and tactics that would be necessary to achieve socialism received relatively little attention. Thus the socialists placed great emphasis on the importance of education and propaganda in their work, but like most British and North American socialists of their time they were prepared to wait with confidence for the gradual growth of socialist strength and the economic and social crises that would have to take place before the socialist commonwealth could be inaugurated.[79]

Stuart never tired of repeating one of the fundamental propositions of the socialist movement. 'We have been looking for justice to come as a gift from the master class,' he stated in an address in Glace Bay in 1904, 'forgetting that, if the workers are ever to be free, *they must free themselves.*' Writing frequently on educational issues, Stuart attempted to educate his fellow teachers to the proper teaching of history. 'The purpose of history,' he wrote, 'is, or should be, to teach the rising generation to avoid the mistakes of their ancestors, and so be able to substantially improve the social, moral, industrial and political system handed down to them by their immediate progenitors.'[80] One Sydney Mines socialist, John MacAllister, eloquently attacked the role of the school and church in propagating capitalist morality. 'As soon as the poor man's child can totter out of doors, it is taught to pull off its cap and pull its hair to the quality.' 'Industry, Honest and Content,' he scoffed. 'The first item is taught because industry gives the rich everything they desire, the second because honesty prevents an iota of the said being taken away again, and the third because content hinders these poor slaves from ever objecting to a system so comfortable to the rich who profit by it.'[81] In addition to attending weekly classes, party members often contributed long reports, letters, discussions, and poetry to socialist and labour newspapers and to the daily press. But ony Roscoe Fillmore could rival Stuart for volume of contributions. His writings ranged from a discussion of the role of labour exchanges in the capitalist economy to a careful study of capitalist development in China, which was published in the *International Socialist Review*. In light of the literature many party members consumed, it was not surprising they impressed visitors with their erudition. In Glace Bay one party member's library featured at least fourteen Kerr editions, including Engels, *The origin of the family*, Emile Vandervelde, *Collectivism and industrial evolution*, Karl Kautsky, *Ethics and the materialist conception of history*, A. M. Lewis, *Evolution social and organic*, John Spargo, *The common sense of socialism*, C. Osborne Ward, *History of the ancient lowly*, Antonio Labriola, *Essays on the materialistic conception of history*, and Karl Kautsky, *The high cost of living*.[82]

But the outstanding feature of the ideology of the early socialists was their continual stress on the primacy of the class struggle. 'Labor produces all wealth,' declared the SPC platform, 'and to the producers it should belong. The present economic system is based upon capitalist ownership of the means of production, consequently all the products of labor belong to the capitalist class. The capitalist is therefore master; the worker a slave.'[83] In election manifestoes, the party's candidates reduced the issues before the electorate to the simple one of 'Capitalism versus Socialism.' In 'Keeping the Issue Clear,' Fillmore characteristically insisted that the party's preaching was restricted to the class struggle: 'Its campaigns are fought on that issue. Campaign speeches of organisers and candidates are not in advocacy of reforms but on the robbery of the slave at the point of production.'[84] Because the party's strategy depended on the conquest of political power in order to enforce 'the economic programme of the working class,' political activity was supervised with some rigour by local, provincial, and dominion executives. The sanctions against Landry and Lavenne in Cumberland County in 1911 provide a dramatic illustration, and on at least three occasions—in Albert County in 1908, in Cumberland in 1911, and in Cape Breton in 1912—party members who supported 'the capitalist ticket' were expelled from the party by their comrades.[85]

By comparison, other issues dividing party members appeared to be less significant. Although issues like religious belief and trade unionism caused tension within the party, they did not result in any open splits among the Maritime socialists. Many party members had become socialists without abandoning strong religious beliefs. H. H. Stuart, who almost personally represented the transition from Christian socialism to Marxism, perceived no contradiction between socialism and Christianity. 'A true Christian could not obey Christ's injunction to "Do unto others as one would be done by,"' he wrote, 'without being an uncompromising foe to the system of wage slavery.' Religious beliefs for Stuart were a private matter: 'Whether a socialist believes in God or no God is his own private business, and the party must tolerate no interference in such matters. If the candidate for membership is sound in his economics, he should be admitted; if unsound thereon, rejected.'[86] Fillmore, however, was a convinced lifelong atheist. Raised a strict Baptist, he had read Ingersoll, Huxley, and Paine in his youth, and after a protracted spiritual struggle, rejected religious belief. But he refrained on principle from undertaking antireligious propaganda. In 1911 the Maritime executive opposed a campaign to have the SPC declare socialism and religion incompatible. Fillmore denounced such efforts for losing sight of capitalism and attacking the effect instead of the cause. In the east, Fillmore pointed out, 'Comrades are up against a different sort of worker, a priest-ridden worker.... These Comrades have not catered to the church—they have simply ignored its insults and antagonism and have gone on their way pointing out the enslavement of the workers and the cure.'[87]

Similarly, on the issue of trade unionism wide differences prevailed within the party. 'The mission of the Socialist Party of Canada,' declared the masthead of the *Western Clarion*, 'is not to further the efforts of the commodity labour-power to obtain better prices for itself, but to realize the aspirations of enslaved labor to break the galling chains of wage servitude.'[88] In practice, however, many of the party's most effective spokesmen were trade-union leaders who consistently defended short-term working-class interests. When millworkers in northeast New Brunswick went on strike in May 1907, H. H. Stuart championed their cause in the *Union Advocate*: 'One workman alone is of no importance in the world today. Only the power that can be exerted by many men moving together with one mind and purpose will avail to elevate and improve the workingmen's condition. Workmen, unite! By doing so, you have everything to gain and nothing whatever to lose.'[89] In Cumberland and Cape Breton counties in Nova Scotia, the socialist movement was dominated by working-class members active in the labour movement. The treatment accorded party organiser Gribble in Glace Bay in 1909 contrasted sharply with the favourable welcomes enjoyed by Simpson and Haywood, socialists for whom trade unionism was an essential component of the socialist movement. The case of the Maritimes suggests that on the trade-union issue the socialists ignored the party's official indifference and pursued vigorous pro-union policies. This may have been the case in other areas as well. As Ross McCormack has pointed out, some 60 to 90 per cent of the party membership were trade unionists, and party leaders often substituted a 'reluctant pragmatism' for the official party 'impossiblism.' Similarly, Tim Buck's recent memoirs have confirmed a picture of a party that operated in a decentralised fashion: 'The Socialist Party of

Canada had been a national organization, but the Dominion Executive had never exerted any great authority. It had, generally speaking, made pronouncements and published the paper, the *Western Clarion*, but each local organization had done pretty much as it wished.'[90]

The Maritime socialists also perceived that the economic and social structure of their region tended to inhibit the rapid progress of the socialist movement. A Saint John socialist, Colin McKay, made an impressive effort to apply 'the laws of expanding capitalism' to the political economy of the region, and addressed the problems of small industry, farmers, and fishermen. 'In a region of small industry, where the employer is obviously not getting rich,' he noted, 'the ideas of Socialism do not meet with a ready reception. It is not easy to grasp the fact that the small employer is a mere vassal in many cases of the larger capitalism.' In general, he concluded, 'the habits of thinking and feeling of the Maritime workers are those peculiar to small-scale industry, and it is not an easy matter to inoculate them with scientific Socialism.' Like most socialists of his time, however, McKay remained confident of the progressive nature of capitalist development and foresaw that the expansion of capitalism in the region would increase the appeal of socialism: 'Still there is no doubt that Socialist ideas are germinating. The provinces are growing more and more industrial, and the new conditions produce new modes of thought.'[91] Stuart shared similar reflections, writing that 'the small business firms are being rudely awakened to the fact that they are doomed to speedy extinction unless something is done to check the freezing-out process that is being applied to them by the big corporations.' Ultimately, this process would bring strength to the socialist movement: 'The Union of all the citizens of the country on equal terms—otherwise known as the Socialist Commonwealth—is the only solution of the industrial problem; but the remedy will not be applied until the majority of the small operators are clean driven to the wall. Then they will turn to Socialism as their only hope.'[92] In his analysis of the fishing industry McKay perceived similar promise for socialism. He observed that the traditions of co-operation in the industry helped the fishermen more readily to 'grasp the possibilities of cooperation generally;' 'among the fishermen of Nova Scotia I have been surprised at the tendency to Socialist modes of thought.' However, he did not expect that co-operative societies were capable of controlling the course of changes in production and marketing methods sponsored by the capitalist fish companies. Instead, he placed his faith in the progressive dynamic of capitalist development: 'there is every reason to expect that the evolution of capitalism within the fishing industry will follow the course it has taken in other industries. In time the workers in the fishing industry will find themselves in the same position as the workers in all capitalistic industries. The laws of expanding capitalism operate to reduce practically all classes of workers to the same status. Capitalism itself develops class conscious workers and creates conditions from which the only way of escape is by the overthrow of the rule of the capitalists and the establishment of the cooperative commonwealth.'[93]

The high tide of the socialist movement in the period 1909-10 did not last.

By 1914 there remained four SPC locals in New Brunswick, two in Nova Scotia, an SDPC local in Amherst, and an independent organisation in Newfoundland. Socialism remained a radical movement supported by small numbers of people in the region. With the beginning of the war, opportunities for socialist influence declined. Still, party locals remained active in 1915 and 1916 in Newcastle, Amherst, Saint John, and Glace Bay. In contributions to the *International Socialist Review*, Fillmore denounced the leaders of international socialism who, he charged, had betrayed the movement: 'When war threatened, in order to have been consistent, the European Socialists should have opposed it even to the point of organized armed revolt.'[94]

Two episodes in the early part of the war indicated the persistence of socialist activity in Saint John and Cape Breton. The Saint John socialists mounted a vocal opposition to the war. Gribble, who had settled in the city and married a local socialist in 1915, remained a prominent speaker. Following a Sunday evening meeting at the Socialists' Hall, Gribble was arrested and charged with making seditious utterances. In the trial it was revealed that Gribble had called the King a puppet and had changed the recruiting motto 'Your King and Country Need You,' into 'Your King and Country Bleed You.' Gribble denied he had spoken these words, but admitted saying that 'Crowns and titled kings are puppets in the hands of the capitalist class.' Socialists around the region rallied to Gribble's defence and collected a substantial defence fund. In January 1916 Gribble was convicted, but the presiding justice imposed a moderate sentence of two months for this criminal offence.[95] In 1916 the Glace Bay socialists nominated McLachlan to run in the Nova Scotia provincial election. An election manifesto proclaimed the principles of socialism and stated that McLachlan was 'nominated by the Socialist Party to contest the election in the interest of the working class alone.' 'The members of the Socialist Party,' the leaflet concluded, 'can do no more than give the worker a chance to express himself.' McLachlan obtained 1,038 votes, 14.1% of the total polled by the leading candidate, John C. Douglas, a substantial increase over 1911.[96]

In the years before the war the socialists opposed the formation of labour parties. In Halifax and Pictou County labour parties contested the provincial elections in 1911, but in Cumberland and Cape Breton the socialists successfully maintained their claim to be the only working-class party. After 1916 the socialists' policy changed. Political frustration, growing industrial militancy and discontent with wartime policies, and the formation of the Canadian Labor Party in 1917 led SPC members in Canada to turn towards the radical One Big Union movement or to make common cause with more moderate elements in the labour movement. In the Maritimes the socialists threw their energy into the election of farmer and labour candidates. In 1917 McLachlan became president of the newly formed Cape Breton Independent Labor Party, whose candidates did better than any other labour candidates in Canada in the 1917 election. In New Brunswick Stuart stumped the countryside advocating 'a truly popular political party by union of the workers, farmers and all others who perform any useful labor with hand or brain.'[97] Labour candidates achieved significant successes in local politics in Moncton, Halifax, Sydney, and the Nova Scotia mining towns. In 1920 six Farmer candidates were elected to the New Brunswick legislature and four Labor and seven Farmer members were elected to the Nova Scotia assembly. In 1921 one Farmer MP was elected in New Brunswick and McLachlan, though defeated, polled more than 8,900 votes in the federal election. But these developments marked a new stage in the history of radicalism in the Maritimes, for the distinctive political identity of the socialists was submerged within a broader movement.

As in western Canada, the radicalism of the postwar period was rooted in the formative experiences of the previous decades. The most prominent radicals of the 1920s and 1930s in the Maritimes included H. H. Stuart, D. N. Brodie, J. B. McLachlan, and R. A. Fillmore, who were all active figures in the prewar socialist movement and subsequently became leaders of the Communist Party and the CCF in the Maritimes. On the invitation of McLachlan, Brodie, and other Cape Breton radicals, in 1921 W. U. Cotton, erstwhile editor of *Cotton's Weekly*, settled in Glace Bay as editor of the *Maritime Labor Herald*. During the 1920s and 1930s, H. G. Ross, a veteran of the Glace Bay local, remained a tireless salesman of radical literature. At the same time, there was also discontinuity, as the deepening underdevelopment of the region accelerated the exodus of population from the region; individual Maritimers such as Sophie Mushkat, P. F. Lawson, and Fred Thompson became prominent in western radicalism.

The emergence of a socialist movement in the Maritimes in the years before the First World War reminds us not only that radicalism in Canada was an established movement prior to 1919, but also that Maritimers played their part in this movement. Available estimates of party membership and newspaper circulation show that Maritimers offered the socialist movement a proportionate share of its nation-wide following. Rooted in the influences and inspirations of the 1890s, the radical movement in the Maritimes, as in Canada as a whole, soon became Marxist in principles and working class in character. The Socialist Party of Canada provided an ideological and organisational rallying point, but the Maritime socialists also exercised considerable autonomy in their activities. The official 'impossiblism' of the SPC guaranteed the party's political purity and proletarian character, but did not prevent the socialists from participating in nonrevolutionary working-class struggles as well. As in western Canada, the strongholds of the radical movement were in the mining and industrial centres where the growth of industrial capitalism was most rapid and the course of class conflict most sharp. This parallel development suggests that the emergence of Canadian socialism owed more to the common conditions of working-class experiences in eastern and western Canada than to any peculiarities of regional life or culture. For thousands of Maritimers, the early socialist movement was an important part of the region's political life, but given the large obstacles imposed by the region's economic and social structure, the achievements of the early socialist movement in the Maritimes were not substantial.

APPENDIX: EARLY SOCIALISM IN NEWFOUNDLAND

Socialist ideas also gained supporters in Newfoundland in the years after 1899. In July 1899 the Socialist Labor Party newspaper, the *People*, carried a long report on conditions among Newfoundland fishermen. A year later another long despatch from Bell Island described the efforts of the iron ore miners to organise against the Dominion Iron and Steel Company.[98] In October 1906 the *Western Clarion* carried reports of the formation of a Newfoundland socialist party. The leading spirit was Robert E. Scott, an itinerant SPC member who in May 1906 had led a 5,000-strong 'Red Flag' parade in Montreal.[99] By January 1907 the new group had held ten meetings. The small socialist society devoted its energies to circulating socialist literature and speaking to local groups on the merits of socialism.[100] One active member of the society was George Grimes, a Methodist lay preacher, who continued to describe himself as a socialist when he was elected to the legislature in 1912 as a member of W. F. Coaker's Fishermen's Union Party.[101] Joey Smallwood has recalled meeting Grimes in St John's as a youth and that Grimes helped spark his interest in socialist literature.[102] In Newfoundland, the circulation of *Cotton's Weekly* reached a peak of 260 copies per week in July 1913.[103] An organisation known as the Newfoundland Socialist League was active in the summer of 1914, but reported 'a large amount of hidebound prejudice to deal with.'[104] Subsequently this group formed the Socialist Party of Newfoundland with a platform and constitution modelled on the SPC.[105] In January 1915 James Stirling, the secretary, reported 50 members in the St John's local and 'in many outside places the gospel of discontent is taking root.'[106] Stirling appealed for donations of literature and continued to correspond with the Dominion executive of the SPC throughout 1915. On one occasion he asked for suggestions on how to discuss socialism with the fishermen: 'They think they would have to work just as hard and long under a cooperative administration as now, fishing in the season; mending nets, etc., when the season is over.'[107]

NOTES

1. E. R. Forbes, 'In search of a post-Confederation Maritime historiography, 1900-1967,' *Acadiensis*, VIII, no 1 (1979), 3-21; and *The Maritime rights movement, 1919-1927* (Kingston, 1978); Don Macgillvray, 'Industrial unrest in Cape Breton, 1919-1925' (unpub. MA thesis, University of New Brunswick, 1971); Nolan Reilly, 'The origins of the Amherst general strike, 1890-1919,' a paper presented before the Canadian Historical Association annual meeting, 1977; A. A. Mackenzie, 'The rise and fall of the Farmer-Labour Party in Nova Scotia' (unpub. MA thesis, Dalhousie University, 1969); J. K. Chapman, 'Henry Harvey Stuart (1873-1952): New Brunswick reformer,' *Acadiensis*, V, no 2 (1976), 79-104.

2. Data on the institutional evolution of the movement and the circulation of *Cotton's Weekly* are presented in tables 4-1, 4-2, and 4-3. The estimate of party membership is from the *International Socialist Review* (April 1910). Circulation data for *Cotton's* was derived from the weekly reports on copies printed and copies sold which appeared in each issue of the newspaper. According to Ross McCormack's important study, national party membership never exceeded 3,000; see McCormack, *Reformers, rebels, and*

revolutionaries: the western Canadian radical movement, 1899-1919 (Toronto, 1977), 68.

3. Martin Robin, *Radical politics and Canadian labour, 1880-1930* (Kingston, 1968) and Norman Penner, *The Canadian left; a critical analysis* (Toronto, 1977) both neglect the regional experience. In addition to McCormack, *Reformers, rebels, and revolutionaries*, important studies of western radicalism are David Bercuson, *Confrontation at Winnipeg: labour, industrial relations and the general strike* (Montreal, 1974) and Gerald Friesen, ' "Yours in Revolt:" the Socialist Party of Canada and the western labour movement,' *Labour/Le Travailleur*, I (1976), 139-57.

4. For instance, a parallel movement emerged in Newfoundland during this period, and we have prepared a short sketch of this movement in an appendix to this chapter. We have not attempted to show the relations between the socialists and other elements in the labour movement, as McCormack's study has done for western Canada. Nor has our study achieved the intensive focus on the region exemplified by F. A. Barkey, 'The Socialist Party in West Virginia, 1898-1920' (unpub. PhD thesis, University of Pittsburgh, 1971).

5. Marshall Saunders, *The house of Armour* (Philadelphia, 1897); John Davidson, *The bargain theory of wages* (New York and London, 1898); Public Archives of Nova Scotia (PANS), A. S. Kendall papers; E. R. Forbes, 'Prohibition and the social gospel in Nova Scotia,' *Acadiensis*, I, no 1 (1971); K. E. Sanders, 'Margaret Marshall Saunders: children's literature as an expression of early twentieth century social reform' (unpub. MA thesis, Dalhousie University, 1978). For examples of the social gospel and interest in George and Bellamy in Halifax, see *Acadian Recorder*, 27 December, 31 May, 18 February 1898; *Halifax Herald*, 30 May 1899; for these references we would like to thank Ian McKay, Halifax.

6. *Butler's Journal*, April 1903, June 1901; H. H. Stuart, 'Socialism in eastern Canada,' *Weekly People* (New York), 24 February 1906.

7. W. F. Hatheway, *Canadian nationality, the cry of labor and other essays* (Toronto, 1906); Public Archives of New Brunswick (PANB), 'New Brunswick political biography,' comp. J. C. Graves and H. B. Graves, VII. Hatheway polled 3,570 votes.

8. PANB, documents from the New Brunswick Assembly papers relating to the Factory Commission and Factory Act 1905, 49, 90-91, and *passim*; Stuart, 'Socialism in eastern Canada.'

9. State Historical Society of Wisconsin, Socialist Labor Party of America Records, Records of the National Executive Committee, 1878-1906, A. M. Muirhead to Henry Kuhn, 24 January 1898.

10. *The People* (New York), 1 May 1899.

11. *Acadian Recorder*, 25 July, 22 August 1899; *Butler's Journal*, June 1901.

12. *Butler's Journal*, June 1901; *Eastern Labor News*, 15 May, 6 November 1909.

13. Stuart, 'Socialism in eastern Canada.' The Socialist Trades and Labor Alliance was a dual trade union federation established by the SLP to challenge the American Federation of Labor.

14. *Ibid.*

15. Joe MacDonald, 'The roots of radical politics in Nova Scotia: the Provincial Workmen's Association and political activity, 1879-1906' (unpub. MS, Carleton University, 1977); University of New Brunswick (UNB), Manuscripts, H. H. Stuart papers, Box 1, No 7, H. H. Stuart, 'Address regarding the ILP,' 24 October 1904. McNeil polled 869 votes in a contest against Liberal Alexander Johnston and Tory William MacKay. In the provincial contest, in which the Tories fielded no candidate, James Boyd polled 2,080 votes against Liberal A. S. Kendall.

16. Stuart, 'Socialism in eastern Canada;' *Sydney Post*, 14, 18, 29 November 1904; for examples of socialist ideas within the PWA, see PWA, Grand Council Minutes, 1904, II, p. 242; 1905, II, p. 485; 1907, III, p. 617.

17. *Butler's Journal*, May 1903. For his poetry, see Martin Butler, *Patriotic and personal poems* (Fredericton, 1898).

18. *Butler's Journal*, July 1891, July 1892, August 1892, May 1895.

19. *Ibid.*, July 1893, December 1899.

20. *Ibid.*, August 1898; *Canadian Democrat*, April 1901.

21. On Stuart, see UNB, Stuart papers, Manuscripts, Box 1, 'Biographical notes,' and Chapman, 'Henry Harvey Stuart.' Hatheway, Stuart, and Butler are the subject of G. H. Allaby, 'New Brunswick prophets of radicalism: 1890-1914' (unpub. MA thesis, University of New Brunswick, 1972).

22. *Citizen and Country*, 21 October 1899; *Butler's Journal*, January 1900; *Western Clarion*, 7 March 1908; Stuart, 'Socialism in eastern Canada.'

23. *Butler's Journal*, February 1899.

24. *The Maine Socialist* (Bath, Me.), 12 March 1904.

25. Stuart, 'Socialism in eastern Canada.'

26. Socialist Party of Canada, *Platform*.

27. McCormack, *Reformers, rebels, and revolutionaries*, 53-61, 70-71.

28. UNB, Stuart papers, Socialist Party of Canada, Local FrederictonNo 1, Charter; *Fredericton Daily Gleaner*, 27 July 1905.

29. UNB, Stuart papers, Manuscripts, Scrapbook No 1, Clipping and handbill, 1907; *Western Clarion*, 24 August 1907. In October 1905 John Taylor of Sydney Mines had sought information about establishing a local, and in 1906 Charlie O'Brien, the prominent Alberta SPC and UMW leader, toured the Maritimes; *Western Clarion*, 21 October 1905, *Cotton's Weekly*, 21 August 1913.

30. *Western Clarion*, 22 February 1908.

31. *Ibid.*, 8 February 1908; Dalhousie University Archives (DUA), R. A. Fillmore, unpublished autobiographical manuscript. We would like to thank Mrs Rosa Skinner for her assistance in discovering this manuscript and for permission to use autobiographical details for this chapter.

32. *Western Clarion*, 8 January 1910.

33. *Ibid.*, 3 April, 22 May, 2 October 1909. On Gribble, see Wayne Roberts, 'Artisans, aristocrats and handymen: politics and trade unionism among Toronto skilled building trades workers, 1896-1914,' *Labour/Le Travailleur*, I (1976), 97; Wilfred Gribble, *Rhymes of revolt* (Vancouver, 1912).

34. *Western Clarion*, 8 July, 2 October 1909, 8 January 1910.

35. *Ibid.*, 20 November 1909, 1 March, 22 November 1913.

36. We would like to thank Mr E. M. Penton, Ottawa for permission to read his unpublished manuscript, '*Cotton's Weekly* and the Canadian socialist revolution, 1909-1914;' *Cotton's compendium of facts* (Cowansville, Quebec, 1913), 94.

37. *Cotton's Weekly*, 22 December 1910.

38. *Ibid.*, 14 October 1909, 15 September 1910; *Western Clarion*, 4 July 1908.

39. *Western Clarion*, 9 October 1909; DUA, Fillmore manuscript.

40. *Cotton's Weekly*, 5 August 1909.

41. *Western Clarion*, 23 October, 18 December 1909; *Cotton's Weekly*, 23 September 1909.

42. UNB, Stuart papers, Scrapbook, 'Articles from Free Speech;' *Western Clarion*, 5 June 1909; *Union Advocate* (Newcastle), 1, 22 September 1909.

43. *Union Advocate*, 9 January 1907, various issues, 1907-19; Chapman, 'Henry Harvey Stuart.'

44. *Western Clarion*, 14 February 1914, 27 August, 19 November 1910.

45. DUA, Fillmore manuscript; *Eastern Labor News*, 27 November 1909.

46. *Western Clarion*, 18 November 1911.

47. *Eastern Labor News*, 2 March, 22 June, 6 July, 27 July 1912.

48. *Western Clarion*, 15 April 1911, 11 October, 22 November, 2 August 1913.

49. *Ibid.*, 30 January, 20 March 1909.

50. *Cotton's Weekly*, 12 August 1909.

51. *Amherst Daily News*, 2 August, 27 July 1909.

52. *Western Clarion*, 5 June 1909.

53. *Ibid.*, 17 July 1909.

54. *Cotton's Weekly*, 6 April 1911.

55. Jim Brennan, interview, Springhill, 1975.

56. DUA, Fillmore manuscript. A similar account is given in *Eastern Labour News*, 18 June 1910.

57. Miner's Museum (Glace Bay), William Watkins to David Coleman, 2 July 1908; *Western Clarion*, 19 December 1908.

58. *Eastern Labor News*, 15 May 1909.

59. *Ibid.*, 15 May, 6 November 1909; *Amherst News and Sentinel*, 9 September 1904, 15 September 1905, 11 April 1905; *Amherst Daily News*, 28 July 1909; *Western Clarion*, 19 December 1908.

60. *Western Clarion*, 19 December 1908; *Eastern Labor News*, 22 May 1909.

61. *Western Clarion*, 11 June 1910.

62. *Eastern Labor News*, 27 November 1909.

63. *Western Clarion*, 11 June 1910.

64. *Ibid.*, 3 June, October 1911, January 1912; *Eastern Labor News*, 27 May 1911.

65. *Cotton's Weekly*, 18 June 1914; *Canadian Forward*, 16 December 1915.

66. *Amherst Daily News*, 2, 29 January, 4 February 1914; *Cotton's Weekly*, 26 February 1914.

67. *Western Clarion*, 28 November 1908.

68. *Ibid.*, 19 December 1908.

69. *Cotton's Weekly*, 10 June, 1 July 1909; *Western Clarion*, 2 October 1909.

70. *Cotton's Weekly*, 10, 17 June, 15, 29 July 1909; *Eastern Labor News*, 18 September 1909.

71. *International Socialist Review*, June 1910, 1,104.

72. *Cotton's Weekly*, 23 December 1909.

73. *Western Clarion*, 13 November 1909.

74. *Eastern Labor News*, 4 June 1910; *Cotton's Weekly*, 9, 16 June, 1 July 1910.

75. *Western Clarion*, 3 June 1911.

76. Nova Scotia, House of Assembly, *Journals*, 1912, appendix no 19, 3-5.

77. *Western Clarion*, September 1911, 61; Canada, House of Commons, *Sessional papers*, 1912, no 18.

78. *Western Clarion*, 2 November 1912; interviews with Murdoch Clarke, 27 September 1975, and Fred Brodie, July 1977.

79. For discussions of the ideology of socialists in Britain and the United States, see Stephen Yeo, 'A new life: the religion of socialism in Britain, 1883-1896,' *History Workshop*, Issue 4 (Autumn 1977), and Paul Buhle, 'Intellectuals in the Debsian Socialist Party,' *Radical America*, IV, no 3 (April 1970).

80. UNB, Stuart papers, Manuscripts, Box 1, No 7, Stuart, 'Address regarding the ILP,' 24 October 1904; *Union Advocate*, 20 October 1909.

81. *Cotton's Weekly*, 4 May 1911.

82. Personal information.

83. SPC, *Platform*.

84. *International Socialist Review*, 1915-16, 614-17.

85. *Cotton's Weekly*, 15 September 1910; *Western Clarion*, 17 February 1912.

86. *Western Clarion*, 22 October 1910.

87. DUA, Fillmore manuscript; *Western Clarion*, 19 November 1910, 28 January 1911.

88. *Western Clarion*, 27 March 1915.

89. *Union Advocate*, 15 May 1907.

90. McCormack, *Reformers, rebels, and revolutionaries*, 55-65; Tim Buck, *Yours in the struggle: reminiscences of Tim Buck* (Toronto, 1977), 122.

91. *Western Clarion*, 2 August 1913; *Eastern Labor News*, 13 September 1913.

92. *Union Advocate*, 20 March 1907.

93. *Western Clarion*, 2 August 1913; *Eastern Labor News*, 13 September 1913.

94. *International Socialist Review*, 1914-15, 398-403.

95. *Saint John Globe*, 8 December 1915, 13, 20 January 1916.

96. *Working class politics* (Glace Bay, 1916); Nova Scotia, House of Assembly, *Journals*, 1917, appendix no 18, 5-7. In Glace Bay McLachlan polled 26.7% // Douglas's vote, in Sydney Mines 22.5%, in Dominion No 6, 43.1%.

97. *Union Advocate*, 9 July 1918.

98. *The People*, 30 July 1899; *The Weekly People*, 14 July 1900.

99. *Western Clarion*, 7 March 1908; *Union Advocate*, 9 January 1907.

100. *Evening Telegram* (St John's), 8 January, 8 February 1907. We would like to thank Bill Gillespie, St John's, for this information.

101. *Cotton's Weekly*, 4 December 1912.

102. J. R. Smallwood, *I chose Canada* (Toronto, 1973), 74.

103. *Cotton's Weekly*, 3 July 1913.

104. *Western Clarion*, 18 July 1914.

105. *Ibid.*, 7 November 1914.

106. *Ibid.*, 30 January 1915.

107. *Ibid.*, 27 March 1915, October 1915.

NOVA SCOTIA

5 Underdevelopment and the Structural Origins of Antigonish Movement Co-Operatives in Eastern Nova Scotia

R. James Sacouman

INTRODUCTION

Directed from the extension department of St Francis Xavier University, the Antigonish Movement involved large numbers of farmers, fishermen, and coal miners in the organisation of numerous forms of co-operative enterprise during the 1920s and 1930s. It achieved its greatest success in the seven eastern Nova Scotian counties of Pictou, Antigonish, Guysborough, Richmond, Inverness, Victoria, and Cape Breton, the geographic boundaries of the Roman Catholic Diocese of Antigonish. Besides pointing to the influence of such external factors as the growth of adult education movements and consumer co-operation in Britain, the United States, and Scandinavia; the existence of the credit-union movement in Quebec and the United States; and the development of an anticommunist Catholic social philosophy through papal encyclicals, early accounts of the Antigonish Movement usually assumed that it was the existence of local conditions of distress and malaise in eastern Nova Scotia that accounted for its success.[1] Impoverishment, rural depopulation, and loss of ownership and control or proletarianisation were cited as conditions underlying individual malaise among the people of the region and the disruptions of industrialism were said to have forged a readiness to join co-operatives among eastern Nova Scotians.

Another factor consistently given great weight by the early sources was the existence of a cadre of dynamic leaders. This cadre developed within an already existing Catholic diocesan network centred around the diocesan university, St Francis Xavier, and its members were strategically located in influential local organisations. Principals among this leadership were two cousins, M. M. Coady and J. Tompkins, both priests who had been educated abroad, and both former teachers at the diocesan university, the focal point for Catholic education in eastern Nova Scotia. In the main, journalists focused upon the leadership of the movement, 'the humble giants,' and exaggerated their impact upon the Maritimes.[2] While this attention was at times an embarrassment to the activists in the movement,[3] early scholarly analyses of the movement maintained this emphasis on personalities.[4]

This dual stress upon generalised distress and dynamic leadership has led to the neglect of those social structural factors that may explain receptivity to the movement's co-operative programme. The social structure of Atlantic Canada has been conditioned by a general, double-edged implication of capitalist underdevelopment: externally owned capitalisation of exportable raw materials and semiprocessed goods, and the creation and maintenance of a surplus population to work at the regional staple industries in times of capital expansion, but particularly to be exported as labour power to more developed areas.[5] In short, capitalist underdevelopment in Atlantic Canada has for many years capitalised two exportable commodities: raw materials and human labour. However, within eastern Nova Scotia at least, underdevelopment has been uneven in effect upon primary production, leading to differing class structures in each of the major sectors of primary production. Understanding these various structures of underdevelopment is crucial in explaining the uneven success of the movement. Eastern Nova Scotia was a region particularly 'beseiged' in the 1920s and 1930s, as capitalism, co-operation, and trade unionism/socialism vied in an organised, though unequal, fashion for hegemony.[6] Since both in scope and dynamism, the 'Antigonish Way,' the 'middle way' between big capitalism and big socialism,[7] rapidly became the dominant social movement among eastern Nova Scotia primary producers during the 1930s, understanding the various structures of underdevelopment may also provide a partial answer to the movement's general success over competing social movements.

ORIGINS OF THE CO-OPERATIVES

The first set of co-operatives begun under the leadership of the St Francis Xavier extension department, together with the provincial department of agriculture fieldmen, were marketing co-operatives on Cape Breton Island in primarily subsistence agricultural areas.[8] These marketing co-operatives were formed in the early 1930s, a period of falling prices for those products which were marketed and yet a period in which 'many of those who had gone from the rural districts to work in the coal mines and in various other industries had to return to their former homes.'[9] Study clubs, mass meetings, and rallies were also organised for the purpose of establishing a marketing organisation to enable Cape Breton farmers to supply a much larger proportion of the requirements of the Sydney market. Throughout the fall and winter of 1930-31, an educational campaign was carried on to convince the largely subsistence-oriented farmers of Cape Breton that such an organisation could efficiently and effectively sell whatever surplus produce was available by promptly delivering to the Sydney market graded quality goods in volume. In 1931, local producer associations established a farm-produce warehouse in Sydney, the Cape Breton Island Producers Co-Operative, under the management of a federal department of agriculture official. It folded in 1933, never having significantly penetrated the Sydney market because of 'irregular deliveries, poorly graded produce, and improper packaging' and because of insufficient capital to carry the organisation through its birth pains.[10]

A second set of Antigonish-inspired co-operative ventures were the producer co-operatives set up among the fishermen.[11] Although the original drive toward fishermen's co-operatives preceded the establishment of the extension department of St Francis Xavier University, it was nonetheless Antigonish-inspired. Principally through the leadership of Fr J. J. Tompkins, the pastor of Canso, a meeting of local people was held in Canso on Dominion Day in 1927 to protest the impoverishment of fishermen in the Maritimes. Support among clergy in other fishing villages was mobilised by Tompkins at the annual rural conference at Antigonish. Through the insistence of these groups, a federal royal commission investigating the fisheries in the Maritimes and Magdalen Islands was appointed in 1928, which recommended the banning of trawlers and the encouragement of fishermen's co-operatives in order to maintain the existence of the many scattered fishing villages and of the owner-operated fisheries along the Atlantic coastline. Fr M. M. Coady, soon to be director of the extension department of St Francis Xavier University, was hired by the federal minister of fisheries to organise the east coast fishermen. During the fall and winter of 1929-30 over one hundred locals were formed and in June 1930 a marketing, educating, and organising centre was formed, the United Maritime Fishermen (UMF).[12]

Lobster canning and marketing was the first specific enterprise undertaken among fishermen, partially because lobster is a delicacy, obtaining higher prices than groundfish per unit processed and marketed. Moreover, lobster harvesting and processing were labour-intensive, small-scale activities. Since lobster harvesting was most suitably carried out by individual fishermen in small boats close to shore, and lobster canning required only a minimum of capital equipment, the lobster industry was particularly suitable for co-operative investment.[13] Between 1931 and 1939, eighteen co-operative lobster canneries were formed out of existing locals of the UMF in eastern Nova Scotia and the organised marketing of UMF produce was aided by provincial department of agriculture fieldmen. Usually following the formation of fishermen's producer co-operatives, consumer co-operatives were initiated. The first Antigonish co-operative store was incorporated at Port Felix in 1932 and others soon followed.

In 1932, the St Francis extension department set up an industrial branch office in Glace Bay and appointed Alex MacIntyre, a former coal miner and executive member of District 26 of the United Mine Workers, as head. MacIntyre, known as 'Red Alex' in the coal strikes of the early 1920s, had been blacklisted after the strike of 1925. He became so strongly converted to the 'Antigonish Way' that he was soon the most virulent attacker of the 'Red Way' in industrial Cape Breton.[14] MacIntyre's prestige and efforts were ably used by the movement to carry its message to the miners and Tompkins was relocated to the parish in Glace Bay to assist in this work. Co-operative stores were soon incorporated in the coal and steel communities at New Waterford (1934), Sydney (1936), Reserve Mines (1937), Little Bras D'Or (1937), and Port Morien in Cape Breton; and at New Glasgow (1935), Trenton (1935, never functioned), Thorburn (1936), and Westville (1935, never functioned) in Pictou County. These were followed by co-operative housing projects at Reserve Mines (1938), Glace Bay (1939), and Dominion (1939).[15]

Some consumer co-operatives in the farming communities of eastern Nova Scotia were also incorporated in the later 1930s and the movement had some success in influencing the reincorporation of such stores in Antigonish County as the People's, Heatherton, and St Andrews. Moreover, a few woodlot-related producer co-operatives were incorporated, such as a timber-marketing and farm-supplies co-operative at Grand Anse (1933) in Richmond, a woodworking co-operative at Iona (1937) in Victoria, and a sawmill at Irishvale (1936) in Cape Breton County. The only non-woodlot-related producer co-operative formed in the agricultural communities in the 1930s was the threshing mill at Lower Washabuckt (1937) in Victoria County. All of these producer co-operatives were very minimally capitalised.

Between 1932 and 1940 over 110 credit unions were organised in eastern Nova Scotia.[16] The credit union was intended to be a mechanism to solve two major structural problems militating against co-operation: the lack of traditions of mutual aid among rural primary producers and the inadequate means of accumulating and circulating savings. Yet, despite the potential utility of credit unions as introductory mechanisms of co-operation, they tended to be formed earliest in communities with people already schooled in mutual-aid organisations. In 1932, 3 out of 4 credit union in eastern Nova Scotia were formed in coal and steel communities; in 1933, 6 out of 12; in 1934, 8 out of 12. By the beginning of 1935, 17 out of 28 credit unions incorporated in the region had been established in coal and steel communities. Even in fishing communities, the communities with no pre-Antigonish co-operative experience, credit unions usually followed other co-operative ventures. Only in the agricultural communities were credit unions more likely to precede other co-operatives,[17] partly because of the relative lack of success of other forms of co-operatives in these communities. As a training ground for further co-operative enterprise, the success of the credit unions was uneven. Of the five fishing communities in which credit unions were the first form of co-operative enterprise, all five had another co-operative later in the 1930s. Of the 27 agricultural communities in which credit unions were the first form of co-operative enterprise, only 10 operated other co-operatives by 1940.

The Antigonish Movement had a substantial impact in eastern Nova Scotia. At the beginning of 1930, the three poorest counties contained no co-operatives, but by the end of 1940 Guysborough had 10, Richmond 6, and Victoria 8—all of which were Antigonish inspired. In Inverness County, 3 co-operatives existed at the beginning of 1930, 16 at the end of 1940—at least 14 of which were Antigonish inspired. In Cape Breton County, the number of co-operatives expanded six-fold from 3 to 18—at least 16 of which were Antigonish inspired. In Antigonish and Pictou counties the growth rate was much less spectacular; there were 6 co-operatives operating at the beginning of 1930 and 9 at the end of 1940 in Antigonish County, 7 of which were initially or became Antigonish inspired. In Pictou County, there were 2 operating by 1930 and 5 at the end of 1940, only 2 of which were Antigonish inspired. In 1940 the report of the inspector of co-operatives showed that 37 out of 42 reporting co-operative stores in Nova Scotia, 14 out of 15 reporting fishermen's co-operatives, and 6 out of 7 miscellaneous reporting co-operatives were located in eastern Nova Scotia.[18] All 4 credit unions incorporated in 1932 were located in this area; all 12 incorporated in 1933; all 13 in 1934; 13 out of 14 in 1935; 24 out of 30 in 1936; 27 out of 36 in 1937; 9 out of 40 in 1938; 10 out of 35 in 1939; and 1 out of 16 in 1940. Nonetheless, while the Antigonish Movement had its greatest organising success in the 1930s in eastern Nova Scotia, success within the region varied between and within types of primary production sectors and subareas depending upon the degree of direct large-scale capitalist underdevelopment.

ECONOMIC CONDITIONS OF EASTERN NOVA SCOTIA

A. Coal and Steel Industry

The structure of underdevelopment of coal and primary steel production in eastern Nova Scotia has been amply documented by others.[19] The industry has been typified by battles between primarily outside capitalists for control of the coal fields and steel plants, by concentration of external capital, by centralisation of productive secondary manufacturing outside eastern Nova Scotia, and by capitalist/working-class conflict. Important effects—of this rivalry, concentration, and centralisation—are exhibited in the uneven growth and decline of the region's coal and steel industry.

Absolute coal production in both Nova Scotia and the Sydney coal fields peaked in 1913 and never recovered.[20] World coal production also reached a peak in 1913 but, unlike Nova Scotian production, peaked at a higher level in 1929.[21] During the depression of the 1930s, Nova Scotia coal production paid the price of world-wide overproduction without ever having regained 1913 levels. The Nova Scotia Royal Commission Provincial Economic Inquiry reported in 1934 that, although coal constituted 90% of the value of mineral production in the province, 'much of the accessible deposits are exhausted and the mines must be pushed deeper, or further under the sea.'[22] The cost of producing a ton of coal, already double that of the United States, increased by fifty cents between 1926 and 1931,[23] and the exhaustion of cheaper coal deposits, without the significant development of secondary industry, adversely affected the work force. While the total average daily work force remained fairly constant during periods of low production (generally, 1921-34), the average number of days worked per man declined between 1926 and 1931 from 230 days per year to 140 days a year, a decline of 39%. The percentage of new workers in the work force declined from 13.3% in 1926 to 1.1% in 1930.[24] Long-term layoffs in the coal industry affected common surface labourers, contract and day-rated miners, and drivers underground drastically and about equally. Between 1 June 1930 and 1 June 1931, 92% of common labourers at coal mines in Nova Scotia (3,241 out of 3,534) had been laid off at least once, with 47% of those laid off losing 25-28 weeks; 91% of coal miners (7,350 out of 8,089) had been laid off with 48% of those laid off losing 25-28 weeks; and 90% of drivers and other haulage workers (835 out of 926) had been laid off with 43% losing 25-28 weeks. A few managers, foremen, and overseers were also laid off.[25]

Even in the pre-depression years, coal production and employment was highly seasonal. December through April were particularly slack owing to a 'considerable dependence' on the St Lawrence market which was only accessible during the winter by higher-cost rail transportation.[26] After 1930, this dependence on the St Lawrence market was increased in the interests of the Montreal-centred owners of Dominion Steel (DOSCO), in order to fuel their central-Canadian concerns in manufacturing, light, heat, and power. While steel facilities in Nova Scotia only utilised, on the average, 25% of local coal production, coal was being transported to central Canada to fuel central-Canadian steel facilities, facilities often owned by DOSCO itself or by some of its owners.[27]

The structure of external concentration and centralisation shaped not only the work place but also whole communities. Twenty per cent of the population of Nova Scotia was wholly or in part dependent on the coal and steel industry.[28] These dependent communities were hard hit by the depression of the 1930s. On 1 June 1931, fully 78% of male wage-earners, 20 years of age and over, were unemployed at Dominion, 71% at Sydney Mines, and 68% at New Waterford.[29] Direct capitalist underdevelopment provided the most fundamental structural basis for the high incidence of Antigonish co-operative formation in the coal and steel communities, given the decline of effective and militant trade unionism/socialism.

B. Agriculture

In sharp contrast to the externally capitalised, concentrated, and centralised coal and steel industry in eastern Nova Scotia, agricultural production between 1871 and 1941 maintained its traditional petit-bourgeois structure: individually held small acreages were worked primarily by the individual owner's family unit in large part for subsistence, noncommercial purposes. This little-changing structure of agricultural production exacerbated a general rural out-migration, particularly by young people, related to the 'shift away from labour-intensive primary occupations, and away from the rural areas in which these activities are carried out.'[30] Regional out-migration was mitigated only partially and only during periods of large-scale capitalisation in the coal and steel industries.

While the actual number of farms declined dramatically between 1891 and 1941, operator ownership of occupied farms in Nova Scotia declined only nominally from a high of 96.3% in 1891 to a low of 92.2% in 1931.[31] The vast bulk of farming in the province and in the region was carried out by owner-operators and their families. The eastern county with the smallest percentage of owner-operated farms was that county with the largest local market, Cape Breton, but even here the percentage of owner-operated farms was never less than 91.7%. The mean size of eastern Nova Scotia farms was about 100 acres between 1871 and 1921. Although there was some enlargement of mean size after 1921, in 1931 the mean acreage per farm was only 0.46% greater than in 1871. The mean farm size varied substantially by county in eastern Nova Scotia, with farms in Cape Breton and particularly Richmond counties substantially smaller than the mean and in Victoria, Pictou, and Inverness counties larger. Between 1891 and 1931 the absolute acreage of improved farmland steadily declined in the province.

Data on mean capitalisation per occupied farm show the small scale of capital investment and capital holdings. Whether taken in total or by its components of land, buildings, implements and machinery, and livestock, the amount of capital invested remained meagre between 1901 and 1941. When mean capitalisation in the province is compared with changes in wholesale price indices for consumer and producer goods, mean capital investment per farm increased only during 1901-11 and 1921-31; it declined between 1911 and 1941. Overall, between 1901 and 1941, there was a net increase of only 356 1926 dollars. (The increase was $356 or $522 depending on whether the consumer or producer wholesale price index is used in the comparison.)[32] Mean capital investment in land per farm, again expressed relative to wholesale price indices, declined between 1901 and 1941 by 316 (or 137) 1926 dollars per farm. Mean investment in buildings increased by 339 (or 394) dollars, and in implements, machinery, and livestock—crucial indicators of productive capital—increased by 229 (or 236) 1926 dollars, yet still stood at only 332 current dollars in 1941.[33] Data on the eastern counties for 1931 and 1941 indicate the even smaller scale of investment here, about 80% of the mean for the province. In terms of investment in means of production, only Pictou County (1931 and 1941) and Cape Breton (1931) show greater mean investment in implements and machinery than the provincial mean. No eastern county shows greater mean total investment than the provincial mean for either 1931 or 1941, while Richmond (1931 and 1941) and Guysborough (1941) showed less than half.

With respect to gross value of production, again only Pictou (1930 and 1940) and Cape Breton (1940) counties were above the provincial average. Mean value of gross production per farm was never more than 935 dollars for any county; Richmond and Guysborough (1930 and 1940) obtained less than half this mean. Of course, these figures greatly understate differences between counties in terms of mean cash incomes. In every case in 1940, the first year for which data are available, the greater the mean gross value of production for any county, the less the percentage of mean value consumed on the farm. Excluding the value of forest produce sold and the value of all produce consumed on the farm, Pictou and Cape Breton counties dominated in mean potentially commercial production per farm relative both to the region and to the province, while Antigonish County was higher than the eastern Nova Scotia mean but lower than the provincial mean. The gaps between counties in terms of this indicator are immense. Pictou had the largest mean potentially commercial value per farm, 3.95 times as large as the county with the lowest mean value, Richmond. Data on hired farm labour confirm intercounty differences in market production.

In 1940, the majority of farms in Nova Scotia had owner-operators and/or members of household earning cash income off the farm. In eastern Nova Scotia a somewhat larger number of farms reported off-farm income, with proportionately more farms reporting income from the fisheries than in the province as a whole. Antigonish, Cape Breton, and Pictou counties had lower percentages of farms reporting off-farm income than the Nova Scotia percentage, while Victoria, Richmond, and Inverness had the largest percentages. However, when income from work off the farm is taken as a percentage of gross farm revenues, only Antigonish has a lower percentage than Nova Scotia, with Richmond and Cape Breton having the largest. The reasons for this can be clarified by looking at the reported length of off-farm work as a percentage of all work done on farms. Cape Breton had the largest percentage of part-time farmers, working 157 days or more a year off the farm or exactly half the number of working days in a year (assuming a six-day work week). Richmond had the highest percentage of farms reporting an off-farm work year of 49-156 days.

Not working for off-farm income can indicate two opposing structures of farm production and marketing: year-round commercial farming or wholly subsistence farming. Data previously cited support the second of the alternatives. Even as late as 1940, 53% of all farms in Nova Scotia were subsistence farms or combinations of subsistence, and generally those counties were most subsistence oriented that were farthest from markets and industrial employment.[34] Eastern Nova Scotia contained 20% more subsistence or combination of subsistence farms than the provincial average. Only Pictou County had proportionately fewer subsistence and combinations of subsistence farms (50%) than Nova Scotia as a whole. When subsistence and combination of subsistence farms are added to part-time farms, they comprise over three-quarters of all farms in the eastern region, a figure that is 18% higher than the comparable figure for all of Nova Scotia. Again only Pictou County (60%) had a smaller percentage than the province(65%). Far and away the vast majority of farms in eastern Nova Scotia, but particularly in Victoria, Guysborough, and Inverness, were noncommercial operations. Subsistence-oriented production offered in times of general crisis more 'stability and security, if at a lower level of living' than industries that were more in the main stream of capitalist development.[35] This helps to explain the turn-around towards slight growth of many rural subdivisions in eastern Nova Scotia during the 1930s. Yet, however well subsistence production mitigated sufferings in times of crisis, long-term maintenance of a subsistence structure of production is the crucial indicator of the underdevelopment of eastern Nova Scotia agriculture, an underdevelopment structurally different from direct capitalist underdevelopment of the coal and steel and the fisheries sectors. This lack of direct underdevelopment by large-scale capital provided the principal structural basis for the lack of Antigonish co-operative formation in the agricultural areas of the region.

C. Fisheries

The structure of the fisheries in eastern Nova Scotia contrasts with both the monopolistic structure of coal and steel and the small-scale nonmarket structure of agriculture. While fish production remained throughout the late nineteenth and early twentieth centuries even less capitalised than agriculture, it was faced with direct destruction by externally owned, vertically integrated fish corporations—firms that employed labour on trawlers, bought fish from independents, and sold gear and other provisions to the independents. Prior to the Second World War, independently owned boat and small vessel inshore fishing always predominated, *in terms of number of fishermen*. Often such inshore fishing was carried on in conjunction with subsistence or part-time farming and woodlot forestry where possible, with wage labour in the fish plants and other industries in the off-season, and with common labour on public works where and when available. Typically, fishermen in eastern Nova Scotia were owners of their means of production, their boats and gear such as they were. They survived the off-season as 'jacks-of-all-trades,' providing the same cheap labour power in the off-season that their wives often provided throughout the year at the fish plant. But during the period of large-scale capitalisation of the coal and steel industries in the eastern counties from 1890 to 1912, the number of fishermen declined by 23% in Nova Scotia and by a massive 43% in eastern Nova Scotia. By 1912, the number of fishermen in the region had declined to a low of 35% of all fishermen in the province, compared to the high of 47% in 1890. Particularly hard hit were Victoria and Richmond counties, which underwent further major losses of fishermen between 1927 and 1939.[36]

Several studies have examined the persistence of boat and small vessel (e.g., schooner) inshore fisheries in Atlantic Canada,[37] and have noted that 'Nova Scotia entered the twentieth century with a *growing* tendency toward the use of small boats.'[38] Small-boat inshore fishing in the region persisted, while the number of fishermen declined partly because of the intrusion of fish buyers and trawler owners upon the fishing banks and the attraction of the eastern Nova Scotia coal and steel industry and of employment in the 'Boston States.'[39] The Royal Commission on Provincial Development and Rehabilitation's *Report on the Fisheries* stated in 1944:

This small-scale condition is partly attributable to the many fish varieties taken on the Atlantic coast, and to the fact that they are landed all along the coast line, which was early settled in small communities; hence the large numbers of small producers, processors, and exporters. Another reason for the small scale is the history of the eastern trade, which grew before the days of canning and refrigerating and which depended on salting for preservation—a method which could be followed effectively by the fisherman himself on the shore: in the past he could be both producer and manufacturer.[40]

A depression in fish prices beginning in 1921, world overproduction in the late 1920s, the general depression of the 1930s, and the incursion of Norwegian, Icelandic, British, Portuguese, Spanish, and Newfoundland trawler fleets into eastern Nova Scotia banks and markets threatened the viability of small-boat inshore fisheries in eastern Nova Scotia.[41] Inshore fishermen were unable to obtain sufficient capital to replace the minimal equipment they did have, let alone to improve and expand their means of production. A vicious circle of capital deterioration and lack of cash set in: 'a melting away of capital resources of all kinds.'[42]

Incursion of foreign trawlers into the fisheries brought, after 1908, a series of 'successful oppositions' by boat and small-vessel owners to the trawler fisheries.[43] A major 'successful opposition' to trawlers led four out of five federal commissioners to recommend in 1928 'the total prohibition of steam-trawlers from operating from Canadian ports, landing their catch in Canadian ports, or obtaining in Canadian ports coal or supplies.'[44] Their report documented the growth of the trawler fisheries and concluded

that they [the trawlers] are responsible for over-production and the consequent 'glutting' of the market, thereby preventing the shore fishermen from disposing of his catch, of superior quality, at a reasonable price; that because of the low prices offered, and the virtual control of the Canadian markets by the companies operating steam-trawlers, the shore fishermen are deprived of an adequate livelihood, with the resultant serious depopulation of the fishing villages in recent years; and that if steam-trawlers are allowed to continue to operate from Maritime Province ports, the fishing villages in these parts will soon be deserted.[45]

Although it is debatable whether the decline can be blamed solely on trawlers, without taking into account the extremely low levels of capitalisation and income in the shore fisheries, the 1928 commission appears to have been correct in its assumption that the fishing communities would decline unless trawlers were condemned.[46]

During the mid1920s, fishermen in the Canso area communities, which had trawler operations and cold storage plants owned by the trawler companies, experienced price-lowering by the buyers and trawler operators. Some were left with no fresh-fish buyers at all as the companies merged and centralised their operations in Halifax (as did National Fish and Maritime Fish in 1931) or became insolvent in the depression (as did Leonard Fisheries in 1933).[47] In either case the local cold storage plants were shut down, leaving no storage for fresh fish or for bait.[48] Some details on the dependence of fishing communities on a cured-fish company were supplied by the president of Robin, Jones and Whitman, which operated at Cheticamp. The company claimed to have 'the second oldest chain store operation' in Canada, next to the Hudson's Bay Company.[49] It had supplied gear and provisions on credit since 1766 and followed a stated policy of paying high for fish and getting it back through the stores. As President Whitman put it: 'We go into anything which will give the fishermen something else to do outside the fishing season— cordwood, pulpwood, wharf timber, lumber. Incidentally, in the export trade we are willing to buy and sell anything on which we can make a dollar.'[50]

Within this monopoly structure, the 'independent' fishermen, the vast majority of fishermen in eastern Nova Scotia, attempted to earn a living. Average *annual* incomes in the fisheries in 1933 ranged from $160 ($110 from line fishing, $50 from lobster fishing) at Canso to about $200 at Queensport in

Guysborough County; $100 in Richmond County at Arichat and Petit de Grat; $75 in Cape Breton County at Glace Bay and $100 at L'Archeveque, North Sydney, Gabarouse, Grand River, and Forchu; and $175 at Louisburg. The extremely low level of cash income to independents can be contrasted to the mean annual earnings of $1,347.60 for trawlermen from 1929 to 1933.[51] The Royal Commission on Price Spreads contrasted the absolute cash impoverishment of the independents with their conditions of labour—often involving 72 hours without rest with 'continuous physical discomfort and serious danger of loss of life.'[52] The extremely low cash income from the fisheries could be only slightly supplemented by part-time farming and forestry. Part-time farming was virtually impossible over large sections of the east coast and even where possible tended to be necessarily of a subsistence nature, to provide food for the table. Part-time forestry, usually in one's own woodlot, was also dependent on geography and the existence of local markets, which were seriously depressed in the 1930s, if they had ever existed. Detailed data on capital investment for 1939 show the results of low cash income.[53] Mean capital investment in boats and vessels in eastern Nova Scotia for 1939 was a mere $142.70 compared to an already low provincial mean of $208.10.[54] Only one fisheries district in the eastern counties, Cape Breton, had a larger mean investment in boats and vessels than the province as a whole, while three districts, Guysborough, Inverness, and Victoria, had a mean investment of under $100 in boats and vessels, although mean investment in gear in eastern Nova Scotia in 1939 was slightly greater than the provincial average because of a greater dependence on strictly inshore activities such as lobstering. With the near market districts of Cape Breton excluded, the mean income in eastern Nova Scotia was $281.20 in 1939 compared to $398.10 for all of Nova Scotia.[55] Although processing by fishermen themselves of their landed catch contributed to a greater proportion of income in the eastern region than in the province as a whole, the contribution, although 14% of mean income, was a mere $38.10 per fisherman in eastern Nova Scotia (ranging from 28 to 2% and from $81.90 to $2.90 in the eastern districts).

Direct underdevelopment of the small-scale 'independent' fisheries in eastern Nova Scotia, together with a high degree of community dependence on the large fish companies, was the principal basis for the higher incidence of Antigonish Movement co-operative formation in the fishing areas of the region. Direct underdevelopment and dependence also provided a structural linkage across class boundaries between the industrial working class of the coal and steel primary production sector and the petite bourgeoisie of the fisheries sector, both class segments having the same structural 'enemy,' capitalist underdevelopment. During the 1930s the Antigonish Movement provided the apparently across-class programme for survival that actually linked these two differing class segments in organised co-operative action.

Capitalist underdevelopment in eastern Nova Scotia included three structures of underdeveloped primary production which were coincident with the three major primary production sectors in the region: a structure of capitalist/working-class social relations in an externally owned coal and steel industry, a structure of capitalist/petit-bourgeois relations in the inshore and offshore fisheries, and a structure of petit-bourgeois relations in agriculture. The structure of ownership of coal and steel tended to determine the extent of secondary processing of coal-fired steel products. With the depletion of coal reserves and the decline of secondary manufacturing in eastern Nova Scotia during the 1930s went the possibility of regional population and employment growth: eventually, with the increase in external ownership went the growth of a strong local market. Independent primary producers both in agriculture and in the fisheries were faced with the same internal underdevelopment dilemma or vicious circle: existing minimal means of production yield minimal returns for investment in means of production. Returns were often insufficient, on the average, even for the replacement of exhausted means of production. However, in the fisheries, this internal underdevelopment dilemma was aggravated by direct control by big fisheries companies over the costs and returns of fishing. The truck system of control and exchange that prevailed in both the coal mining and fishing communities was a major contributor to the growing dependence of those communities on big capital. By being forced to purchase their consumer supplies from company stores 'on the tab' for high prices, coal miners and fishermen were kept dependent on the respective companies.

Within the independent farmer segment, structural variations occurred along a subsistence-commodity production continuum. Those least polarised by big capital underdevelopment were the subsistence farmers and the wealthiest commodity producing farmers in eastern Nova Scotia. Subsistence farmers tended to experience fewer of the indirect financial and market controls of big capital since their production was not market-oriented and their need to expand not dictated by the laws of capitalist development. The wealthiest commodity producers were sheltered from the harshness of the direct controls since they could obtain credit more easily and could afford to transport to better-paying markets. Those farmers in the middle of the subsistence-commodity production continuum (in semisubsistence, semicommodity production farming, and farming-and-fishing) were the most structurally polarised of the independent farmer class segment. Confronted with the full force of indirect financial and marketing controls, they were not wealthy enough to obtain easy credit and yet had to expand in order to remain viable. They generally did not produce enough of one product or have large enough shipments to command better prices for their produce.

The central theme of this study has been that varying structures of capitalist underdevelopment in eastern Nova Scotia underpinned the incidence of Antigonish Movement co-operative formation. To substantiate this theme, the likelihood of movement co-operative formation in differing types of census subdivisions, up to 1940, was compared.[56] It was expected that coal and steel and fishing subdivisions would be overrepresented with respect to movement co-operative formation in both depressed subdivisions in general (operationalised by depopulation) and farming subdivisions and that middle-range farming subdivisions would have a greater likelihood of movement

TABLE 5-1

SUMMARY TABLE: COMPARATIVE LIKELIHOODS OF
CO-OPERATIVE FORMATION

Types of subdivisions compared	ALL SUBDIVISIONS INCLUDED		ONLY SUBDIVISIONS WITH CO-OPS OR CREDIT UNIONS	
	Incorporated and operated co-operatives	Incorporated co-operatives	Incorporated co-operatives	Incorporated credit unions
Coal and steel subdivisions compared to depopulated subdivisions	3.0	3.0	2.9	2.8
Fishing subdivisions compared to depopulated subdivisions	2.3	2.2	2.3	1.6
Fishing subdivisions compared to farming subdivisions	3.0	3.2	2.9	2.0
Middle-range farming subdivisions compared to larger farming subdivisions	9.7	10.9	6.7	1.5
Middle-range farming subdivisions compared to smaller subdivisions	2.0	2.3	2.9	1.3

NOTE: Cell entries represent the increased likelihood of co-operatives in one kind of subdivision as compared to another kind; for instance, coal and steel subdivisions were three times as likely to have incorporated and operated co-operatives than depopulated subdivisions were.

co-operative formation than either of the extremes. As Table 5-1 indicates,[57] these expectations were convincingly fulfilled.

The emphasis in earlier accounts of the Antigonish Movement on generalised conditions of distress in eastern Nova Scotia was an overemphasis. Conditions of distress were prevalent before, during, and after the formative years of the Antigonish Movement. But why some distressed areas formed Antigonish-inspired co-operatives and credit unions and not others is unanswerable without an understanding of varying structures of underdevelopment. Why coal and steel and fishing subdivisions were greatly overrepresented remains a mystery with a mere emphasis on generalised distress—as does why farming-and-fishing and semisubsistence farming subdivisions were greatly overrepresented relative to subsistence and commodity farming communities. Similarly, earlier writers overemphasised the powers of a dynamic leadership. The leadership was unquestionably dynamic. But why the leadership ignited the fishing and not the farming villages is problematic to the dynamic approach, especially since the biographies of many of the leaders are rooted in eastern Nova Scotia farming villages. The magic of the Antigonish leadership and programme was potent or impotent depending on the structural bases upon which it acted. Of course, an emphasis on underdevelopment and structural origins of the Antigonish Movement can itself be an overemphasis if it leads to dogmatic structural (or economic) reductionism. If, however, structural conditions are viewed as principal bases upon which other more directly social considerations are phrased, then a myriad of questions left unanswered in this study become more readily solvable. Why did the Alumni Association of St Francis Xavier University, the diocesan Catholic clergy, and the Scottish Catholic Society come together in the late 1920s to form the core of the movement? Why did the movement win, during the 1930s, over militant trade unionism/socialism in the region? Why did the movement ultimately fail in reaching its expressed objectives in eastern Nova Scotia and the Maritimes?

With capital expansion in coal and steel in eastern Nova Scotia between 1890 and 1910, unskilled and semiskilled wage labour became available for male members of subsistence and semisubsistence farming or farming-fishing families and for male members of independent fishing families. Because of the seasonal nature of the coal mines, agriculture, and the fisheries, many of these people became in fact part-time farmers and/or fishermen *and* part-time wage labourers. Proletarianisation within the region was thus mitigated as a stratum of semi-petit bourgeois, semi-proletarians was produced. 'Jack-of-all-trades Bluenosers,' combination farmers-fishermen-proletarians, were produced and class differences—differences in relationship to the means of production—were lessened. During periods of crisis within the coal and steel industry, the independent proletarian and his full-time proletarian children had the farm and/or the boat to which to return for at least subsistence purposes and during the Great Depression a significant return to the rural subdivisions, a process of 'subsistencisation,' appears to have occurred, although available evidence is sketchy. Both partial proletarianisation during expansion and subsistencisation during industrial crisis were the results of underdevelopment. Both served to lessen interclass differences through the establishment of an intermediary stratum of farmers-fishermen-proletarians. Perhaps this particular process of underdevelopment best explains, at the structural level of analysis, the development of an apparently across-class leadership and programme, the success over trade unionism/socialism in the 1930s, and the ultimate failure of the movement.

NOTES

I wish to thank the Canada Council for the doctoral funding that made this study possible.

1. Of the sources written by activists and impressed visitors, the most extensive are A. F. Laidlaw, *The campus and the community: the global impact of the Antigonish Movement* (Montreal, 1961) and his edited volume, *The man from Margaree* (Toronto, 1971); M. M. Coady, *Masters of their own destiny* (New York, 1939); G. Boyle, *Democracy's second chance: land, work and co-operation* (New York, 1944) and *Father Tompkins of Nova Scotia* (New York, 1953); B. B. Fowler, *The Lord helps those...* (New York, 1938); M. E. Arnold, *The story of Tompkinsville* (New York, 1949); L. R. Ward, *Nova Scotia—land of co-operators* (New York, 1942); and J. T. Croteau, *Cradled in the waves* (New York, 1951). Other early histories published by the extension department of St Francis Xavier University include Coady, *Mobilizing for enlightment* (1940), *The Antigonish way* (1942) and *The social significance of the co-operative movement* (1945); and H. G. Johnson, *The Antigonish Movement* (1944). As well, various issues of the Antigonish weekly, the *Casket*, between 1917 and 1940, and each issue of the bi-weekly information arm of the extension department of St Francis Xavier University, the *Extension Bulletin*, between 7 November 1933 and 19 May 1939 and its successor, the *Maritime Co-operator*, document the growth of the movement's programme and organisation. See also J. Lotz, 'The Antigonish Movement: a critical analysis,' *Studies in Adult Education*, V (1973), 97.

2. J. Hernon, 'The humble giants,' *Atlantic Advocate* (February 1960); D. MacDonald, 'How F. X. saved the Maritimes,' *MacLean's Magazine* (June 1953).

3. *Extension Bulletin*, 18 October 1938; Laidlaw, *The campus and the community*, 91-93.

4. C. P. MacDonald, 'The co-operative movement in Nova Scotia' (unpub. MA thesis, McGill University, 1938); H. P. Timmons, 'An analysis of the religio-cultural aspects of the Nova Scotia adult education movement' (unpub. MA thesis, Catholic University of America, 1939); M. T. Murphy, 'The study-action group in the co-operative movement' (unpub. PhD thesis, Fordham University, 1949).

5. Seminal pieces on Atlantic Canadian underdevelopment include B. P. Archibald, 'The development of underdevelopment in the Atlantic provinces' (unpub. MA thesis, Dalhousie University, 1971); and David Alexander, 'Development and dependence in Newfoundland, 1880-1970,' *Acadiensis*, IV (1974), 3-31. For a lengthier discussion of a Marxian theoretical approach to underdevelopment and social movements, see R. J. Sacouman, 'The social origins of Antigonish co-operative associations in eastern Nova Scotia' (unpubl. PhD thesis, University of Toronto, 1976), 56-75.

6. For analyses of the trade union response, see D. MacGillivray, 'Cape Breton in the 1920s: a community besieged,' *Essays in Cape Breton history*, ed. B. D. Tennyson (Windsor, Nova Scotia, 1973), 49-67, and D. A. Frank, 'Coal masters and coal miners:

the 1922 strike and the roots of class conflict in the Cape Breton coal industry' (unpub. MA thesis, Dalhousie University, 1974). For an analysis of a capitalist-oriented response among eastern Nova Scotians, see E. R. Forbes, 'The origins of the Maritime rights movement,' *Acadiensis*, V (1975), 54-66.

7. Coady, *The Antigonish way*.

8. The best summary of pre-Antigonish co-operation in Nova Scotia is R. J. MacSween, 'Co-operation in Nova Scotia' (unpub. MS in Public Archives of Nova Scotia, n. d. [about 1952]). A brief look at pre-Antigonish co-operation is in I. MacPherson, 'Patterns in the Maritime co-operative movement, 1900-1945,' *Acadiensis*, V (1975), 67-83.

9. MacSween, 'Co-operation in Nova Scotia.'

10. *Ibid.*, n. p.

11. See *ibid.* and the files of the inspector of co-operative associations at the Nova Scotia Department of Agriculture, Markets Branch, Truro for all incorporation dates.

12. See the office files of United Maritime Fishermen Ltd., Moncton. The leadership role played by the Catholic clergy and by the St Francis Xavier extension department within the UMF is evident in the minutes of all UMF conventions in the 1930s.

13. That co-operative lobster canning was suitable to small-scale owner-operated production is evident in the independent formation of lobster canneries in Yarmouth County as early as 1922. These two canneries in Yarmouth County were the only instances of formal co-operation among fishermen prior to the Antigonish Movement.

14. See the issues of the *Extension Bulletin* and *Maritime Co-operator* for 1938, 1939, and 1940.

15. For the story of early co-operative housing, see Arnold, *The story of Tompkinsville* and F. J. Mifflen, 'The Antigonish Movement: a revitalization movement in eastern Nova Scotia' (unpub. PhD thesis, Boston College, 1974).

16. See the files of the Nova Scotia Credit Union League at their office in Halifax.

17. From 1935 to 1940, the incorporation of credit unions in agricultural communities predominated in gross numbers and by the end of 1936, there were more credit unions in agricultural communities than in coal and steel communities in eastern Nova Scotia.

18. Nova Scotia Department of Agriculture, Markets Branch, *Report of co-operative associations* (Halifax, 1940).

19. J. M. Cameron, *The Pictonian colliers* (Kentville, 1974); B. D. Tennyson, 'Economic nationalism and confederation: a case study in Cape Breton,' *Acadiensis*, II (1972), 39-53; Frank, 'Coal masters and coal miners;' C. O. MacDonald, *The coal and iron industries of Nova Scotia* (Halifax, 1909); T. W. Acheson, 'The National Policy and the industrialization of the Maritimes, 1880-1910,' *Acadiensis*, I (1972), 3-28; Eugene Forsey, *Economic and social aspects of the Nova Scotia coal industry* (Toronto, 1926); D. Schwartzman, 'Mergers in the Nova Scotia coal fields: a history of the Dominion Coal Company, 1893-1940' (unpub. PhD thesis, University of California at Berkeley, 1952); Nova Scotia, Royal Commission on Coal Mines, *Report*, 1932; Nova Scotia, Royal Commission Provincial Economic Inquiry, *Report*, 1934; Nova Scotia, Royal Commission on Trenton Steel Works, *Report*, 1944.

20. See Royal Commission on Coal Mines, *Report*, Chart C; and Frank, 'Coal masters and coal miners,' 229, 230.

21. See S. A. Saunders, *The economic welfare of the Maritime provinces* (Wolfville, 1932), 30.

22. Royal Commission Provincial Economic Inquiry, *Report*, 192.

23. Royal Commission on Coal Mines, *Report*, Chart C.

24. Calculated from *ibid.*

25. See Canada, *Census, 1941*, VI, 812-13.

26. Saunders, *Economic welfare,*, 35, 36; also Royal Commission Provincial Economic Inquiry, *Report*, 30.

27. See Royal Commission on Trenton Steel Works, *Report*, 21-23.

28. Nova Scotia, Royal Commission on Provincial Development and Rehabilitation, *Report on minerals*, 1944, 71; Canada, Royal Commission on Canada's Economic Prospects, *The Nova Scotia coal industry*, 1956, 32. In 1956, New Glasgow was said to be 30% dependent, Stellarton 50%, Westville 50%, Sydney 50%, North Sydney 30% dependent, all others 'wholly dependent.' These estimates, while probably roughly correct for 1956, just as probably underestimate impact for the 1930s.

29. Calculated from Canada, *Census,1931*, VI, 1269-71.

30. K. Levitt, *Population movements in the Atlantic provinces* (Halifax, 1960), iii, 140.

31. All data on the characteristics of agricultural production are taken or calculated from Canada, *Census,1941*, VIII, 144-201; *Census,1931*, VIII, 84-109; *Census,1921*, V, 131, 176, 678.

32. Given in *Historical statistics of Canada*, ed. M. C. Urquhart and K. A. H. Buckley (Toronto, 1965), 296.

33. The position of the seven eastern counties relative to each other with respect to mean investment in implements, machinery, and livestock in 1931 exactly corresponds to the position of these counties with respect to mean gross value of production in 1930. Total investment exactly corresponds in only three out of seven pairing cases.

34. Percentages are calculated from Canada, *Census,1941*, VIII, 197. Definitions of types of farms are in *ibid.*, xxv, xxvi. 'Farms on which the value of products consumed or used by the farm household amounted to 50% or more of the gross farm revenue were classed as "Subsistence Farms." "Combinations of Subsistence Farms" are farms where the value of products used or consumed and the revenue from another main type, such as poultry, livestock, etc., were required to form 50% or more of the gross farm revenue. "Part-time Farms" are farms where 50% or more of the gross revenue was obtained from work performed off the farm (such as lumbering, fishing, road work, custom work), from overnight lodgers, boarders, campers, etc.'

35. J. F. Graham, *Fiscal adjustment and economic development: a case study of Nova Scotia* (Toronto, 1963), 22.

36. Data in this paragraph were calculated from Canada, Royal Commission Investigating the Fisheries of the Maritime Provinces and the Magdalen Islands, *Report*, 1928, 96; and Royal Commission on Provincial Development and Rehabilitation, *Report on the Canadian Atlantic fisheries*, 1944, 157.

37. Most notably, H. A. Innis, *The cod fisheries* (Toronto, 1954).

38. Nova Scotia, Department of Trade and Industry, *A brief review of the fisheries of Nova Scotia*, 1963, 10; emphasis added.

39. See R. F. Grant, *The Canadian Atlantic fishery* (Toronto, 1934).

40. Royal Commission on Provincial Development and Rehabilitation, *Report*, 26.

41. Grant, *The Canadian Atlantic fishery*, 30-34; Department of Trade and Industry, *Brief review of fisheries*, 15.

42. Department of Trade and Industry, *Brief review of fisheries*, 17. See also 31-33.

43. See *ibid.*, 24-31.

44. Royal Commission Investigating the Fisheries, *Report*, 98, 99.

45. *Ibid.*, 92-95.

46. See W. G. Ernst, *Submission on behalf of the fishermen of the province of Nova Scotia to the Royal Commission on the Fisheries*, 1928, 4-5.

47. See F. A. Nightingale in Canada, Royal Commission on Price Spreads, *Minutes of proceedings and evidence*, 1934, I, 327-82.

48. See A. Hanlon and B. L. Wilcox in *ibid.*, 51-68 and 89-100.

49. See H. H. Whitman in *ibid.*, 471-86.

50. *Ibid.*, 477.

51. See Hanlon in *ibid.*, 51-68. These figures represent no deductions for gear but deductions for other operating expenses (gas, oil, and bait), eight months' labour with, in most communities, 'nothing whatever to do during the other four months.' 'Some little farming' was reported for L'Archeveque, Gabarouse, Grand River, and Forchu: 'just large enough to carry them over the winter.'

52. See Royal Commission on Price Spreads, *Report*, 1935, 183.

53. See Royal Commission on Provincial Development and Rehabilitation, *Report*, 142, 143.

54. Commenting on the Nova Scotia mean, the provincial royal commission stated: 'the kind of boat and engine that this would provide, even if men worked in pairs and groups, is self-evident to anyone who compared it with the investment in the family car,' *ibid.*, 35.

55. Royal Commission on Provincial Development and Rehabilitation, *Report*, 167.

56. For definitions and a methodology for identifying and comparing types of census subdivisions, see Sacouman, 'Social origins,' 76, 80-83, 195-217.

57. The data for this summary table are from Tables 5, 10, 15, 21, and 23 in Sacouman, 'Social origins,' 270-76, 281, 297-300, 209-10, 313. 'Depopulated' subdivisions accounted for 90 of 167 subdivisions (53.9%), 37 of 88 incorporated-and-operated co-operatives, 43 of 99 merely incorporated co-operatives, 28 of 66 subdivisions with co-operatives, and 49 of 111 subdivisions with credit unions. Figures for other types are presented in *ibid.*, 195-217.

6   Underdevelopment and Social Movements in the Nova Scotia Fishing Industry to 1938

L. Gene Barrett

INTRODUCTION

The link between the development of capitalism on a world scale and underdevelopment in most third world countries has been discussed at length in a large body of literature.[1] In particular, both Marxist and non-Marxist academics have become increasingly interested in how regional disparities emerge *within* the framework of national capitalist development.[2] Within the Canadian context, lines of debate similar to those found in the broader 'dependency' literature, are being drawn between neo-classical and Marxist approaches to regional underdevelopment, on the one hand[3] and, on the other, between those Marxists who emphasise unequal regional *exchange*[4] and those who focus on the underlying conditions of regional *production*.[5]

This paper will focus on one staple industry within an underdeveloped region: the fishing industry in Nova Scotia. The process of production, of capital accumulation and exploitation, will form the basis of the discussion so that the reproduction of certain characteristics of regional underdevelopment in a particular industry may be clearly understood. In this context the social history of two fishermen's organisations will be traced. Whereas several authors have shown, in this volume[6] and elsewhere,[7] a positive correlation between participation in social movements and exposure to 'direct capitalist underdevelopment,'[8] this paper will attempt to delineate a broader relationship over time: between changing 'forms' of underdevelopment and social movements. How the Fishermen's Union of Nova Scotia grew out of the backward conditions exploited by 'late developing'[9] *salt*-fish capital; and how the Fishermen's Federation of Nova Scotia battled the worst conditions perpetuated by a newly developed, but under-capitalised, *fresh*-fish capital[10]— these will be our major concerns.

CAPITAL AND THE FISHING INDUSTRY OF NOVA SCOTIA

The history of the fishing industry in Nova Scotia presents a very clear and interesting case of capital in transition. Two analytically distinct forms of capital appear in the course of its history, each vying for hegemony.[11] In the nineteenth century an indigenous merchant-trader class dominated the salt fishery. A branch of this class was later responsible for the development of large-scale salt-fish companies and the offshore schooner fishery, both of which dominated the industry until the late 1920s. The second form of capital in the industry was invested in a few large-scale Canadian fresh-fish companies which were formed in the years immediately preceding World War I, but which did not gain strength until the 1930s and 1940s.

A. SALT-FISH CAPITAL

The mercantile elite which emerged in Nova Scotia in the eighteenth and nineteenth centuries was a 'junior partner' in the lucrative triangular trade between British North America, New England, and the West Indies.[12] The fishing industry as such provided only one staple good among many in the merchant's export cargo.[13] Innis cites the case of a merchant from Liverpool, Simeon Perkins, as a typical example:

In the years following 1783 Simeon Perkins sent lumber from Liverpool to Port Roseway, Port Mouton, and the newly settled areas. Vessels left for the West Indies with lumber and fish. The fish were shipped at Liverpool or purchased at points along the Atlantic coast, and the lumber came from Frenchman's Bay and kindred points; later from the Bay of Fundy and New England. Vessels returned either directly with salt, molasses, and rum, or, after calling at American ports, with flour, corn, and provisions. Schooners proceeded in the spring to Newfoundland and the Labrador for salmon.... In the summer ... for mackerel to Crow Harbour, Margaret's Bay, Deep Cove, and the South-West Harbour, and to Prospect for herrings.... The flexibility which characterised the New England fishery became more evident in Nova Scotia.... The divisibility of both vessels and cargoes and the relatively small size of the ships made it easy for merchants and others along the coast to take a very extensive part in trade.[14]

The 'carrying' or 'coasting' aspect of mercantile trade, as opposed to the fishery, was dominant in Nova Scotia in this early period. Towns such as Arichat, Cheticamp, Halifax, and Lunenburg, were the foci of trade well into the mid-nineteenth century. In fact, mercantile firms such as Jason Eisenhauer and Company of Lunenburg, which by the 1860s was considered the 'best known fish firm in Canada,' originally had only a modest interest in the fishery.[15]

These types of companies exploited the fishery in two ways: through a 'truck' or barter-exchange system with small inshore communities (chiefly in the western counties, around Canso, and on the eastern edge of Cape Breton)[16] and through direct control of the offshore, schooner fishery.

However, the inshore fishery remained the dominant form of production in the fishing industry until the 1880s. The 'unit' of production[17] was a two-fold domestic[18] type involving the inshore fisherman and his family in forms of primary and secondary petty commodity production.[19] Salt- or dried-fish, or fresh lobsters, were the surplus products produced by the domestic unit. These were appropriated by merchant capital at the level of exchange: in differentials between costs, values, and prices. For example, merchants could potentially realise profits through four unequal transactions: (a) The difference between the *price*—i.e., cash, credit, or supplies—paid to the domestic unit in exchange for fish and the reproduction *costs* of the labour-power within the unit. As long as one aspect of domestic production remained subsistence production, then domestic labour's lack of organisation and the monopoly control of market access by merchants ensured that the price of the labour of the domestic unit was lower than its value. (b) Merchants could also realise a profit in the market, on the difference between the market *price* of fish and its *cost*. In this case the cheap labour of the fisherman and his family cushioned the merchant against fluctuations in market demand.[20] (c) The difference between the *cost* of supplies purchased on the wholesale market by merchants and the retail *price* received for them from the domestic unit. (d) The absolute difference between the *value* of the fish received and the *value* of the supplies sold. These 'cost-price' differentials systematically denuded the inshore fishery of an investible surplus: its primitive accumulation of capital.[21] It remained to be seen whether the merchants who appropriated this surplus used it to develop the fishery as a whole.

As long as the West Indian market for Nova Scotia trade remained captive, and as long as wooden ships remained the primary mode of transportation, the schooner coasting trade remained dominant. However, by the 1880s and 1890s, two factors effected a dramatic change in this situation. First, the US entered the fresh-fish industry and Nova Scotia experienced an increase in demand for high quality salt-fish. Second, the extension of steam and steel ships eclipsed the schooners as cargo vessels.

Unlike the case of Newfoundland, where the 'planter' fishery declined in favour of a 'household' fishery and capital relinquished production control to individual families in exchange for savings elsewhere,[22] the merchant-trader fishery in the Maritimes wrested *more* control over the production of salt-fish from the domestic unit. In the face of intense competition and rising demand, Innis commented that

The advantages of large-scale organisation in the dried-fish industry made itself felt in that supervision of curing which large-scale organisation could offer in its effective control of the product until marketed and its ability to compete in a wide variety of markets, with their varying grades.... Independent fishermen were able to give smaller quantities of fish better supervision, and to cure a better product; but differences of skill and capacity in the individual and fluctuations of weather and catch inevitably produced wide variations. The risks that lay alike in extended credit, the careless grading of fish, and the intense competition in foreign markets made for both the disappearance and the amalgamation of companies.[23]

In 1881 a steamship service to the West Indies and Brazil was inaugurated, which spelled the decline of schooners in the West Indies trade.[24] From this point on, schooners were adapted primarily to the offshore fishery[25] and certain of the key salt-fish companies in the region moved to control primary production, in addition to secondary production.

In 1870, for example, a key partner in the Jason Eisenhauer Company, Lewis Anderson, left the firm with the one-third interest ($10,000) he controlled and with most of the company's schooners, to form his own company.[26] His new enterprise helped spearhead the expansion of the bank fishery and in 1873, his best captain, Benjamin Anderson, became one of the first to take his schooner to the banks.[27] Instrumental to his success was the innovation of a system of trawl fishing which became the wherewithal for a general expansion of the offshore fishery in the entire province.[28]

A boom in shipbuilding followed the expansion of the schooner fishery, and to overcome high construction costs an equity share system known as the 'Lunenburg 64' was developed and capital was raised through the sale of 64 shares in each vessel. The *Progress Enterprise* claimed in 1907 (24 April) that quite often the shareholders in a schooner sailed as fishermen on their own vessels, thus receiving both a 'lay' income (from fishing) and a dividend income on their shares. Moreover, fishermen would where possible own shares in several vessels to minimise their risk.

Mercantile companies, in order to consolidate control over primary production, developed certain insurance mechanisms themselves. For instance, according to a Lunenburg captain, an outfitting firm would own a small portion of the 64 shares, 'investing [just] enough money in the boat for certain captains to get their outfits from them.'[29] This system was formalised in the position of the 'managing owner' of each schooner. The managing owner was normally a representative of the company that controlled the largest block of shares in the vessel and was empowered to arrange all purchase of supplies and equipment, as well as all sales of fish, settlements with fishermen, and payment of debts.[30] By 'controlling' ownership of schooners, companies were able to ensure a market for their supplies and provisions.

To assure themselves of a constant supply of fish, companies often took another tack. The case of W. C. Smith and Company of Lunenburg is instructive in this respect. Incorporated in late 1899 with an operating capital of $15,000, the firm competitively managed and outfitted schooners for the salt 'bank' fishery, and by 1914 'grew to be one of the largest and most aggressive fishing units in the province.'[31] By World War I the company's fleet of vessels had increased from six to twenty and it had branched out into the lucrative West Indian and European winter charter trade. Central to their success was the method whereby the company locked skippers into their business operation as a whole. They transposed and interlocked the traditional Lunenburg 64 system of schooner ownership with the land operations of their commercial business. All six skippers of the original six vessels they outfitted in 1900 were also shareholders in the company.[32] According to an account in the *Yarmouth Herald*,

young and ambitious skippers, attracted by the prospect of the work for their vessels after the season was over, came to outfit with the new firm. They were offered stock and became shareholders in the business.[33]

An overall sense of the control which companies such as W. C. Smith exercised over the offshore fishery is evident from the following. First, the company was the exclusive outfitter of a number of schooners. It provided credit for outfitting at the beginning of each trip and deducted portions of the debt outstanding when the fish were brought in after each trip. Usually the legally designated 'managing owner,' selected from among the schooner's shareholders, was either one of the company's shareholders, or a member of the Smith family. He had sole authorisation to make purchases for each trip.[34] Second, the Lunenburg Coal and Supply Company, formed in 1920 as a subsidiary of W. C. Smith, supplied all coal and wood to 'their' schooners, similarly deducting portions of the debt outstanding after each trip.[35] In addition, W. C. Smith and later Lunenburg Sea Products Ltd (another subsidiary formed in 1926 to handle the parent's growing fresh-fish business) supplied all bait and ice for each trip. Third, W. C. Smith and Lunenburg Sea Products bought the entire catch of all the schooners.[36] And fourth, the firms of W. C. Smith and Lunenburg Coal and Supply gave extensive personal credit to most crewmen and their families during the year, crediting their accounts from their wages after each trip.

Under these conditions free competition and independent commodity production were myths. What existed was, rather, a form of oligopolistic control of primary production and offshore 'schooner' fishermen who were dependent primary commodity producers. The price of fish, and all purchasing and selling transactions, did not reflect the unfettered operation of supply and demand, nor were profit calculations made for each vessel. Instead the logic of production reflected the profit requirements of an entire company's integrated operations.

Other companies wrested control over primary production not by independent expansion into the offshore fishery, but by transforming the traditional coasting system *and* the domestic unit of production. For example, the Atlantic Fisheries Company of Lunenburg ran a very profitable dried-fish business. William Duff, later mayor of Lunenburg and MP for the county,[37] was credited with establishing an immense business with the financial backing of the Bank of Montreal. With headquarters in Lunenburg, the company had branches in Canso, La Have, Bay of Islands, and Barrington, each specialising in a different department of the business. Two steamers and a large number of schooners would collect the fish from various inshore fishing communities and convey them to the factories. At the Lunenburg and La Have plants the fish would also be bought 'green' directly, and dried in mechanised dryers, later to be shredded and packaged.[38] With distributing and wholesale agents in Montreal and points west, and hundreds of employees, this company represented a very advanced organisational type for the time in the industry.[39] It attempted to integrate vertically the functions of production, processing, distributing, and marketing as well as to maintain and exploit certain aspects of the older domestic form of production and in particular its primary production aspect—inshore fishing.

Other firms, notably Robin, Jones and Whitman Ltd, adopted a complex system of collection—a system whose precise contours varied according to the region and fishery involved. Thus in the Gulf of St Lawrence and Gaspé regions alone, the company and its antecedent companies controlled fish supplies through patronage relations with inshore fishermen,[40] directly *employed* inshore fishermen on company-owned boats, and operated schooners in a fashion similar to that mentioned above in Lunenburg.[41] Production became so important, and quality control so decisive, that by the 1930s the company handled four refined cures of salt-fish.[42]

From disparate origins in the mercantile trade, the development of large-scale capital in the salt-fish industry marked a clear transition from merchant to industrial capital in Nova Scotia. The mercantile-trader class had been primarily an 'agent' of capitalism in Britain and had profited through an unequal trade in staple products, which lowered the costs of production and reproduction for British capital in the West Indies. Pushed from this lucrative niche by external conditions of free trade, merchant capital moved from exchange into production and transformed various production methods in its drive to develop the fishing industry.

While this process may seem to parallel closely the 'classical' transition of merchant to industrial capital,[43] it is useful to point out briefly some unique aspects of underdevelopment as they were reflected in the salt-fish industry: (a) Industrial development in the fish industry was far behind that of New England. In some crucial respects New England can be said to have 'underdeveloped' the Nova Scotia fishery in the seventeenth and eighteenth centuries by reducing Nova Scotia to a convenient outpost or 'way station.'[44] However, this was primarily due to the peculiar position of Nova Scotia within the British mercantile system: it represented capital concentrated in an unproductive entrepôt trade—capital which was often drained out of the area altogether.[45] Industrial development in the fishing industry occurred late and was consequently restricted to narrow and insecure markets. (b) Two major consequences followed: the fishing industry came early to depend on cheap labour and cheap raw material to enter markets. And low wages and low prices, as well as high costs for gear and provisions, contributed early on to the migration of labour to New England.[46] (c) Despite the consolidation of the production process, various other costs, such as the *social* costs associated with training, and subsistence food production, which the domestic unit of production continued to shoulder, remained windfall gains to capital. This was especially true as market fluctuations in the demand for salt-fish and high seasonal variations in the demand for labour created tremendous social security costs which households, not the companies, had to bear.[47] For example, while the schooner fishery was developed by capital to increase productivity, it aggravated unemployment problems for shore workers. Stewart Bates commented that

the plant operators could throw [the] risk [of gluts and scarcities] on the shore labour; there was a great pool of shore labour, and operators employed or dismissed plant labour according to the landings. Thus one of the social costs of using schooners was the employment variations among plant labour.[48]

B. FRESH-FISH CAPITAL

Historically, the growth of various fish processing centres such as North Sydney, Canso, Halifax, and Lockeport closely followed the development of bait freezing facilities in these centres by fishermen's bait associations. By 1908 there were 37 freezers in operation in Nova Scotia, supplying bait to inshore and offshore fishermen and to foreign vessel fleets.[49] However, the uncertainty of demand for bait weakened the competitive position of these associations and contributed to their consolidation in the hands of private interests beginning to produce fresh-fish for an expanding domestic market.[50]

The fresh-fish industry necessitated large-scale capital investment in cold storage and packing equipment, processing facilities for by-products, and transportation services.[51] It also required a large, dependable supply of fish.[52] By 1910 steam trawlers had been introduced to provide this reliable supply. The trawlers had the advantage over inshore and schooner operations of being able to fish under widely varying weather conditions, of catching larger volumes, and of supplying an expanding market regularly on certain days of the week.[53]

In 1908 the industry was aided by a federal government subsidy of transportation costs, whereby shipments to points west were charged only one-third of normal express duty. In addition, the government increased the duty on competitive American fish from one-half to one cent per pound.[54] By 1910 a rail line to Mulgrave, Nova Scotia, had been built, and in 1913 a government subsidised refrigerated express to Montreal was inaugurated. One car left Mulgrave on the Saturday of each week, and shipments from Halifax and elsewhere were consolidated in this car at Truro. By 1917 ten refrigerator cars were travelling between Nova Scotia and Montreal; and in 1918 a 'Sea Food Special' provided refrigerated fast freight service between Mulgrave, Halifax, and Toronto.[55]

Two significant technological developments in the United States during the 1920s revolutionised that country's fish-products industry and gave two large companies—General Seafoods Corporation of New England (a subsidiary of General Foods Corporation), and the Atlantic Coast Fisheries Company of Groton, Connecticut and New York—a tremendous competitive advantage.[56] The first of these breakthroughs came in 1922 and involved the development of a filleting operation at the point of production rather than at the retail outlet. It was now possible to eliminate the excess weight of bones and heads, and thus decrease transportation costs; the manufacture of by-products such as fish meal was now possible; quality control and improvement was facilitated; the transformation of packaging and commercial handling was encouraged; large-scale marketing and advertising were given new impetus; and the brand name of the producer (rather than the retailer) was publicised on a wide scale.[57] In other words, filleting allowed the fish products industry to catch up with, and in some cases, out-compete, other parts of the food industry. It facilitated the industrialisation of the production process, and the consolidation of processing, marketing, and retail concerns into vertically integrated enterprises.

The second development, an advanced technique for fast freezing, was equally revolutionary. It was invented simultaneously by two men working independently in the mid 1920s. However, both General Seafoods and Atlantic Coast Fisheries claimed immediate patent rights to the process and assumed a virtual monopoly of the technology.[58] The process was important since it assured standardised quality control and allowed easy transportation to distant markets. It also gave the processor some measure of insulation from the worst effects of market fluctuations since gluts of fish could be frozen and stored immediately, to be marketed when conditions allowed greater profit taking.[59]

By 1910 three sizable Canadian companies dominated the fresh-fish industry: National Fish Company of Halifax and Port Hawkesbury, Leonard Fisheries Ltd of Saint John and North Sydney, and Maritime Fish Corporation of Canso and Digby.[60] These three firms were responsible for the growth in the number of Nova Scotian trawlers from four to eight during World War I and to ten by 1927. Of these ten, six were owned and registered in Canada—one each to Leonard Fisheries and Maritime Fish, and four to National Fish. Three were English owned—two chartered to Maritime Fish and one to Leonard. The last was a Newfoundland trawler chartered to the National Fish Co.[61]

With the end of the war, salt-fish markets were substantially taken over by Norway, Great Britain, and Iceland because of their greater efficiency, improved technology and higher quality product, and in some cases, because of government subsidisation.[62] Newfoundland also lost its European and Brazilian markets and was forced to concentrate on Nova Scotia's West Indian market. Nova Scotia retreated from its newly found Havana and south Brazil markets and steadily lost ground to Newfoundland in other parts of Cuba, Puerto Rico, and Trinidad.[63]

In this turbulent climate, W. C. Smith and Company sniffed the winds of change and introduced fresh fishing and fresh-fish processing in Lunenburg. In February of 1925 a town meeting was called in order to generate investment capital to construct a cold-storage plant.[64] The firm of Lunenburg Sea Products and Cold Storage Ltd, was incorporated and began operation under W. H. Smith, president. The original financing consisted of $40,450 common stock, all owned by W. C. Smith and Company, and an issue of $85,000 twenty year, six per cent, first mortgage sinking fund bonds, the interest on which was guaranteed by W. C. Smith and Company, and 94% of which was immediately bought by members of the Smith family.[65] To assure itself of a steady year-round-supply of fish, Lunenburg Sea Products, not possessing its own trawler fleet, convinced one of its captains, Newman Wharton, to install an auxiliary diesel engine on his schooner,the *Jean and Shirley* and to fish during the winter.[66] The fresh and frozen trade concentrated capital in certain areas of the province. By 1939, two-thirds of the freezing capacity in the industry was concentrated in nine freezing plants between Halifax and Shelburne.[67] In addition, 52% of the filleting trade was concentrated in Halifax, 16% in Lockeport, 10% in North Sydney, 10% in Lunenburg, 4% in Shelburne, and 3% in Canso.[68] Of the eleven main fishing centres landing over five million pounds of fish in 1939, nine lay on the south shore between Halifax and Digby

Neck. This region accounted for 75% of all fish taken in Nova Scotia, 68% of the total value of landings, and 57% of the fishing equipment in the province.[69]

The depression years of the 1930s signalled disaster for numerous fish companies and the consolidation of the fresh-fish industry into two very large concerns: (a) the Maritime-National Fish Co. of Halifax, which controlled both the National Fish Co. of Halifax and its trawlers,[70] and the Maritime Fish Co. of Digby and its subsidiaries;[71] and (b) Smith Fisheries of Lunenburg, which operated plants in North Sydney, Port Hawkesbury, Lockeport, Liverpool, and Lunenburg.[72] According to Harold Innis,

Being closer to Halifax as a terminal point for transportation to the interior and possessing dominance in the bank fishery, the latter firm was able more effectively to combine the frozen- and fresh-fish with the salt-fish industry. This diversity [had] been extended by the acquisition of [smaller] plants in the eastern and western parts of the province. The larger organisation had the advantage of connections with Saint John at Digby which became the centre of a varied industry including salt-fish ... and, in 1934, a fish meal plant. Halifax, however, was the chief centre of its frozen- and fresh-fish industry. It ... operated trawlers, and, since their numbers were reduced by Dominion regulations, Lunenburg power schooners, for supplies of fish to be handled fresh, frozen and fish meal.[73]

The impact of the development of fresh- and frozen-fish production on labour in the fishing industry can be summarised in two main points: (a) The concentration of capital in specific areas of the province aggravated rural depopulation, which had been blamed on centralised salt-fish processing. Inshore fishing communities, isolated geographically from cold-storage facilities, were particularly hard hit. However, while these communities were marginalised, their people became part of a large mass of rural dispossessed— Marx called such people the 'latent surplus'[74] of labour—who roamed the province and county during the 1920s and 1930s as part of a large reserve of labour that acted,

during the periods of stagnation and average prosperity, [to weigh] down the active labour army; during the periods of over-production and paroxysm, [to hold] its pretensions in check.[75]

(b) The mechanisation of the vessel fishery—in addition to the small number of trawlers—created a full-time offshore labour force which no longer had the winter season off.[76] The small cash income from fishing which had been supplemented by the 'dole' or other wagework during the off-season now had to form the sole cash contribution made by the household head to the domestic unit. At the same moment this development increased the fisherman's dependence on the price of fish, and therefore the company which owned the vessel and paid for the fish, and it pressured other members of the domestic unit either to raise the level of domestic subsistence production, or to participate further in the cash/wage economy.[77] In other words, under conditions of underdevelopment, whereby fishermen were forced to work for extremely low incomes, a proletarianising development acted to *increase* the relative importance of the reproduction function performed by the domestic unit.

However, the impact of the consolidation process of fresh- and frozen-fish processing was less 'revolutionary' in Nova Scotia than it was in the US. As Stewart Bates observed 'private investible funds that might have flow[ed] into the fishing industry ... tended ... to move into the central provinces where greater profitability was promised.'[78] Despite initial development, the Nova Scotia fresh-fish products industry became saddled with antiquated and inefficient technology and modes of organisation in an increasingly competitive food industry. The fishing industry was able to respond with only relatively minor adjustments, such as the addition of engines to schooners in Lunenburg, rather than, for instance, a large-scale expansion of trawler technology.[79] Filleting techniques remained primitive and no massive transformation of the fresh-fish industry occurred to keep pace with American competition.[80] Even the potential created by filleting for brand-name production remained undeveloped as fillets continued to be wrapped in parchment, the traditional way, the processor trusting the care given his products by separate distributors, hundreds of miles away, to advertise his name.[81] 'The catching of fish, unloading of vessels, cutting of fish, handling and packing in plants, all [depended] almost entirely on hand labour ... even in the largest plants.'[82] While the production of fresh and frozen fish increased from 9% to 34% of total fish production between 1920 and 1939, according to Bates 'this change was forced on the industry more by the decline in the salt-fish markets than by any revolution in the methods of catching, processing, or distributing the product.'[83]

The report of the Royal Commission of Price Spreads[84] provides corroborative evidence of the degree to which the very structure of the fish products industry accentuated its own problems, a situation made all the more clear during the depression. In an examination of the price spreads in cod and haddock fillets and steaks shipped to the Montreal and Toronto retail markets by Nova Scotia companies, the commission gathered the following data on middlemen and their relationship to high prices. In October 1934, to take one example, the average price charged the wholesaler by the processor was 174% higher than what he had paid the fisherman. The average price received by the wholesaler from the retailer was 355% greater than that given the fisherman, and 45% higher than that paid to the processor. The price charged the consumer was 117% higher than the processor's original price and 510% greater than the price paid to the fisherman.[85]

The consequences of the underdevelopment of the fresh- and frozen-fish industry for labour were many and widespread. As companies were undercapitalised, and processing facilities and the distribution system for fresh fish inefficient, the larger landings characteristic of trawler fishing only created huge gluts of fish and extremely low prices for all fishermen—inshore and offshore alike.[86]

The adaptation of schooners to fresh fishing carried over to the new industry seasonal employment problems for plant workers which had been characteristic of the salt-fish industry. The multiplicity of middlemen in the structure of the industry aggravated the problem of low prices to fishermen by depreciating the value and price of fish even further. For example, during the 1920s, market expansion consisted almost entirely of growth *within* the Canadian market since 90% of the fresh and frozen trade was in Canada. Shortly thereafter, however, faced with a saturated Canadian market in which fish steadily lost ground to meat and poultry, the fresh-fish industry entered the US market by cutting the price of its product—not by streamlining its mode of organisation. Capitalising on the lack of organisation among labour in the industry, each middleman was able to pass along the costs of this price cut to fishermen and fish-plant workers.[87] Stewart Bates summarised the situation as follows:

The price reductions that had to be made to widen the American market reflected themselves in the low standard of living to which the Canadian fishermen became increasingly subject. In other words, the usual method adopted by the industry in trying to widen its market, was to cut the export price. Practically no attention was given to any other possible way of achieving the same end—the power of organisation among processors and exporters that might have prevented panic price-slashing, or the search for cost-reducing innovations in the industry itself. The labour of fishermen and plant workers was too cheap to force the industry into such alternatives, and in the milieu that existed, labour could be made to bear the incidence of low prices.[88]

As was the case with salt-fish capital, fresh-fish capital also survived by the exploitation of a reserve army of cheap labour. This exploitation operated at three distinct levels: (a) Inshore fishermen and their families continued to provide the best quality product[89] at below-subsistence prices since the domestic unit continued to shoulder reproduction costs. (b) Shore workers—whose function had been 'torn away' from the domestic unit and was now under the direct control of capital—were also available at below-subsistence wages, thanks to the continued function of the domestic unit as a reproductioin agent. (c) Offshore fishermen, who were now the main primary producers,[90] were still paid low prices as a consequence of capitalist underdevelopment in the industry. Subsistence production by the domestic unit also supplemented low prices enough to cover the social costs of the reproduction of labour for the vessel fishery.

LABOUR AND THE FISHING INDUSTRY OF NOVA SCOTIA

As we have seen, the transition from mercantile to industrial capital in the fishing industry and the evolution within industrial capital from salt-fish to fresh-fish capital marked the transformation of the domestic unit of production, and the development of two full-time labour forces: offshore fishermen and fish-plant workers. These developments can be interpreted as a process of proletarianisation in a broad sense.

We have also seen that because of unique regional conditions the nature of salt-fish and fresh-fish capital was distorted and backward. Various manifestations of this, such as archaic technology, inefficient organisation, overdependence on volatile markets, etc., persisted since capital was able to rely on cheap labour, whether on land or on the water. This labour, varied as it was, continued to be cheap because of its lack of organisation and the unrewarded reproduction service provided to capital by the domestic unit.

However, the variations among these two characteristics were quite considerable. The domestic unit of production, for instance, under some localised conditions of stagnation and high unemployment, blossomed into a virtual mode of production independent of any others. Under other conditions, in urban centres such as Halifax, for instance, its traditional functions diminished and it became primarily a labour-recruitment mechanism for capital. However, a discussion of such variations is beyond the scope of this paper.

In like manner fishermen's organisations varied considerably. In some circumstances inshore fishermen organised independent marketing and producer co-operatives in a populist fight against the worst effects of underdevelopment.[91] In other circumstances inshore fishermen identified with working-class trade unionism and fought alongside fish-plant workers and offshore fishermen for trade union rights.[92] A discussion of two organised responses by fishermen to the worst effects of underdevelopment follows: inshore fishermen and the Fishermen's Union of Nova Scotia, and offshore fishermen and the Fishermen's Federation of Nova Scotia.

THE FISHERMEN'S UNION OF NOVA SCOTIA

The first fishermen's union was formed in Nova Scotia in 1905. It was an organisation for inshore fishermen and excluded all 'hired hands on private vessels'—offshore fishermen.[93] With approximately 12,000 native-born people, or 10,000 families, engaged in the inshore fishery in Nova Scotia, organisers felt that inshore fishermen should seek 'official guidance and assistance.' According to the 'unpaid sponsor of the association,'[94] Moses H. Nickerson:

The status of the fishermen as an industrial class ... will be improved, and their common interests promoted by organising on lines similar in certain respects to those of other unions, but with the objects more particularly in view of securing more expeditious means of presenting their views to the governmental authorities, and of obtaining greater freedom from restrictions in the preparation and marketing of their 'catches.'[95]

One of the chief concerns of the union was to arrange a satisfactory system with government assistance to combat rapacious speculation and middleman control. In addition, the union sought to gather and communicate the latest information on technology, processing, transportation, and marketing; and to make representations and furnish information 'to the proper authorities.'[96]

The union was never a trade union in the normal sense. An act outlining the aims and structure of the union's 'stations' was passed in 1905. Its provisions secured the issuance of a certificate of incorporation by the registrar of joint-stock companies under the name 'Station No.... Fishermen's Union of N.

S.' where not fewer than fifteen fishermen wanted a station.[97] Three of the first 4 stations—Wood's Harbour, Little Harbour, and Clarke's Harbour—were organised through the personal efforts and direction of M. H. Nickerson.[98] By 1906 the union claimed to have added 6 new stations in Digby County and 6 in Cape Breton. By 1907 the total number had reached 20 stations[99] and by 1909, 25—representing 375 fishermen across the province.[100]

Information pertaining to the union's local practice and success can be gleaned from reports of the union's annual conventions. Initially one is struck by the central role played by Nickerson, who was, significantly, a fish merchant and politician. He was instrumental in organising the union and various stations, as well as promoting its educational goals as a 'special lecturer' from 1908 on.[101] One might draw the conclusion from this that the union was run by a patronising merchant *for* the fishermen, a view that was indeed not far from what Nickerson himself seemed to think. In 1938 he was quoted in the press as saying that when he left Nova Scotia for Gloucester, Massachusetts, in 1930, the union 'without a leader and by the inroads of politicians ... fell to pieces.'[102]

Resolutions petitioning the government for control and assistance were continuously reiterated at the union's annual meetings with no apparent effect. At the 1911 convention, for example, frustration seems to have finally surfaced in the sardonic remark made by the delegates to the federal superintendent of fisheries, whose attention was drawn 'to resolutions which had been adopted at previous annual meetings.'[103]

The effectiveness of the union's programme is further called into question if one examines the history of one of its stations. In 1909, 300 members of the union's Main-A-Dieu, Cape Breton, Station No 13 were faced with a cut in the price of lobster by $1.50 per case.[104] The lobster industry of the area, like that of the region, had been transformed by large-scale foreign capital in the 1880s and 1890s.[105] Main-A-Dieu became dominated by the Portland, Maine company of Burham and Morrell Ltd. It was the largest of the American lobster companies operating in Canada, with 30 canneries by 1910.[106]

Some elderly fishermen of the village recalled their early experiences with the company as follows:

in my young days there was no money paid for lobsters, it all went in and when you were finished lobster fishing you'd do down and get settled up, your bill was kept off.[107]

They used to first pack around 1100 cases during the season ... and it was costing them $25 a case but they were getting $50 a case for lobsters.[108]

By 1907, I started to fish lobsters with my brother. The fishermen of Scaterie and Main-A-Dieu formed a Union and we struck for 3 cents per pound. When the packers came (the 1st of May) they wouldn't pay that much so they offered us 2 1/4 cents. Well by the 15th May they were going to close up the factory and go back to the States. It was an American company, Burham and Morrell, so the fishermen had to accept it or starve.[109]

Two years later four companies, with Burham and Morrell in the lead, attempted to enforce the decrease in the price of lobster. The fishermen from Main-A-Dieu[110] and Gabarus struck for a month attempting to pack and market their own lobsters. While this was indeed a novel and valiant attempt to defy the control of a foreign company, its short-term success was limited.[111]

These strikes were never mentioned at the annual meetings of the Fishermen's Union and it seems certain that the union gave little or no effective support to the workers. One is left with the conclusion that in the face of 'direct underdevelopment,'[112] (whereby large-scale foreign capital extracted a cheap resource, exploited extremely cheap labour at the point of production, and distorted the local economy), information exchange and government lobbying were ineffective tactics. Co-operative production in the context of strike action were tactics quite foreign to the corporative aims of the union. This principle had been codified in a resolution passed at the union's first convention:

The assistance of organisers of other trade union bodies will not be accepted, on the grounds that the objects of the fishermen's union differ in a number of material points from those of other trade unions and that they could not be so effectively served if the union were affiliated in any way with international trade unions.[113]

The late 1910s and 1920s were telling times for the Fishermen's Union of Nova Scotia. In the context of a drastic postwar recession, the decline of salt-fish markets, the rise of the large fresh- and frozen-fish companies, and the growth of labour militancy in Nova Scotia and elsewhere, the union—or, more precisely, its leadership—became an outspoken champion of an idealised past. Marketing problems, loss of control in production, and low prices were all consequences of capitalist underdevelopment in the salt-fish industry. This fact was antithetical to Nickerson's beliefs, however; he saw the rise of militant trade unionism as the real enemy of the fishermen. Labour militancy was without doubt on the rise in Nova Scotia. Centring mainly in Cape Breton among coal and steel workers, a number of violent and at times revolutionary strikes and confrontations for union recognition and better wages marked a progression to a new level of militancy and class consciousness among these workers.[114] A farmer-labour coalition arose to become the official opposition in the House of Assembly between 1921 and 1925.[115] And in general the worsening effects of the recession, which added wage cuts and unemployment to an already long list of grievances, stoked the fires of industrial unrest in the province.

In Newfoundland, fishermen were drawn together in the Fishermen's Protective Union and moved beyond protective economic association into politics in the 1910s and 1920s.[116] In New England, fishermen, trawlermen, and fish handlers shut down their entire fishery during the summers of 1917, 1918, and 1919.[117] The leaders of the Fishermen's Union of Nova Scotia came under strong criticism from their rank and file members for not calling a sympathy strike in support of the New England workers.[118] The response of the leadership was unequivocal. In addressing a regular meeting of the Fishermen's Union of Clarke's Harbour on 20 August 1919, Nickerson observed that the Fishermen's Union 'lives and moves and has its being' on a basis different from that of the Boston union, given their differing conditions of work:

The conditions are entirely different. You are owners of the boats and gear you handle, judging your own times, seasons, and hours of labour. You are on the same industrial plane as the farmers or fruit-growers.[119]

He went on to point out that not only did their provincial charter imply the promotion of the common interests of fishermen, 'but also it would tend to stimulate and assist local business of any kind to a considerable extent.'[120] According to Nickerson there were no antagonisms between owners, dealers, crews, and speculators: the union was simply a self-helping order whose duty it was to serve the community as a whole. There was nothing to strike against and, if this were done, the fishermen would be breaking the laws and their charter would be forfeited:

We sympathise with the Atlantic Union and wish them success.... But any effort in their behalf on our part would not have helped the course in the least, but it would have blasted our prospects forever.[121]

Ironically, Nickerson even went on to draw attention to the lucrative market openings which the strike would create for Nova Scotia fish.[122] And he urged Maritimers in New England 'to return to the Provinces to which most of them belong, and if they still choose to follow the calling, make themselves as independent of owners and operators as most of our boat fishermen, and the crews of the Lunenburg banking fleet.'[123] The Lunenburg 64 concept of profit-sharing co-operation, a scheme developed for the offshore fishery, presented Nickerson with a golden illustration around which to expound his ideals: an ironic situation indeed, since offshore fishermen were still considered 'hired hands on private vessels,' and excluded from the union. It seems that only when it served Nickerson's purposes were offshore fishermen to be considered on the same 'industrial plane' as inshore fishermen.

Before discussing Nickerson's manipulation of the Lunenburg 64 scheme, it is instructive to investigate the realities of its operation in the offshore fishery of Lunenburg, twenty years after its inception. By the end of World War I construction costs had increased by 450% over their level in the early part of the decade,[124] and shares which would have cost fishermen $62.50 in 1907 were selling for $525.00 in 1921.[125] A vessel which cost $970 a year to outfit in 1903, cost $5,850 to outfit in 1919.[126] These increases in cost, apart from the worsening standard of living and income levels of fishermen during this period,[127] underlay a structural change in the ownership of schooners in the 1920s.

According to testimony by Captain Knickle of Lunenburg before the Royal Commission on Price Spreads:

when the vessels went into debt they were in debt to the firm and they just figured out to let them go far enough until they saw they could probably realize the amount of the debt, and they put them up for sale, by public auction, and what happened was the firms bought them back and they eliminated the ordinary man.[128]

This testimony is corroborated by a sample of ownership data of schooners outfitting with W. C. Smith and Company between 1921 and 1924. Only one vessel, in one year (1921), had a majority of crewmen who were also shareholders, of an average of ten vessels outfitting per year. In fact, on the average, only three of twenty crewmen were shareholders at all.[129] On the other hand, the Smith family (with approximately 23 members) owned, on the average, 22% of the shares of each vessel. This number increases to 50% if one considers the number of shares owned in vessels by the company's shareholders.[130] The Lunenburg 64 concept of profit-sharing can therefore be considered to have been dead, in its original form and intent, by the post-war years. Its resurrection and use by a union thatnever associated itself with the offshore fishery is far-fetched enough; however, its flowering as a social philosophy divorced from all reality in either the inshore or offshore fishery reveals its function as an ideology.

As we have seen, the beginnings of the campaign emanated from Nickerson's attempts to squelch sympathy among his union's membership for militant trade unionists in the New England fishery. The strains of this tune were echoed in these turbulent years by members of the press, clergy, private business, and government.[131] For instance, an editorial writer for the *Maritime Merchant* commented:

In these days when labour troubles are reported on all sides; when the employees in various industries are holding meetings, and forming industrial organisations to fight their battles for higher wages, it is refreshing to turn to one industry in this province in which ... there have been no signs of discontent.[132]

Referring explicitly to the Lunenburg fishing fleet, the editor proclaimed the fishermen, their families, and friends to be their own bosses, and further pointed out that the industry saved a million dollars because of this co-operation in the previous year. According to him there was 'no watered stock in the fishing industry; no bonus for the promoter, everyone [got] in on the ground floor, everybody [got] his share of what [was] going.'[133] The journal reiterated this view in a similar editorial in 1922, esteeming the

capacity of the Lunenburg 'banker,' not only as a fisherman but as a trader. Taking one season with another, he gets about all that is coming to him in the latter connection and therefore needs not to join up with the O. B. U. idea of Mr. McLachlin in order to get equa[l] with the tyrannious capitalist.[134]

The myth of the Lunenburg 64 should be seen as an attempt by persons in the Nova Scotia elite—Moses H. Nickerson included—to protect their class interests in an important sector. However, while the intent of this campaign is clear, its success is rather less so. The fact that no large militant trade unions arose in the fishing industry in the 1920s is somewhat telling. However, this cannot be attributed automatically to the acceptance of this ideology by fishermen, as indeed during the 1920s, many took the position that it was better to 'quit than fight' and entered more lucrative occupations such as rum-running, wage labour in the cities, or fishing in the United States.

Shortly thereafter the Lunenburg 64 campaign was given new impetus. Not only was the traditional independence and co-operation characteristic of Nova Scotia fishermen said to be in clear antipathy to trade unions, it was also seen to be in opposition to trawler technology. For example, J. J. Kinley, MLA for Lunenburg, argued in 1920 before the legislature that there was an 'inherent contradiction' between the co-operative share system of ownership and the new beam trawlers that required huge capital expenditures which were beyond the means of fishermen.[135] In addition, the *Halifax Herald* and Nickerson mounted a vociferous attack against the trawlers and their chief promoters, the National and Maritime Fish companies and the Canadian Fisheries Association.[136]

As we have seen, in the absence of extensive modernisation of fresh-fish processing and distribution facilities, the large landings of fish characteristic of trawler fishing only created gluts of fish and low prices. The so-called trawler problem therefore had more basis in reality than the Lunenburg 64 concept even did, especially for inshore fishermen. Not missing an opportunity, the Nova Scotia elite attempted to link both campaigns in order to capitalise on the grassroots opposition to trawlers. From 1910 onward, the three fresh-fish companies operating trawlers did so out of the Canso and Port Hawkesbury area. And from 1911 the fishermen in Canso held meetings and organised protests against these trawlers.[137] The protests culminated in 1927[138] with the appointment of the MacLean Commission to investigate the entire fisheries, but its central concern quickly became steam trawlers. This issue split the commission, but its majority report recommended that legislation be enacted prohibiting trawlers as of 1929.[139] However, the legislation that was passed imposed only a tax of one cent per pound on all fish caught on foreign-built trawlers and two-thirds of a cent per pound on all fish caught on Canadian-built trawlers.[140]

It may seem that this opposition was an oddly successful populist response by independent commodity producers to encroaching industrialism. And indeed, Stewart Bates characterised it as largely the traditional opposition of hand labour to mechanisation.[141] However, the power behind this irregular government action must be seen in terms of the *combined* action of inshore fishermen *and* schooner owners and salt-fish merchants against large-scale fresh-fish capital.[142] For most of the existing fish producers, a trawler licence would have been a valuable asset, but realising that the government could not wholly ignore public sentiment and consequently would not permit the wholesale issuance of licences, salt-fish merchants allied with the opposition. They were not against the trawlers as such, but against giving advantages to their competitors.[143] A second group, the owners of schooners, feared that the wholesale development of a trawler fishery would have spelled the obsolescence of their schooner technology and would have placed them in an even worse competitive position.[144]

The inshore fishermen feared the widespread use of trawlers for two reasons, both of which later proved to be well founded. First, the technique might shift the industry's centre of gravity to the main fishing ports and into the hands of large financial interests, a process that was certainly already taking place, not necessarily because of the trawler, but because of the shift in the industry from salt- to fresh-fish production which required large-scale centralised technology.[145] Second, inshore fishermen feared that the use of trawlers would jeopardise their economic position as suppliers of fish. Bates[146] explained that this would have been true not so much because they were competing for the same species of fish (the schooner was, after all, their main competitor in this regard), but because the industry was underdeveloped and the traditional salt-fish trade was on the wane and alternative markets for their fish were drying up. The argument used by the fresh-fish companies was that the trawler would have been able to expand the market for fish by offering regular supplies and would have thus benefitted the inshore fishermen. However, Bates showed that in itself the introduction of trawlers would *not* have expanded the market since this would have also required modernised fish plants, transportation, and wholesale and retail distribution. As the plants and the distribution system of the Nova Scotia fresh-fish industry were underdeveloped in this respect, the inshore fishermen had a valid point in arguing that a wide extension of trawlers would merely increase supplies, causing a glut of fish, and lower prices for all.[147] In fact, in testimony before the MacLean Commission, inshore fishermen pointed out that the heart of the trawler problem was one of overproduction, of the glutting of markets, of lower prices and *restricted* markets for fishermen—and consequently of the depopulation of fishing villages.[148]

The two cases in point, the Lunenburg 64 concept and the trawler controversy, while linked, can be seen to have served two different functions. The first was utilised as an ideological tool by capital against working-class militancy encroaching on the fishing industry.[149] The second was an effective weapon to prevent a new fraction of capital (fresh-fish) gaining advantage at the expense of an older, established fraction (salt-fish).

The domestic unit of production steadily lost control over secondary production from the last decade of the nineteenth century on, first with the penetration of large American lobster companies, later with the centralisation of salt-fish production and large-scale fresh- and frozen-fish companies. While domestic *petty* producers put up little or no fight to retain control over salt- and dried-fish production, the Fishermen's Union of Nova Scotia was the defensive response of *primary* producers in the domestic unit—inshore fishermen—to threats to their dominant position as primary producers from offshore technology. Initially this took the form of an active strategy to stay competitive with offshore technology through efficiency measures. The success of this strategy presupposed a well-developed industrial structure, however, and in the face of a real drop in living standards due to the combined effects of trawler overproduction and underdeveloped fresh-fish capital, their strategy changed to an active fight *against* large-scale competition. In retrospect it is ironic that inshore fishermen, forced into this position by underdevelopment, only succeeded in restricting trawler expansion by allying with one fraction of the very class that was responsible for the problem in the first place.

Insofar as the Fishermen's Union of Nova Scotia was run and spoken for by a merchant—Moses H. Nickerson—with outside class allegiances, one can judge the extent of the union's *real* opposition to labour unions. As we have seen, the Lunenburg 64 campaign was initiated and orchestrated by Nickerson with little or no apparent rank and file support. In the cases of the Main-A-Dieu strike and the New England strikes this ideology was actively ignored. However, Nickerson's intentions were a success to the extent that he managed to prevent the union from developing trade union links and therefore kept it on the corporative road. This was evident in the predisposition of union stations in eastern Nova Scotia[150] to the corporatism of the Antigonish Movement, and its arm in the fishing industry, the United Maritime Fishermen, which developed in 1930.[151]

THE FISHERMEN'S FEDERATION OF NOVA SCOTIA

The depression brought a further drastic drop in the price of fish and in the income of fishermen.[152] At the same time, the price of equipment and bait was rising so that Lunenburg fishermen and captains alike faced a worsening economic situation. Under conditions which grew more difficult daily, the Lunenburg fishermen responded spontaneously in 1933 with a 'primitive' strike. Captain Knickle of the Lunenburg fleet described the situation leading up to this event:

the price is made in the fall before we start, and there is no advance in the price unless the masters get together and say,'We cannot afford to fish for that price....' We had an instance of that last winter [1933]. They did not go on strike because they are not organised in our part, but around Christmas they all came home, and last fall from September until Christmas the highest boat made $90 and the lowest boat made $60. That was from September through October and November up until the 20th of December. They got disgusted. The men could not get any money to pay their bills and they went on a sort of strike. Then it was agreed to give them half a cent more, but the men forgot about the bait, and when they went to pay for the bait next time they found it was raised half a cent a pound.[153]

The mid to late 1930s was a very militant period for workers in the New England fishing industry. The brief influx of American capital into Nova Scotia during the 1930s and tariff changes that lowered the duty on Canadian fish entering their market, were calculated attempts by American capital to improve their competitive situation at home. The position in which this put Canadian fishermen during the early 1930s is clear from the following account of two strikes in New England:

They had a strike there at one time and there was a Canadian boat come in there and the union spattered them with a couple of cases of rotten eggs: they won't allow us in. In other words, the union would not consider the duty at all; they would not allow us into the dock.... They have a strike on in Boston now [October 1934]; we had some firms ship fish to Boston recently about a week ago and they would not allow them to land them on the docks; that is, the Eastern Steamship Co. The strikers made them take them off the dock and return the fish to Canada again.... The labourers would not allow any men to go to work and handle these fish, and the police had no power at all; they were afraid to interfere and the fish were returned to N. S. and in that case the merchants had to lose that freight.[154]

As we have seen, as a consequence of their underdeveloped structure, Canadian companies were also exploiting the cheaper raw materials and labour of the Nova Scotia fishery to gain an advantage in the US market. In early 1937 Captain James Whynacht of Lunenburg returned from working in the New England fishery out of Gloucester.[155] Having been a member of the union there, having seen what a trade union could do for fishermen and having witnessed the ingratiating position that unorganised Nova Scotia fishermen were in relative to striking New England fishermen, he suggested that a similar union be started in Nova Scotia.[156] Acting with another local fisherman, Ben MacKenzie of Lockeport, himself just returned home after fourteen years fishing out of Gloucester,[157] and a sympathetic Halifax lawyer, W. Pitt Potter, KC,[158] the dormant Fishermen's Federation of Nova Scotia was rejuvenated. Initially, 36 schooner fishermen and captains[159] were organised into three stations at La Have, Riverport, and Lunenburg in January 1937.[160] Subsequently, Lockeport was organised under MacKenzie as station No 105,[161] and by the end of 1937 nine stations existed in fishing communities and towns around the south shore.[162]

In late December 1937, Captain Angus Walters called for a united front of Nova Scotia fishermen from Cape Sable to Cape Breton to demand an increase of one quarter cent per pound in the price of haddock.[163] When the fish buyers refused to recognise or negotiate with the Fishermen's Federation, and with the news of a sharp increase in outfitting charges for the impending voyages, a 'tie-up' ensued affecting nine companies in Lunenburg and Halifax and involving 800 fishermen.[164]

Behind slogans such as 'We might as well starve ashore as starve out at sea,'[165] both inshore and offshore fishermen flocked to support and to join the federation. On the very first day of the strike, 130 new members were signed up, bringing the total membership of the Lunenburg station to 250. By the fourth day of the strike (3 January 1938), membership had swollen to close to 600 as a result of a mass influx of enthusiastic inshore fishermen.[166] This brought the membership of the federation to over two-thirds the total number of fishermen in the area.[167] The same day, Walters left for Liverpool, North Sydney, and other points to help establish stations of the federation in response to local requests from fishermen.[168]

The union reported also that work on organising trawler crews was proceeding apace, and it was expected that the three trawlers out of Halifax would tie up shortly. The fervour of these early days can be judged from the following account in the *Halifax Chronicle*:

Some idea of the general confusion resulting from the tie-up may be gleaned from the fact that while the *Muriel Isabel* was trying to slip away to sea this afternoon, Captain James Whynacht, original organiser of the union a year ago, was in her forecastle signing on the crew as union members, and might have been carried off to sea if the attempt had been successful.[169]

Later the *Chronicle* speculated:

There are about 35,000 fishermen in the Atlantic Region of Canada, of whom it is estimated there are enough in Nova Scotia alone to recruit a union numerically half as strong again as the U. M. W. [United Mine Workers] which has accomplished so much for the workers in the mining field.[170]

Most important, this vigour was a clear expression of the fishermen's potential to identify with working-class interests and militant tactics. It was also a clear representation of the degree of frustration and indignation felt by fishermen over their impoverished and exploited condition. On 8 January, when the 'prize' schooner of W. C. Smith and Co., the *Jean and Shirley*, landed her fish, W. H. 'Billy' Smith of Lunenburg Sea Products appeared and requested the crew not to join the union, 'for it wouldn't feed them when they were out of work.'[171] A number of the crew replied: 'You won't feed us either, Mr. Smith. So we may just as well loaf and starve as work and starve.'[172] Ben MacKenzie received a 100% vote of agreement from his Lockeport station to tie up in support of the Lunenburg strike on January 4th, despite the fact that one of the Lockeport companies, Swim Brothers, had decided to pay the union prices.[173]

The overwhelming majority of the membership in the Lunenburg station were rank and file fishermen, while the majority of captains, apart from a few militant leaders, were only tacitly or involuntarily complying with the strike. In a number of cases they even attempted to break it. As the *Chronicle* reported:

The staunchness of the dorymen of the fleet is one of the most conspicuous features of the tie-up on all occasions. When one or two skipper members have issued the call for the sea they have unanimously refused to stir.[174]

As the strike progressed and the contradictions within the union between captains and crew deepened, more and more captains, initially attempting to remain impartial, sided with the companies and tried to sail with scab crews. The fishermen picketed the company wharves, preventing the vessels from baiting. On one occasion a Captain Watson Greek was prevented from baiting by 200 to 300 angry picketers who claimed they would 'tear the boat to pieces' if he tried anything.[175] On another occasion a captain threatened 200 pickets with a gun if they interfered with his vessel. Perhaps the most curious incident involved a Captain Calvin Tanner, who slipped away from Lunenburg to Wood's Harbour and hired a bus to return to Lunenburg for a scab crew. The bus was intercepted outside Lunenburg by an infuriated group of over 50 union members who took the driver's keys and drove the bus back to union headquarters. Here the bus owner was called and instructed to get his bus out of town within twenty minutes or the union would not be responsible for what might happen to it. The owner and driver complied forthwith.[176]

Eight days into the fishermen's strike, Walters met with the recently formed Fish Handlers' and Fish Cutters' Union of Halifax at a general meeting in the Halifax Labour Temple. This resulted in an 'ironclad offensive and defensive alliance' between the two unions for the promotion of their mutual interests by direct action.[177] The fish handlers promised to refuse to handle scab fish while the Lunenburg fleet was on strike, and to endeavour to unionise the local trawler fleet in support of the general interest of the fishing industry workers.[178] The fishermen, for their part, promised to 'back up to the hilt' the Fish Handlers' Union in their longstanding dispute over recognition with the Halifax companies, especially Maritime-National Fish Company.[179] The union members claimed that this alliance heralded the dawn of a new day for Nova Scotia fish workers; and the *Halifax Chronicle* called the treaty 'one of the most significant developments in the fishing industry in the last century and one-half.'[180]

As a result of this show of solidarity, the very next day the Maritime-National Fish Company took decisive retaliatory action. Eighty employees, 60 of whom were the most active union members, were fired, ostensibly because of the shortage of fish caused by the Lunenburg strike. These members included all those on the union executive who worked for the company, all plant committeemen, and the most active rank and file members.[181] At 5:30 a.m. on 7 January, the entire union went on strike for the reinstatement of the 60 union members and for union recognition.[182] On Tuesday the 11th of January, in an attempt to break the coalition, the fish buyers acceded to the fishermen's demand for an increase in the price of haddock averaging one-quarter of a cent per pound. However, they unanimously refused to recognise the federation as a bargaining agent for the fishermen. Despite the fact that the main issue over which the captains had entered the strike, and indeed had allied with their crews in the federation, had been resolved, the federation, under pressure from its rank and file, decided to stay out. The federation stated that it would do so until a three-cornered agreement was reached with the companies. This involved: (a) recognition of the Fishermen's Federation of Nova Scotia; (b) recognition of the Halifax Fish Handlers' and Fish Cutters' Union; and (c) some arrangement to provide work for the three Lunenburg vessels left idle because General Seafood Ltd of Halifax was still holding out on the price agreement.[183]

The fish buyers were intransigent, despite the willingness of the federation leadership to compromise. Perhaps anticipating a complete victory, the Lunenburg dealers reneged on all union proposals—even the price increase—and forced the confrontation to a head.[184] Infuriated at this brazen attempt to flout and ridicule their traditional authority, the captains ordered vessels loyal to the federation to moor end to end, forming a solid floating boom across Lunenburg harbour.[185] Arming their crews with axes, they ordered the men to chop to pieces any boat that attempted to break for the banks.[186] Organising dory patrols of every dock, and stationing 50 picketers along the railway on the land side of the W. C. Smith plant—the owners of which particularly incurred their wrath by leading the buyers—the federation reinforced its stand.[187]

Friday the 14th also marked a distinct escalation of tensions in Halifax. The workers, none of whom had savings, were hard hit by a strike lasting even a few days, and, disqualified from receiving relief aid from the city, were living a day-to-day existence on charitable donations made by other trade unionists and citizens of the city and province.[188] Their desperation with the company's arrogance vented itself in property damage and spontaneous outbursts of violence on the picket lines. Strikebreakers, who actually lived inside the plant, feared an invasion and armed themselves with clubs, pipes, and, in one case, a sword.[189] That night, the picket line, swelling to 300 people, launched an offensive against the National Fish Laboratories across the street from the plant. However, upon hearing that the upstairs of the building was rented out as tenements to working people, the picketers returned to their line.[190]

In Lunenburg, the intervention of the town council and local members of Parliament and the Legislature produced a verbal agreement from Lunenburg Sea Products not to ship fish to National Fish in Halifax while the fish handlers were still on strike. This concession provided some captains with enough incentive to renew efforts to break the coalition. However, at a general meeting of the federation on Saturday the 15th, the rank and file voted 98% in favour of remaining tied up.[191]

When it became clear that the fishermen would stay out, the executive of the Trades and Labour Council in Halifax was authorised to seek the intervention of Premier Angus L. Macdonald. In view of the strike's importance to provincial labour as a whole,[192] D. W. Morrison, representing 12,000 miners, was asked to become part of a delegation to the premier.[193]

On Monday the 17th, an urgent meeting of Trades and Labour Council representatives, the Fish Handlers, the department of labour, and the premier took place at Province House.[194] Charles Murray acted as liaison between the fishermen in Lunenburg, the fish handlers in Halifax, and the government.[195] In the midst of the meeting, a radio report announced that the Lunenburg strike had been settled, and that the schooners had been ordered to break the blockade and head for the banks. This was in spite of the agreement that no group would go back to work until both strikes had been settled. Calling Walters, Murray suggested that the vessels should make for Halifax instead of the banks, and blockade the National Fish plant from the water. Walters was hesitant, but the intimation of this threat to the companies was enough to settle the strike even though it is doubtful whether Walters would have carried it out.[196]

Subsequently, the fish handlers' union in Halifax lost a certification vote since the Maritime-National Fish Company retained a significant number of its new employees long enough to sway the vote against the union.[197] The Fishermen's Federation, on the other hand, died a 'natural' death: a victim of internal divisions and contradictions between the schooner fishermen and captains.[198] Charles Murray observed that, at the end of the strike,

the fishermen who joined [the federation], who worked in it, who helped organise it, [and] who fought for it ... were convinced that it prevented them from achieving anything.... It wasn't a healthy sort of thing anyway: it was dominated by the captains, and by and large the interests of the captains and the interests of the companies were much closer than the interests of the captains and the crews.... The crews weren't happy about it.[199]

One station of the Fishermen's Federation continued in existence for another year in Lockeport under Ben MacKenzie. However, with no trade union status or bargaining power, the federation was not able to combat various unfair labour practices that the Lockeport Cold Storage Company was committing against member fishermen. Consequently, when the Canadian Seamen's Unionn offered the Lockeport station a direct charter in 1939, it was enthusiastically accepted.[200]

The strikes of 1938 in Halifax, Lunenburg, and Lockeport are very important for understanding labour's response to underdevelopment and development in the fresh- and frozen-fish industry. The Fishermen's Federation of Nova Scotia was organised in Lunenburg County to combat the extremely low prices which prevailed as a result of the efforts of an underdeveloped industry to expand its American market. As a consequence of these attempts, Canadian fishermen were put in an antagonistic position relative to American fishermen who were striking for higher prices. Fishermen such as James Whynacht and Ben MacKenzie, driven to the United States in the first place by poor conditions in Nova Scotia, came home to roost.

The major element of capitalist development which influenced the course of these events was the fact that two very large companies dominated the fresh- and frozen-fish industry and, as a consequence of the drastic decline of salt-fish, the entire fishing industry in Nova Scotia. Inshore and offshore fishermen in the Halifax, Lunenburg, and Lockeport areas were faced by similar prices and conditions. The reality of dealing with a small, powerful group of fish buyers destroyed the traditional hope of alternative buyers paying better prices. Instead, the range of options open to fishermen looking for a better price was narrowed to just one: bargaining with the buyers or starving.

Co-operation, education, and lobbying reform programmes became as obsolete in this context as the idea that inshore and offshore fishermen did not face the same problems. In fact, as we have seen, the federation even went so far as to forge ties with the fish handlers in Halifax and the Trades and Labour Council. Pro-working-class and trade-union sympathies were by no means all-pervasive in the federation. This problem was reflected in the frequent divisions caused by some captains and in the fact that the federation's lawyer dropped proceedings for trade-union certification mid way through the strike.[201] However, the fishermen were definitely tempered in working-class struggle, as became clear in the following years by the massive support they gave to the Canadian Fishermen's Union.

CONCLUSION

Direct underdevelopment in the fishing industry of Nova Scotia was most evident in the form of undercapitalisation, and archaic methods of production and organisation. These in turn were a consequence of regional backwardness and the outflow of investment capital to metropolitan centres. Profitability relied on the excessive exploitation of labour rather than the manipulation of prices and costs (economies of scale) through vertical and horizontal integration. The lynchpin of the entire industry was abundant, cheap labour—both on the land and on the water.

The two social movements under review have been seen as responses to these two forms of underdevelopment. The Fishermen's Union of Nova Scotia was initially a response to the problems of a 'late developing' and backward salt-fish industry. It attempted to combat excessive speculation, transportation and marketing inefficiencies, and, in general, the insecurities that accompanied overdependence on one product in a volatile market. By the 1920s the union became allied with one fraction of capital against another. It waged an effective short-term fight against one symptom of fresh-fish capitalist underdevelopment—trawler overproduction—only to lose in the long run to another—inefficient, undercapitalised organisation. The Fishermen's Federation of Nova Scotia was clearly an organised labour response to the worst conditions created by inefficient fresh-fish capital in its frantic bid to enter the American market at cut-throat prices. Members of an impoverished labour force, proletarianised in a very real sense by monoploy conditions in the industry, rose up to fight for basic trade union rights and a decent price for their labour.

NOTES

1. P. Baran, *The political economy of growth* (New York, 1962); A. G. Frank, *Capitalism and underdevelopment in blatin America* (New York, 1967); S. Amin, *Accumulation on a world scale* (Hassocks, Sussex, 1974) and *Unequal development* (Hassocks, Sussex, 1976); A. Emmanuel, *Unequal exchange* (London, 1972); F. H. Cardoso, 'Dependency and development in Latin America,' *New Left Review*, no 75 (1972), 83-95 and 'Associated-dependent development: theoretical and practical implications,' *Authoritarian Brazil: origins, policies, and future*, ed. A. Stepan (New Haven, 1973), 142-96; T. Dos Santos, 'The crisis of development theory and the problems of dependence in Latin America,' *Underdevelopment and development*, ed. H. Bernstein (Harmondsworth, 1973); D. Booth, 'Andre Gunder Frank: an introduction and appreciation,' *Beyond the sociology of development*, ed. I. Oxaal et al. (London,1975), 50-85; P. J. O'Brien, 'A critique of Latin American theories of dependency,' *Beyond the sociology of development*, Oxaal, 7-27; A.

Foster-Carter, 'The modes of production controversy,' *New Left Review*, no 107 (1978), 47-77.

2. For Marxist analyses of regionalism, see Ernest Mandel, *Capitalism and regional development*(Toronto, 1971); Henry Veltmeyer, 'Dependency and underdevelopment: some questions and problems,' *Canadian Journal of Political and Social Theory*, II (1978), 55-71; and I. Carter, 'The highlands of Scotland as an underdeveloped region,' *Sociology and development*, ed. E. Dekadt and G. Williams (London, 1974), 279-311. For dualist and neo-classical approaches, see, for instance, S. Holland, 'Regional underdevelopment in a developed economy: the Italian case,' *Regional Studies*, II (1971), 71-90 and *Capital versus the regions* (London, 1976); G. Myrdal, *Economic theory and underdeveloped regions* (London, 1957); and A. G. Green, 'Regional aspects of Canada's economic growth, 1890-1929,' *Canadian Journal of Economics and Political Science*, XXXIII (1967), 232-45.

3. B. Archibald, 'Atlantic regional underdevelopment and socialism,' *Essays on the left*, ed. Laurier Lapierre et al. (Toronto, 1971), 103-120; A. M. Sinclair, 'Problems of underdevelopment in Atlantic Canada,' *Symposium on problems of development in Atlantic Canada*, ed. S. D. Clark and P. G. Clark (Sackville, New Brunswick, April 1975); and David Frank, 'The Cape Breton coal industry and the rise and fall of the British Empire Steel Company,' *Acadiensis*, VII (1977), 3-34 and 'The nine myths of regional disparity,' *Canadian Dimension*, XIII no 2 (1978),18-21.

4. K. Campbell, 'Regional disparity and inter-regional exchange imbalance,' *Modernization and the Canadian state*, ed. D. Glenday et al. (Toronto, 1978), 111-31.

5. Henry Veltmeyer, 'Dependency and underdevelopment: some questions and problems,' and chapter 1 in this volume.

6. See chapters 2, 5, and 9 in this volume.

7. R. J. Brym, 'Regional social structure and agrarian radicalism in Canada: the cases of Alberta, Saskatchewan, and New Brunswick,' *Canadian Review of Sociology and Anthropology*, XV (1978).

8. See chapter 2 in this volume.

9. R. Dore, 'The late development effect,' Institute of Development Studies (University of Sussex), Communication 103 (1972).

10. These two forms of capital come under Sacouman's general category of direct capitalist underdevelopment (see chapter 2 in this volume) in that the fishing industry of the twentieth century in Nova Scotia—whether 'salt' or 'fresh'—was dominated by large-scale capital, and involved the exploitation of fishermen—inshore and offshore—through the appropriation of a surplus product in the sphere of production. The distinction between 'late developing' salt-fish capital and undercapitalised fresh-fish capital is made to illuminate ceetain unique points in the history of the industry, and in the courses taken by each fishermen's organisation which might otherwise be missed.

11. One can actually distinguish among three forms of capital, the third being foreign-owned. The latter consisted primarily in American companies that were concentrated in the lobster canning industry from the 1880s onward, and after 1929, in the fresh- and frozen-fish industry. Gaining hegemony in the fresh-fish industry briefly in the years 1929 to 1936, American capital dominated the lobster canning industry from its beginnings through to the depression. For an extended discussion of this interesting subject see H. A. Innis, *The cod fisheries* (Toronto, 1940), 245, 437, 428; and L. G. Barrett, 'Development and underdevelopment, and the rise of trade unionism in the fishing industry of Nova Scotia, 1900-1950' (unpub. MA thesis, Dalhousie University, 1976).

12. Innis, *The cod fisheries*; H. H. Robertson, 'The commercial relationship between

Nova Scotia and the British West Indies, 1788-1822: the twilight of mercantilism in the British empire' (unpub. MA thesis, Dalhousie University, 1975).

13. While this mercantile-trader class seems comparable to the eighteenth- and nineteenth-century trader class which controlled fish markets in Newfoundland, the existence of the same type of 'planter class' at the community level which mediated control between the traders and the fishermen in Newfoundland is less clear in the case of Nova Scotia. For the Newfoundland case, see E. Antler, 'Maritime mode of production, domestic mode of production, or labour process: an examination of the Newfoundland inshore fishery,' a paper presented before the Northeastern Anthropological Association (24-26 March 1977), 6-7.

14. Innis, *The cod fisheries*, 231.

15. *Progress Enterprise* (Lunenburg, Nova Scotia), 1 May 1907.

16. J. W. Watt, *A brief review of the fisheries of Nova Scotia* (Nova Scotia, 1963), 11, 12, 42; Innis, *The cod fisheries*, 275.

17. The term 'unit of production' is used cautiously to stress a unique form of capitalist production which utilised an integral unit of organisation at the domestic level. This term is used instead of the more common expression 'mode of production.' See, for example, M. J. Hedley, 'Transformation of the domestic mode of production,' a paper presented before the annual meeting of the Canadian Sociology and Anthropology Association (Fredericton, 1977); Veltmeyer, 'Dependency and underdevelopment,' 60-63; and chapter 2 in this volume.

This is done in order to stress the focus of this paper which concerns capitalist development in the fishing industry and the changing functions performed by a domestically organised unit of production rather than the equally important focus which analyses the domestic unit, in all its dimensions, as a unique mode of production. See Hedley, 'Transformation of the domestic mode of production.' In particular, the domestic unit is discussed from the limited perspective of its function in the reproduction of labour-power for capitalism, rather than the integrity of the reproduction of the unit (mode) itself. See Hedley, 'Transformation of the domestic mode of production,' 2, 3.

In addition, the term 'unit of production' is used instead of 'mode of production' to stress the analytical similarities between the labour-rent functions performed by domestic units under widely varying circumstances. This exposes the functional similarities of such seemingly diverse subjects as, for example, inshore fishing families in nineteenth-century Nova Scotia and nuclear families in modern day, developed Toronto. See M. P. Connelly, *Last hired, first fired: Canadian women and the labour force* (Toronto, 1978). In either case the unifying tenet is that capital accumulation everywhere requires and reproduces a wide variety of *non*-capitalist *relations* of production in a drive to offset declining rates of profit. See E. Laclau, 'Feudalism and capitalsim in Latin America,' *New Left Review*, no 67 (1971), 34-36; and Veltmeyer, 'Dependency and underdevelopment,' 58-63.

18. The term 'domestic unit of production' is used only to stress the close relationship between the household/family kinship unit and the productive unit. It is not used as a synonym for independent commodity production—although it may entail at some stages, 'ownership, operation, and control of the means of production ... [by] ... the actual producer' (Hedley, 'Transformation of the domestic mode of production,' 19) or for subsistence, feudal (Veltmeyer, 'Dependency and underdevelopment,' 61), pre-capitalist or noncommodity modes of production (Sacouman, chapter 2 in this volume).

19. Inshore fishermen operated small boats manned by one or two men. They would fish by setting trawls, or lines of baited hooks, from one to fifteen miles from shore to catch 'line' fish (i.e., groundfish such as cod, haddock, halibut, hake, etc.). In addition,

inshore fishermen also fished closer to shore, setting long nets to catch pelagic fish such as mackerel or herring, and traps to catch shellfish such as the lucrative lobster (*Progress Enterprise*, 30 April 1925; *Labour Gazette*, Ottawa, 1905, 412).

Groundfish and pelagic fish would, in most cases, be brought to home port to be split, cleaned, and either salted or dried by the fishermen's family. Lobster, on the other hand, was sold directly to a company buyer or cannery: see G. White, 'Moderniza- tion and the small fishing community: a case study in Cape Breton County' (unpub. MA thesis, Dalhousie University, 1976).

In either case the product—whether raw, semi-processed, or finished—would often not be sold for cash, but exchanged for credit in a general store. The relations of production in the salt fishery were between mercantile capital and dependent *petty* commodity producers. As long as some form of secondary production remained in the domestic unit this remained true and the appropriation of a surplus product was indirect, through the unequal exchange of commodities. Relations of production in the lobster fishery—insofar as lobster fishing was the dominant line of fishing for the domestic unit—were between industrial capital and dependent *primary* commodity pro- ducers. In these circumstances the domestic unit no longer performed any secondary production function in terms of the fishing industry and a primary commodity was appropriated under conditions of extreme dependence and routinised production.

One can therefore specify that under conditions of capitalist development the domestic unit comes under considerable pressure to specialise and rationalise produc- tion: Hedley, 'Transformation of the domestic mode of production,' 3, 6. Any reduc- tion in either or both of the domestic unit's production functions transforms the rela- tions between the unit and the capitalist mode of production in general. (Sacouman stresses the importance of the change away from secondary production; see chapter 2. See also J. C. Faris, 'Primitive accumulation in small-scale fishing communities,' *Those who live from the sea*, ed. M. E. Smith (St Paul, 1977), 246.) Appropriation of a surplus, and exploitation, move from relations of exchange to the realm of relations of produc- tion, a transformation which Sacouman has termed the change from indirect capitalist underdevelopment to direct capitalist underdevelopment: chapter 2 in this volume.

20. C. Wadel, *Marginal adaptations and modernization in Newfoundland*, (St John's, 1969), 18.

21. Faris, 'Primitive accumulation in small-scale fishing communities.'

22. Antler, 'Maritime mode of production, domestic mode of production, or labour process,' 8-10.

23. Innis, *The cod fisheries*, 427-28.

24. *Ibid.*, 372.

25. The offshore fishery in Nova Scotia was concerned solely with the operation of fishing schooners up to 1910, and mainly with the operation of schooners, in addition to a handful of wooden steam trawlers up to 1945. Schooners were wooden sailing vessels manned by sixteen to twenty men. They fished the 18,000 square miles of fishing grounds ('banks') within 200 miles of the coast, as well as the 70,000 square miles of Grand Banks which lay off the southeast corner of Newfoundland: B. Atlee, 'Hands off the trawler,' *McLean's Magazine*, 15 April 1930, 9, 76. Each vessel carried six to eight two-man dories which left the mother ship each day to lay eight trawls, 20,000 feet long each, with 800 hooks per trawl. Each doryman was responsible for four trawls which meant rigging and baiting some 3,200 hooks possibly three times per day. The trawls were then set and pulled and fish was taken to the parent ship to be cleaned, split and salted, or buried in ice; *Argus* (Lunenburg, Nova Scotia), 20 April 1925.

For the most part, vessels out of Lunenburg made two trips a season: the first called the 'Spring Baiting Trip,' which commenced 'the morning succeeding the Sabbath nearest the 21st of March;' and the second beginning about the 7th of June. Upon return from the first trip at the end of May, a few days would be spent in port unloading the semi-processed fish at 'curing' stores and taking on supplies for the second trip which lasted until late autumn. In the interval lasting the duration of the second trip, the fish would be processed and marketed by numerous wholesale agents and companies in the town: *Progress Enterprise* (Lunenburg), 24 April 1907. Only after this long process of 'making' the fish were crewmen or their families paid cash or given credit in general stores: Barrett, 'Development and underdevelopment,' 26-29.

26. *Progress Enterprise*, 1 May 1907.

27. *Ibid.*

28. *Ibid.*, 24 April 1907; 27 February 1907.

29. Canada, Royal Commission on Price Spreads, *Minutes of Proceedings and Evidence*, No 1 (Ottawa, 1937), 31.

30. For concrete examples of this system, see Public Archives of Nova Scotia (PANS), Lunenburg Sea Products Collection, 1931 Correspondence.

31. PANS, Lunenburg Sea Products Collection, W. W. Smith, *History of the company* (n. d.), 18.

32. *Yarmouth Herald*, 10 February 1925.

33. *Ibid.*

34. PANS, Lunenburg Sea Products Collection, 1931 Correspondence.

35. *Ibid.*, 1921; 1924; 1931.

36. *Ibid.*, Schr. *Astrid W.* files.

37. *Progress Enterprise*, 9 November 1917; 20 July 1927.

38. *Ibid.*, 20 April 1907.

39. *Ibid.*

40. R. J. Sacouman, 'The underdevelopment of primary production dependent rural communities in Maritime Canada,' a paper presented before the Ninth World Congress of Sociology (Uppsala University, Sweden, August 1978), 13-14.

41. Innis, *The cod fisheries*, 426-29.

42. *Ibid.*, 428. Robin, Jones and Whitman Ltd present possibly the best case of a salt-fish company which attempted to combine numerous forms of production under varying conditions in order to combat a fluctuating and insecure market. From a survey of its methods of operation it becomes clear that the maintenance and exploitation of the domestic unit of production was a very mutable process reflecting in particular the capitalist business cycle and regional underdevelopment, but also geographical conditions, ethnicity and religion, etc. Changes in the functions of the domestic unit of production by no means followed a linear progression over time.

43. For an extended discussion of the relationship between merchant capital and underdevelopment, see G. Kay, *Development and underdevelopment: a Marxist analysis* (London, 1975), 100, 101, 119-24.

44. H. A. Innis, 'An introduction to the economic history of the Maritimes, including Newfoundland and New England,' *Essays in Canadian economic history*, ed. M. Q. Innis (Toronto, 1956); W. S. MacNutt, *The Atlantic provinces* (Toronto, 1965); G. A. Rawlyk, *Nova Scotia's Massachusetts* (Toronto, 1973).

45. Atlantic Provinces Economic Council, *Atlantic Canada today* (Halifax, 1977), 19.

46. Innis, *The cod fisheries*, 330-34.

47. Antler, 'Maritime mode of production, domestic mode of production, or labour process,' 10; Innis, *The cod fisheries*, 334.

48. Stewart Bates, 'Report on the Canadian Atlantic sea fishery,' Nova Scotia, Royal Commission on Provincial Development and Rehabilitation, *Report*, 1944, IX, 44.

49. Innis, *The cod fisheries*, 432, 435.

50. *Ibid.*

51. *Ibid.*, 435.

52. *Ibid.*

53. *Ibid.*

54. J. W. Watt, 'A brief review of the fisheries of Nova Scotia,' Nova Scotia, Dept of Trade and Industry (1963), 20; Nova Scotia, Economic Council, Nova Scotia Fisheries Conference, 1938, *Proceedings*, 30.

55. Nova Scotia, Economic Council, NS Fisheries Conference, 1938, *Proceedings*; Fisheries Council of Canada, *Annual Review, 1967*,65.

56. Barrett, 'Development and underdevelopment,' 48-49, 90.

57. Bates, 'Report on the Canadian Atlantic sea fishery,' 76.

58. Watt, 'A brief review of the fisheries of Nova Scotia,' 22; Innis, *The cod fisheries*, 424.

59. Bates, 'Report on the Canadian Atlantic sea fishery,' 76.

60. Innis, *The cod fisheries*, 433; Nova Scotia, Economic Council, NS Fisheries Conference, 1938, *Proceedings*, 29.

61. Canada, Royal Commission Investigating the Fisheries of the Maritime Provinces and the Magdalen Islands, *Report*, 1928, 89.

62. For example, Norway paid $600,000 in subsidies to secure the Havana market; Watt, 'A brief review of the fisheries of Nova Scotia,' 14.

63. In 1926 Newfoundland was said to have supplied very nearly half of Puerto Rico's dried cod requirements, practically all of which a few years earlier had been supplied from Lunenburg; Watt, *ibid.*, 14.

64. *Argus*, 26 February 1925; PANS, Lunenburg Sea Products Collection, 1925 Correspondence.

65. Fisheries Council of Canada, *Annual review, 1967*, 74; PANS, Lunenburg Sea Products Collection, Smith, *History of the company*,19, 21.

66. Smith, *ibid.*, 21; Innis, *The cod fisheries*, 436.

67. Bates, 'Report on the Canadian Atlantic sea fishery,' 79.

68. *Ibid.*

69. *Ibid.*, 48.

70. Canada, Royal Commission on Price Spreads, 1937, *Proceedings and Evidence*, No 1, 328,384.

71. *Ibid.*, 383; Innis, *The cod fisheries*, 434.

72. Innis, *The cod fisheries*, 434.

73. *Ibid.*

74. Karl Marx, *Capital*, I (London, 1970), 642, 663.

75. *Ibid.*, 639.

76. Canada, Royal Commission on Price Spreads, 1937, *Proceedings and Evidence*, No 1, 7, 14; Innis, *The cod fisheries*, 436.

77. Brox has discussed at length the importance of the 'nuclear' role of cash in the 'outport household economy.' O. Brox, *Newfoundland fishermen in the age of industry; a sociology of economic dualism* (St John's, 1972), 9-19.

78. Bates plays down the brief but important part played in this under-capitalisation by US capital: Bates, 'Report on the Canadian Atlantic sea fishery,' 39. For example, both General Seafoods and Atlantic Coast Fisheries took over Canadian companies in order to develop Nova Scotia as 'the "Fish Pier of America:' " Atlee, 'Hands off the trawler,' 76. General Seafoods failed in this initial bid (see Barrett, 'Development and underdevelopment,' 96-98) but Atlantic Coast Fisheries remained in Nova Scotia from 1929 to the mid 1930s: Canada, Royal Commission on Price Spreads, 1937, *Proceedings and evidence*, No 1, 328, 383-84, 392; Fisheries Council of Canada, *Annual review, 1967*,

79. An amalgamation of nine companies—all subsidiaries of either Maritime Fish or the National Fish Company—was forged in 1929 by A. H. Brittain, president of Maritime Fish Corporation, under the name of Maritime-National Fish Co., and it became a wholly owned subsidiary of Atlantic Coast Fisheries Ltd. It thereby became the largest processor of fresh- and frozen-fish in Atlantic Canada. Between 1931 and 1934, $67,500 was paid in 'administrative services' to the American parent for rights to the latter's 'quick freezing' technology and some new techniques in cod and halibut liver oil production. In addition, Maritime-National Fish supplied halibut livers and all of its 'surplus' fresh fillets—amounting to 80% of the company's U. S. trade—to Atlantic Coast Fisheries *at cost*: Canada, Royal Commission on Price Spreads, 1937,*Proceedings and evidence*,No 1, 328, 338-39, 383-84, 386, 388-89, 392. In other words, the region's single largest fresh- and frozen-fish processor was selling fully 20% of its entire output at sacrificial prices to its American parent. Hardly insignificant at such a crucial juncture in the history of the industry.

79. Bates, 'Report on the Canadian Atlantic sea fishery,' 67. The peculiar restriction of trawler expansion is discussed at length below.

80. *Ibid.*

81. *Ibid.*

82. *Ibid.*

83. *Ibid.*, 29.

84. Canada, Royal Commission on Price Spreads, 1937, *Report*, 192.

85. See also Nova Scotia, Royal Commission on Provincial Development and Rehabilitation, 1944, *Evidence*, 1685.

86. Bates, 'Report on the Canadian Atlantic sea fishery,' 41.

87. *Ibid.*, 64.

88. *Ibid.*

89. R. Williams, 'Fish ... or cut bait,' *This Magazine*, XI, no 3(1977), 7.

90. Barrett, 'Development and underdevelopment,' 7-19.

91. See chapter 5 in this volume.

92. Barrett, 'Development and underdevelopment,' and S. D. Cameron, *The education of Everett Richardson* (Toronto, 1977).

93. *Halifax Chronicle*, 4 January 1938.

94. *Ibid.*

95. *Labour Gazette*, 1905, 413.

96. *Ibid.*, 412, 413.

97. Nova Scotia, *Statutes*, 1905, Chap. 39; An act to provide for the organisation of fishermen's unions.

98. *Labour Gazette*, 1905, 414.

99. *Ibid.*, 1906-07, 414.

100. *Ibid.*, 1909-10, 479.

101. *Ibid.*, 1906-07, 415.

102. *Halifax Chronicle*, 4 January 1938.

103. *Labour Gazette*, 1911, 301.

104. Canada, Depart of Labour, *Report on strikes and lockouts in Canada* (Ottawa, 1913), 213; and *Report on labour organisation in Canada 1911* (Ottawa, 1912), 34.

105. Innis, *The cod fisheries*, 437.

106. White, 'Modernization and the small fishing community,' 38; and Innis, *The cod fisheries*, 437.

107. White, *ibid.*, 42.

108. *Ibid.*, 39.

109. *Ibid.*, 36.

110. This Main-A-Dieu station later bacame a strong local of United Maritime Fishermen; White, *ibid*.

111. Canada, Depart of Labour, *Strikes and lockouts*, 213.

112. See chapter 5 in this volume.

113. *Labour Gazette*, 1905, 115.

114. David Frank, 'Class conflict in the coal industry, Cape Breton, 1922,' *Essays in Canadian working class history*, ed. G. S. Kealey and P. Warrian (Toronto, 1976).

115. E. R. Forbes, 'The origins of the Maritimes rights movement,' *Acadiensis*, V (1975), 54-66; G. A. Rawlyk, 'The Maritimes and the Canadian community,' *Regionalism in the Canadian community*, ed. Mason Wade (Toronto, 1969) and 'The Farmer-Labour Movement and the failure of socialism in Nova Scotia,' *Essays on the left*, ed. Laurier Lapierre (Toronto, 1971), 31-41.

116. See chapter 9 in this volume, and G. E. Panting, 'The Fishermen's Protective Union of Newfoundland and the farmers' organisations in western Canada,' Canadian Historical Association, *Annual report*, 1963, 141-51; S. Noel, *Politics in Newfoundland* (Toronto, 1971).

117. Barrett, 'Development and underdevelopment,' 73-74. For a more detailed discussion of these strikes and the unions involved, see D. J. White, *The New England fishing industry: a study in price and wage setting* (Cambridge, Mass., 1954), 44.

118. *Progress Enterprise*, 3 September 1919.

119. *Ibid*.

120. *Ibid*.

121. *Ibid*.

122. *Ibid*.

123. *Ibid*.

124. *Progress Enterprise*, 9 January 1918.

125. PANS, Lunenburg Sea Products Collection, 1921 Correspondence: M. M. Gardner to F. B. McCurdy, MP, 28 February 1921.

126. Canada, Royal Commission Investigating the Fisheries, 1928, *Report*, 125.

127. Barrett, 'Development and underdevelopment,' 25-29.

128. Canada, Royal Commission on Price Spreads,1937, *Proceedings and evidence*, No 1, 31.

129. PANS, Lunenburg Sea Products Collection,Office files, 1921-24.

130. *Ibid*.

131. Barrett, 'Development and underdevelopment,' 74-80.

132. *Progress Enterprise*, 10 September 1919.

133. *Ibid*.

134. *Ibid*., 22 January 1922.

135. *Ibid*., 17 March 1920.

136. *Argus*, 21 January 1926; *Progress Enterprise*, 20 January 1927; 2 November 1927.

137. Canada, Royal Commission Investigating the Fisheries, 1928, *Report*, 91.

138. In fact the Canso station of the Nova Scotia Fishermen's Union became the first station of the Fishermen's Federation of Nova Scotia in 1927 under the leadership of Captain John Kennedy, Jr. However, since it differed from the Fishermen's Union in name only, and since it was rapidly supplanted by United Maritime Fishermen in 1930, I have continued to call it the Fishermen's Union for simplicity's sake: both were maifestations of the same phenomena. See Barrett, 'Development and underdevelopment,' 81-83.

139. Canada, Royal Commission Investigating the Fisheries, 1928, *Report*, 99.

140. Watt, 'A brief review of the fisheries of Nova Scotia,' 28.

141. Bates, 'Report on the Canadian Atlantic sea fishery,' 42.

142. *Ibid.*, 41.

143. *Ibid.*

144. *Ibid.*

145. *Ibid.*, 42.

146. *Iibd.*

147. *Ibid.*

148. Canada,Royal Commission Investigating the Fisheries,1928, *Report*, 95.

149. Even if the Lunenburg 64 scheme of profit-sharing had been functional in the 1920s in the offshore fishery, one can still argue that it would have been detrimental to the development of trade unionism in the industry. (Thanks to J. Sacouman for this point.)

150. The question of why corporatism was *not* rekindled in southwestern Nova Scotia among inshore fishermen has, as yet, not received sufficient attention by Marxist scholars in the region.

151. See chapter 5 in this volume.

152. Bates, 'Report on the Canadian Atlantic sea fishery,' 30; H. R. Forsey, 'Distribution of income in the Maritimes,' *Canadian Forum*, XXI (1942), 253.

153. Canada, Royal Commission on Price Spreads, 1937, *Proceedings and evidence*, No 1, 19.

154. *Ibid.*, 17.

155. *Halifax Chronicle*, 4 January 1938.

156. *Ibid.*, 5 January 1938.

157. Interview with Charles Murray, Lower Sackville, Nova Scotia, 1975.

158. *Halifax Chronicle*, 5 and 8 January 1938.

159. *Ibid.*, 30 December 1937.

160. *Ibid.*, 5 January 1938.

161. *Ibid.*, 4 January 1938.

162. Canada, Depart of Labour, *Labour organisation in Canada 1937* (Ottawa, 1938), 78-81. At some point in January 1938, the three original stations amalgamated into one at Lunenburg under the illustrious Captain Angus Walters, famed skipper of the schooner *Bluenose*: *Halifax Chronicle*, 5 January 1938; interview with Charles Murray; interview with K. D. Parker, Halifax, Nova Scotia, 1975.

163. *Halifax Chronicle*, 30 December 1937.

164. *Ibid.*, 31 December 1937; *Labour Gazette*, 1938, 13.

165. *Halifax Chronicle*, 3 January 1938.

166. *Ibid.*

167. *Ibid.*

168. *Ibid.*

169. *Ibid.*, 4 January 1938.

170. *Ibid.*, 5 January 1938.

171. *Ibid.*, 9 January 1938.

172. *Ibid.*

173. *Ibid.*, 4 January 1938; *Labour Gazette*, 1938, 135-36.

174. *Halifax Chronicle*, 5 January 1938.

175. *Ibid.*, 4 January 1938.

176. *Ibid.*, 10 January 1938.

177. *Ibid.*, 6 January 1938.

178. Requiring little persuasion, the fifteen-man crew of the trawler, *Viernoe*, struck for union recognition with a full list of grievances: *Halifax Chronicle*, 12 January 1938; *Labour Gazette*, 1938, 136-137; H. A. Logan, 'Report on labour relations,' Nova Scotia, Royal Commission on Provincial Development and Rehabilitation, 1944, *Report*, XV, 95.

179. *Halifax Chronicle*, 6 January 1938.

180. *Ibid.*

181. *Labour Gazette*, 1938, 136; *Halifax Chronicle*, 8 January 1938.

182. *Halifax Chronicle*, 8 January 1938.

183. *Ibid.*, 11 January 1938.

184. *Ibid.*, 14 January 1938.

185. *Ibid.*, 15 January 1938; interview with Charles Murray; interview with K. D. Parker.

186. Interview with Charles Murray.

187. *Halifax Chronicle*, 11 January 1938.

188. Interview with K. D. Parker; *Halifax Chronicle*, 11 January 1938.

189. *Halifax Chronicle*, 15 January 1938.

190. *Ibid.*, 18 January 1938.

191. *Ibid.*

192. In April 1937 the provincial Liberal government of Angus L. MacDonald passed Nova Scotia's first trade union act: Nova Scotia, *Statutes*,1937, 115-19; *Halifax Chronicle*, 17 January 1938 and 9 November 1939. Labour in the province watched with keen interest to see if the Government would 'put teeth into the act' and the fish-plant workers' strike marked its first legal test: *Halifax Chronicle*, 10 January 1938; see also issues of 13 January and 18 January 1938.

193. *Halifax Chronicle*, 17 January 1938.

194. *Ibid.*, 18 January 1938.

195. Interview with Charles Murray.

196. *Ibid.*

197. Interview with K. D. Parker.

198. The divisive and anti-trade-union activities of captains has been a recurrent theme through the decades since 1938. For example, Lunenburg captains actively kept the Canadian Fishermen's Union out of Lunenburg in 1939 (interview with Charles Murray); captains around the province united to form the Master Mariners' Association in 1947 to assist National Sea Products Ltd in its attempt to break a strike by deep-sea fishermen (Barrett, 'Development and underdevelopment,' 194-207); and in 1968-69, National Sea Products' trawler captains actively campaigned on behalf of a company union to undercut attempts by the United Fishermen and Allied Workers' Union to unionise trawlermen: United Fishermen and Allied Workers' Union (Vancouver), union files, correspondence, 1969; H. Stevens to J. Thompson, 10 February 1969.

199. Interview with Charles Murray.

200. Interview with Charles Murray; *Halifax Chronicle*, 24 October and 9 November 1939; Logan, 'Report on labour relations; H. A. Logan, *Trade unions in Canada* (Toronto, 1948), 293; J. A. Sullivan, *Red sails on the Great Lakes* (Toronto, 1955), 60.The Canadian Fishermen's Union, as it came to be called, flourished for eight years in Nova Scotia and endured two tremendous strikes: one in 1939, and another in 1947. It was organised through the efforts of the Communist Party of Canada and the Canadian Seamen's Union and represented a very militant trade union unifying all workers in the fishing industry: Barrett, 'Development and underdevelopment,' 173-207; and Sullivan, *Red sails on the Great Lakes*.

201. Barrett, 'Development and underdevelopment,' 165-67, 170.

7 Inshore Fishermen, Unionisation, and the Struggle against Underdevelopment Today

Rick Williams

INTRODUCTION

As other articles in this book clearly affirm, issues of class are central to any effective understanding both of the development of social movements in the Atlantic region and of their successes and failures. Since it is our goal not just to understand our history but to change it, we must attempt to uncover the dynamics of change and stability so that new possibilities become realities. The themes of class, class interest, and class consciousness are central to those dynamics.

While other contributors to this volume have documented and analysed social movements in our history, I will deal with a movement that is only just beginning. Inshore fishermen in the Maritimes have since early 1977 been moving in ever greater numbers to unionisation as a means of dealing concretely and effectively with issues of survival and development in their industry. But, although their organisation and many of their problems are new, the impediments and potentials for the creation of a powerful social movement are familiar reflections of movements and struggles in our past. In particular, it seems that movements of petty primary producers manifest very complex problems of class structure and of interclass relationships; the contradictory internal class relations of petty primary production have often severely limited the efficacy of political and economic struggles. It may be of interest then to look at these complexities in the context of contemporary developments of unionisation and political mobilisation.

The fishing industry on the Atlantic coast has entered a period of very substantial change—indeed, of transformation. It is thus a critically important time to re-examine the concrete realities and on this basis to reconsider and evaluate our theoretical approaches.

I have been involved in these theoretical complexities more as a minor actor than as a theoretical analyst. I am doing research on the structure of the industry and on the organisational needs of inshore fishermen so as to provide the newly formed Maritime Fishermen's Union with technical and strategic support for their work in Nova Scotia. It is on the basis of this work that I hope to develop some theoretical perspectives on the possibilities of successful mobilisation of inshore fishermen at the present time.

ONE FISHERMAN

As a means of situating this discussion, let me start out by describing in some detail one of the fishermen I have come to know quite well in my work with inshore fishermen's organisations. He is about 30 years old and lives with his wife and two children in a tiny village on Nova Scotia's south shore. He owns and operates a two-year-old, 35-foot long-lining and lobster boat. He fishes by himself on inshore and near-shore grounds within roughly a 75-mile radius of his home wharf. For convenience I will refer to him by the pseudonym 'Don.'

As a teenager Don started fishing with his father who still lives nearby and still operates a smaller boat for hand-lining and lobster fishing. When he left school, Don decided that he wanted to stay in his home area and that he wanted to be a fisherman. In order to get started he needed capital, which was not available locally. Therefore, together with several contemporaries, and following an established pattern, he set out for Prince Rupert, British Columbia. There, through contacts from Nova Scotia, he went to work on a variety of large vessels fishing salmon, herring, and halibut. Some five years later he returned home with a wife and enough money to get a loan to buy an old 35-foot Cape Island fishing boat. He fished lobster in the spring and fall and hand-lined for cod and haddock in the early summer. He continued the pattern of winter and summer fishing in British Columbia as an experienced crewman making 'big money.' After five more years, he had enough saved to get a mortgage to build his new house himself and to get a boat loan to have built a $40,000 Cape Island fishing boat. This all amounted to a life of incredibly hard work and sacrifice.

By outlining the course of his activities over a year, we can get a sense of the production process in which Don is involved. Lobster season in his area opens some time in March, depending on tides and weather conditions. While the season lasts two months, the fishermen know within the first week whether it will be worthwhile to continue to fish. Catches have declined seriously in recent years owing mainly to extensive overfishing by both inshore and offshore operators. As will be described below, lobster has been the mainstay for south shore fishermen and this decline is hitting the area very hard. Don has been the 'high liner'—the most productive fisherman—in his area for a couple of years and he usually does best on the lobster. If the catch is poor in the first week, he will very likely haul all his traps and catch a plane to Prince Rupert. If he finds he can make a little money, he will decide to stay at it for a month or so until ground-fishing starts. While lobster catches are down, the prices are understandably at an all-time high; there is, therefore, a closely calculated gamble as to what can be accomplished financially in a given period.

Traditionally, perhaps the majority of fishermen have made most of the income they will get from fishing by the end of the spring lobster season. They will spend the summer and fall doing some fishing when weather, prices, and stocks are all favourable, but will also be occupied in numerous other income-producing activities. But Don is a full-time professional fisherman—more a result of exceptional stubbornness and determination than any economic or ecological factors. After the lobster season he gears up for long-lining, a method for catching groundfish (cod, haddock, halibut, hake, etc.) in which he believes adamantly. Other fishermen use less laborious methods, such as those using gill nets and drag nets, while the less adventure-some and less capitalised fishermen use hand-lining ('jigging') techniques close to shore. Don believes the nets to be very destructive of the environment and the stocks and therefore not in the best interests of fishermen in the long run. In the early summer the fish stay far off on the small banks and then move inshore as the water warms up. Don, therefore, has to go 50 to 75 miles offshore in the cold and foggy months of May and June. He goes every day that the weather allows him to do so, leaving the dock at midnight and steaming four to five hours. When he gets to the area he has chosen, he spends another hour searching for likely looking bottom and other signs of fish on his sonar. Having chosen an exact location, he 'sets his trawl;' i.e., strings out mile-long lines of baited hooks across the bottom. Because the bait is a major operational cost, the amount he sets involves a gamble upon how much he will likely catch. After setting the trawl, Don has a half-hour break to eat his lunch and catch a nap. The Cape Island boat is famous for its seaworthiness and payload, but in any kind of sea it bobs like a cork. Don still gets seasick regularly, as do many fishermen.

The work of hauling the fish back in and gutting it can take from three to six hours depending on the size of the set and of the catch. It is punishing work handling up to 30-pound fish on the heaving, offal-strewn open deck. Most long-liners have worked with two or three crew members, but increasingly the smaller-boat owners who only go out for a day have been going it alone because of the cost factor.

Don gets home with his gutted and cleaned load of high quality fresh groundfish usually in the late afternoon. He sells the fish at the wharf to the agent for a plant in the nearby town, and then goes to the bait shed to bait his trawl for the next trip. He hires high school students to help him bait, but has problems because the job requires considerable skill and concentration so that the line will not tangle. He usually does most of it himself and gets home in the early evening. After supper and some time with his family, he gets a few hours sleep before leaving again. If the weather or tides are bad, he will miss trips. This allows him to get caught up with his huge garden, his house building, and his gear maintenance. As the summer wears on, the fish are more plentiful inshore and the weather more stable, so although he does not have to steam so far the trips are more regular and the work of handling the fish becomes heavier. On a poor day he will land under a thousand pounds of mainly smaller cod, hake, and other 'shack;' i. e., low priced species. On a good trip he will get upwards of three thousand pounds with lots of 'steakers'—big cod, haddock, and especially halibut. Through this busy time, his wife is very much a partner in the operation, doing the prodigious bookkeeping and government form-filling correspondence, keeping in touch with fish prices and market conditions, and buying gear and supplies. They make joint decisions about investments, work in B. C., weather conditions, and so on. She also earns income through work outside the home on an occasional basis. In this respect she is no exception. Many of the fishermen's wives work in fish plants along with other nonfishing members of their families.

In the fall, groundfishing tails off as the weather worsens and the stocks recede. Don again goes farther off in more dangerous conditions. But in November the fall lobster season starts and there are a few weeks of work close to shore. By Christmas, it is over. Don either heads to B. C. if he is short of cash to pay his season-end debts, or he gets unemployment insurance and spends the winter repairing his boat and gear and attending fisheries' meetings and conferences.

Don's economic situation is, to say the least, unstable. He requires nearly a thousand dollars a month income just to carry his debt load. Operating costs for bait, gear, and gasoline range between one and two hundred dollars per groundfishing trip. He considers that fish prices today are not bad—he would get a larger boat and share with crew members if the stocks were adequate—but the biggest problem is the unpredictability of the catch. With an operation that is, on his scale, very demanding of both capital and labour, he is threading the needle between rising costs, precarious income, and the physical limits of his endurance. Again, the only thing that keeps him on the rails is his willingness to work hard, and his above-average production and management skills. And yet, we find that he is not unique among inshore fishermen. There are many older fishermen further down the same road he is on, with larger investments and greater incomes combined with the same insecurities and pressures. But there are also very substantial numbers of young fishermen trying to get in and stay in by very much the same methods.

Because in the past few years Don has defined his major problem as that of stocks and conservation, he does not see the small fish companies he sells to as a severe limitation on his situation. In his political analysis, it is the government and the monopoly companies that are his 'enemy'—government because of bureaucracy and confusing and counterproductive policies, and the companies because of the needless abuse of the resource base caused by their offshore fleets, linked to their more powerful influence on government policy. Don is very active in fishermen's meetings and attempts to organise, and has been an effective leader of criticism and protest from time to time. He is a strong believer in unionisation, having seen what has been accomplished on the west coast. He directly attributes the relative backwardness of the Atlantic coast fishery to the lack of an effective fishermen's organisation. His father was active in fishermen's union struggles in the thirties and forties, and Don has grown up with a radical and militant commitment to the overall redevelopment of the industry for the betterment of all. There is an intense and unstable intermingling of cynicism and populist morality, individualism and collective spirit, in his world view. In short, he manifests the consciousness of a person whose whole being hangs in transition, balanced between different cultures, class allegiances, and modes of production.

By examining in some detail the economic status and the work experience of one fisherman, I hope to have provided the basis for a wider analysis of the structure of the inshore fishery in southwest Nova Scotia. As will be shown below, Don is highly representative of inshore fishermen in his region in terms of his production methods and his levels of investment. I would also add, based on my own observations, that his experience of migration, of work in other regions and in other industries, and of the relations of production of wage labour are completely typical of the experiences of most younger fishermen in his region. Don epitomises for me the stratum of fishermen who occupy the most important position in the structure of the inshore industry, and whose views are crucial to the prospects for unionisation of inshore fishermen.

THE INSHORE FISHERY IN SOUTHWEST NOVA SCOTIA

The most developed inshore fishery in Atlantic Canada is undoubtedly in southwest Nova Scotia. Geographically and ecologically the region is highly favoured. The Gulf stream moves close to the land to warm the water and air (and to produce copious amounts of fog) and thus allows for fishing nearly ten months a year. Within reach of small boats are numerous banks which are rich feeding grounds for groundfish. In addition, the area, including the Bay of Fundy, has long been Canada's most productive source of lobster, scallops, and herring.

The relatively long season, proximity to the American market, and the richness and variety of the resource base have made possible over the past decades a prosperity unknown to inshore fishermen in most of the Atlantic region. In fact, their affluence has taken on mythical proportions, with frequently heard stories of millionaire fishermen spending their winters in Florida. Many fishermen in the southwest try to live up to the image—they are prominent in fisheries' conferences calling for free competition, an end to all subsidies to small operators, or the closure of the industry to part-timers in other areas. The arrogance of these ambassadors has done much to fragment and undermine regional efforts at organisation and other attempts to promote a unified inshore fishermen's position on the development of the industry.

There is no question that the advantages of this area are real and that the industry is more developed in terms of incomes, capital investment, and infrastructure than elsewhere. But this does not gainsay real weaknesses and problems. In the summer of 1978, this writer and two colleagues, Nils Kuusisto and Sandy Siegel, did an analysis of these conditions and problems in order to produce a report for the Maritime Fishermen's Union on the prospects for unionisation in the southwest. We limited our observations to Shelburne County, which contains the largest proportion of inshore fishermen, and focused specifically on Cape Sable Island, which is the most developed area within the whole southwest region. Tables 7-1 and 7-2 give a breakdown of boat size and fishing activity in the county.

TABLE 7-1

FISHING BOATS IN SHELBURNE COUNTY

Length of Boat	Cape Sable Island		Remainder of Shelburne County		Total	
Not given	2	(.5%)	—		2	(.2%)
20' or less	81	(21.9%)	115	(21.9%)	196	(21.9%)
21' to 31'	14	(3.8%)	36	(6.8%)	50	(5.6%)
32' to 37'	93	(25.2%)	134	(25.6%)	227	(25.4%)
38' to 45'	168	(45.3%)	194	(36.9%)	362	(40.4%)
46' to 65'	9	(2.4%)	29	(5.5%)	38	(4.2%)
66' to 100'	2	(.5%)	11	(2.1%)	13	(1.4%)
101' and up	1	(.2%)	6	(1.1%)	7	(.8%)
TOTAL	370	(100%)	525	(100%)	895	(100%)

NOTE: 41.3% of the fishing boats in Shelburne County are located in Cape Sable Island, leaving 58.7% in the remainder of the county.

Boat size is a critical factor in analysing the development of the inshore fishery. Almost all the boats between 31 and 65 feet in length are 'Cape Island' boats—a locally designed and built vessel ideally suited to carrying heavy loads in open seas. The boats are made of wood, although fibreglass construction at significantly higher cost is a growing trend. The wooden boats can cost up to $100,000, depending upon size and equipment. (The most frequently built boat is a 39 footer which, with Loran navigational equipment, ship-to-shore radio, radar, sonar, and auto-pilot, will range in cost between $50,000 and $75,000.) Because of heavy use of the boats in all weather conditions, the most productive fishermen usually sell them after three or four years, either to new fishermen locally or to fishermen from outside the southwest area. To give a sense of the scale of capital investment involved and of the backward linkages to the local economy, a conservative estimate would have some ten million dollars of boat construction in the county annually.

To examine the number of vessels of each size is a somewhat crude but generally reliable way to get a sense of the different classes or strata of inshore fishermen. The type and size of boat a fisherman will own will be determined by his investment capabilities on the one hand—his return on previous production, his access to credit, the condition of stocks and markets—and, on the other, by the type of fishing he is in a position to do—lobster, groundfish, or other, inshore, near-shore, or offshore. Boat size in turn determines the kind and quantity of gear used, the kind and quantity of catch handled, the range of territory fished, the number of workers employed in the operation, and the scale of operating capital required. Successful fishermen will move from larger to smaller boats and back because of finely calculated changes in operating costs, fish prices, and so on. There is no simple formula that says bigger is always better, and there is no particular technology that guarantees success under different conditions at different times. As will be seen, the popularity of the intermediate size boat is a direct function of its flexibility and adaptability, and is an indication that general conditions in the industry favour certain levels of investment and certain productive methods at this time. It must be borne in mind that the existence of the inshore fishery in general, and of the particular types of capital employed in it, are expressions of economic conditions and productive relations rather than of some purely technological determinism. It is the *productivity* of particular methods and productive relations that sustains their viability within an overall, socially determined division of labour.

Boats of 20 feet or less are often built by the fisherman himself and are powered by outboard motors. They are used for raking Irish moss, for lobster, and for hand-lining, all within a mile of shore and only in fine weather. Boats between 21 and 31 feet may be sturdier and more professionally constructed, but are similarly limited in their uses. Fishermen operating these vessels tend to be marginal producers—older fishermen on the verge of retirement, occasional producers with substantial employment elsewhere, or young people getting started or just making a bit of money on the side. There will also be a number of fishermen who fish as crew members on larger vessels, but who keep a small boat for lobster or moss-raking.

Boats between 32 and 45 feet are the backbone of the inshore fishery. Depending upon their beam and displacement, they may be capable of two- or three-day-long trips to George's Bank, or manoeuverable enough for one man by himself to fish lobster close to the rocks. Approximately one-half of this fleet will consist of occasional and part-time fishermen (usually in very old boats) who just go for lobster and some hand-lining. However, the great majority of the full-time or professional inshore fishermen (of whom Don is a good example) operate in these boats: approximately 300 fishermen in Shelburne County.

Vessels of 46 to 65 feet operate under more restricted licences and require a three- or four-person crew. The most numerous type of vessel in this class is rigged for long-lining only and will go all-year-round to the farthest reaches of the offshore banks for trips of up to a week. The boats of 65 feet or more are in the great majority of cases owned by fish companies and are operated by full-time wage-earning skippers and crews. There are long-lining, offshore lobster and other trawl (or 'dragger') vessels in this class. Boats above 100 feet in length are company-owned side draggers and the newer steel, stern draggers.

Of the vessels based in Shelburne County (which contains three large fishing ports with medium-sized fish processing facilities—Lockeport, Shelburne, and Clark's Harbour), only six percent are larger than 45 feet. This clearly illustrates the small number of large-scale entrepreneur-operators and of wage-earning skippers and crew members. Among the intermediate-sized boats there are a number that are company owned, or that employ wage-earning crew members (as opposed to the more usual share method—one equal share to the skipper, each crew member, and to the boat for operating costs above and beyond the bait and supplies for the trip), or both. Indications are that while company-owned boats under 65 feet were a rarity in the past, they are now increasingly common. We were not, however, able to get good statistical information on this trend.

TABLE 7-2

FISHING ACTIVITY IN SHELBURNE COUNTY

	Cape Sable Island	Remainder of Shelburne County	Total
Lobster only	272 (73%)	144 (27.3%)	
Lobster and Hand-lining	0 (0)	142 (26.9%)	
			558 (62.1%)
Lobster and Long-lining	74 (19.9%)	177 (33.6%)	251 (27.9%)
Long-lining only	17 (4.6%)	36 (6.8%)	53 (5.9%)
Otter trawl only (under 65')	6 (1.6%)	16 (3%)	22 (2.4%)
Offshore Lobster		8 (1.5%)	8 (.9%)
Herring Seiner	1 —		1 —
Other	1 —	4 —	5 —

Turning to Table 7-2, we see how fishing effort is distributed across different methods and technologies. The most striking characteristic of the industry in Shelburne County[1] is the overwhelming dependence on lobster. Nearly three-quarters of the fishermen on Cape Sable Island and nearly two-thirds of those in the county are licensed for lobster only. Altogether, 93% of the fishermen in Cape Sable and 96% of those in the county, fish lobster. This dependence on lobster is responsible for the profound vulnerability of the inshore industry in southwest Nova Scotia. As mentioned above, because of overfishing the catches have dropped by as much as 50% in the past three years. While the shock has been somewhat cushioned by a very substantial rise in price, the more marginal fishermen—setting fewer than 100 traps—have been hit very hard. In the summer of 1978 there was much evidence of fishermen switching their effort to other products, particularly herring, and to more remunerative methods of catching groundfish. As this transition proceeds, there will be growing strains on stocks for other species. However, there is little possibility of any other product being sufficient in quantity and value to replace lobster as the income staple.

These pressures are evident in other parts of the industry as well. The effects of the generalised overfishing of groundfish stocks throughout the Atlantic fishery are being felt keenly in the southwest. One major consequence of this is the shift away from the traditional hook and line methods. The growing use of otter trawl and gill nets is considered irresponsible[2] by committed long-lining fishermen, and there is serious disunity and often open conflict within fishing communities on this issue. There is also growing conflict between communities as fishermen crowd in on each other's traditionally defined territories. As with lobster, where poaching and overtrapping (beyond prescribed limits) are growing phenomena, there seems to be a tendency for 'end game' attitudes to emerge as catches decline and economic insecurity grows.

An additional source of concern for these fishermen is the current instability of Canadian-American trade relations in the fishery. The declaration of 200-mile zones has generated a dispute over access to and ownership of George's Bank, the richest fishing ground in the region. This issue has exacerbated a more basic competitive conflict between American and Nova Scotian fishermen over markets. The American fishermen have recently agitated to have the border closed to Canadian imports that undercut their own products in the Boston market. They argue that government subsidies keep Nova Scotian fish much cheaper than their own, and that the unfair competition has seriously inhibited the development of a domestic inshore fishery. For fishermen in the southwest, easy access by truck to the Boston market is crucial to the higher than average prices they get for their fresh product, and is the basis on which they have maintained some independence in spite of the emerging monopoly structure of production, processing, and marketing for the Atlantic Canadian fishery as a whole.

In summary, then, the inshore fishing industry in Shelburne County at this time exhibits the following major characteristics: (1) While being unquestionably the most developed inshore fishery in the Atlantic region, it is very unevenly developed internally and depends for both direct productivity and labour supply on a very substantial number of marginal and near-marginal producers. In spite of its many advantages, the county is distinguished from other parts of the Atlantic inshore fishery more by the presence of a few high-income fishermen than by better incomes and working conditions and more secure futures for all or most of the fishermen. (2) Two of the major advantages of the southwest area—abundance of fish stocks and proximity to the American market—are seriously threatened at the present time. Should present trends continue, fishermen will experience, together with the rising production costs that are general throughout the industry, substantial drops in income due to smaller catches. They will also have fewer options for the marketing of their fish, which may adversely affect price and bring them into more direct relationships of dependency with the monopoly fish companies. (3) Following from the above points, the industry in Shelburne County is in the process of internal restructuring. While occasional and part-time fishermen may be reduced in numbers, the full-time professional fisherman is also under severe pressure and is being forced to change operating methods and technology, and to increase continually his capital investment. This process is giving rise to contradictory attitudes and behaviour. On the one hand, there is greater competition and conflict, and evidence of less responsible treatment of the resource base. On the other hand, there are many indications of interest on the part of fishermen in collective action to defend their positions in the industry and to increase their control over policies, prices, markets, and so on. This growing consciousness of the need for collective organisation and action is most in evidence among the younger full-time fishermen struggling to stay in fishing and committed therefore to the overall development of the industry as the prerequisite for their own individual progress.

THE STRUCTURE OF THE INDUSTRY

As has been seen, the industry in Shelburne County is predominantly a small-boat fishery. But it must be emphasised that this is not in itself necessarily a justification for assuming the backwardness or underdevelopment of the fishery in the area. The reality is more complex. While there are many marginal producers utilising marginally productive methods and technology, there are also cases where a small but relatively highly capitalised vessel operated by a highly skilled fisherman is the most productive, cost effective, and environmentally sound way to catch particular products in particular locations. It is not by accident that there are so few large vessels located in Shelburne County (or for that matter in the southwest generally).

This point has relevance to the entire fishery in the Atlantic region. For authority on this matter, we need only turn to an analysis presented by no less a figure than the former federal minister of fisheries, Romeo LeBlanc:

Although none of the following definitions is hard and fast, generally the Atlantic 'offshore' fleet means the 250 or so large steel vessels, mostly processor owned, over 150 gross registered tons and over 100 feet in length. With crews of twelve to fifteen, offshore vessels employ perhaps 3,500 fishermen, and they bring in 35 or 40% of the landed value of Atlantic Canada's fishery.

Next come 900 intermediate vessels between 25 and 150 tons and generally ranging from 50 to 100 feet. Mostly owned by fishermen, they can cost anywhere between $40,000 and $900,000. Of intermediate range, they may leave home for a day or a week or longer. They typically fish one-third to one-half of the days of the year, taking part in the groundfish, scallop, herring, shrimp, crab, seal, and other fisheries. With a usual crew of five to eight men ... they employ perhaps 6,000 or 7,000 fishermen. They bring in about 15% of the Atlantic landed value....

Finally come the true inshore vessels, under 25 tons and generally under 50 feet. Gillnetters, line-fishing craft, trap-tenders, and the like, they generally cost from the low thousands up to $40,000.[3] They usually stay within a day's sail of home, although some make longer trips well offshore, and they fish one-quarter to one-third the days of the year. They dominate the $50 million lobster fishery, they take perhaps half the groundfish, and they fish for almost every other species: herring, scallops, squid, salmon, Irish moss, whatever you care to name. *They bring in about one-half the Atlantic fishery's value*. These boats number about 28,000—some 95% of all Atlantic fishing vessels, and they employ roughly three-quarters of Atlantic Canada's 40,000 fishermen.[4]

LeBlanc goes on to describe the inshore and near-shore (50 to 100 foot vessels) fishery as the 'backbone of the industry' and reports that it far exceeds 'the offshore fleet in value of landings, numbers of boats, and number of fishermen.' He further notes that offshore fishermen earn between $15,000 and $22,000 per annum 'thanks to year round fishing and collective bargaining,' and that near-shore and inshore fishermen have reached income levels averaging between $9,000 and $12,000 per annum from all sources (including UIC) in the very recent past.

While we would dispute the romanticism with which the minister espouses the cause of the 'individual, independent owner-operator,' and can find fault with some of his facts, the core of his argument still holds; small-boat fishermen are a critically important element in the overall structure of the industry. They are important in terms of the gross quantity of their production, in terms of the quality of that product compared to other methods of producing it, and in terms of their (to this point) exclusive ability to harvest certain resources, in particular lobster. While modernisation of the industry over the past two decades has put considerable pressure on the more marginal producers, it has seen the consolidation of a position in the production process by inshore fishermen utilising advanced methods and technology on a small scale.

In discussing underdevelopment in the Atlantic fishing industry, and the struggle against it, we should be led therefore to consider issues of ownership and control, returns to labour and to investment, market distortions and inadequacies, and rational use of the resource base, rather than focusing intensely on the linear transition from labour-intensive to capital-intensive large-scale methods.

The real issue with respect to development is to identify the social and political conditions under which a maximal safe utilisation of the resource can proceed over the long term through the most rational integration of appropriate techniques and labour/capital mixes. The creation of such political and social conditions implies the mobilisation of a social base for real development of the industry as one important dimension of a struggle for the real development of the region as a whole.

STRATEGIES FOR ORGANISING INSHORE FISHERMEN

There is no question that inshore fishermen are turning to unionisation in increasing numbers. Over the past three years, close to 2,000 fishermen have joined the Maritime Fishermen's Union in New Brunswick (where the union began) and in Prince Edward Island and northeastern Nova Scotia. Organisational work is just now beginning in southwest Nova Scotia, and is showing substantial signs of success. What is equally notable is the decline of several well-established fishermen's associations in these areas and outside. As in agriculture and other industries, associations have been a government- and company-favoured approach in which fishermen participate on an individual, voluntary basis in discussions about local management and policy without collective bargaining or any structured role. As in the federations of agriculture, the fishermen's associations have tended to be dominated by the biggest operators who profit most from close consultation with government. Associations have also served as important networks for political patronage. Their decline is indicative of the increasing impotence of such traditional mechanisms of social control among inshore fishermen.

Unionisation could be a process that mobilises fishermen to participate in the transformation and redevelopment of the whole industry. This would imply the wresting of control over the shape and direction of development from the monopoly corporations. The achievement of rights and capacities to bargain for the price of their products is only a partial step in this direction, and one fraught with dangers. If the producers get a higher return, this will accelerate the process by which the companies switch to labour-saving technology which will displace small producers and re-establish corporate control over the production process. Besides creating unemployment and abusing the resource base, the high technology approach to development would intensify the overall indebtedness of the industry and thereby further entrench foreign control: in other words, the continuing 'development of underdevelopment.' Up to now, all that has offset total commitment to this form of development has been the relative ease with which the companies have been able to exploit small producers. Unionisation disturbs this delicate arrangement.

This is not to say that unionisation should not address the question of the price of fish, for this is indeed a crucial issue for most fishermen, but rather that the issue of price should never be separated from problems of control and structure in the industry. This raises questions of class interest and class consciousness among inshore fishermen.

Contrary to prevailing Marxist approaches, this writer has concluded that straightforward delineations between petit bourgeois, independent commodity producer, and proletarianised worker are not necessarily useful in trying to understand the political economy of inshore fishing today. The simple fact is that most inshore fishermen operate within all of these relationships to the production process through the course of a year, or most have had substantial experience with the range of positions. They own their own capital, and their income comes from exchange. However, they frequently move in and out of the wage-labour market, are regularly unemployed, and have very unstable incomes. Most have experienced extended periods of very low incomes and of marginal status as producers. While they have often had substantial work experience outside the fishing industry altogether, they have also experienced a wide range of production relations within the industry. They have served as crew members on other boats and have rented out their own capital and labour. They often still produce within their family unit a finished or semifinished product (such as lobster traps and other nets; salt, dried, or pickled fish; dressed fish, etc.) if market opportunities dictate. Many fishermen also engage in hunting and small-scale agriculture. They may have fished for a co-operative, or on contract to a company, or within the traditional truck system. Perhaps most important, if they do not do all of these things themselves, other people around them do and these experiences are all part of the culture of inshore fishermen. Any particular productive relationship is therefore over-determined by knowledge or experience of alternatives. Any particular consciousness of class interest is qualified by contradictory objective and subjective factors. This complexity generates within the political and economic struggles of inshore fishermen a dialectical intensity that obviates simple resolutions and predictable outcomes.

The ideological pitch of inshore fishermen's associations, most of them goverment-sponsored, has been to the fisherman as independent producer. Free and competitive markets and a consultative relationship with government were held out as the most effective mechanisms for the development of the inshore industry. Collective bargaining was posed as a threat to the independence of the individual producer. The failure of this line of argument to mobilise fishermen into associations (or, more accurately, to demobilise fishermen's unions) in the past few years has been manifest. In southwest Nova Scotia, the Nova Scotia Fishermen's Association is maintaining a tenuous existence by modelling itself more and more along union lines. It has severed its financial dependence on government, and is attempting to rebuild a membership base through militant public postures on policy issues and through involvement in price negotiations. However, it still maintains an anti-unionisation posture and promotes an ideology of harmony of interest among all strata in the industry. It remains to be seen whether it can hold th se contradictory tendencies together, and whether it can attract sufficient membership to sustain itself financially. My own expectation is that rising pro-unionisation sentiment among small and intermediate operators will split the association irreparably in the very near future.

Co-operatives have similarly addressed the petit-bourgeois and independent-producer interests of the fishermen. They have held out the promise of control over markets and processing as an alternative to monopoly structure, and have subtly appealed to the most productive fishermen to consolidate their advantages over their fellow fishermen. Again, the appeal of this ideology has suffered serious setbacks in the immediate past throughout the Atlantic region. Fishermen have accepted the reality of monopoly structure, and they understand well the role and limits of reformist institutions within that structure. In fact, fishermen joining the union in New Brunswick and Prince Edward Island have made it abundantly clear that their main motivation has been to gain leverage over the co-ops of which they were members. The co-ops have responded with a virulent red-baiting, anti-union campaign.

While these developments indicate the clear preference of fishermen for unionisation, the fishermen obviously do not approach this alternative with a straightforwardly proletarian consciousness. As small producers with a strong mythology of independence and individualism, they are highly oriented to control and local-power issues as well as to the struggle over the exchange value of their labour or their products. They are therefore very suspicious of highly centralised forms of organisation, of integration with workers outside the fishing industry (as for example in the Canadian Food and Allied Workers Union), or of leadership within their organisation by persons who have not proven themselves as fishermen.

The crucial point in all of this is that the unionisation process must take into account these complexities and must aim to make the most of the possibilities arising out of the overall struggle for development of the industry. From the point of view of their productivity, both actual and potential, inshore fishermen represent a solid base for development. Unionisation must mobilise the social and political power to defend this base against the incursions of the monopoly sector backed by the state. Once their position with respect to policy issues, the structuring of the industry, marketing, the division of the resource base, and so on has been defended, the organised inshore fishermen can then address economic issues of price and return for labour without the inevitable trade-off of income for reduced control over the production process. Within this process of collectivisation and integration of inshore fishermen, consolidation of political and economic power, and therefore enhanced returns for products and labour, it is quite likely that modernisation will continue to alter the capital/labour ratio in an authentically developmental way. Thus the multiple relationships of fishermen to the production process will be gradually rationalised without the usual generation of substantial surplus labour.

In short, the contradictory nature of the class experience and therefore of the class consciousness of inshore fishermen, if approached correctly, can be a very positive factor in the unionisation process. Because they are not alienated from production to the point where their labour is in their own consciousness a commodity, inshore fishermen are preoccupied with issues of power, control, and autonomy. Their objective experience provides a basis for understanding that these values cannot be realised or defended through individual relationships to the state and the monopoly sector. On the other hand, collectivisation is only acceptable to the extent that it does not subsume goals of self-determination. On the basis of considerable contact with inshore fishermen and direct analysis of their productive relations and class consciousness, this writer has concluded that what is required is a movement in which a democratic, decentralised unionisation process is integrated with a political struggle for the restructuring and rational development of the fishing industry as a whole. While the movement is not at this stage a self-consciously socialist one, the logic of both the struggle itself and the requirements of modernisation and development will place socialism squarely and inexorably in our paths.

NOTES

1. We were not able to get figures on hand-lining on Cape Sable Island, but for the remainder of the county it is singled out as a discrete activity. Until recently, fishermen did not have to have a licence for hand-lining, which part-time and occasional fishermen engage in irregularly. We can assume that most of the fishermen listed as 'lobster only' on Cape Sable also do some hand-lining and also put out nets for herring or mackerel to be used for home consumption and for bait.

2. This is a complex issue that cannot be analysed here in detail. In general, it is argued that fish caught by long-lining methods are of a more uniform size, are fresher, and are undamaged in the catching process. Drag nets may damage bottom feeding and breeding grounds, kill the fish prematurely, and catch many sizes and species indiscriminately. Gill nets also kill the fish prematurely, are somewhat indiscriminate, and are a serious hazard to fish life when they get cut free in storms. Fishermen turn to these latter methods because they require less labour and lower operating costs after initial investment.

3. These figures on cost of boats and on length of season more accurately describe parts of the region other than southwest Nova Scotia.

4. Quoted from a speech by the Hon. Romeo LeBlanc, then minister of fisheries, at the regional conference for the 50th anniversary of the extension department of St Francis Xavier University, 5 July 1978. Emphasis added.

NEWFOUNDLAND

8 The Capitalist Underdevelopment of Nineteenth-Century Newfoundland

Steven Antler

INTRODUCTION AND PRELIMINARY ISSUES

Conventional economic wisdom often has it that regional economic disparities express little more than fundamental disparities in the physical economic potential of regions. Climate, economic accessibility of natural resources, location, and so on, are, according to this view, the ultimate determinants of a region's wealth or poverty. Given the presence of genuine economic potential within a region, it is sometimes explicitly but more typically implicitly argued that appropriate levels and types of capital and labour will automatically either develop within or find their way to the region, through the workings of the free market.

Like so much of conventional wisdom, the geographical determinist explanation of regional economic disparities is circular which explains, perhaps, why is is seldom put forward explicitly. The contention that a region is poor owing to its physical geography cannot be disproved, for the simple reason that it cannot be *proved*, except in such clear-cut cases as deserts or polar regions. We have with geographical determinism a simple, appealing, and completely useless theory of regional economic disparities. It is with this theory, however, that many discussions of the striking disparities between Newfoundland and the rest of Canada begin and end. This is most unfortunate for Newfoundland itself, since the province regularly faces an array of proposed and sometimes implemented policies based upon the conventional wisdom of geographical determinism.[1]

Newfoundland is Canada's newest and poorest province. Its physical geography resembles that of Norway and Iceland, while its standard of living is significantly lower than theirs. Newfoundland is a political unit formed from North America's oldest community, and its history includes a fascinating set of contradictions and puzzles. Retarded colonisation, sparse public versus large private provision of economic infrastructure, self-imposed political, economic, and to some degree social isolation, the rise of household production coupled with the decline of economic activity mediated by the market mechanism, are all facets of Newfoundland's history. Like the economic stagnation of the island throughout much of the nineteenth century, these facets have yet to be fully explained in published literature dealing with this history.[2] The purpose of the present essay is to fill this gap in the literature.

THE BASIC ISSUE

At issue is why one province of Canada—Newfoundland—is distinctly poorer than the rest of the nation. The casual visitor to Newfoundland may have no problems resolving the issue, since, relative to most places in North America, Newfoundland is bleak, somewhat depressing in terms of weather patterns, and apparently deficient in economic potential.

Newfoundland's most striking geographic characteristic is, and always has been, its intolerance for any but the most accommodating forms of agriculture. With the retreat of the last glacier, Newfoundland lost almost all of its topsoil, and the same weather patterns that give Newfoundland a damper yet more temperate climate than that of central Canada give Newfoundland far less sunshine.

It interesting that the only genuinely comparative data regarding economic performance (and perhaps potential) of the various regions of British North America during the first decade of the nineteenth century seem to rank Newfoundland as the most promising in all areas but agriculture.[3] Acreage cleared in per capita terms is strikingly lower in Newfoundland (by at least 50%) than in the rest of British North America. Per capita value of all commodities produced, however, runs from over 100% to a bit over 35% higher in Newfoundland than in the rest of British North America. Similarly, per capita trade surplus and per capita value of capital stock are much higher in Newfoundland (see Table 8-1).

A great deal of fragmentary but still persuasive data suggest that these figures reflect an early wave of diversification and growth in the Newfoundland economy that was not reversed until the mid 1830s. Shipbuilding had been established in Newfoundland by 1718,[4] and was maintained throughout the eighteenth century. By the first decade of the nineteenth century, Newfoundland may well have been able to maintain her fleet intact through domestic economic activity alone.[5] Copper mining was first attempted in 1776-77, and within sixty years Newfoundland also had three operating corn mills, established limestone quarries, and a modest export trade in planks, oars, and other wooden smallwares.[6] D. W. Prowse's description of the early seal fishery, as well as James Murray's lamentful contrast of economic conditions in late nineteenth-century Newfoundland to those existing much earlier in the century tend to confirm what these and other data suggest: the first three decades, relative to the rest of the nineteenth century, were ones of growth, prosperity, and diversification for the Newfoundland economy.[7]

The basic issue addressed by this study can be stated as follows: given—even according to the rather shaky logic of geographical determinism—that early nineteenth-century Newfoundland showed every sign of economic potential relative to the rest of British North America, how is

TABLE 8-1

INDICATORS OF ECONOMIC PERFORMANCE
FOR REGIONS OF BRITISH NORTH AMERICA, CIRCA 1812

| | PER CAPITA VALUE (£) | | | | Acres cleared |
	Output, including that of the fisheries	Exports	Imports	Capital Stock	per capita
Upper and Lower Canada	24	1	4	27	13
New Brunswick	32	12	10	38	10
Nova Scotia	26	6	5	59	10
Cape Breton	23	3	2	79	10
Prince Edward Island	43	23	19	159	10
Newfoundland	59	39	32	368	5

SOURCE: P. Colquhoun, *A treatise on the wealth, power and resources of the British Empire, in every quarter of the world including the East Indies* (New York, 1965).

it that the Newfoundland economy tended toward stagnation and decline from approximately 1835 to the mid 1880s?[8]

TWO UNSATISFACTORY EXPLANATIONS OF ECONOMIC STAGNATION IN NINETEENTH-CENTURY NEWFOUNDLAND

Two of the most compelling and ultimately most puzzling aspects of Newfoundland's economic history are England's anticolonisation policy towards the island, and the rather bizarre credit system under which the Newfoundland fishery operated during much of the nineteenth century. These aspects, combined with explicit or implicit geographical determinism, have all too often been deemed sufficient to explain Newfoundland's poor economic performance.

Newfoundland was discovered by John Cabot in 1497. It was the regular workplace for certain of the British people by the reign of Henry VIII, and by the time of James I, if not earlier, there were British people who might well have called Newfoundland their home. Despite all this, it was not until 1832 that Newfoundland was granted representative government by Great Britain. Up to that point colonisation was in many respects illegal, the existence of a flourishing community on the island notwithstanding. This anticolonisation policy is typically explained as stemming from: a combination of chance and circumstance (e.g., England's reaction to the American revolution prevented a reversal of her policy toward Newfoundland); the victory of lobbying by special interest groups like the 'western adventurers,' those West Country masters who wished the continuation of the visiting Bristish fishery at Newfoundland; and the triumph of mercantilist ideology that saw in the visiting fishery a 'nursery for seamen,' and thus an economic activity that contributed to British naval supremacy. This rather striking policy—unique in British history—has yet to be fully explained. Special-interest and lobbying groups existed elsewhere in the Empire, yet nowhere did their activities appear more successful, at least in affecting *official* thought on the matter, than in the issue of Newfoundland's colonisation.[9] Similarly, other areas in the Empire were valuable in the training of seamen, and clear as the mercantilist rationale[10] for the original exclusion of Newfoundland from the plantation system might have been, the maintenance of this early policy for over one and a half centuries is difficult to understand.

Just as curious is the sustained existence of the truck system, a nonmarket barter system of credit under which the Newfoundland fishery operated for much of the nineteenth century.[11] The question of how prices and market systems are formed haunts the history of economic thought like Banquo's ghost. Where history itself is used to illustrate the nature and origins of prices and markets, the exposition usually takes the form of apocryphal stories showing how truck and barter gave way to market exchange. During the first decades of the nineteenth century, as Newfoundland's truck system began to be legitimised through various court decisions,[12] Newfoundland moved from a situation in which economic exchange was more typically mediated by prices to one in which truck and barter were, if not universal outside urban areas, then nearly so. In effect, we have with nineteenth-century Newfoundland an economy that gave up the price mechanism. As the price mechanism declined in the Newfoundland fishery, wage labour gave way to household production. Insofar as it is typical, historically, for household production to precede production organised through the employment of wage labour, we have here another example of how the 'typical' flow of events was reversed in nineteenth-century Newfoundland.

Britain's anticolonisation policy—identified in much of the literature as 'retarded colonisation'[13]—has been incorrectly credited with being fully responsible for economic stagnation in nineteenth-century Newfoundland. Harold Innis, applying his general interpretation of Canadian economic history[14] to Newfoundland in too eager a fashion, suggested that

the growth of the [resident] Newfoundland fishery and the increasing importance of resident commercial interests brought to an end the influence of the West Country ports ... and established government machinery designed to stimulate agriculture, industry, and trade by such developments as steamship services, the beginnings of railway construction, and the adoption of tariff protection.[15]

Innis's Canadian model ascribed to central government the roles of mediator of varying class interests, and of agent fostering economic development. Applying his general model to the specific Newfoundland case, he unintentionally glossed over an extremely important point: there was at least a fifty-year gap between the decline in influence of the West Country ports and the government activities he described. The most striking feature of New-foundland's resident government throughout much of the nineteenth century was its apparent interest in hindering, rather than fostering, diversification and development.[16] The activities noted by Innis were more the reversal than the culmination of a trend.

As with retarded colonisation, so the truck system and the rise of household production have been given perhaps too much credit for having produced economic stagnation and decline in nineteenth-century Newfoundland. Basing his argument on an 1882 document, S. Ryan writes that

the general insecurity arising out of the cod fishery led to the disappearance of the large [employers of fishermen] and the development of small family enterprises with the men catching the fish and the wives and children doing the [jobs of curing the fish on shore]. This apparently resulted in a deterioration in quality. Thus the [period during which this took place, the 1830s], was probably the major turning point in the internal operations of the fish trade.[17]

While he identifies external factors related to marketing as being important in explaining declines in Newfoundland's codfish trade during the nineteenth century, Ryan suggests that deterioration of the product, caused by the rise of household production, was a primary cause of Newfoundland's declining share of the world market for dried cod.[18]

There is no question that retarded colonisation and the rise of household production (accompanied by the truck system) had important economic consequences for Newfoundland. Yet to explain economic stagnation in nineteenth-century Newfoundland as being simply the predictable outcome of retarded colonisation and household production is to avoid the most interesting questions of all: *why* was the colonisation of Newfoundland retarded, and what were the *causes* of the decline of the price mechanism and the rise of household production?

The answers to these questions lie not in the physical geography of Newfoundland, but rather in the general political economy of colonial frontiers. 'A new colony,' observed Adam Smith, 'must always for some time be under-stocked in proportion to the extent of its territory, and more under-peopled in proportion to the extent of its stock, than the greater part of other countries.'[19] Relative to the mother country, great disproportions exist among factors of production along the colonial frontier. The economic history of the colony cannot be understood except in the light of these disproportions.

THE PURE ECONOMIC THEORY OF COLONIAL EXPLOITATION—BACKGROUND

Framing its questions in terms of the economics of international trade, A. C. Pigou's *The economics of welfare* (1918) is perhaps the most well known orthodox treatment of certain analytical issues, central to the economics of colonial frontiers, that were first raised by E. G. Wakefield in 1833 and later dealt with in some detail by Marx.[20] These issues centre around the question of whether the market mechanism, when left solely to its own devices, can actually guide economic activity in such a way that resources allocated to uses in increasing-cost industries are utilised economically, rather than overutilised.[21] Framed in terms of an elaborate analogy, Pigou's reasoning is a convenient starting point for our discussion of the pure economic theory of colonial exploitation.

Take two roads, both going from point 'a' to point 'b.' The first road is wide, perfectly able to carry all the traffic that might care to utilise it, but bumpy, poorly graded, and generally unattractive. The second road is narrow, subject to congestion, but built smoothly, well graded, and quite attractive in contrast to the first road. Let a sufficiently large number of trucks needing to go from 'a' to 'b' decide, independently, which road to take. The outcome is that the smooth and well-graded road congests to the point that transport costs are the same on both roads. The last trucks to arrive will find themselves to be indifferent as between the two roads. Yet were some outside agency (e.g., government) wisely to reroute some traffic from the narrow to the wide road, welfare would undoubtedly be increased. Trucks routed from the narrow to the wide road would experience no increase in transport cost, since the wide road is not subject to congestion. Trucks *not* rerouted from the narrow to the wide road find congestion decreased, and consequently find transport costs lower than would otherwise have been the case.

We have here not an obscure exercise in the economics of transportation, but rather a fairly powerful argument favouring government intervention in the long-run operations of capitalist economies. The wide and bumpy road may be considered analogous to any constant-cost industry, or to any region or country having industries, economic activities, etc., subject to constant costs; the narrow road, analogous to any increasing-cost (or decreasing-returns) industry, or again, to any region with economic activities subject to increasing costs. The argument thus leads to the apparent conclusion that fixed-factor rent can be maximised only through appropriate government taxation of the increasing-cost industries, or through appropriate taxation of economic enterprise within the country or region with industries subject to increasing costs.

Whether it effectively put to rest what Pigou saw as the major issues, F. H. Knight's response to Pigou, originally published in 1924, unintentionally demonstrated how sound Pigou's reasoning was when applied to specific social and historical circumstances.[22] Knight, with his nearly perfect faith in the ability of the price system to assess costs and parcel out rewards correctly, argued that Pigou implied that his

argument holds good over the whole field of investment whether investment is free to choose between uses subject to cost curves of different slope. Take, for example, two farms, one of superior quality, the other marginal or free land. Would not labor and capital go the the better farm, until the product per man became equal to the product to be obtained from the marginal land? If so, it is clear that the total product of all the labor and capital could be increased, as in the case of the roads [in Pigou's two-road analogy], by transferring some of it from the superior to the inferior farm. This application of the reasoning will probably suggest the fallacy to any one familiar with conventional economic theory. The statement does in fact indicate what would happen *if no one owned the superior farm*. But under private appropriation and self-seeking exploitation of the land the course of events is very different. It is in fact the social function of ownership to prevent this excessive investment in superior situations.[23]

Social scientists might dispute Knight's contention that the social function of ownership is to prevent investment in superior situations—they might, indeed, suggest that ascribing social functions to various institutions is a bit teleological. No one, however, would dispute that along a colonial frontier, where it is very likely that the superior farm in Knight's farming analogy is in fact owned, initially, by no one, it is Pigou's rather than Knight's reasoning that is more applicable. Unlike the natural resources of the Old World, the resources of the colonial frontier are still being appropriated. No guarantee exists that they will be appropriated in such a way that they will ultimately be utilised economically. Colonial governments may or may not act in such a way as to ensure that settlement proceeds slowly enough that the colony's resources are not overutilised.

Conventional microeconomic theory, then, suggests that colonial frontiers face an inherent barrier to economic development. Given rapid settlement of a frontier, it is likely that rent accruing to resources will be spread among many owners. These resources will thus be utilised, in the aggregate, less economically than would have been the case had there been fewer owners[24] to manage the rate of utilisation of the colony's resources. If output in the colony increases, it does so not because of changes in the organisation or technique of production, but rather because more resources are appropriated by more producers using the same techniques as all others.[25] Growth may take place, but economic development—in the textbook sense of the term, namely, a sustained change in the technique of production which gives rise to sustained increases in the average productivity of labour—will not materialise. Further, if an important element in economic development is the accumulation of economic surplus (or profit, or surplus value, or whatever one chooses to call it), colonial frontiers face another barrier to development: since resources are overutilised, rent is spread among many owners and is, in the aggregate, much smaller than it could be. There is, to put the matter simply, less economic surplus to accumulate than would otherwise be the case.

Colonial frontiers, where relatively abundant natural resources are combined with relatively scarce capital and labour, have a natual tendency towards resource-based growth, rather than resource-based development. The pure economic theory of colonial exploitation explains how a colony's economic history will be informed by this natural tendency.

THE PURE ECONOMIC THEORY OF COLONIAL EXPLOITATION

As with so many other aspects of Marx's work, his treatment of economic development is one that rightly may be judged as having exerted extensive influence on later work, be this work appreciative or critical. While a comprehensive review of Marx's influence on the economics of development is not yet available, it can be said that his insight into the question of why economic development occurs has informed the entire literature dealing with this problem. Among the critical literature, Rostow's continuing assertion that a 'non-Communist manifesto' can better explain the economics of development provides the best example of popular yet unpersuasive treatments of the issues involved.[26] J. Hick's *A theory of economic history*—self-consciously non-Marxist yet willing to admit that it deals with the 'kind of thing that was attempted by Marx'—provides what is perhaps the best sympathetic non-Marxist treatment of the same issues.[27] The very fact that Rostow and Hicks each feel the need to spell out the relationship between their views and those of Marx underlines the point just made.

The current textbook distinction between development and growth can be traced to Marx's work, although he did not use these particular terms. Recognising that output might expand when smallholding is extended, Marx suggested that handicraft industries, cottage industry, and so on, could be regarded more as a potential impediment to industrial development than as its 'first stage.' He wrote:

The transition from the feudal mode of production is two-fold. The producer becomes merchant and capitalist, in contrast to the natural agricultural economy and the guild-bound handicrafts of the medieval urban industries. This is the real revolutionising path. Or else, the merchant establishes direct sway over production. However much [the latter] serves historically as a stepping-stone—witness the English 17th-century clothier, who brings the weavers, independent as they are, under his control by selling their wool to them and buying their cloth—it cannot by itself contribute to the overthrow of the old mode of production, but tends rather to preserve and retain it as its precondition.... This system presents everywhere an obstacle to the real capitalist mode of production and goes under with its development.[28]

So often incorrectly identified as a technological determinist, Marx stresses in this extract technical inertia rather than change. Where increased orders can be met by more enterprises sharing a common technique, technique tends to stagnate even though the number of enterprises tends to expand. Growth, not development, is the tendency.

Marx's emphasis when he deals with the development versus growth issue is, in contrast to modern non-Marxist treatments of the matter, both pessimistic and sound. If any current ruling class can continue to capture economic surplus[29] without directing its attention to the tasks of technical change, there is no reason *why* it should bother, to use Marx's terms, to 'revolutionise the means of production.' Rostow's tautological system of stages of economic growth—traditional society, preconditions, take-off, etc.—has no apparent basis in theory, relying instead on the reader's sharing the author's implicit assumption that economic progress is the 'natural' state of affairs of mankind. Hicks's *A theory of economic history*, providing as good a set of insights as any orthodox treatment of western economic history, disappoints resoundingly when it deals with the growth versus development issue. What is the source of the transition from handicrafts to industrial production? Hicks asks. He answers:

It is science. It has always been true that the economy grows by the exploitation of new opportunities for investment ... but while in the former phase the exploration was mainly geographical, in the latter it has been scientific exploration of the physical world in a much wider sense. It is science, especially physical science, which has opened up such seemingly illimitable prospects for industry.[30]

As with Rostow, progress is assumed by Hicks to be the natural state of affairs of mankind. All orthodox economic history sees history as the succession of differing and progressively 'better' ways mankind has succeeeded in meeting its material needs. The engine of progress—science for Hicks, time for Rostow—is outside the model, acting as a prime mover. In contrast, Marx's works, and that of those influenced by him, emphasises that history is best understood as a succession of differing ways that various classes have been exploited by other classes. As something of a byproduct, varying economic systems, which meet people's material needs, in various ways, have arisen.

Thus Marx comes up with no clearcut explanation of the transition from handicraft production to early modern industrial production. He sees this transition as fundamentally a movement from one mode of *exploitation* to another; his explanation, on close examination, amounts to the contention that the technique of production remains unchanged up to that point in history when exploitation cannot by carried out *without* some such change. The continuing reality of exploitation in precapitalist as well as capitalist society led Marx to emphasise, in his discussion of early industrialism, the *stability* of industrial technique rather than the propensity of later capitalism to revolutionise constantly the means of production. Thus modern orthodox treatments of the transition to industrial society tend to treat unconvincingly a problem which Marx, given his direct concerns, had no need to deal with. History for Marx was not the record of increasing prosperity for all. He could, without diminishing the rigour of his main argument, rely on the simply circular proposition that the transition from preindustrial to industrial capitalism took place when it was no longer possible for the former system to continue.

Where early industrial capitalism developed rather than grew, Marx argued, two movements occurred simultaneously. First, accelerated commerce exerted a dissolving influence on the old mode of production —i.e., the very acceleration of all forms of economic activity put stress on social and economic institutions that formerly stabilised such activity. Second, the widening of markets (this widening being either identical to or causing the accelerated commerce) and increased volume of sales pressured merchants and producers alike to seek out new techniques of production, in aid of meeting the demands of wider markets.[31] Exploitation is an element of both preindustrial and industrial capitalism, and under both systems the owning class captures economic surplus through its ability to exploit nonowners. Industrial capitalism replaces preindustrial capitalism, according to Marx, not simply because owners wish to grow more wealthy, but because they can no longer continue to do as well as in the past without carrying out changes in the techniques of production. Once the transition to industrial capitalism has been completed, sustained technological progress is the rule by the very nature of the new system; prior to the completion, stagnation of technique is the rule.

Changes in the techniques of production are necessary but not sufficient for economic development along a colonial frontier. The most efficient factory in the world produces nothing without workers to staff it. Along a colonial frontier, where resources are abundant and smallholders may proliferate, some socio-economic process similar to primitive accumulation in the Old World must come about before a propertyless class of wage labourers can be brought into existence.

This process according to Marx was best exemplified by the policy prescriptions advocated by Gibbon Wakefield. Natural resources being abundant, resource-based growth—the proliferation of smallholdings—was the natural tendency along the frontier. Resource-based development—sustained 'revolutionising' of the means of production by the capitalist class—could only take place once this tendency was countered. It could be countered, Marx suggested, if potential smallholders were somehow barred from ownership of land. On a colonial frontier, this would be accomplished when colonial government placed a high enough price on farm land. On the one hand, such a policy would eradicate subsistence production and provide capitalists with wage labourers. On the other hand, the fund from land sales could be utilised by government to import additional labourers, and to further cement the laws and regulations needed to maintain and protect the institutions of private property. Marx wrote:

How, then, to heal the anti-capitalistic cancer of the colonies? If men were willing, at a blow, to turn all the soil from public into private property, they would destroy certainly the root of the evil, but also—the colonies. The trick is how to kill two birds with one stone. Let the Government put upon the virgin soil an artificially high price, independent of the law of supply and demand, a price that compels the immigrant to work a long time for wages before he can earn enough money to buy land, and turn himself into an independent peasant. The fund resulting from the sale of land ... the Government is to employ, on the other hand, in proportion as it grows, to import have-nothings from Europe into the colonies, and thus keep the wage-labour market full for the capitalists.[32]

The actual influence of Wakefield on British colonial policy is far from obscure. S. B. Ryerson sums up his influence on Upper and Lower Canada as follows:

To extend [capitalism] ... to North America, all that was needed ... was to *incorporate land companies*, give them unsettled lands for speculation and profit—and thus a respectable number of immigrants would be kept in their 'place'—in the ranks of the propertyless. The solution adopted was to charter the Canada Company (1825) and the British American Co., in Upper and Lower Canada, with some three million acres of land between them. These institutions were 'aids to immigration' of a kind that lined the pockets of speculators, kept up the price of land, and ensured that a portion of the immigrant population should remain landless—and hence available for hire.[33]

More obscure, probably, is the general *principle* underlying Wakefield's various policy prescriptions, and those of his later admirers.[34] This principle, observable in much of British colonial as well as strictly US history, is that some form of monopoly—created privately, or through government action—must accompany settlement and regulate the rate at which natural resources are appropriated by settlers. If the basis of colonial settlement is resource-based development—that is, if this basis is other than the proliferation of smallholders, practising the colonial equivalent of simple commodity production in the Old World—some form of monopoly must stand between the settlers and the otherwise plentiful natural resources. Monopoly is neither a barrier to economic development in the early history of the colony,[35] nor a generator of less desirable economic consequences than would be produced by competition. Rather, monopoly must be viewed in many instances as an essential characteristic of settlement. If those wishing to settle and presumably develop the resources of the colonial frontier are—as they must be—aware of the colony's natural tendency towards resource-based growth, their first priority as the new territories are governed is to erect monopolies such as those advocated by Wakefield and Durham.

It is the generalisation that monopoly is an essential characteristic of settlement that we put forward as the 'pure economic theory of colonial exploitation.'

The initial settlement of a colony, regulated as it most likely will be by the sort of monopoly described immediately above, *is* economic development in the sense that structural change in the colony's economy is taking place. Whether sustained economic development will be the rule after this point is, of course, a different matter.

It might be mentioned parenthetically that our view of monopoly as an essential characteristic of settlement places a great deal that has been written about Canada's economic history in a new and, we hope, useful perspective. Innis's generalisations concerning the central government's unique role in fostering Canadian economic development make a great deal of sense if the central government is viewed as the agency that serves the same role as, or itself creates, monopoly in aid of settlement. As Innis sought to explain the central government's unique role in a theoretical rather than an empirical context, his argument tended toward unfalsifiable hypotheses centring on cultural characteristics of Canada as a whole.[36] The view that monopoly is an essential characteristic of settlement may explain more of Innis's own empirical work than was explained by his late attempts to formulate a theoretical basis that might tie together his earlier work.[37]

The economics of our pure theory of colonial exploitation lies within the realms of both orthodox microeconomic theory and Marxist economic theory. According to orthodox theory, with no government intervention resources along a colonial frontier will be overutilised; according to Marx's logic, should government fail to form some barrier standing between resources and settlers, these resources will be occupied by those who would otherwise be the colony's proletariat. Both approaches suggest that colonial government—if it is influenced by those settlers or potential settlers with relatively large amounts of economic power—will have, as its first priority, the construction of certain monopolies designed to counteract the colony's natural tendency toward resource-based growth. To use the jargon of Marxist economics: capitalism 're-creates' itself along the colonial frontier by constructing these monopolies.

RETARDED COLONISATION REVISITED

While certain details and points of emphasis are still in dispute,[38] it certainly appears that serious doctrinal differences existed between those favouring settlement of Newfoundland and those who opposed it, wishing instead the continuation of the visiting British fishery at Newfoundland. Lounsbury characterised the Westerners—the West-Countrymen opposed to settlement—as prone to 'narrow localism ... and an extreme conservatism which prevented their accepting with ease any new practices.'[39] He characterised those favouring settlement as representing the new spirit of 'economic nationalism.'[40] Innis objected:

It might be argued not that the west country adventurers supported the old medieval conception of trade and the London merchants the spirit of economic nationalism ... but that the west country merchants were insistent on the advantages of freedom of trade and opposed to proposals of monopoly from London.[41]

Whether one wishes to take exception to both Innis's and Lounsbury's view that the conflict represents one of *ideologies*, one can almost certainly object to the fact that neither view is sensitive to the fundamental *similarities* between the policies advocated by those favouring settlement and those opposed. Both viewpoints may or may not have been representative of ideologies, yet both were most certainly alternative plans for regulating the rate at which Newfoundland's fisheries resources would be exploited. The Westerners wished to continue hiring labour, outfitting ships, and, in general, regulating access to the Newfoundland fishery by ensuring that all fishing operations (and all legal obligations arising from these operations) began and ended in England. Under these circumstances, yearly calculations of the likely success of the voyage were essential. Settling with their employees in end-of-season shares of the season's catch rather than in fixed wages,[42] the decisive factor determining the profitability of the Newfoundland fishery was the rate at which the resource itself was utilised. While it may have been phrased in the language of mercantilism,[43] Britain's anticolonisation policy toward New-foundland amounted to nothing more than the creation of a monopoly regulating the rate of utilisation of the Newfoundland fishery. The monopoly was held not by anything resembling a land company, but rather by a region of England; the resource's use was regulated not by selling it at artificially high prices,[44] but by ensuring that only those who could afford the cost of the yearly voyage to Newfoundland would (in law at least) be the ones to prosecute the fishery.[45] Similarly, the Londoners' plans for settlement involved the creation of monopolies and the granting of patents—once again, in aid of regulating the use of the resources of Newfoundland. Their proposals included at least one innovation to counter the risks occasioned by increased settlement:

Selfish though [those favouring settlement] may have been, [they] had a much larger vision than did the West Country group.... The Kirke group in particular was convinced that the fishery could be made more efficient by substituting the wage system for the old West Country practice of fishing on the share basis.... True capitalists in the modern sense of the word, they were certain that the individual merchant was deprived of a considerable profit because of the payment of labor on a share basis, and, therefore, was unable to obtain additional funds to expand his business.[46]

Seeking a monopoly on much, if not all, economic activity in Newfoundland, and advocating a wage rather than a share system, the Londoners designed their economic proposals to serve the same purpose as the anticolonisation policy: to regulate the rate of exploitation of Newfoundland's resources. There might be settlers in Newfoundland, but with a wage rather than a share system, and with the Londoners' monopoly control of the economy, they would arrive as, and remain, a proletariat.

The dispute between the Londoners and the Westeners was not one between monopoly and competition, as suggested by Innis, since both groups were proposing varying forms of monopoly. Neither was this dispute one beween medieval and mercantilist economic thought, as suggested by Lounsbury; both strategies for exploiting Newfoundland's resources had major elements that might be easily called mercantilist. The dispute, rather, was over the best way to regulate the rate at which the Newfoundland fishery was exploited. We see in this history not the struggle of ideologies, but rather a struggle between two regions, each wishing to erect a different form of monopoly control over the resources of Newfoundland.

THE-UNDERDEVELOPMENT OF NINETEENTH-CENTURY NEWFOUNDLAND

I have suggested elsewhere that the coexistence of policies advocated by the Londoners and the practices of some of the late eighteenth-century settlers in Newfoundland accounts for the early wave of diversification described above.[47] The Londoners' inability to obtain monopolies and patents notwithstanding, a wage system arose in Newfoundland alongside the visiting British fishery's share system, and alongside the practices of resident masters within the Newfoundland fishery who paid in shares. It was the combination of a settled resident population and this wage system that accounted for the early wave of diversification. Settlers paying wages to their employees were able to capture the economic surplus generated during the fishery's best years. Legislation creating the Newfoundland Savings Bank was not enacted until 1834, and as in other frontier areas, savings in many locations could only have taken two forms: hoarded currency, or fixed investment. Whatever the causes, the early wave of diversification appears to demonstrate that the potential for economic development did in fact exist in nineteenth-century Newfoundland. This conclusion is underlined by the fact that Newfoundland's truck system and its accompanying system of household production developed not out of custom and practice, but rather in response to actions brought by merchants before Newfoundland's newly established court system.

Undoubtedly the new system was highly favourable to the merchants. Under the truck system

each fisherman went to a merchant in the spring and obtained from him, on credit, supplies of equipment and food to enable him and his family to live, not for the whole year, but during the three or four months of the fishing season. At the end of the season, the fisherman returned to the merchant with his catch of fish, dried and cured, to set off against his account. The price of fish was fixed by merchants, as also was the price of provisions, etc., supplied to the fisherman and his family in the spring. In cases where fish was valued according to quality, the quality of the fish tendered by the fisherman was determined by a 'culler' or valuer who himself was the employee of the merchant. In good years a balance was left to the fisherman, after deduction of the debt due to the merchant; this balance was paid to him in cash. In bad years the value of the fish tendered by the fisherman was not sufficient to pay for his supplies and he, therefore, remained in debt to the merchant. The balance available to him in good years was often such as to leave him with no margin after he had provided for himself and his family for the rest of the year, and the same process was, therefore, repeated in the following spring. In bad years, there was no balance at all and while in some cases, which were considered specially deserving, merchants continued to make advances to assist a man over the winter, thus adding to the burden of debt to be repaid during the ensuing year, the majority had no resource to fall back upon and, in default of other employment, were compelled to turn to the Government for relief.[48]

That it was favourable was no accident. Every element of the system was constructed by a different decision of the Newfoundland Supreme Court. Between 1817 and 1828, the court brought down the following rulings:

(1) Whenever supplies had been advanced for the prosecution of the cod fishery, accounts were payable only in fish and cod-liver oil, rather than in cash.

(2) Cod were *not* legal tender 'in payment of a debt contracted for articles furnished [by merchants to fishermen or those employing fishermen] for the prosecution of the seal-fishery [rather than the cod fishery].'

(3) The urban area of St John's may be an 'open and customary place of sale,' but rural areas in Newfoundland are 'unusual places of sale,' areas in which cash payments for goods does not take precedence over prior liens in determining the ownership of goods.[49]

These decisions, plus an additional decision that effectively eliminated the employers' power to ensure that their supplying merchants would pay the season's wages out of their realised season's earnings,[50] seemed to guarantee that in those areas where supplying merchants wished to conduct the purchase of cod and oil and the sale of supplies through truck, they were legally free to do so.[51]

It is ironic that Newfoundland's nineteenth-century economy has been described by some as a 'traditional economy.'[52] It was the court system of Newfoundland, and not tradition, that constructed the truck system.

THE TRUCK SYSTEM REVISITED

Why should a society discard the market mechanism in its most active economic sector? The answer may well lie in the logic of the pure economic theory of colonial exploitation, and in the open-access nature of any fishery.

Once settlement was accomplished and legitimised, and once a certain transitional period—marked, among other things, by the court decisions outlined above—had taken place, the Newfoundland merchants' monopoly on the island's foreign trade apparatus appears to have served an economic function similar to Britain's earlier anticolonisation policy. As long as merchants failed to compete with each other, and as long as the average fisherman's operation was sufficiently small to make direct foreign trade on his part impractical if not impossible, the rate at which Newfoundland's fisheries resources were exploited depended directly upon the merchants' willingness to extend credit to fishermen.

It might reasonably be asked at this point why the average fisherman's operation should, necessarily, have been small enough to make direct foreign trade on his part impossible. The answer lies in the open-access nature of the fishery, as well as in the nature of the merchants' economic interests.

A large vessel, with sole access to a given area of sea, having its own nonmigratory fish population, will be utilised by a 'rational' owner in such a way that fishing effort ceases at the point where the additional value of catch equals the additional cost of present effort. This is the same principle applied by the rational landowner, farming his land in such a way as to maximise fixed-factor rent. But take the same landowner, and place him in a social milieu wherein land is viewed by his class not as a resource, but rather as a simple source of income. Joan Robinson describes this situation quite well:

In order to have no trouble with cultivation, the landlords let out the land to tenants, the rent being a traditional proportion, say, half, of the gross output of the land. The landlord has no direct control over the work that the share croppers do. Tenants have neither the means nor the motive to maintain the productivity of the land, while the landlord can get his income without bothering about it. In these conditions, *the greater the number of workers on his estate, the larger is the landlord's return*. The landlord gains most when the holdings are so small and the level of intensity of cultivation so high as to maximize output per acre, i.e., [at the point where] the marginal product of an additional tenant would be zero.[53]

The economic interests of Newfoundland's merchants of the nineteenth century were similar to those of Robinson's landlords. The rational merchant wished to supply many low-productivity enterprises rather than a few high-productivity ones. With the costs of fishing gear, and the risks of ice, poor fishing seasons, etc., being borne by the fishermen rather than by the merchant, the fundamental economic problem faced by a merchant in a given locale went not much farther than deciding how many low-productivity enterprises he should supply. This decision, so long as the merchant was not bothered by the competition of other merchants, regulated the rate of utilisation of Newfoundland's fisheries. And merchants were not bothered by competition, for the simple reason that the truck system itself tied fishermen to their supplying merchants, and forbade competition among merchants in outport Newfoundland.

GEOGRAPHICAL DETERMINISM REVISITED

Above we have presented a pure economic theory of colonial exploitation, and have suggested that this theory explains two otherwise puzzling aspects of Newfoundland's economic history: retarded colonisation, and the rise of the truck system (with its concomitant household production). Marx suggested that in the capitalist system, when serious discrepancies exist between labour and capital on the one hand, and natural resources on the other, monopolies will form. These monopolies enable owners of capital to develop the natural resources through the employment of wage labour. In the pure economic theory of colonial exploitation, monopoly is thus an essential aspect of the settlement of new and relatively unpopulated territories. In the case of Newfoundland, two forms of monopoly served during the island's early history to enable capitalists to develop the fishery. These were prohibition of colonisation, and the truck system.

Relying implicitly on geographical determinism, much that has been written on Newfoundland's economic history has contended that her nineteenth-century merchants were not much better off than the fishermen they supplied. In examining the question of whether merchants were distinctly better off than fishermen, we will note incidentally that their economic status, compared with Canada as a whole at the same time, was astoundingly superior.

The 'merchant and fisherman have but one common interest and are bound together by one tie of mutual dependence,' reads a mid nineteenth-century merchants' petition dealing with Newfoundland's electoral franchise.[54] In defence of the merchants' apparent profiteering at the fishermen's expense, Governor Bannerman claimed in 1863 that if 'the fisherman is unsuccessful, or partly so, [he is tempted to] cheat his supplier, and the [merchant] must necessarily exact high prices [for supplies] to cover the great risks which ... he must run.'[55] Indeed, from the nineteenth century on, it has repeatedly been suggested that while merchant and fisherman may have held some mutual hostility, in fact a mutually beneficial rather than mutually exploitative relationship existed between the two classes.[56]

We have already shown, however, that there was a significant divergence of interest between the two classes. The merchants' interest lay in supplying many low-productivity fishing enterprises, while the fishermen's interest, clearly, lay in expanding the size of the average enterprise and increasing its average productivity. The common-property nature of the resource, as well as the various court decisions favouring the merchants, tended to structure the fishery more in the merchant's rather than the fisherman's interests.

All this notwithstanding, the strict geographical determinist view of Newfoundland would contend that the doctrine of mutual dependence—with its corollary that merchants as well as fishermen tended to be relatively poor in nineteenth-century Newfoundland—is in fact a correct assessment of the island's nineteenth-century economic situation. The question can only be settled quantitatively: was the fishery profitable for the supply merchants, and if so, how profitable was it? Data for a direct answer have not yet been gathered, yet sufficient data for an indirect yet persuasive answer are available. They demonstrate the nineteenth-century Newfoundland fishery to have been extremely profitable for the supply merchants.

Using simple national-income accounting techniques and available data,[57] it can be shown that Newfoundland was a net capital exporter rather than importer through much of the nineteenth century. Net capital exports averaged roughly 4.5% of net national product for the entire period 1845-84. Taking net capital exports to have been the entirety of merchants' income (their incomes would have been substantially larger, since net capital export measures, essentially, savings flowing abroad), and allowing half of the 895 merchants and traders listed in the averaged 1845-84 Newfoundland census returns to have had operations large enough to have exported three-quarters of average 1845-84 net capital export, we obtain an average income for this group of almost $600 per year (see Table 8-2). This compares quite favourably with, for example, an approximate Canadian income per capita of $135 in the year 1880. It is likely that fewer than half of the merchants and traders listed in the census were large enough to have been substantial exporters of capital, and it is also likely that this smaller group exported more than three-quarters of Newfoundland capital flowing abroad; therefore, it can be safely concluded that the merchants' average income in nineteenth-century Newfoundland was substantially greater than 439% of the Canadian average. Because Newfoundland's per capita income in 1884 was approximately 42% of the same Canadian average,[58] we can conclude that merchants and fishermen were certainly not on an equal economic footing.

For the skeptic, Table 8-2 details a wide variety of possible values of yearly net capital export per merchant, produced by available data on the number of merchants and traders and the amount of net capital export for Newfoundland during the years 1845-84. Those more comfortable with the doctrine of mutual dependence between fisherman and merchant would be more comfortable with, say, the first two rows and last two columns of data in Table 8-2. If 100% of all merchants' operations were sufficiently large to export capital from Newfoundland, economic power was fairly widely dispersed throughout the merchant class. Row 1 of Table 8-2 yields data that would obtain had this in fact been the case. If 25% of all net capital exports had been sent abroad by merchants, then on the whole merchants' economic activities could not be judged responsible for the export of capital from Newfoundland. This would indicate some degree of dispersion of economic power between Newfoundland's various classes. Column 4 of the table yields data that would obtain had this been the case. The entry under row 1, column 4, shows per merchant net capital export from Newfoundland under assumptions that are, probably, as favourable as possible to those espousing the doctrine of mutual dependence. The data say that if 100% of Newfoundland's merchants were responsible for only 25% of net capital export, net capital export per merchant

TABLE 8-2

POSSIBLE VALUES OF AVERAGE ANNUAL
NET EXPORT OF CAPITAL PER MERCHANT

PERCENTAGE OF MERCHANTS[a] EXPORTING CAPITAL	PERCENTAGE OF CAPITAL[b] EXPORTED BY MERCHANTS			
	100%	75%	50%	25%
100%	$395	$297	$198	$99
75%	527	395	263	132
50%	791	593	395	198
25%	1,582	1,187	791	395

SOURCES: Newfoundland, *Census Returns*, 1884; S. Antler, 'Colonial exploitation and economic stagnation in nineteenth century Newfoundland' (unpub. PhD thesis, University of Conneticut, 1975)

[a] Group of 895 individuals counted as 'merchants and traders' in the 1884 Newfoundland census.

[b] Average of 1845-84 net capital exported (i.e., $354,000).

NOTE: Cell entries give the net capital export per merchant if the specified conditions had occurred. Thus if 75% of merchants had been responsible for exporting 50% of the capital that was sent out of Newfoundland, the average amount per merchant would have been $263.

averaged $99 during the years 1845-84. While this figure can probably be better described as *savings* rather than income (i.e., income was almost certainly substantially greater than funds sent abroad), and while a per merchant figure is not strictly comparable to a per capita figure, it must be noted that the $99 figure compares favourably with the average Newfoundland per capita income during the years 1845-84 of $56. For those convinced that economic power in nineteenth-century Newfoundland was highly concentrated between economic classes as well as within the merchant class, it should be mentioned that the figure noted in column 1, row 1 provides striking support for the contention that the fishery was very profitable for at least some of the supply merchants.

Exactly which entry in Table 8-2 is the correct one is a matter we need not agonise over. The table demonstrates that assumptions *most* favourable to the hypothesis of mutual dependence yield data that contradict the hypothesis about as clearly as one might imagine possible.

The nineteenth-century Newfoundland fisherman was exploited; he faced this exploitation differently than the factory worker faced his, in that he faced monopolistic merchants rather than factory owners. Still, the structure of the fishery was such that surplus was captured by the merchants— Newfoundland's bourgeoisie—rather than by the fishermen.

The consequences of this exploitation were all those that would lead us to describe the Newfoundland economy in the mid 1880s, when the government began to take an active role in fostering qualitative economic change, as underdeveloped. The total value of factory production listed in the 1884 Newfoundland census returns is on the order of magnitude of $1.2 million. (This is total value of, and not value of additions to, capital stock.) But if net capital export from Newfoundland had remained in the country from 1845 to 1884, and even if this economic surplus had been invested in nondurable capital equipment—say capital equipment with an average life span of five years (i.e., capital with an average rate of depreciation of 20%)—Newfoundland's 1884 capital endowment would have been nearly $3.2 million rather than $1.2 million.[59] The figures grow more impressive if we assume a still conservative but more reasonable rate of depreciation of 15%. Under these circumstances, Newfoundland's 1884 capital endowment would have been something on the order of $3.7 million. The figure climbs to $4.7 million with an assumed rate of depreciation of 10%.

Nineteenth-century Newfoundland remained underdeveloped through the mid 1880s, not because economic surplus was not generated in Newfoundland, but rather because the surplus that might otherwise have been utilised for industrialisation was exported. It appears that Newfoundland's class structure, rather than her geography, accounted for her poverty.

SUMMARY: DEVELOPMENT, GROWTH, AND COLONIAL EXPLOITATION

The pure economic theory of colonial exploitation, explaining how a colony's economic history is informed by its natural tendency towards resource-based growth rather than resource-based development, suggests that generally speaking, monopoly is an essential characteristic of settlement itself.

In nineteenth-century Newfoundland, resource-based growth was first countered by Britain's anticolonisation policy. Later the truck system—a system that in effect encouraged resource-based growth (the proliferation of smallholdings)—regulated the aggregate rate at which fisheries resources were utilised, and captured for Newfoundland's merchants the economic surplus generated by the fishery.[60] For the merchants, rewards were substantial; for Newfoundland, the cost was a capital endowment that might have increased her late nineteenth-century industrial capacity fourfold.

Those unsympathetic to the Marxist point of view might well object at this point, insisting that if profitable opportunities for investment were available in Newfoundland, then capital would have remained in the country and would not have flowed abroad. The objection can be rephrased as follows: was not the export of capital from Newfoundland the responsibility of the invisible hand, rather than of Newfoundland's class structure?

This objection can be answered quite simply. We can say with confidence that, in terms of orthodox economic theory, capital (or any other resource) is being utilised optimally if and only if all markets that affect the decisions involved in its allocation are perfectly competitive. To the extent that markets even *existed* in nineteenth-century Newfoundland, they were about as far from perfectly competitive as markets can be. The export of capital from Newfoundland, when viewed in the light of orthodox microeconomics, can be judged to have been an optimal use of economic surplus only in the perfectly tautological sense that merchants generally felt it more in their best interest to invest abroad than at home. Economic orthodoxy offers us no real means to judge the wisdom of their decision. For all we genuinely know of the matter, the most economic use of capital exported from Newfoundland may actually have been fixed-capital formation at home.

The point can be generalised: its general form is both an excellent endpoint to the present essay, and a useful insight into the economics of development. Geographical determinism is a nontechnical, nonrigorous version of the doctrine of Pareto optimality. Implicit in geographical determinism is the belief that if it is in the Pareto-optimal sense economic for development to occur in a nation or region, then development will take place. Poverty, economic backwardness, low capital endowment, and so on, are, according to this view, the logical outcome of the workings of the free market interacting with the physical geography of the region. Underdevelopment may be an ugly phenomenon, but given the workings of the invisible hand, it must be judged to represent the best of a wide variety of less appealing possibilities.

Yet by the logic of Pareto optimality *itself*, the wisdom of the market, as it allocates resources, is *nonexistent* so long as markets are imperfect. The pure economic theory of colonial exploitation—based on the logic of both Marxism and economic orthodoxy—suggests that market imperfections are fundamental characteristics of colonial frontiers. To the extent that the theory is sound, the conclusion pointed to is that in areas such as British North America, to claim that a relationship exists between economic performance and economic potential is to put forward an assertion that is unscientific, and one that is supported by neither Marxist nor orthodox economic theory.

NOTES

1. Cf. P. Copes, *The resettlement of fishing communities in Newfoundland* (Ottawa, 1972).

2. The most influential work that might be said to have been influenced by geographical determinism is D. Alexander, 'Newfoundland's traditional economy and development to 1934,' *Acadiensis*, V, no 2 (1976), 56-78.

3. P. Colquhoun, *A treatise on the wealth, power, and resources of the British empire, in every quarter of the world, including the East Indies* (New York, 1965).

4. It was reported about 1720 that nearly all the Poole vessels engaged in the Newfoundland trade were built in Newfoundland: D. W. Prowse, *A history of Newfoundland from the English, colonial, and foreign records* (Belleville, 1972), 165n. For a complete survey, see E. W. Sager, *Sailing ships and the traditional economy of Newfoundland* (St John's, 1977).

5. An average life span of twenty years (or less) per vessel engaged in the Newfoundland trade would mean that Newfoundland's shipbuilding activity, at about the turn of the century, was sufficient (or more than sufficient) to maintain her fleet intact: R. G. Lounsbury, *The British fishery at Newfoundland, 1634-1763* (Hamden, 1969),

314; Prowse, *ibid.*, 378, 711. Sager, *ibid.*, 9, reports 63% of all newly registered tonnage during the years 1820-29 as representing vessels built in Newfoundland. By mid century this percentage had been more than halved and only by the penultimate decade of the century did the figure once again climb to near its earlier level.

6. R. M. Martin, *Statistics of the colonies of the British empire* (London, 1839), 271, 269.

7. Prowse, *A history of Newfoundland*, 450-52; James Murray, *Commercial crisis in Newfoundland* (St John's, 1895).

8. A colleague has suggested that the case for the early nineteenth-century prosperity and diversification may be overstated; in his opinion Colquhoun's data reflect little more than temporary war-related prosperity for Newfoundland. Yet while the Napoleonic war must certainly be taken into account in evaluating any data of this period, it seems to me that there exists sufficient additional evidence to allow us to conclude that the war was not the only factor involved. Further, one must not forget that British North America as a *whole* enjoyed a good deal of war-related prosperity during the period of Colquhoun's study: cf. P. Knaplund, *The British empire, 1815-1939* (New York and London, 1941), 65ff. The effects of the war are reflected not only in the Newfoundland data, but also in the data regarding the economic performance of the *rest* of British North America. The striking discrepancy between Newfoundland's economy and that of the rest of British North America reflected in Table 8-1 cannot be accounted for simply by war prosperity.

9. It has been argued that with the exception of a few 'hysterical' years in the 1670s, during which the West-Countrymen opposed all settlement, most of the early years of Newfoundland's history were marked by only 'passive hostility' to settlement on the part of this group. Further, it has been suggested that by the end of the seventeenth century the Westerners came to depend upon settlement of Newfoundland themselves: K. Matthews, 'A history of the west of England-Newfoundland fishery' (unpub. PhD thesis, University of Oxford, 1968), 10-11. It appears by this argument that a well defined special-interest group opposed to settlement may not have even existed, and that, to the extent that some West-Countrymen may have opposed settlement, their opposition was far less effective than has generally been believed.

10. With the 1675 report of the Lords of Trade, the principle was laid down that unlike the enumerated commodities produced in the West Indies and mainland North America, cured cod produced in Newfoundland could be marketed economically only by transporting it direct to market. Thus trade in Newfoundland cured cod was a part of Great Britain's foreign trade, rather than a branch of her domestic commerce. Taking as given the mercantilist axiom that colonies may not prosecute foreign trade, it logically follows that Newfoundland could not have become a colony. On this see Lounsbury, *The British fishery*, 144ff. For a direct and simple diagrammatic treatment of mercantilist trade patterns and thought see W. R. Brock, *Britain and the dominions* (Cambridge, 1951), 26.

11. On the whole, literature attempting to deal with the origins of the truck system obscures more than it reveals. Regarding those who contend that its origins lie in feudalism [cf. Newfoundland Royal Commission, *Report*, 1933; St J. Chadwick, *Newfoundland: island into province* (Cambridge, 1967)], we might be charitable and interpret 'feudal' to mean 'backward,' and not feudal in the literal sense. A significant portion of the literature tends to attribute the origins to man's basically avaricious nature and be done with the matter: cf. McLintock, *Constitutional government in Newfoundland*, 122-23. The actual origins of the system are most easily understood in light of the fact that prior to, say, 1800 it was taken as dogma by the British Government that any and all contractual obligations arising from the prosecution of the Newfoundland fishery would originate and terminate in Great Britain. Thus by the Act of 1775, and by provisions of the act renewed in 5 Geo. IV, cap. 51 (1824), fishermen were given a lien on the physical

proceeds of the voyage until such time as wages were paid; counterbalanced against these provisions were court decisions maintaining the principle that any boatowner or fisherman's current supplier held a lien on the physical proceeds of the season's voyage, to the value of the supplies advanced.

12. The most crucial of these was *Nowlan* v. *McGrath* in 1840, reported in some detail in Newfoundland, Legislative Council, *Journal*, 1841, 6th session, 2nd general assembly, 33. The decision specified that, even where a contract existed, the lien exerted upon the season's catch by the fisherman's wages was dissolved when the fish left the fisherman's possession.

13. This term seems to have originated with McLintock, *Constitutional government in Newfoundland*. As McLintock used the term, one senses a meaning closer to 'retarded economic development' than retarded settlement. It is not uncommon to find the two senses of the term confused in the literature. The upshot of McLintock's argument is that with settlement *and* colonial government, Newfoundland might have developed economically. Matthew's, 'History of the fishery,' argues that poor weather, not the western adventurers, was responsible for a slow rate of settlement in Newfoundland. The latter argument stresses the demographic aspects of the history, while the former stresses the political economy of the matter. On close examination, the two arguments do not appear to speak to each other.

14. Innis's view—often presented wrongly as being nothing more than a vulgarised staples thesis (i.e., the argument that development requires simply the export of staples)—was one of a nearly dialectical relationship between staples exports, concomitant expansion of the frontier, and government policies in aid of economic development. See, for example, pp. 400-401 in his *The fur trade in Canada: an introduction to Canadian economic history* (Toronto, 1970).

15. H. A. Innis, *The cod fisheries* (Toronto, 1978), 384-85.

16. T. Talbot, *Newfoundland* (London, 1882), 43; S. D. Antler, 'Colonialism as a factor in the stagnation of nineteenth century Newfoundland: Some preliminary notes,' ACEA, *Papers*, no 2, 89ff.; S. D. Antler, 'Colonial exploitation and economic stagnation in nineteenth-century Newfoundland' (unpub. PhD thesis, University of Connecticut, 1975), 89-91.

17. S. Ryan, 'The Newfoundland cod fishery in the nineteenth century' (unpub. MA thesis, Memorial University of Newfoundland, 1971), 87.

18. *Ibid.*, 194.

19. Adam Smith, *An inquiry into the nature and causes of the wealth of nations* (New York, 1937), 92.

20. A. C. Pigou, *The economics of welfare* (London, 1918); E. G. Wakefield, *England and America* (1833; New York, 1967).

21. In the jargon of welfare economics, a resource is being utilised economically if its marginal product would be no higher if it were utilised elsewhere.

22. F. H. Knight, 'Some fallacies in the interpretation of social cost,' *Readings in welfare economics*, ed. K. O. Arrow and T. Scitovsky (Homewood, Ill., 1969), 213-27.

23. *Ibid.*, 215.

24. Anticipating orthodox microeconomics as it addressed this point, Marx, as noted below, observed that government-created monopoly would 'solve the problem' being discussed.

25. One might ask why innovation would not take place. The answer is that if expansion is taking place, producers can already sell as much as they wish to without taking the risks of innovation.

26. W. W. Rostow, *The process of economic growth* (New York, 1962), 9, chapter 13.

27. J. Hicks, *A theory of economic history* (London, 1973), 2.

28. Karl Marx, *Capital* (3v., New York, 1967), III, 334.

29. It is proper to use Baran's term here, not because we necessarily accept his framework, but rather because we are speaking of a time prior to the emergence of uniform national labour markets. Only in limited areas, at this stage of the emergence of modern capitalism, is labour power a commodity. See Paul Baran, *Political economy of growth* (New York, 1957).

30. Hicks, *Theory of economic history*, 145.

31. Marx, *Capital*, III, 332ff.

32. *Ibid.*, I, 772.

33. S. B. Ryerson, *Unequal union* (New York, 1968), 35.

34. For example, Durham's insistence that the disposal of unoccupied lands remain under the control of the British government.

35. In the colony's later history, monopolies may in fact form such barriers.

36. Cf. R. Neill, *A new theory of value: the Canadian economics of H. H. Innis* (Toronto, 1972).

37. It might also be mentioned that the framework suggested above takes a much sounder approach to monopoly itself than is often the case in studies of Canada's economic history. With no apparent justification, for example, Ryerson's generally excellent *Unequal union* asserts that land monopoly on Prince Edward Island operated to retard progress for more than a century (p. 205). Presumably everyone knows that monopolies are 'bad' and unprogressive. Therefore, since economic development is 'good' and progressive, land monopolies must necessarily retard progress. Q. E. D. Monopoly certainly does hinder development under some circumstances. But one cannot assume it does so under any and all circumstances.

38. Whether the West-Countrymen were consistently antisettlement has, as was mentioned above, been questioned by Matthews. He suggests that the West-Countrymen's only consistent political aim was absence of government rather than absence of settlement: Matthews, 'History of the fishery,' 4-5.

39. Lounsbury, *British fishery*, 91.

40. *Ibid.*

41. Innis, *Fur trade*, 326.

42. Cf. Lounsbury, *British fishery*, 90.

43. Ambiguities in the definition of mercantilism have resulted in serious confusion in much of the literature dealing with the issues involved. The westerners were mercantilist in that their emphasis was on the fishery's acting as a training ground for seamen, while the Londoners were mercantilist in that they wished to be granted patents or monopolies or both.

44. The open-access nature of the fishery would have made this impossible, of course.

45. While it might be objected that the laws against settlement were ineffective (it remains a matter of controversy whether they were), it must be remembered that what is at issue here is the economic objective of the law, and not its actual effects.

46. Lounsbury, *British fishery*, 89.

47. Antler, 'Colonial exploitation and economic stagnation,' chapters 3-5.

48. Newfoundland Royal Commission, *Report*, 1933, 79-80.

49. *Decisions of the Supreme Court of Newfoundland: the reports, 1817-1828*, ed. B. Dunfield (St John's, 1916), 219-20, 228-29, 29ff.

50. Antler, 'Colonial exploitation and economic stagnation,' 86-88.

51. Robert Brym has suggested that along Newfoundland's northeast coast, as of at least the early twentieth century, the household-based fishery that these decisions gave rise to was not the predominant form. He suggests that here, where fishermen were engaged in the Labrador fishery, the seal fishery, and logging operations, capital-

intensive operations employing wage labourers either continued or arose again as of the early 1900s.

52. Cf. Alexander, 'Newfoundland's traditional economy.'

53. J. Robinson and J. Eatwell, *An introduction to modern economics* (London, 1973), 70; emphasis added.

54. Quoted in Ryerson, *Unequal union*, 208.

55. Newfoundland, House of Assembly, *Journals*, 1863, appendix, 502.

56. For example, R. A. MacKay doubted whether 'the total accumulation from the fishery and the mercantile business built thereon has ever been much more than sufficient to finance these activities and subsidiary industries and services:' see MacKay, *Newfoundland: economic, diplomatic and strategic studies* (Toronto, 1946), 117. See also C. Wadel, *Marginal adaptations and modernization in Newfoundland* (St John's, 1969), 21.

57. See Antler, 'Colonial exploitation and economic stagnation,' 127-37. Sager objects to my argument, saying that 'although capital may have been exported from Newfoundland, it is unlikely that the island was deprived of access to its own economic surplus:' see his 'The merchants of Water Street and capital investment in Newfoundland's traditional economy,' a paper presented to the Maritime History Group conference (St John's, 1978), 20. Having re-examined my data and my original argument I am satisfied that the initial conclusion is sound. Sager's own work (*ibid.*, and *Sailing ships and traditional economy*) suggests that if vessels used in the Newfoundland fishery or in the coastal trade were to be counted as 'imports' as my initial model evaluated net capital export, my figure for net capital export would be diminished by no greater than one-third, and quite likely by something substantially less than a third. This would not alter the conclusions presented in my initial study, nor would it alter the conclusions given above.

58. Calculated from Antler, *ibid.*, 114, 136.

59. Calculated from *ibid.*, 132, as simply the sum of net capital export—with an unrealistically low initial value in 1844 of zero—less 20% on a year-by-year basis. The endpoint year 1881 (from the original data the five-year average centred on 1881) has been added to value of capital stock listed in the 1884 census. Even with an unrealistically low initial value of capital stock of zero, and even with a near impossible rate of depreciation of 20%, the discrepancy between Newfoundland's actual 1884 capital endowment of $1.2 million and her potential endowment of nearly $3.2 million is understated rather than overstated. Fixed-capital formation increases income, which in turn increases consumption, investment, and savings. None of these indirect effects is taken into account by the $3.2/$1.2 million discrepancy. Only if the multiplier's effect operated *entirely* outside Newfoundland—quite unlikely to say the least—would the discrepancy have been as small, even under the restrictive assumptions imposed upon the calculations.

9 Regional Factors in the Formation of the Fishermen's Protective Union of Newfoundland

Robert J. Brym and Barbara Neis

INTRODUCTION

The prevailing image of Atlantic Canada is that of a political wasteland: a region where the stability ensured by economic stagnation has precluded all forms of radicalism and produced a political system marked only by 'immemorial conservatism.'[1] Mid-nineteenth century St John's is not known for the frequent and violent riots of its urban 'crowd;' Victoria and Carleton counties are not famous as the seat of the United Farmers of New Brunswick, a party that provided, together with labour candidates, a quarter of all provincial legislators after the 1920 election; Antigonish is not widely perceived as the source of a co-operative movement that swept eastern Nova Scotia in the 1920s and 1930s. Yet these and other manifestations of political radicalism did occur in Atlantic Canada—a fact that clearly belies Frank Underhill's sardonic comment that 'as for the Maritimes, nothing, of course, ever happens down there.'[2]

The Fishermen's Protective Union of Newfoundland was one of these 'unknown' cases. Formed in 1908, the FPU saw eight of its nine candidates win seats in the 1913 Newfoundland election: almost 24 per cent of the total. And in 1919 more persons voted for the FPU than for any other party in the colony.[3] First as the largest opposition party and then as junior partner in a coalition government, this collective opponent of what was sometimes called the 'fishocracy' sought to achieve many of the same objectives endorsed by the farmers' movement in Canada.[4] Taken together, these aims may conveniently be viewed as an attempt to alter the distribution of economic rewards in society by challenging the dominant class of businessmen, particularly those engaged in financial and mercantile activities. This involved the establishment of consumer co-operatives; the abolition of the merchant's right to grade and thereby set the price for fish; an increase in state intervention in the regulation and rationalisation of the fisheries; the elimination of the so-called 'credit system,' whereby the exchange of fish for supplies was marked not by the exchange of money, but by the often arbitrary 'adjustment' of the fisherman's account book by the merchant; and so forth. Along with other administrative, constitutional, educational, and economic reforms of a progressive nature, these demands were made in the FPU's 1912 Bonavista Platform—the Regina Manifesto of Newfoundland.[5]

In this paper we want to provide neither a short political history of the FPU nor a discussion of its etiology. Rather, we shall focus mainly on the question of why the movement emerged *where* it did. Support for the FPU was far from being evenly distributed across the island, and although this fact has attracted the attention of some historians and political scientists, there still remains the task of placing it within some theoretically consistent explanatory framework.

The framework we employ in the following analysis is based on a deceptively simple and almost tautological insight generated by recent work on social movements: attempts to engage in collective political action involve struggles for power between partisans of the movement and authorities. Viewed in this manner, the question of why political movements emerge where they do does *not* focus attention on the strains and deprivations that incite partisans to engage in collective action; in contrast to Durkheim's stress on anomie or the more recent emphasis on relative deprivation as the chief causes of collective unrest,[6] the power models most closely associated with the names of Anthony Oberschall and Charles Tilly pay particular attention to the *structural* conditions that shift balances of power between potential partisans and authorities, thereby upsetting institutionalised arrangements for the conduct of political life and promoting the creation of new ones.[7]

In our analysis of the FPU we shall be particularly concerned with regional variations in only one structural determinant of power—level of social organisation.[8] It will be demonstrated that (a) fishermen in Newfoundland were affected by two broad types of economic underdevelopment, each of which produced different forms of labour organisation, and only one of which produced a form conducive to collective political action; and (b) only in one area of the island was a principal opponent of the FPU, the church elite, insufficiently organised to suppress the involvement of potential partisans in the movement. The combination of these two factors—regional variations in the power of fishermen and in the power of opposing elites—explains well, we submit, why the movement succeeded and failed where it did.

Before presenting our analysis of the problem it will prove useful first to indicate just where the FPU met with success and where it did not. The accompanying map and table (Figures 9-1 and 9-2) demonstrate that, whether we measure FPU support by per cent FPU vote in the 1913 election, by FPU membership as a percentage of registered voters, or by number of branch stores of the FPU's Fishermen's Trading Company in 1917, the movement's strength was to be found along the northeast coast of the island, especially the constituencies of Twillingate, Fogo, Bonavista, Bay de Verde, and Port de Grave. Why?

STRUCTURES OF UNDERDEVELOPMENT IN NEWFOUNDLAND

A large part of the explanation for regional variations in the strength of the

FIGURE 9-1

NEWFOUNDLAND ELECTORAL DISTRICTS, 1913
AND FISHERMEN'S TRADING COMPANY BRANCH STORES, 1917

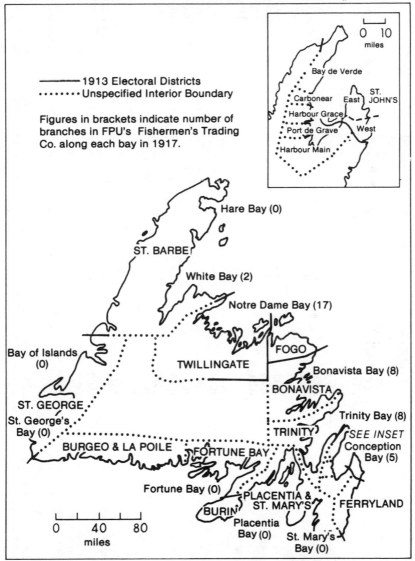

SOURCE: J. Feltham, 'The development of the FPU in Newfoundland (1908-1923)' (unpub. MA thesis, Memorial University of Newfoundland, 1959), 166-67.

NOTE: This map was constructed by Gerald McManus of the Department of Geography, Memorial University of Newfoundland.

TABLE 9-2　　SELECTED STATISTICS ON NEWFOUNDLAND AND THE FPU

Constituency	Ratio of Roman Catholics to Protestants, 1911	Percent FPU vote, 1913	FPU membership as % of registered voters, 1913	Persons employed in Labrador fishery and logging, 1911, as % of registered voters, 1913
St. John's East	1.06	0.0	**	0.0
St. John's West	1.02	0.0	**	0.3
Harbour Main	2.33	0.0	**	14.1
Port de Grave	0.35	55.5	41.5	66.3***
Harbour Grace	0.26	0.0	23.1	48.9***
Carbonear	0.34	0.0	**	77.2***
Bay de Verde	0.29	25.1*	59.9	15.8
Trinity	0.08	37.1*	65.0	47.6
Bonavista	0.16	68.6	64.2	43.2
Fogo	0.16	69.2	73.2	19.2
Twillingate	0.12	32.9*	67.9	36.9
St. Barbe	0.30	0.0	37.4	10.2
St. George	1.58	0.0	**	9.0
Burgeo and La Poile	0.02	0.0	**	1.0
Fortune Bay	0.28	0.0	**	6.0
Burin	0.53	0.0	**	3.5
Placentia and St. Mary's	4.16	0.0	**	1.0
Ferryland	36.62	0.0*	**	0.0

* Three-party contests.
** Membership in these constituencies was insignificant — a total of only 300.
*** About a third of the Labrador fishery 'stationers' from these constituencies were non-voters (i.e., women and children). In other constituencies this percentage was insignificant (i.e., less than 1%). See Staveley (1973).

SOURCES: *The history of the Fishermen's Protective Union, from 1909-1929*, ed. W. Coaker (St. John's, 1930), 64; Newfoundland, *Census, 1911* (St. John's, 1914), tables I, 496-8; II, 442-3; IV, 302; 'Newfoundland general election results, 1900-1932,' ed. M. Graesser (unpub. MS, Dept. of Political Science, Memorial University of Newfoundland).

FPU has to do with the character of underdevelopment in Newfoundland.It has frequently been noted that underdeveloped regions perform several important functions in capitalist economies: on the demand side they act as markets for manufactured goods produced in industrially more developed regions; on the supply side they provide developed regions with ready sources of cheap raw materials and cheap labour.[9] However, it is less often recognised that the twin supply functions are chiefly responsible for the creation of varying patterns of work organisation in different parts of underdeveloped regions. Those areas that specialise in supplying raw materials *tend* to be characterised by relatively high levels of capital investment and the creation of a solidary, legally free, wage-labouring class; those that specialise in supplying cheap labour, by relatively low levels of capital investment and the maintenance of an atomised working population partly or even largely engaged in subsistence production and available for migration should industrial expansion warrant it.

The social organisation of fishermen in nineteenth and early twentieth century Newfoundland was by no means immune to this 'law of uneven economic underdevelopment.'[10] The first form of labour organisation that deserves our attention in this connection was that of the inshore fishery, which originally evolved as a means of depressing the share of value accruing to fishermen and increasing the share accruing to merchants. If the typical relationship between a wage labourer and his employer is such that the full cost of the labourer's subsistence is borne by the employer in the form of a wage, then the relationship between the Newfoundland inshore fisherman and the merchant (who, through the credit system, supplied the fisherman with his gear and other necessities in exchange for the right to dispose of his product) was in no sense typical. For in Newfoundland merchants were able to effect 'a shifting of the actual costs of subsistence onto households' by eliminating wage relations with inshore fishermen and thereby encouraging the latter to garden, hunt, tend livestock, construct their own boats and homes, etc. [11]

Increasing the share of value accruing to the merchant through the replacement of wage relations by the credit system prevented significant capital accumulation on the part of inshore fishermen. Moreover, the existence of the credit system meant that the interest of the merchant tended to focus more on the profits to be gained from supplying the fisherman with his necessities than on encouraging the fisherman to increase his productivity. After all, the merchant

paid out not season's wages, but rather end-of-season payments [in the form of credits against the fisherman's account] varying directly with the size of the catch itself.... If the catch was poor, payments were low: so long as the value of the catch stayed sufficiently above the value of supplies advanced at the start of the season, the merchant had no interest in whether or not average levels of productivity of labour in the fishery were rising or falling.[12]

The result: merchants tended to invest their capital in wholesale and retail trade, or in safe overseas securities, rather than making their capital available for upgrading the productivity of the fishery. This, together with the fact that fishermen were unable to accumulate savings, 'meant that the countryside was denuded of capital and access to capital.'[13]

The inshore fishery therefore tended to be undercapitalised. Typically, it was prosecuted in small open boats with crews of only two to six men.[14] As we shall see, it is of some considerable significance that along the south coast fishing crews were even smaller: partly, it seems, because environmental conditions along the south coast necessitated the use of hook and line rather than the net or the trap, so that 'the most efficient productive unit (hence ideal crew) was felt to be that of the lone fisherman.'[15] This explains why, along the northeast coast, inshore fishing crews were recruited from extended family and, when necessary, friendship networks; while along the south coast work organisation was based on the individual rather than the family and the 'crowd.'[16] But notwithstanding this regional variation in the size and organisation of the crew, it may safely be said that, overall, the inshore fishery, which was prosecuted in virtually all parts of the island, tended to involve a relatively atomised form of work organisation, in which mere handfuls of men were brought together for the fishing season.

It is quite true that, along the south coast at the turn of the century, at least two factors were responsible for the growth of a more capital-intensive offshore fishery on the Grand Banks. First, relatively cheap technological innovations, notably the trawl and the gasoline engine, were increasingly adopted, occasioning overcrowding in the inshore fishery. Second, rising prices for cod on the world market (see Figure 9-3) provided local merchants with the incentive to become directly involved in the fishery by financing the construction of intermediate-size 'skiffs' and large 'bankers' and by employing men to do the fishing. But even here one cannot speak of a highly solidary form of work organisation for, despite the relatively large size of crews, they comprised transient men who shifted back and forth between the Nova Scotia or Boston schooner fishery and the Banks.[17] More important perhaps, the Banks fishery operated until the mid 1930s on the basis of the 'count' system of remuneration. Rather than receiving a share of the value of fish caught by *all* dories working from a mother ship, a fisherman's income was computed according to the number of fish caught by him in his *single* (two-man) dory. As a result, there was intense rivalry and competition among two-man dory crews, the least co-operative gesture being withheld since co-operation might decrease one's earnings and increase someone else's. One fisherman and skipper on the Banks fishery recalled:

How unhappy it would be sometimes. I've seen people go days and not spoke to one another. Aboard the same schooner, sit to the same table, lookin' at one another, and yet cuttin' one another's throat.[18]

Hardly a context in which one would expect to find much collective action, political or otherwise.

FIGURE 9-3

EXPORT PRICES PER QUINTAL OF DRIED COD, YEARLY AVERAGES, 1890-1940

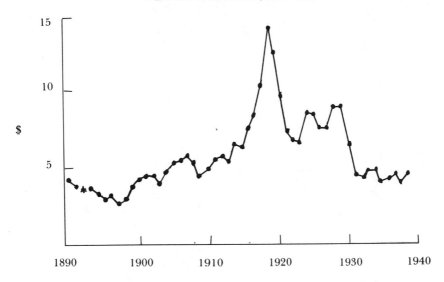

SOURCE: *Newfoundland: economic, diplomatic, and strategic studies*, ed. R. MacKay (Toronto, 1946), 143.
NOTE: No figures available for 1892.

If one wanted to find highly solidary forms of labour organisation in early twentieth-century Newfoundland, one would have to travel to the northeast coast: the area of the FPU's predominance. In addition to having an inshore fishery which, as noted above, employed larger and more concentrated crews than along the south coast, this area was the recruitment base for the Labrador fishery, as much as a thousand miles to the north. When it reached its maximum development during the first decade of this century, the Labrador fishery accounted for one-quarter to one-half of Newfoundland's total production of salt cod.[19] As on the Grand Banks, rising prices and inshore overcrowding provided the main incentives for the expansion of the Labrador fishery. Merchants invested capital either by financing the construction and operation of 'floaters' (i.e., schooners with roughly ten-man crews),[20] or by establishing permanent fishing stations along the Labrador coast and transporting crews of 40 or more men on large steamers for the season.[21] The use of steam vessels to transport 'stationers' to Labrador actually posed a grave threat to the livelihood of those engaged in the floater fishery: it was feared that the more powerful steamers would be able to overcome ice conditions with relative ease, arrive in Labrador early, and monopolise the choicest fishing 'berths.' Heavy capital investment thus raised

FIGURE 9-4

MEAN TONNAGE OF SEALING VESSELS
1900-1912

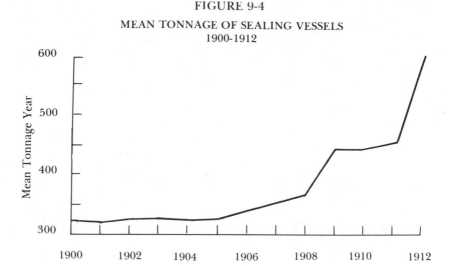

SOURCE: L. Chafe, *Chafe's sealing book: a history* (St John's, 1924), 67, 79.

the spectre that 'unless there is some prohibition against steam all the Labrador coast from Cape Harrigan south must fall into the hands of [large]
capitalists.'[22] It was also responsible for the creation of the most concentrated
and solidary segment of the work force (paid in cash or in shares of the
season's catch) in Newfoundland's fisheries. S. J. R. Noel correctly links this
fact with the spread of the FPU on the northeast coast:

It was thus among a unique breed of fishermen (they were commonly known as 'floaters') that the FPU was born, and the relevance of their occupation to the union's
precipitous advance is that they alone of Newfoundland's fishermen constantly inter-
mingled in the course of their work. Unlike the inshore fishermen, who worked in
isolation, or the banking crews, who worked far out to sea and never touched port until
the end of a voyage, the floaters joined in a great seasonal migration. Before sailing
they met at merchants' wharves for the loading of supplies; while pushing their way
north they often anchored in clusters to ride out a storm in a safe harbour; and once
the Labrador coast was reached there were frequent rendezvous at bait depots, in
sheltered creeks, and on the actual fishing grounds where dories from many schooners
mingled indiscriminately. In all these places the contagious union idea spread without
hindrance.[23]

Noel neglects to mention that stationers, too, were, for much the same reason,
very likely to join the FPU.[24] But he does point out that fishing was not the
only activity on the northeast coast that involved relatively solidary forms of
labour organisation.

Receptivity of persons living around the northern bays to the FPU was
also enhanced by participation in the sealing industry. Dominated by many of

the same mercantile firms as the Labrador fishery, the seal fishery was similarly experiencing increasing large-scale capitalisation at the turn of the century (see Figure 9-4). The introduction of steel steamers in 1906 had an impact on the antiquated wooden steamers going to the sealing grounds much the same as the introduction of steamers had upon the Labrador floater fishery. The steel steamers were able to travel to the sealing grounds more quickly and were thus more certain of a profitable voyage.[25] They were large—about 1,500 to 2,000 tons each—and carried crews of up to 270 men, whose cash wages were based on the size of the catch. Given the horrendous working conditions and the high level of social interaction among the thousands of sealers nimbly making their way along the ice floes and constantly courting disaster,[26] it is hardly surprising to learn that strikes were not unheard of in the sealing industry in the early part of this century[27] and that the FPU found eager supporters among the sealers.

A second type of seasonal work that deserves our attention in this connection was to be had in the logging camps near the northeast coast, where many sealers and inshore and Labrador fishermen were employed for wages during the winter months. Increased investment in the timber resources of the area began around 1890 after the construction of the Newfoundland railway. Many of the more valuable timber stands, as well as the water systems that provided both access and power, were rather quickly taken over by a few large lumber companies, financed in considerable measure by Newfoundlanders. However, they soon became disillusioned with their businesses; and the threat of their pulling out, together with the loss of railway revenues that this would entail, made William Reid, financier of the Newfoundland railway, responsive to the plans of one H. J. Crowe: Crowe bought out most of the mills and thereby acquired their timber rights. Then, with the support of Reid, he went to Britain and convinced the Harmsworth enterprise to establish a pulp and paper mill in central Newfoundland and buy *him* out. In this manner, control of many logging camps became concentrated in the hands of only one firm.[28] Hence the repetition of a by now familiar pattern: substantial amounts of capital investment created a segment of the Newfoundland work force sufficiently concentrated to facilitate the communication of radical ideas and the organisation of a radical movement. It was only along the northeast coast that logging, sealing, the Labrador fishery, and even (because of environmental conditions that allowed the use of the relatively capital-intensive cod trap) the inshore fishery provided fishermen with the structural basis necessary for involvement in the FPU.[29] This is, at least, part of the explanation for the relationships expressed by the data in Figure 9-2.

THE ORGANISATION OF CLERICAL ELITES

Some of the differences in labour organisation discussed above have attracted the attention of a few scholars interested in explaining the regional basis of recruitment to the FPU; but, we might add, these scholars have failed to appreciate the overall context of uneven economic underdevelopment that produced the differences in the first place.[30] We now want to discuss the importance of a second variable—this one having to do with religion—that has not failed to interest scholars either. But here, too, we must add an important qualification: for the most part the influence of religion on political behaviour has been viewed in cultural rather than social organisational terms. And this is not without its explanatory difficulties.

Typically, Richard Gwyn notes that the FPU 'swept the island, except for the merchant stronghold of St. John's and the ... Catholic districts where clerical conservatism proved more powerful than material populism.'[31] The implication of Gwyn's statement is plain: the presence of Catholic religious beliefs sufficed to block the spread of the union idea. But there are problems with this explanation. First, it fails to take account of the fact that some Catholic settlements on the northeast coast (Boyd's Cove and Fortune Harbour in Twillingate; Tilting in Fogo; St Brendan's, Keels, and Red Clift in Bonavista; etc.) had strong FPU local councils.[32] Second, it ignores the emergence of eleven FPU councils in the overwhelmingly Catholic constituencies of south coast Ferryland and Placentia/St Mary's.[33] Third, it does not recognise that variations by constituency in the ratio of Roman Catholics to Prostestants are too small to explain variations in FPU membership (see Figure 9-2).

This suggests that, rather than focusing on the political consequences of Catholicism as a system of beliefs, we would be well advised to examine how the various religious denominations were organised in Newfoundland. For just as fishermen who were more highly organised in their places of work had more power to translate their ire into action, so too did more highly organised clerics have more power to suppress their parishoners' involvement in the FPU.[34]

That there existed more of less general ecclesiastical opposition to the FPU in Prostestant as well as Catholic church hierarchies is beyond question.[35] But consider for a moment the advantages that the Catholic church, especially in the archdiocese of St John's (which included the constituencies of St John's East, St John's West, Ferryland, and Placentia/St Mary's) had in this regard. The population within the boundaries of the archdiocese was predominantly Catholic, overwhelmingly so outside the city of St John's itself, and the Catholic church had been established in this area for a longer period than anywhere else on the island. Nor did the Catholic church restrict its domain to spiritual matters. Even in those parts of the southern shore where a priest visited only once or twice a year, he was (if the reader will pardon the *double entendre*) the sole institutional leader, and exercised his prerogatives 'in a variety of contexts: not only religious, but social, economic and political as well.'[36] Priests controlled the educational system. They were not infrequently members of local economic elites, engaged in activities ranging from land speculation to the marketing of vegetables.[37] They dominated many voluntary associations, such as the Irish Benevolent Society and the Star of the Sea Association, and banned others, like the Irish Christian Society, which they could not control.[38] They regularly admonished their congregants to vote for particular candidates and parties.[39] And they possessed the capacity to enforce their political predilections because they, together with members of the mercantile elite, effectively prevented the emergence of a lay leadership by monopolising leadership positions in the community. When eleven FPU locals were sponataneously formed in Ferryland and Placentia/St Mary's,[40] the authority of the church was quickly deployed in order to put an end to such activities. The FPU was banned. An open letter was circulated by the bishop of the archdiocese of St John's, Dr M. F. Howley, who angrily asserted that the FPU's purpose was 'of an insidious nature ... calculated to cause great confusion, and an upheaval of our social fabric; to set class against class, and to end in the ruin and destruction of our commercial and business system.'[41] Notices denouncing the FPU were hung in every church of the archdiocese. And in the face of this opposition, the FPU councils on the south shore soon folded.

In contrast, the diocese of St George (which included the constituencies of Burin, Fortune, Burgeo/La Poile, St George, and St Barbe) had been organised only in 1904, and many parts of the diocese had only poorly developed religious institutions. Therefore, even if the diocese had contained some 'exceptional' area (like Ferryland and Placentia/St Mary's in the St John's archdiocese; see note 40) where labour organisation facilitated opposition to the 'fishocracy,' it is entirely questionable as to whether the church could have stifled it. The problems faced by the church in the constituencies of the northeast coast, which formed the diocese of Harbour Grace, certainly lend weight to this interpretation.

Not only was the Catholic church less able to exercise centralised control over its priests along the northeast coast—the historical record notes organised resistance against the bishop's authority on the part of Irish priests of the region[42]—but the area was fragmented into several religious denominations—chiefly Catholic, Anglican, Methodist, and Salvation Army—with no one denomination clearly predominant. As a consequence, the FPU could 'play one group of clergymen off against another if they openly opposed the movement.'[43] There developed, in other words, what might be termed parallel religious organisations, a situation that facilitated the FPU's capacity to engage in that ancient practice of *divide et impera*.

This was the case at least in longer-established parts of the northeast coast. In the new towns that grew up along with the development of timber resources, church structures in general were less complete and institutionalised, as is evidenced by the fact that the only nonsectarian churches and schools on the island were located in some of these towns. Similarly, on the rare occasion when a clergyman visited persons working in the Labrador fishery, his congregants typically belonged to various denominations. In fact, the absence of clergymen permitted the emergence of lay leaders, thus further undermining centralised ecclesiastical control.[44]

If the existence of multiple denominations on the northeast coast generally meant that religious organisations were split into several vertically atomised hierarchies, so that the power of clerics to enforce their will in political and other matters was weakened, the congregants themselves were able to create associations that displayed relatively high levels of horizontal (i.e., interdenominational) solidarity. The organisation with the greatest significance in this regard was the Loyal Orange Association, the most extensive voluntary association in the area. The LOA 'provided a common ground for Anglicans and Methodists to meet, for people ... were Orangemen first and denominational adherents second.'[45] It further permitted the emergence of a nonclerical leadership.[46] And it furnished the FPU with a network of social relations that proved most useful in recruiting members to the movement.[47] The same appears to have been true of several mutual aid societies, which may have had both Catholic and Protestant members.[48]

The general picture that emerges from the above discussion is that of a splintered clerical opposition to the FPU on the northeast coast and a united clerical opposition in the south. Where the clergy possessed the power that derives from organisation they were able to counter the threat of the fishermen's movement. Where they did not, they were unable to do so. In a like manner, it was only those fishermen who were based on proper organisational foundations who could actively struggle against the difficult conditions that circumscribed their lives: those who formed solidary segments of the work force because they suffered from 'direct capitalist underdevelopment,'[49] or the investment of capital for purposes of supplying developed regions with cheap raw materials. Those who suffered from 'indirect capitalist underdevelopment'—which involved the noninvestment of capital for purposes of maintaining a reserve labour force—were socially atomised and therefore unable to attempt an overthrow of the merchant oligarchy in Newfoundland.

CONCLUSIONS

The foregoing discussion suggests that regional variations in the balance of power between movement partisans and opposing authorities explains well the geographical distribution of the FPU's successes and failures. We use the word 'suggest' advisedly, for a full discussion of this relationship would require that we consider not just a single determinant of social power—level of social organisation—but other determinants as well, notably degree of access to those resources (economic, normative, etc.) that can be used to mobilise or suppress movement partisans. It would further require that we pay careful attention to the political actions of *all* authorities: our focus on the clerical elite would have to be augmented by an examination of the merchant elite. And while we have assumed an essential unity of interest between clerics and merchants, any comprehensive discussion would have to demonstrate the existence of social linkages between them; the assumption that the two naturally act in harmony is immediately gainsaid if we consider, for example, that clerics in other Atlantic regional social movements, such as the Antigonish movement, supported and led movement partisans. It would, finally, be useful to have at least a rough idea of how much of the variance in level of FPU support each independent variable explains. Thus, a great deal more sociological work remains to be done on the FPU.[50]

These shortcomings notwithstanding, we believe that this paper makes two theoretical contributions to the study of social movements in Canada. First, it emphasises the importance of taking what might be called a comparative political economy approach to the problem. We still very often read historical and sociological accounts of Canadian social movements that purport to explain incidents of collective unrest as consequences of strain, anomie, or relative deprivation. Sometimes, although by no means always, this has led to a form of psychologistic reasoning which takes individuals rather than social processes as objects of analysis. And even if this Durkheimian rule of sociological method is not broken, such approaches tend to draw attention away from the fact that strains of one sort or another may be endemic to a region, whereas collective reactions to these strains tend to be localised. In contrast, our approach is inherently comparative: we would agree with Charles Tilly's observation that in order to explain why a social movement emerges somewhere we must be able to explain why it does not emerge somewhere else. And it has centred on political-economic processes: we have sought to demonstrate the connection between different patterns of economic underdevelopment, labour organisation, and collective political action; and between the social organisation of authority and the suppression of political dissidence.

The second contribution of this paper, we should judge, is that it takes a small step toward correcting the centrist and western bias of students of Canadian social movements. As is evident from Frank Underhill's statement, quoted in the first paragraph of this paper, our ignorance concerning Atlantic Canada has led us to believe that 'nothing much ever happens down there.' This view is altogether misleading. Atlantic Canadians have not passively accepted the underdevelopment of their region, and their collective reactions to underdevelopment, whether political or not, must become a subject of sociological inquiry if we are to gain a comprehensive picture of the evolution of Canadian social movements.

NOTES

The authors thank Raoul Andersen, Clinton Herrick, Robert Hill, Robert Paine, and the two anonymous reviewers for the *Canadian Journal of Sociology*, in which this article originally appeared, for their critical comments on an earlier version of this paper; and Clinton Herrick and Gerald McManus for helping with the cartography.

1. W. L. Morton, *The Progressive Party in Canada* (Toronto, 1950), 83; cf. S. M. Lipset, *Agrarian socialism: the Cooperative Commonwealth Federation in Saskatchewan* (Berkeley, 1968), 47.

2. F. Underhill, *The image of Confederation* (Toronto, 1968), 63.

3. 'Newfoundland general election results, 1900-1932,' ed. M. Graessner (unpub. MS, Dept of Political Science, Memorial University of Newfoundland, 1977), 17-20.

4. G. Panting, 'The Fishermen's Protective Union of Newfoundland and the farmers' organisations in western Canada,' *Canadian Historical Association, Report, 1963*, 141-51.

5. *The history of the Fishermen's Protective Union of Newfoundland, from 1909-1929*, ed. W. Coaker (St John's, 1930), 44-63.

6. E. Durkheim, *The division of labor in society* (New York, 1965); T. Gurr, *Why men rebel* (Princeton, 1970).

7. A. Oberschall, *Social conflict and social movements* (Englewood Cliffs, N. J., 1973); C. Tilly et al., *The rebellious century, 1830-1930* (Cambridge, Mass., 1975).

8. Cf. R. Bierstedt, 'An analysis of social power,' *Power and progress: essays on sociological theory* (New York, 1974), 220-41.

9. E. Mandel, *Capitalism and regional disparities* (Toronto, 1973).

10. We borrow the phrase—and the idea that uneven underdevelopment produces intraregional variations in labour organisation—from R. Sacouman; see chapter 5 in this volume.

11. E. Antler, 'Maritime mode of production, domestic mode of production, or labor process: an examination of the Newfoundland inshore fishery,' a paper presented before the Northeastern Anthropological Association (Providence, 1977), 7 and *passim*.

12. S. Antler, 'Colonial exploitation and economic stagnation in nineteenth century Newfoundland' (unpub. PhD thesis, University of Connecticut, 1975), 113.

13. D. Alexander, 'Development and dependence in Newfoundland, 1880-1970,' *Acadiensis*, IV (1974), 19.

14. A. Martin, *The economic geography of Newfoundland* (n. p., 1938), 79-84; T. Philbrook, *Fisherman, logger, merchant, miner: social change and industrialism in three Newfoundland communities* (St John's, 1966), 31.

15. M. Gaffney, 'Crosshanded: work organization and the development cycle of the south coast Newfoundland domestic groups,' a paper presented before the Northeastern Anthropolological Association (Providence, 1977), 6.

16. *Ibid.*, and M. Gaffney, 'Resistance to unionization on the south coast of Newfoundland,' a paper presented before the Institute of Social and Economic Research, Memorial University (St John's, 1977); M. Firestone, *Brothers and rivals: patrilocality in Savage Cove* (St John's, 1967); Philbrook, *Fisherman, logger*; R. Schwartz, 'The crowd: friendship groups in a Newfoundland outport,' *The compact: selected dimensions of friendship*, ed. E. Layton (St John's, 1974).

17. Gaffney, 'Crosshanded,' 17-18.

18. Quoted in R. Anderson, 'The "count" and the "share:" offshore fishermen and changing incentives,' a paper presented before the Canadian Ethnology Society (Halifax, 1977), 13.

19. W. Black, 'The Labrador floater cod fishery,' Association of American Geographers, *Annals*, L (1960), 267.

20. *Ibid.*, 286; G. Briton, 'Fishermen and workers: the process of stability and change in a rural Newfoundland community' (unpub. PhD thesis, Columbia University, 1974), 37, 41; P. Devine and J. Lawton, *Old King's Cove* (n. p., 1944), 11.

21. 'Report of the select committee on the bill entitled "An act to prohibit the prosecution of the Labrador fishery in steam vessels," with the evidence taken in connection therewith,' Newfoundland, House of Assembly, *Journals*, 1905, 225 and *passim*.

22. *Ibid.*, 249.

23. S. J. R. Noel, *Politics in Newfoundland* (Toronto, 1971), 91-92. Noel is slightly inaccurate. The banking crews did in fact return to shore periodically for ice and bait.

24. Black, 'The Labrador floater cod fishery,' 286, writes that floaters had crews ranging in size from three to seventeen men. Using 1911 census data, districts with an average of seventeen or fewer men per ship going to the Labrador fishery we classified as predominantly floater districts, those with an average of more than seventeen per ship as predominantly stationer districts. Among the latter, FPU support was also high;

e.g., the constituency of Port de Grave, which had an average of over 45 persons per ship going to the Labrador fishery, was a stronghold of the union.

25. H. MacDermott, *MacDermott of Fortune Bay* (London, 1938), 196-202.

26. C. Brown with H. Horwood, *Death on the ice: the great Newfoundland sealing disaster of 1914* (Toronto, 1974).

27. L. Chafe, *Chafe's sealing book: a history of the Newfoundland seal fishery from the earliest available records down to and including the voyage of 1923* (St John's, 1924), 38.

28. *The book of Newfoundland*, ed. J. Smallwood (6v., St John's, 1937-67), II, 417-29.

29. The idea that social solidarity promotes political participation (and, among disadvantaged groups, radicalism) has of course a long history in sociology. It goes at least as far back as Marx and Engels' discussion in the *Manifesto of the Communist Party* of how the concentration of workers in large industry facilitates the development of political radicalism. The importance of this variable has been affirmed in a host of studies, many of which are discussed or cited in R. Brym, *The Jewish intelligentsia and Russian Marxism: a sociological study of intellectual radicalism and ideological divergence* (London, 1978); C. Smith and A. Freedman, *Voluntary associations: perspectives on the literature* (Cambridge, Mass., 1972); W. Spinrad, 'Correlates of trade union participation,' *American Sociological Review*, XXV (1960), 237-44; Tilly et al., *The rebellious century*.

30. J. Feltham, 'The development of the FPU in Newfoundland (1908-1923)' (unpub. MA thesis, Memorial University, 1959), 27-28; Noel, *Politics in Newfoundland*, 90-94.

31. R. Gwyn, *Smallwood: the unlikely revolutionary* (Toronto, 1972), 22; cf. Feltham, 'The development of the FPU,' 37-38.

32. *The history of the FPU*, ed. Coaker, 44.

33. I. McDonald, 'Coaker the reformer: a brief biographical introduction' (unpub. paper, Dept of History, Memorial University, n.d.), 25.

34. One of the few students of the subject who paid some attention to the social organisation of the churches with regard to the issue addressed here is the late Ian McDonald, whose suggestions in *ibid.*, 25-26, have proven most helpful in framing our argument.

35. Roman Catholic Archives (St John's), file ('The fisheries: Fishermen's Union, etc.'): Society of United Fishermen, *Annual Report* (March 1909); *Fisherman's Advocate*, 12 November 1910, 16 March 1912.

36. T. Nemec, 'The fishermen of St. Shores: leaders in context,' a paper presented before a research colloquium on community aspects of political development with special reference to Newfoundland, Institute of Social and Economic Research, Memorial University (St John's, 1971), 2; 'Trepassey (1840-1900): historical perspectives on social stratification,' *Perspectives on Newfoundland society and culture*, ed. M. Sterns (St John's, 1974), 87.

37. Devine and Lawton, *Old King's Cove*, 50-51; *The book of Newfoundland*, ed. Smallwood, II, 422.

38. Roman Catholic Archives, file ('The fisheries: Fishermen's Union, etc.'): Archbishop M. F. Howley to Mr Wallace, 20 September 1908. See also N. Veitch, 'The contribution of the Irish Benevolent Society to education in Newfoundland from 1823 to 1876' (unpub. MEd thesis, St Francis Xavier University, 1965).

39. P. Cashin, *My life and times, 1870-1919* (St John's, 1976), I, 76.

40. Why did they emerge at all, given the population's low rate of participation in the Labrador fishery, sealing, and logging? Unlike most parts of the south coast, this area was making increased use of the cod trap, which required larger boat crews; and the traps were frequently put out by merchants, or even operated by hired crews paid in cash. Moreover, increasing capitalisation, direct merchant control, wage payments, and labour concentration were occurring at this time and in this area in the ice trade (which

involved the supply of ice to bankers for purposes of freezing their catch) and, to a lesser extent, in the bait fishery and in wrecking activities. The existence of the local whale fishery may also have been important in this regard. Finally, the use of forty-quintal-capacity 'jack boats' to prosecute the Cape Ballard Banks fishery was probably of some significance for, unlike crews aboard ships working the Grand Banks, those on the jack boats displayed a higher level of social interaction since they had to come to shore frequently and fished closer together. See Cashin, *ibid.*, and R. Crane, *Ferryland* (St John's, 1973).

41. Quoted in McDonald, 'Coaker the reformer,' 26.

42. Devine and Lawton, *Old King's Cove*, 41-42.

43. McDonald, 'Coaker the reformer,' 25.

44. R. Moynes, *'Complaints is many and various but the odd divil likes it:' nineteenth century views of Newfoundland* (Toronto, 1975), 126-27.

45. H. Batstone, 'Methodism in Newfoundland: a study of its social impact' (unpub. MA thesis, McGill University, 1967), 50-51.

46. *Ibid.*, 17, 152.

47. Feltham, 'The development of the FPU,' 131, notes that William Coaker, the top leader of the FPU, had become a member of the Orange Lodge in early manhood, and his 'association with the Orange Lodge proved a great advantage to him during the formative years of the union, for he was given the use of the Orange Hall in every community which had one. He could also claim the kinship of brother members in almost every northern community.'

48. C. Chaulk, *Fogo, Twillingate and dependencies* (St John's, 1974).

49. The terms direct and indirect capitalist underdevelopment are used by Sacouman, chapter 5 in this volume, to distinguish between different modes of surplus appropriation. Our usage is focused on the question of the level of capital investment and resultant form of social organisation. For an attempt to combine both sets of concerns, see chapter 3 of this volume.

50. See B. Neis, 'The Fishermen's Protective Union of Newfoundland: a sociological analysis' (MA thesis, Memorial University, in press).

10 Towards a Critical Analysis of Neo-Nationalism in Newfoundland

James Overton

INTRODUCTION

Recent years have witnessed the growth of a number of what are variously called neo-nationalist, regionalist, or separatist movements in a number of countries.[1] Some of these movements are of a fully fledged nationalist-separatist nature while others are less developed, less powerful expressions of autonomist sentiments. They are particularly prominent in such European countries as Britain, France, Spain, Switzerland, and the Low Countires, but they are also in evidence in Canada, Australia, India, and so on.[2] They exist at a variety of scales, from the tiny Shetland Islands[3] to Quebec in Canada.[4] And they focus on a variety of more or less well defined political-economic-cultural units; some are quite distinct, having been fully constituted nations in the past, but others are based on quite fuzzy concepts with little historical, political, or even distinct cultural validity. A good example of the latter type is Occitania in France where there is little evidence that common characteristics outweigh internal heterogeneity.[5]

How can such widespread movements be accounted for, both as a general phenomenon and in specific instances? What is the nature of such movements and what are their implications? This paper begins to explore some dimensions of these questions, concentrating on the development of neo-nationalist sentiment in the province of Newfoundland.[6] As the title of the paper suggests, however, this is an effort 'towards' an analysis, much of which remains to be fully worked out. Conclusions, therefore, are of a tentative nature and should be treated with some considerable degree of caution.

SOME THEMES

In trying to understand embryonic nationalist or regionalist movements, it may be useful to focus on the following themes: (1) The *conditions* under which such movements occur and the *forces* that produce them. This should be approached from both a general point of view and by examining particular movements. (2) The *form* that the movement takes: i.e., its economic, political, and cultural components and the relationship among these. What is being protested (for example, economic inequalities and domination)? What is the form of the protest? What is being asserted (for example, local distinctiveness and identity)? What is being advocated (more local autonomy, control of resources, for example)? Why? This will involve a study of the embryonic ideology or ideologies of the movement. (3) The origins of the movement in terms of the groups of people that *initiate* and *facilitate* its development. How are workers, capitalists, politicians, and intellectuals involved in the movement? How is it managed and legitimised by these people? Special attention should be given to determining which classes and strata in society have their interests embodied in the movement. (4) The *theoretical basis* of the movement; that is, examining the views of change, of interregional or national relations, of rural-urban relations, of regional or ethnic identity, and of development, which are implicit or explicit in such movements. (5) The *implications* of such movements. This again involves the question of ideology. What kinds of theoretical and practical confrontations are taking place with regard to development? What is the dominant theory and practice of development? What is the nature of the critical break with this pattern that the new movement represents, and what kind of image of the future is contained within its viewpoint? A critical evaluation of the proposals advocated by the movement is particularly important. If regionalism or nationalism arises in opposition to a particular orthodox theory of development, the question of whether it will be able to bring about fundamental change or have its energy sapped and absorbed as it is forced back into an accommodation with the existing dominant ideology and power relations must be asked. Will the new opposition in development have its essence transformed while its appearance remains unaltered as has been the case with so many ostensibly radical movements?

The kinds of questions outlined above suggest a particular approach to understanding neo-nationalism, regionalism, or indeed any localism. The approach is one that seeks to analyse such movements as specific historical phenomena within their paticular social context, rather than viewing them as abstract expressions of the human spirit or the spirit of the nation.[7]

A NOTE ON IDEOLOGY

Before proceeding it is important to make a few comments about ideology which should be borne in mind in the context of the themes outlined above.

Ideology is not to be viewed as 'empty fancy.'[8] It must always be treated as a material force. Ideology consists not simply of a set of ideas, but of practical activities as well: how ideas 'work in the world.' In addition, it must be made clear that ideology, in the sense it is being used here, is *not* something that gives meaning to events, but rather it is the events as we experience them.[9] It follows that in trying to understand struggles between particular perspectives on development, central attention should be paid to the fact that the 'enemy of a theory or doctrine' is not simply a 'rival or competing theory.' It is 'the world of social practice' in which the rival theory is grounded, and it is this that must be countered in theory and in practice.[10]

Ideologies are firmly rooted in the interests and experiences of particular social classes, these classes being constituted at the level of relations of production.[11] In class societies, however, the ideology of the ruling class dominates. But this is not a result of simple manipulation by the dominant class although this does occur. More important, dominant ideology depends for its effectiveness on not being generally seen as the expression of certain class interests. For any ideology to be accepted even partially by a dominated class, it must render reality intelligible and make sense of people's everyday experiences. It must provide a guide for action and consequently it must 'work' at some level. Ideologies are never mere subjective illusion imposed on the subordinate classes by the dominant ones.[12]

To understand any particular ideology we must be able to demonstrate why things appear as they do for particular classes; that is, to analyse the forms of appearance of social relations. At the same time, the way in which these appearances are related to and conceal the fundamental relations of production and the central dynamic of capitalist society, the accumulation of capital, must be made clear. In the context of examining any nationalist or regionalist movement, it becomes important to ask how such an ideology makes sense of a particular situation and provides a guide for action for certain classes and strata. But, the way in which the ideology is an expression of certain struggles centred on, and constituted in terms of, the basic relations of production must also be examined.[13] Thus, in trying to understand any movement, it becomes important to distinguish what it claims to be about, the 'phrases and fancies' of the parties concerned,[14] and its basic determinants and real interests. This may be an especially crucial consideration in attempting to understand how movements of opposition become co-opted and have their potential for change diffused by the very social reality they challenge.[15]

Finally, it should be pointed out that in practice the identification of any ideology may be extremely difficult. Any developing ideology may not be in all respects mature, coherent, and free from contradictions. It may be an 'embryonic ideology,' which, though amorphous and ambiguous, is in opposition to the existing dominant ideology in certain critical respects.[16] Awkward and inconvenient as it may be for those who would study them, ideologies are never pure ideas. They are, after all, the ideas of people who live and struggle in actual social and historical contexts. Ideas influence and are influenced by the events that shape and are shaped by people.[17]

NEO-NATIONALISM

What are the forces that are producing neo-nationalist movements? Perhaps this question can best be approached first by discussing the nature of nineteenth-century nationalism.[18] This was characteristically a movement of integration focusing on building national economies. It involved the creation of national systems of infrastructure (transport and communications), money and banking, and administration. National markets, national identity, and centralised political systems were also created. All this was to provide a framework within which national capitalism could grow and develop (e.g., Canada's National Policy). Nationalism, then, aimed at achieving economic development, and constituted the nation state as the main building block of world capitalism. The opposite side of this nation-building was, of course, the decline of regional economies, local industries and institutions, and the growth of regional specialisation within the national division of labour.[19] In a nineteenth-century context, economic viability depended to a large extent on size; that is, on a country's having sufficient territory and population to provide a large internal market and a wide range of goods. These kinds of trends continue today with the formation of various economic unions (the Common Market).

The nationalist movement of today, however, although similar in some respects, is typically separatist in nature. This situation reflects, first, changes in the nature of world capitalism, which have led to the weakening of the nation state and of the national economy as the basic elements of the world economy.[20] The growing internationalisation of capital, represented especially by the multinationals and international economic management, has led, according to Martinelli and Somaini,[21] to a 'lower degree of unification of the capitalist interests within a country.' The internal economies of nations are losing their integration and cohesiveness. In addition, criteria of economic viability are changing, partially as a result of post-World War II decolonisation experiences. Small states are now seen as more viable. What is increasingly important is for the nation, however small, to find a strategic position somewhere along the circuits of the complex world economy.[22] A strategic resource like oil, or even being a tourist paradise or a good military location, can provide an adequate national income for states, according to this view. Second, since World War II, we have seen in developed countries a massive increase of state involvement in the economy in order to try to iron out some of the cyclical, social, and spatial unevenness in capitalist development and thus prevent some of the political problems associated with such unevenness. It has recently become obvious, however, that the efforts of the capitalist state to manage the economy, produce full employment, and end regional disparities have failed. These issues have consequently become politicised, especially since the advent of the current economic crisis. One result of this, Nairn argues, is that areas experiencing relative deprivation have 'increasingly been drawn into political action against this.'[23] The action often takes the form of neo-nationalism. In general, then, it is uneven economic development that is the cradle for political competition over the fruits of economic development, and regionalism, or neo-nationalism can be seen as a reaction against the tendencies to concentration and centralisation that are inherent in capitalism.

THE NEWFOUNDLAND CONTEXT

Although nationalist sentiment in Newfoundland has existed since the early nineteenth century, and since that time has continued to be an important political, economic, and cultural force,[24] the current phase of nationalism is rooted in post-Confederation (1949) developments in the province.[25]

In the post-World War II period, struggles in underdeveloped countries around the world moved from anticolonial ones towards a 'demand for development.'[26] This was partly because the war drew such areas out of their isolation and thus created an awareness of development issues among their inhabitants. In Newfoundland, economic problems and the desire for a higher standard of living provided much of the impetus for Confederation with Canada. Following Confederation, Newfoundland was jerked even more out of its relative isolation than it had been by the war and it underwent a process of rapid integration into the Canadian economic and political systems.[27] In the 1950s, there was initiated in the new province, under the leadership of J. R. Smallwood and the Liberal Party, a period of rapid social and economic development in which the state acted as the motor of change. This consisted of an attempt to prepare for and promote economic development by means of creating an economic, administrative, and cultural infrastructure of the kind appropriate to an advanced capitalist society.[28] The concentration was on the provision of transportation facilities (the Trans-Canada Highway and 'Roads to Resources'), rural electrification, the creation of cheap hydro-electric power for industrialists, and the development of a modern communications system (see Table 10-1). An administrative bureaucracy and a technocracy were

TABLE 10-1

SELECTED STATISTICS ON
NEWFOUNDLAND, 1950-1975.

	Paved Road (miles)	Telephones (Per 1,000 population)	Registered Motor Vehicles	Population (1,000s)
1950	121	6.1	16,375	361
1955	130	8.1	39,766	415
1960	380	12.6	61,952	458
1965	1009	17.6	92,885	493
1970	1337	26.0	118,641	522
1975	2605	36.1	173,642	558

SOURCE: *Historical Statistics of Newfoundland and Labrador, Supplement,* Volume 2 (1), (St. John's, 1977)

formed and educational facilities were provided to train the new bureaucracy and the less-skilled workers that were also needed. In addition, the period saw the development of the mass media, new institutions catering to the arts, and other leisure-time activities (camping and tourism). In fact, *all* the facets of the modern state and of modern capitalist society, including unions, where appropriate,[29] were developed in preparation for a period of rapid industrial growth. Even a potential workforce was made available by such means as the resettlement of isolated fishing communities in 'growth' centres.[30] Industrial development initially took the form of small-scale import-substituting industry; however, by the late 1950s most of these enterprises had failed. Later developments concentrated on large-scale industrial schemes, especially those exploiting resources.

Of course, the growth of a strong provincial state structure in Newfoundland, as in the rest of Canada, must be seen in the context of the postwar boom and the changing nature of the state.[31] Since the war the Canadian economy has undergone a substantial 'piecemeal absorption' into the American imperial system.[32] Manufacturing in Canada (often in American branch plants to begin with) has been reoriented from internal markets to export ones in the USA (e.g., the Autopact). This has been accompanied by a process through which Canadian regions have become increasingly appended to the American market, in many cases as suppliers of primary products. Concomitant with these economic changes, dialectically related political changes have taken place. There has been what many have seen as a steady attrition of the power of the central government and this 'weakness at the centre'[33] has encouraged political disintegration. Consequently, there has been a massive growth in the importance of provincial and even municipal structures for the promotion of economic growth. Using the state as the motor of economic growth, provinces have engaged in a scramble for investment, enticing capital by massive expenditures on infrastructure, grants, and concessions. As a result, there has been a substantial increase in state debt in Canada at the provincial and municipal levels. According to Deaton,[34] in the period 1950 to 1968, federal government debt increased only 136% while provincial debt increased 505%, and municipal debt 511%.

Provincially directed growth has further increased fragmentation in Canada as each province develops its particular interests. In the postwar period, there have been attempts at economic management by means of government participation in the economy, to try to achieve full employment and eliminate regional disparities. Both the welfare state and strategies for industrial development were regarded as ways of dealing with poverty, unemployment, and low productivity in a period when the main ideology of development was progress, industrialisation, modernisation, and the creation of jobs.

This period saw massive changes in Newfoundland. There occurred a substantial shift in the spatial division of labour: in 1951 about 60% of the province's population lived in settlements with fewer than 1,000 inhabitants, whereas by 1971 the figure was approximately 40%.[35] Changes in production and the changes in the province mentioned earlier resulted in a broad shift in class relations. This was, in turn, related to an expansion of people's horizons and the development of their needs. The whole process of change was accompanied by the breakdown of the traditional economy of the outports as the fishing industry was modernised and a capital-intensive sector of the fishery

FIGURE 10-2

ADVERTISEMENT PLACED BY THE
NEWFOUNDLAND DEPARTMENT OF ECONOMIC DEVELOPMENT, 1959

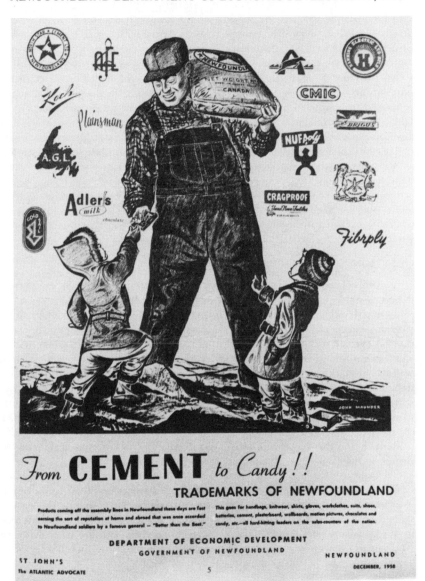

concentrating on frozen fish, mainly caught offshore, was developed. The inshore fishery and the salt-fish trade, which had been associated with it, declined in importance.[36] Many of the changes that resulted in the destruction of rural life appeared to stem directly from government policies, with the consequence that these issues became politicised.

That people accepted for so long what Canning has termed 'the illusion of progress'[38] is not surprising, considering the force with which the illusion was projected by politicians, academics, business people, the media, and government employees. A glance at government and business advertisements for the 1950s provides a clear illustration of the way in which the majority of the population was mobilised and given a stake in the utopia for all that was supposed to result from ties with Canada and industrial growth (see Figure 10-2). By the mid to late 1960s, however, it had become clear that this drive for development was far from a success. It was the grave state of affairs in the fisheries in the late 1960s that led to the birth of a number of development associations around the province, all seeking to ameliorate the situation. Since then, the failure of many development schemes and the advent of the present economic crisis have given rise to an increasing questioning of past development policies and a general search for alternatives. Confederation, not wholeheartedly or uniformly embraced in the first place, is increasingly being questioned.

QUESTIONING DEVELOPMENT

It is within the context of the changes since Confederation that the present debate over development in Newfoundland must be examined.

On a world scale, development is the subject of considerable debate at the present time; a controversy exists over its very meaning in theory and practice.[39] Very often criticism of development focuses on the contradictions between economic growth, on the one hand, and overall concern with human welfare and cultural and spiritual values, on the other. In Newfoundland, the debate has in many ways followed the same lines, being explicitly concerned with what can be identified as an opposition between cultural and economic values. This is at the core of the neo-nationalist movement, which focuses on (1) control of resources and economic and political decision-making; and (2) what is identified as the 'Newfoundland way of life.' In fact, in most cases, the two principles are linked, as in the key issue of the fishery.

The kind of questioning we are talking about is part of a quite broadly based, though diffuse, movement that includes the grassroots development associations, people working in the state bureaucracy, the media, the university, and other educational institutions. People in these institutions are increasingly expressing concern over the undermining of the traditional Newfoundland way of life with its distinctive activities, values, and settlement patterns. As one writer to the St John's *Evening Telegram* put it:

Fellow Newfoundlanders,
    Due to recent trends in our political systems and in particular, our social system, I

feel that now, more so than ever before, we as Newfoundlanders, interested in the preservation of our culture, tradition and heritage, must organize ourselves to fight the foreign factions now adversely influencing our country (Newfoundland).

Would Newfoundland nationalists, separatists, interested in attending an organizational meeting to outline the policies of our group, please write ... to 'The True Newfoundlanders.'[40]

Often included in the concern is a sense of loss and nostalgia for outport life and a questioning of the values expressed in the 'urban dream and the industrial goal.'[41] This kind of reaction also corresponds in many cases with a tendency to romanticise the traditional economy and way of life and the rural community,[42] a tendency which, Nigel Harris notes,[43] is not uncommon in similar situations and which, he suggests, is an expression of nostalgia and current alienation.[44]

The whole question of the resettlement of isolated fishing communities is a key aspect of the modernisation of the province on which much of the debate has focused, and the issue has stimulated many exchanges on the meaning of development, cultural versus economic values and ethics (ideology) in social science and policy research.[45] The reaction against resettlement is summed up well by Martin in his statement that 'the people of rural Newfoundland no longer silently permit their governments to conduct social genocide.'[46]

Among a certain section of the population in Newfoundland, then, there is a growing reaction against changes that are seen as being imposed from outside (with the assistance and encouragement of an inept government). These changes have arrived in the form of alien lifestyles and values; what O'Flaherty calls 'the continual inrush of North American vulgarity'[47] and what Alexander[48] and Canning[49] see as imported, inappropriate development strategies, which destroy rather than reinforce the cultural distinctiveness of the area. According to Canning[50] it is 'our great affinity for the CFA—the Come From Away'—that has led to the acceptance of alien values and inappropriate large-scale development schemes.

Changes since Confederation, expecially the flowering of the welfare state, are also seen as having sapped independence, self-reliance, and self-sufficiency, creating a massive dependence on 'crumbs from the rich man's table' that is 'psychologically debilitating.'[51] The increasing dependence on Ottawa (over half the province's revenue comes in transfer payments) is very much resented by some people. As a recent observer notes, 'our Newfoundland pride is slipping away, thanks to Canada's dole.'[52] In fact, all this adds up to a general feeling that, within Confederation, 'the centre has failed to come effectively to grips with the real problems of the local economy,'[53] while there has been a substantial loss of control over local conditions.[54]

It is no accident that the question of control of resources is a central issue in the debate over development. As Harris points out, there is a feeling among Newfoundlanders that they are the 'victims of exploitation' and that 'their resources have been alienated to satisfy the ineffable greed of their imperial masters and the multinational corporations whose puppets they are.'[55] And

Conservative politician John Crosbie argues:

It would turn your stomach to see what American Smelting [and Refining Company] took out of Buchans in the years they have operated there, and Price [Company], without paying to this province hardly anything in taxes and employing people there at miserable wages and miserable conditions in a company town with miserable housing. [It] would really cause you to become a savage—you know, Marxist.[56]

Others suggest that it was the loss of local control over the fishery resource with Confederation (the federal government has responsibility for offshore resources) that led to the neglect of the fishing industry. More local control of this resource is consequently seen as a prerequisite for the future development of the fishing industry so as to maximise benefits to the province. Similarly, with the discovery of oil and gas off Newfoundland and Labrador, a strong case has been made by the provincial government for control of this resource.[57] The desire for greater control over resources and for greater benefit from them has recently stimulated the provincial government to issue nationalist slogans such as 'Vive la Terre Neuve Libre!' and 'we're going to be masters in our own house.'[58] Whether such statements can be viewed as leading towards independence for Newfoundland, they do indicate that the threat of separatism can be used in the interests of building a stronger state in Newfoundland and getting a better deal for the province.

The kind of questioning taking place in Newfoundland is summarised well by the statement issued by the April Fools at the time of the celebration of the 25th anniversary of Newfoundland entry into Confederation:

WHY ARE WE CELEBRATING?

BECAUSE major decisions affecting Newfoundland's development are being made in Ottawa?

BECAUSE these decisions have not been in the best interests of Newfoundland?

BECAUSE key positions in Newfoundland have been consistently given to outsiders rather than Newfoundlanders of equal ability?

BECAUSE Newfoundland society is being steadily absorbed into North American mediocrity?

BECAUSE we are paying the highest prices in Canada for everything?

BECAUSE our resources have been sold out to foreign and mainland interests?

BECAUSE our people are forced to emigrate through a failure to develop local opportunities?

BECAUSE our fisheries are dying?

Signed,
THE APRIL FOOLS

The stated objectives of the April Fools were (1) to sponsor new approaches and ways in which Newfoundland might regain control over its own development and destiny, and (2) to provide a forum for individuals and groups who wish to promote a more realistic approach to Confederation.[59]

What is happening in Newfoundland and Labrador is common to a very large number of areas in North America and Europe. For example, oil development and the growing power of the multinationals have been closely related to the revival of Scottish nationalism. Similarly, it is the threat and promise of oil development in the tiny Shetland islands that have raised important questions about local control of development and stimulated an interest in separatism.[60]

Associated with the kind of questioning of development in Newfoundland discussed above, a cultural revival or renaissance has been taking place over the past few years: a renewal of interest in rural life and folk culture (art, music, customs, crafts, theatre, speech) and local history.[61] Much of this movement of rediscovery and popularisation of local culture is directed by, and intended for, the consumption of the new urban middle class, a class which—paradoxically—was created by the very process of modernisation that has been (and is) regarded as a threat to the traditional culture. According to Martin, the cultural revival is a sign of 'a society on the rebound.'[62] There is a lament for a vanishing way of life:

Today ... the vitality of this folk culture is being steadily sapped by the pervasive influence of North American values, the influence of social and economic forces undermining the traditional pattern of outport life.[63]

The roots of this culture are seen to be 'withering away' as the 'folk arts of the past' are lost for 'the opiates of the present.'[64]

The cultural dimension of this neo-nationalism is not surprising. In virtually all cases such movements involve significant cultural revivals. This is certainly true of the Shetland case where the revival must be seen, as in Newfoundland, as a way of mobilising local sentiment on the basis of perceived cultural distinctiveness either to resist or control forces that are shaping the local economy and restructuring a way of life. Similarly, as Nairn points out for nineteenth-century nationalism, sentimental or romantic culture 'always went hand-in-hand with the spread of nationalism.'[65] And, as Ernst Fischer has concluded: 'the romantic idealization of folklore and folk art became a weapon for stirring up the people against degrading conditions.'[66] Associated with neo-nationalism, therefore, we often find a rediscovery or invention of national or regional history and culture, all of which is part of an attempt to discover and define an identity as a prelude to political mobilisation. In Newfoundland, such an identity already exists, for, as Martin notes, 'an independent Newfoundland ... is not history but the common experience of many living Newfoundlanders.'[67] Such a national identity, called by Gwyn the Newfoundland 'mystique'[68] and by Neary 'an incipient nationalist sentiment,'[69] has long been present and has been a powerful force in politics. But behind the consciousness of Newfoundlanders as being a 'distinctive breed'[70] with a unique cultural heritage, and the myth of the 'hardy Newfoundlander,'—both of which are partly the sentimental creation of the elite of the late nineteenth and early twentieth centuries—lie feelings of inferiority and insecurity.[71] Such feelings have been translated into a 'fierce patriotism' which has been a significant force in Newfoundland, especially in anti-Confederation movements.[72]

To summarise: The central questions that are being asked in Newfoundland about development can be expressed in the following terms: (1) Does the province have to follow the usual paths of economic development? If so, can the negative effects of this development be minimised? (2) Is it possible to have some form of economic development that is compatible with what are seen as worthwhile cultural values? If not, then what are the barriers to this, and under what conditions would it be possible? These questions, implicitly or explicitly stated, run through just about every development issue discussed, whether it be the establishment of national parks, oil development, or the future of the fisheries.

THE THEORETICAL BASIS OF NEO-NATIONALISM

The neo-nationalist ideology that is emerging in such areas as Newfoundland contains a number of complex theoretical strands. As Nairn has commented, such 'neonate separatism ... has equipped itself speedily with New Left populist and environmentalist ideologies of the 1960s ... mixed up with elements from traditional nationalism and "Third Worldism." '[73] Newfoundland is no exception to this pattern (see Figure 10-3, for example) and a list of the ideological elements of the movement in the province, even if impressionistic and partial, can be usefully introduced at this stage in order to understand the theoretical basis of neo-nationalism. Some of these elements have already been outlined in the previous section; others have not. They include (1) An emphasis on economic, political, and cultural independence and autonomy. (2) An emphasis on lifestyle solutions to problems of underdevlopment. It is suggested that restricted consumption patterns be combined with traditional patterns of 'occupational pluralism' in a way that is reminiscent of proposals from the 1930s.[74] (3) Concern with small-scale industry using local resources and alternative technology.[75] (4) Community development—i.e., grass-roots, bottom-up decision making rather than top-down decision making and large-scale development schemes—as a strategy for progress. Associated with this are the ideas of self-sufficiency, self-help, and self-reliance—in short, what is known as the 'small is beautiful' model of development.[76] (5) An emphasis on obtaining more revenue from resource development and on using income from, say, multinational corporations' exploitation of oil to help seed development; that is, to help maintain, develop, or revitalise industry that will fit in with the local culture.[77]

What this adds up to is a diffuse populism, the two main strands of which are an economic/cultural nationalism or regionalism and what may be called 'economic romanticism.'[78]

Populism is common in underdeveloped areas within the capitalist system.

FIGURE 10-3

PROGRAMME COVER FOR THE PLAY
THE PRICE OF FISH, 1976

DIRECT TO YOU
FROM THE NATION'S TENTH FRONTIER
THE MUMMERS
OF NEWFOUNDLAND
IN
(WHAT'S THAT GOT TO DO WITH)
THE PRICE OF FISH
BEING A FISH EYE'S VIEW OF CANADA'S THIRD WORLD.
SAMPLE THIS
EAST COAST REMEDY FOR
CHRONIC INTERNAL
DISORDERS & DISRUPTIONS
CAUSED BY
· ATTACKS OF FOREIGN CAPITAL ON NATURAL RESOURCES
· INVASIONS OF MAINLAND TROJAN HORSES BEARING
WELFARE GIFTS
· TRANSPLANTS TO TORONTO
· AND MANY MORE UNHEALTHY ASSAULTS ON THE
NEW—FOUND—LAND
TRULY AN ELIXIR FOR THE NEW
INTERNATIONAL ECONOMIC ORDER
BEWARE
FALSE CURE-ALLS FOR ECONOMIC PARALYSIS

Quite often it occurs during periods of rapid change in which small-scale, independent production is eliminated as capitalist development and industrialisation take place. During such changes there is great disruption and the rural population undergoes social and political mobilisation. Populism generally represents a critique of capitalist development from the point of view of the small producer whose existence is being threatened by the changes that are taking place, yet who also hopes to participate in, and benefit from, them. While using a vision of the good old days to measure the limitations of the developments that are taking place, populists project the past into the future and use it in an attempt to bolster or reintroduce small-scale production and rural regeneration.[79]

The most recent expression of this populism is the report of the People's Commission on Unemployment.[80] This speaks out against the overwhelming and impersonal forces that are seen to be shaping people's lives and creating economic problems in Newfoundland. These forces are big business (multinationals), North American materialistic values, and centralised government with its policies that are inappropriate to Newfoundland and unresponsive to the needs of ordinary people. It is these outside forces that have undermined the economic and social basis for life in rural Newfoundland. The report harps back to a pre-Confederation Golden Age before these alien forces took hold of Newfoundland and destroyed the inshore fishery, which had been 'a reliable source of employment for centuries.'[81] It is Confederation, then, that is viewed as the breach in the dam that led to the destruction of the viability of rural life and to a situation where 'our natural and human resources have become the fuel for someone else's development'—Ontario, Alberta, Quebec, and the United States are mentioned in this respect.[82]

If the problems of Newfoundland are seen as stemming from foreign control, inappropraite large-scale development, integration into the mainstream of North American life, and exploitation, then the solutions implicit and explicit in the report are consistent with this view. For the future, they point towards more local control, or at least a government that is responsive to local needs, and small-scale capitalism using local resources and expertise. Such a programme will be the basis for regional/rural revitalisation, rather than the 'pipe dream ... of an industrial Newfoundland.'[83]

Whether clearly stated or not, the theoretical basis for this kind of perspective is a version of the dependency theory of development and underdevelopment.[84] According to this theory, underdevelopment in Newfoundland results from its being a peripheral or hinterland region within Canada and the world economy. Such areas are dominated by regions that are economically and politically more developed, and they are kept in a state of 'colonial servitude;'[85] their development is not for the benefit of local people (at best only a small local elite benefits); but is dictated by the needs of the metropolitan society. An area like Newfoundland is, therefore, dependent on the metropolis for capital investment, technology, consumer goods, planning models, expertise, and welfare and transfer payments. In this unequal relationship, the periphery is exploited: its undervalued raw materials and surplus labour go to feed development at the centre. The dominated society receives a few low-paying jobs, limited revenue for the state, and experiences environmental destruction.

This theoretical perspective became popular in New Left circles in the 1960s. It was developed in opposition to the conservative modernisation theories that prevailed at the time. Much of the radicalism that was initially associated with the use of dependency theory has been diffused, and now, at least in its less virulent forms, it is used by quite conservative analysts.[86] This is certainly true in Newfoundland, where elements of the perspective are frequently used even by Conservative politicians. Such a theory is increasingly popular in Newfoundland because it does seem to make sense of the experiences of many people in the last thirty years, and it does provide a guide for action. An understanding of development that rests on this theory almost inevitably leads to certain kinds of solutions to the economic and other ills of peripheral areas. If dependency and domination are the problem, then independence, or at least greater autonomy, is the solution. Such a theory is, then, usually the ideological basis for some kind of regionalist or neo-nationalist movement.

This is not the place to provide an in-depth critique of dependency theory; this has been done effectively by others.[87] It is, nevertheless, useful to outline some of the limitations of this theory for understanding uneven regional development. First, the concept of dependency is too vague and unspecific to be of effective use in an analysis of uneven development: it is unclear exactly what kinds of social relationships are actually being described by the term. The same problem exists with the concepts of metropolis and hinterland or centre and periphery. All these concepts lack historical and social specificity and could refer to any social and economic system from advanced capitalism to the Inca empire. Second, dependency theory places great emphasis on spatial relations. One region is said to dominate another region. But, what basis is there for accepting the region as a unit of analysis, how is this region defined, and at what scale should the analysis operate?[88] What lies behind this space fetishism are social relations of production, which are *class* relations. Related to the above point is the assumption that the problem is 'them'—that is, metropolitan society—and that more control by an unspecified 'us' would solve the problems. In this view, the 'us' is usually the local state structure, which is assumed to represent the people. The state is thus *not* seen as the essential instrument of class domination in capitalist society, but as an institution that stands above production relations and can be used in the interests of the people rather than capital. But, the most important criticism of dependency theory, and one related to the points made above, is that it operates with a market definition of capitalism. This means that the analysis operates in terms of relations of exchange rather than relations of production. The concept of exploitation is used, but in a rather loose way to describe what are often called trade 'rip-offs.' This use of the term conceals the basis of exploitation in capitalist society: the extraction of surplus value from the working class in the production process. Dependency theory, then, operates with a concept of production as basically a technical process rather than a social one. It contains no concept of mode of production and fails to analyse the relations of production, which are at the heart of uneven regional development in capitalist society. Focusing on exchange relations, such a perspective leads to areas resisting exploitation in trade and trying to get a better deal for their resources within the capitalist system.

In moving from 'dependency to development,'[89] that is, in trying to gain greater independence and autonomy, it is recognised that it is important to have a strong economic base, as the author of a letter to the editor of the St John's *Evening Telegram* indicates:

The time will soon be coming when as Newfoundlanders [we] will choose to rid ourselves of the Confederation with Canada and I would like to reassure all the doubters out there, that we will not do it until we can financially stand on our own two feet.[90]

Greater control of existing resources, such as hydro-electric power and the fisheries, and the development of such strategic resources as oil, will provide the financial basis for more independence according to the neo-nationalist scenario. The present provincial government's attempts to gain control of offshore oil can be seen as the provincial equivalent of economic nationalism. After all, oil is the magic commodity that transforms 'have not' provinces and countries into 'have' ones overnight. Revenue from such resources could even, in theory, be used as part of a provincial/national development programme to revitalise the decaying traditional sector of what is regarded as New-foundland's 'dual economy.'[91]

A COMMENT ON THE CLASS BASIS OF NEO-NATIONALISM

Throughout this paper, a few comments have been made about the class basis of neo-nationalist sentiments in Newfoundland; however, this important issue needs to be explored in greater detail. Here we are concerned with the class basis of neo-nationalism from two points of view: first, identifying the social class of its supporters and, second, examining the class nature of its content and grievances. This is the most speculative and impressionistic part of the paper, owing to the lack of hard data to support the argument. Consequently, I intend to state more than can be proven at this time and thus simply to suggest some relationships.

Since Confederation there have been substantial changes in class structure in Newfoundland, although existing data offer only a rough impression of them. Many of the most important changes are in the fishing industry, which has undergone a long-term decline as a source of employment. In the 1890s over 50,000 people (80% of the labour force) were engaged in fishing; this declined to 35,000 (40% of the labour force) in the mid 1930s, to just over 18,000 (17% of the labour force) in 1951, and to just under 18,000 (13% of the labour force) in 1970.[92] There have also been substantial changes in the structure of the industry since Confederation. The role of the independent operator and family production in the fishery has declined in importance and, with this, inshore fishing and the production of salt fish. Offshore trawler fishing and the production of fresh frozen fish in local fish plants now predominates. According to the *Financial Post*,[93] there are now only 12,000 inshore fishermen in the province, while 1,500 work offshore and 6,500 are employed in fish plants. Of the other primary industries, mining has expanded in terms of production, but not significantly in terms of employment (see Table 10-4), while forestry and agriculture have declined substantially as providers of jobs. In forestry, in particular, mechanisation of logging operations has led to the

TABLE 10-4

SELECTED LABOUR FORCE STATISTICS BY INDUSTRY
FOR NEWFOUNDLAND AND LABRADOR,
1951-1971 (IN THOUSANDS)

	1951	1961	1971
All Industry	106.7	112.2	147.9
Agriculture	3.5	1.6	1.2
Forestry/Logging	10.5	6.9	2.5
Fishing/Trapping	18.5	8.4	6.8
Mining	3.7	4.3	4.9
Manufacturing (All)	14.6	12.2	17.6
Fish	3.2	3.4	8.0
Sawmilling	1.6	3.4	8.0
Pulp & Paper	4.6	3.5	3.2
Other	5.2	4.4	5.8
Construction	7.3	9.5	15.5
Transport, Communications and Utilities	10.7	15.2	16.4
Trade	14.3	18.9	23.1
Finance, etc.	.6	1.4	2.6
Service (All)	21.6	30.3	44.2
Community	6.5	10.7	20.1
Business & Personal	5.6	7.1	12.3
Government	9.5	12.6	11.8
Unspecified	1.4	3.5	13.1

NOTE: Persons 14 years of age and over in 1951. In 1961 and 1971 persons 15 years and over.

SOURCE: Canada, *Census*, 1951, Volume 4, Labour Force by Occupation and Industry, Table 16; Canada, *Census*, 1961, Volume 3, Part 2, 3, Fart 4, Labour Force by Industry, Table 1; Canada, *Census*, 1971, Volume 3, Part 4, Labour Force by Industry, Table 2.

great loss of employment. In the past thirty years the most significant growth in the numbers of people employed has been in the service sector of the economy. In 1977 the production of goods provided only an estimated 42,000 person-years of employment compared with services, which provided 118,000, including 48,000 in government employment.[94] Rapid expansion in employment has taken place particularly in construction, transport, communications and utilities, trade and community, business and government service (Table 10-4). Even with a growth in employment opportunities, unemployment has remained high and has in recent years risen to about 18% according to official statistics. This figure would undoubtedly be very much higher but for the fact that total net migration from the province amounted to about 45,000 people in the period 1961-75.[95]

During the period since Confederation a new middle class has developed in Newfoundland. One part of this class, which evolved from the controlling elite of pre-Confederation days, has abandoned its entrenched position in the fish trade for new business opportunities in construction, transportation, communications, and various kinds of merchandising. This class is small and relatively powerless in national and international terms and is clearly dependent on the state and the few basic industries (mainly run by multinationals) that form the productive base of the economy.

The other main section of the new middle class consists of what may be called a technocratic fraction. This is a broad stratum of people employed in state and state-related agencies (education, the civil service, the media, the arts, the social services, etc.) and also, to some extent, in industry and in unions. In underdeveloped regions of developed capitalist nations, it is state-related employment that is the most important arena for the new middle class.

The crucial question of whether the new middle class is indeed a class, in terms of being constituted by the relations of production, rather than being determined by its technical function in production and by political, ideological, and social factors, will not be discussed here.[96] Suffice it to say that this is a significant new stratum, or set of strata, in society generally, and in Newfoundland in particular. It will be argued here that it is this group that is especially the focus of neo-nationalist sentiments in Newfoundland as in many other areas with similar movements.[97] But first, what are its main characteristics?

One of the main functions of the technocratic fraction of the new middle class within the social division of labour is an intellectual one. The basis for understanding intellectuals as a social category in capitalist society has been suggested by Gramsci.[98] This group consists of all those who exercise technical or directive capacities—managers, administrators, bureaucrats, politicians, and organisers of culture such as educators and artists. Intellectuals consist of both people who are specialists, such as managers, and those who organise society in general by creating the most favourable conditions for the progress of the class whose interests they serve. Gramsci also distinguishes between 'traditional' and 'organic' intellectuals. The former group is the one we normally think of as intellectual. It is composed of learned people who think of themselves as autonomous and independent of the dominant class in society (teachers, artists, priests, etc.). The second group is more directly related to the economic structure. It is made up of industrial managers, scientists, innovators, and so on. It is a group that is rarely hostile to the interests of the dominant class.

Intellectuals, as a group, are an increasingly powerful force in society. But how can the central position of the group be explained? According to Enzensberger, the petit bourgeoisie, of which intellectuals are a part, is a class that has little economic power. Its importance can be attributed to the cultural hegemony that it exercises in modern capitalist society. In particular, it is a class that 'produces the forms of daily life on a mass scale and imposes them on everybody else.'[99] The petite bourgeoisie is swarming with innovators. It invents ideologies, and inspires, supports, and implements practically all schools, trends, and movements. In great measure it determines what people think, what is considered good and worth striving for. A supplanting class, it is continually striving 'to become.' For the new middle class, the key to advancement (within occupational spheres finely graduated by status and professional grouping) is education. The importance of this cannot be underestimated. Education represents accumulated 'cultural capital.'[100] Members of the new middle class see work as a career in which individual effort will be rewarded by promotion. This is the dominant view of work in our society, which should be contrasted with the attitude to work of the working class.[101] Within the middle-class perspective on work, failure to succeed is attributed either to personal inadequacy or natural disaster, but in certain circumstances it can also become politicised.[102]

The emergence of the new middle class in Newfoundland, a significant group of intellectuals, has been made possible by the substantial development of the economic and cultural infrastructure that has arisen since Confederation. The number of occupations for intellectuals has expanded rapidly as a result of Newfoundland's bureaucratic revolution, much like the 'quiet revolution' in Quebec and similar developments in Alberta.[103] As Gramsci points out:

Every state has its own functionaries: one of the functions of the state is to raise the mass of the population to a particular cultural and moral level, a level which corresponds to the needs of the productive forces for development, and hence to the interests of the ruling classes.[104]

The past period of state-directed development in Newfoundland has produced an upwardly mobile, skilled, and highly educated stratum of people with expanded horizons and an awareness of the possibilities for, and the barriers against, their advancement (see Table 10-5). This group is largely urban-based and propertyless (in terms of owning the means of production) and its interests are obviously linked to the state. As long as the dominant class remains progressive and appears to advance the interests of society and of the new middle class, the latter group is likely to remain supportive. But if there is a lack of direction in society and if economic growth and the possibilities for advancement falter, this ambitious and restless section of the population is likely to become increasingly critical of the state of affairs.

That changes in the class structure since Confederation have had a far-reaching effect on politics in Newfoundland is widely recognised. By the late 1960s, it had become clear that much of the political power of those engaged in fishing, who had provided Smallwood's main source of support, had been eroded. It was the new middle class that provided the major new force in politics; a force that Matthews describes as 'urbanism.'[105] It was this group that, in the economic climate of the late 1960s and early 1970s, the Progressive Conservative Party was able to mobilise in order to oust the Liberals from power. In the words of Peter Neary, 'Smallwood the modernizer fell victim to the modernized.'[106] The new middle class has also become an important force in other areas of Newfoundland politics. For example, sections of it have been involved in the rise in popularity of the New Democratic Party as well as having become involved in city politics (e.g., the recently formed Civic Reform Group in St John's). This group also provides the seedbed for the growth of neo-nationalist sentiments.

TABLE 10-5

SELECTED STATISTICS ON EDUCATION
AND GOVERNMENT-EMPLOYED TAXPAYERS
NEWFOUNDLAND AND LABRADOR, 1950-1975

	Degrees granted at Memorial University	Teachers in public schools	Number of taxpayers in federal, provincial, and municipal government employment
1950	16	2,499	3,240
1955	49	3,106	5,960
1960	151	4,317	11,149
1965	287	5,543	12,323
1970	1,097	6,437	17,296
1975	1,735	7,621	26,809

SOURCE: *Historical Statistics of Newfoundland and Labrador, Supplement*, Volume 11 (1), 1977, Table H-3.

It was intellectuals, especially in education, who emerged in the 1960s as the source of opposition in its articulated form to the contradictions of post-Confederation development. Much of the focus of attention, as previously pointed out, was on the demise of rural Newfoundland. Often this was also seen as very much a cultural question—the elimination of a unique way of life—by the urban-based, middle-class intellectuals. The interpretation of Newfoundland history and society, and the critique of development pioneered by this group, has become widespread. It has been diffused through the university to the government, to rural development agencies, the media, and the unions. To provide one last example of this perspective it is worthwhile to quote from a brief presented by the Newfoundland and Labrador Rural Development Council to the Task Force on Canadian Unity (1977). According to the brief, at the time of Confederation,

lack of imagination, greed avarice and stupidity had brought us to the brink of rack and ruin but instead of taking stock and starting anew, we threw away our one chance for independence and gave up in despair, revelling in the sweet death of welfare, unemployment insurance and mother's allowance. We turned belly up and Canadian wolf was quick to rip out our guts. Canada gave us security, or so we felt, and for that we were induced to sacrifice everything, our culture, our resources, indeed the very spirit of our people. A bespectacled messiah handed us the hammer and we gleefully nailed ourselves en masse to a comfortable cross.[107]

Newfoundland was 'pillaged and raped' in the period after Confederation, while the victims remained 'without a voice.'[108] Now, 'we are forced to view the vast riches that could have been ours if only we had had the foresight,' and 'we are beginning to realize that the main barrier to Newfoundland's future development may in fact be the nature of confederation itself.'[109]

The cultural dimension of this perspective is not really surprising, considering its intellectual origins and the nature of the new middle class. Members of this class are particularly sensitive to cultural issues, and most resent cultural slurs concerning the inhabitants of underdeveloped areas, which are characteristic of uneven social and economic development and colonialism.[110] It is an attribute of a rising middle class that its members feel that they are 'as good as anyone' and the the disparaging comments made about people living in underdeveloped areas do not really apply to *them*. The roots of many members of the new middle class are, in addition, actually or emotionally still in the traditional social and economic structures of rural Newfoundland—Patrick O'Flaherty, a university professor and politician, says he is a 'transplanted bayman.' The romanticisation of rural life and the idealisation of the independence and natural life of the rural producer, have long been a feature of middle-class culture. It is precisely this romantic view of rural Newfoundland that has been more and more promoted in tourist literature throughout this century to attract middle-class urban dwellers to the country/province.[111] For many of the new middle class, the post-Confederation changes that have brought them into existence have also threatened to destroy 'the Real Newfoundland.'[112] Many come forward to defend the folk against alien hostile forces. The sealing issue is a particularly good example of this. The attack on the sealers by the conservationists is seen as part of a long history of cultural deprecation. It is a strike at the mythical heartland of Newfoundland culture by 'bleeding hearts' and 'urban strangers,' and members of the new middle class respond with fury to the threat.[113] The press and politicians have been only too eager to make the defence of the sealhunt a popular nationalist issue. It has become a highly visible diversionary tactic for politicians, drawing attention away from economic problems, especially unemployment, and from their inability to do anything about these problems. Attention is turned towards a common foe, and the premier of Newfoundland can travel around the world playing white knight by defending the province's honour. As a cultural nationalist issue, which mobilises sentiments for 'the people' (the people and the nation are synonymous) and against outside threatening forces, this builds on a long history of nationalism and resentment and fear of outsiders.[114] It is interesting that some of the more radical cultural chauvinists have united with conservative politicians over the sealing issue in a strong display of nationalist feeling;

for example, the Mummers Troup's Sealing Show was financially supported by the Progressive Conservatives.

While neo-nationalism in Newfoundland has focused on cultural issues, political and economic concerns have become increasingly important, especially in the context of the current economic crisis. The cultural question ultimately comes down to a question of political and economic control.

Neo-nationalism is a phenomenon that reflects the aspirations and anxieties of both the new dependent business community in Newfoundland and the intellectual strata that have been created since Confederation. As Larry Pratt has argued for Alberta, the provincial equivalent of economic nationalism is the 'ideological emblem of a rising middle class.'[115] It must be seen, Pratt continues, as the product of a 'frustrated sense of subordination and dependency among elites in the periphery.'[116] Such elites have high aspirations, yet their progress is blocked by 'uneven diffusions of growth.' These observations, which are paralleled by studies of Quebec separatism (cited earlier), would seem to be most useful for understanding the Newfoundland situation.

Expressions of neo-nationalist sentiment are increasingly to be found amongst the new business and professional strata in Newfoundland. In many ways this is an ambiguous sentiment, both a protest against restricted opportunities for advancement and lack of concern in central Canada for local interests, and an acknowledgement of the realities of Newfoundland's dependence on the federal government for revenue. In the present crisis, however, local business interests are more and more seen to be at odds with national priorities and policy. Actions in the national interest are often seen to favour Ontario capitalists, for example. The interest in greater political and economic independence among the entrepreneurs of the new middle class and their associated professional groups is grounded in the need for improved conditions of trade and capital accumulation. A strong local state, along with 'Buy Newfoundland' campaigns and the like, can help further and protect the interests of local capital. The economic crisis brings intensified competition in all spheres of life, for profits especially, but also for jobs. There is a scramble for development, in which separatism is used as a threat to central governments, but is also held out as a possible solution to problems for aspiring, supplanting middle-class groups in areas like Newfoundland.

But neo-nationalist sentiment is not confined to the business section of the new middle class. The economic crisis is having a profound effect on intellectuals. Opportunities for employment in both public and private sectors have begun to dry up in the 1970s. A body of people with highly developed career expectations is becoming frustrated. As federal politician James McGrath said recently in an interview,

separatism is even beginning to rear its ugly head amongst young Newfoundlanders who are beginning to question the system because, after all, you look at all these young kids that are coming out of our beautiful university ... out of our beautiful trade schools, and there are no jobs for them and they don't want to leave, and they are wondering why there are no jobs.[117]

Currently, for example, there are some 1,000 unemployed teachers in the province. These people are part of a group that is not fully integrated into the new Newfoundland either as beneficiaries or as victims, and it is among such intermediate strata of the population that, as Hobsbawm notes,[118] nationalist sentiments often arise. Given the problems that are being experienced by this group and their exposure to various interpretations of them—dependency theory and neo-nationalism—it is not surprising that this group might view independence as a possible solution to some of these problems.

In an area like Newfoundland, the new middle class can only really maintain its material base during periods of state expansion and state-directed growth. Hence the importance attached, in the neo-nationalist scenario, to resource development and to more local control of such developments (the fishery, oil, etc.). Such a period of growth would be one in which state enterprise takes the form of public works for the benefit of the business community and the urban middle class.[119] Such a strategy is already in evidence in the policies of the Progressive Conservatives. They have a dual development strategy of major resource exploitation and small business promotion.[120] Multi-national development of such resources as oil and fish will provide spin-off opportunities for local capital, in this strategy, while state development of other industries, such as tourism, will open up other avenues for investment, and also provide a few jobs. To ensure that such a policy would work, however, there is a move towards more provincial control of such developments.

In general, then, a section of the new petite bourgeoisie sees an increased degree (as yet undetermined) of political independence as a prerequisite for its economic and cultural goals. Such a programme would, however, depend on having strategic resources that could be exploited and could provide the financial basis of a strong state structure: it would also have to gain more widespread support to become a reality.

In fact, elements of this programme are already being established. Considering its position in the social division of labour and its role in the production and distribution of the ideological and cultural context of life, the new middle class is in a strong position to colour the interpretation of events. It is thus possible for a neo-nationalist programme to fill the political vacuum that exists in the province.

It is significant in this regard that the intellectual section of the new middle class is important in union leadership. Working-class leadership has very often come from middle-class intellectuals. In underdeveloped areas where there is little in the way of a heritage of independent working-class initiative and action, it is quite usual for unions to be led by members of the middle class; for example, lawyers. There is, therefore, a danger that union policy can come to reflect the interests and aspirations of the new middle class rather than the self-interests of workers. The new middle class may offer the working class a planned utopia, most likely along the lines of Scandinavian social democracy. This would involve more industrial democracy and union involvement in planning as well as more control over capital, and more local autonomy. This kind of programme, playing on fears of unemployment and offering a possible way out of economic problems, may be able to attract working-class support (at least until it is clear that the programme is not working). Such support depends, however, on the possiblity of workers' being persuaded that their interests are similar to those of the local capitalists, or at least that they will benefit from the development of small business.

Finally, it is worth mentioning that the new middle-class intelligentsia contains within it a broad spectrum of opinion, including conservatives, social democrats, separatists, and socialists. That it is drawn politically towards neo-nationalism and to a generally populist perspective is not really surprising. In areas where the working class is politically underdeveloped and small, the lessons of the working-class movement are not part of the agenda for those wishing to alter society. In such situations it is quite common for a kind of populism to be developed in an effort to mobilise other social groups—the unemployed, small producers, rural inhabitants, and other underprivileged and dissatisfied sections of the population—in order to try to alter society.

CONCLUDING COMMENTS

In this paper it has been argued that neo-nationalism in Newfoundland is basically the expression of the activities and interests of a particular class, the new petite bourgeoisie. It has also been suggested that neo-nationalism cannot solve the general problem of underdevelopment in Newfoundland. What appears, for some, to be a radical movement for change does, in fact, only marginally challenge the basic institutions and structures of our economic system: private ownership of the means of production, multinationals, etc. The neo-nationalist interpretation of the causes of regional underdevelopment does not get to the root of those causes. The political programme is basically a reformist one. The class that has its interests embodied in such a programme simply seeks promotion of its own interests and a better deal *within* the system. It should also be noted that while such a movement can force some changes on the state and even on international capital, both are capable of accepting such changes and turning them to their own advantage.

The independence and autonomy that the neo-nationalists advocate would appear to be unattainable, judging from experiences elsewhere. Such a programme would simply reconstitute a new kind of dependency. New independent states would still exist under the sufferance of the major powers and would still be economically dependent on an international capitalist system, which they can have little hope of influencing.[121]

The challenge from the periphery in fact consists of a series of pinpricks against the imperialist system, separate in time and space, rather than a unified assault. The challenge is particularistic and chauvinistic when applied to both areas and groups of people. The 'centres' remain powerful and can ward off, accommodate, co-opt, or diffuse the assault.[122]

International capitalism has to a very considerable degree already adjusted to economic nationalism and in many parts of the world turned it to its favour. As Norman Girvan[123] and Eric Hobsbawm[124] point out, there are positive advantages for international capital in having new states with formal ownership and administration of resource industries. First, for a multinational economy, the optimal strategy may be one where the number of autonomous political units is maximised and their strength and size minimised. Under such circumstances, it is easier for foreign capital to negotiate to further its interests. Second, states directly assume the risks of fluctuations in international markets and of economic crises. Third, this strategy neutralises a number of political problems for international capital. The ownership issue is defused and stability of supply is thus made more likely; i.e., because the question of ownership is no longer a source of conflict. Multinationals are also freed from the task of having to deal with labour problems (this will be done by the state) and from being accused of foreign exploitation of indigenous labour.

Not only capital, but also the state structure in most countries, can also accommodate nationalist-separatist movements by granting certain reforms. Change from above, in the form of the centralised state's granting more regional autonomy, even if it is a result of pressure from below, can help defuse neo-nationalist sentiment. What Christopher Lasch calls a 'repressive decentralization'[125] may be used to ease the cultural problem. However, this might simply allow for community control of culture while centralised control of production remains and the underlying reality of class domination is unchanged. In light of the comments made above, however, it seems generally that any devolution of economic and political power will do little to solve the basic problems of inequality, poverty, and unemployment in underdeveloped areas. Neo-nationalism, in addition, may divide the working class at a time when unity in the fight to protect their interests in the face of the worsening economic situation is more and more important.

NOTES

The original version of this paper was prepared for the annual conference of the Atlantic Association of Sociologists and Anthropologists (St John's, March 1978). Many people have provided encouragement and assistance during the preparation of this paper. In particular, I would like to thank Judith Adler, Bob Brym, Richard Fuchs, Jim Sacouman, and Lee Seymour.

1. A variety of terms are used. See, for example, Tom Nairn, *The break-up of Britain: crisis and neo-nationalism* (London, 1977); Eric Hobsbawm, 'Some reflections on *The break-up of Britain*,' *New Left Review*, no 105 (1977), 3-23; Ernest Mandel, *Capitalism and regional disparities* (Toronto, 1973); and N. Poulantzas, *Classes in contemporary capitalism* (London, 1975). The terms are used interchangeably here; however, it can be argued that because Newfoundland was once a nation-state, the term neo-nationalism is the most appropriate one.

2. Nairn, *The break-up of Britain*; Hobsbawm, 'Some reflections on *The break-up of Britain*;' S. Chandra et al., *Regionalism and national integration* (Jaipur, 1976); Nicole Arnaud and Jacques Dofny, *Nationalism and the national question* (Montreal, 1977).

3. Paul Harrison, 'The Shetland's separate state,' *New Society*, 27 January 1977, 169-71.

4. Gilles Bourque and Nicole Laurin-Frenette, 'Social classes and nationalist ideologies in Quebec, 1760-1970,' *Capitalism and the national question in Canada*, ed. G. Teeple

(Toronto, 1972), 184-210; 'The November 15 elections and Quebec: an editorial statement,' *Our Generation*, XI, no 4 (1976), 3-10; Henry Milner, 'The decline and fall of the Quebec Liberal regime: contradictions in the modern Quebec state,' *The Canadian state: political economy and political power*, ed. Leo Panitch (Toronto, 1977), 101-132.

5. E. Le Roy Ladurie, 'Occitania in historical perspective,' *Review*, I (1977), 21-30; Hobsbawm, 'Some reflections on *The break-up of Britain*.'

6. The province of Newfoundland includes Labrador, where, in turn, there is a growing separatist movement; W. A. Fowler, 'The growth of political conscience in Labrador,' *The Newfoundland Quarterly*, LXXII, no 4 (1976), 38-44.

7. Eugene Kamenka, 'Political nationalism—the evolution of the idea,' *Nationalism: the nature and evolution of an idea*, ed. E. Kamenka (Canberra, 1973), 6.

8. Karl Marx, *The eighteenth Brumaire of Louis Bonaparte* (Moscow, 1967); Nigel Harris, *Beliefs in society: the problem of ideology* (Harmondsworth, 1968); N. Poulantzas, *Political power and social classes* (London, 1973).

9. Harris, *Beliefs in society*, 44.

10. G. Nowell-Smith, 'Commonsense,' *Radical Philosophy*, VII (1974), 15.

11. Kevin McDonnell, 'Ideology, crisis and the cuts,' *Capital and Class*, IV (1978), 34-69; Simon Clarke, 'Marxism, sociology and Poulantzas' theory of the state,' *Capital and Class*, II (1977), 1-31.

12. McDonnell, 'Ideology, crisis and the cuts,' 35.

13. Simon Clarke, 'Capital, fractions of capital and the state: "neo-Marxist" analyses of the South African state,' *Capital and Class*, V (1978), 32-77.

14. Marx, *The eighteenth Brumaire*, 38.

15. E. P. Thompson, 'Romanticism, moralism and utopianism: the case of William Morris,' *New Left Review*, no 99 (1976), 83-111.

16. Harris, *Beliefs in society*, 87.

17. Thompson, 'Romanticism, moralism and utopianism.'

18. Eric Hobsbawm, 'Some reflections on nationalism,' *Imagination and precision in the social sciences*, ed. T. J. Nossiter (London, 1972), 385-406; Eric Hobsbawm, *The age of capital, 1848-1875* (London, 1975), 82-97; Hobsbawm, 'Some reflections on *The break-up of Britain*;' Nairn, *The break-up of Britain*.

19. For some information on this for Atlantic Canada, see Tom Naylor, *The history of Canadian business, 1867-1914* (2v., Toronto, 1975); and T. W. Acheson, 'The National Policy and the industrialisation of the Maritimes, 1880-1910,' *Acadiensis*, I (1972), 3-28.

20. Hobsbawm, 'Some reflections on *The break-up of Britain*.'

21. Alberto Martinelli and Eugenio Somaini, 'Nation states and multinational corporations,' *Kapitalstate*, I (1973), 71.

22. Hobsbawm, 'Some reflections on *The break-up of Britain*,' 6.

23. Nairn, *The break-up of Britain*, 28.

24. Peter Neary, 'Democracy in Newfoundland: a comment,' *Journal of Canadian Studies*, IV (1969), 43; J. H. Calhoun, 'The national identity of Newfoundlanders' (unpub. PhD thesis, University of Pittsburgh, 1970); K. Matthews, Lectures on the history of Newfoundland, 1500-1830, 'The origins of Newfoundland nationalism' (unpub. MS, Memorial University, 1973), 249-54.

25. According to Matthews, the first phase of nationalism in Newfoundland was focused on members of a newly formed colonial elite, many of whom were from Britain and were carving out a place for themselves within the British imperial system. Nationalism became widely adopted and the appeal to local identity and prejudice was a weapon for the elite. It was a nationalism that cursed outsiders while at the same time took pride in being part of the British Empire. See Matthews, 'The origins of Newfound-

land nationalism.'

26. Harry Cleaver, 'Internationalisation of capital and mode of production in agriculture,' *Economic and Political Weekly*, 27 March 1976, 3.

27. In fact, Newfoundland has been the province of Canadian banks since the 1890s.

28. Richard Gwyn, *Smallwood: the unlikely revolutionary* (Toronto, 1968); Parzival Copes and G. Steed, 'Regional policy and settlement strategy: constraints and contradictions in Newfoundland's experience,' *Regional Studies*, IX (1975); Ralph Matthews, 'Paths of change: Newfoundland's social and economic development 1949-1974' (unpub. paper, Dept of Sociology, McMaster University, 1974); D. Alexander, 'Development and dependence in Newfoundland, 1880-1970,' *Acadiensis*,IV (1975), 3-31; James Overton, 'Uneven regional development in Canada: the case of Newfoundland,' *Review of Radical Political Economy*, X no 3 (1978), 106-116.

29. Parzival Copes, 'The fishermen's vote in Newfoundland,' *Canadian Journal of Political Science*, III (1970), 585-88.

30. Ellen Antler and James Faris, 'Adaption to changes in technology and government policy: a Newfoundland example (Cat Harbour)' (paper presented before the Ninth International Congress of Anthropological and Ethnological Sciences, September 1973).

31. G. Stevenson, 'Federalism and the political economy of the Canadian state,' *The Canadian state*, Panitch, 71-100.

32. C. Gonick, *Inflation or depression* (Toronto, 1975), 94-98; Gary Teeple, 'The limits of nationalism,' *Canadian Dimension*, XII, no 6 (1977), 30-31.

33. D. Alexander, 'Weakness at the centre,' *Canadian Forum*, LVI (1976), 15-17.

34. R. Deaton, 'The fiscal crisis of the state in Canada,' *The political economy of the state*, ed. D. Roussopoulos (Montreal, 1973), 18-58.

35. Matthews, 'Paths of change,' 13.

36. For a discussion of changes in the Nova Scotia fishing industry, including fishermen's reactions to conditions in the salt-fish trade and the newly developed fresh-fish trade, see chapter 6 of this volume.

37. D. Alexander, *The decay of trade: an economic history of the Newfoundland salt fish trade, 1935-1965* (St John's, 1977).

38. Stratford Canning, 'The illusion of progress: rural development policy since 1949,' *Canadian Forum*, LIII (1974), 22-23.

39. Ivan Illich, *Tools for conviviality* (London, 1973); E. F. Schumacher, *Small is beautiful* (London, 1974); Denis Goulet, 'Ethical strategies in the struggle for world development,' *Sociological Inquiry*, XLVI (1976), 281-90.

40. St John's *Evening Telegram*, 6 April 1968.

41. Ralph Matthews, *There's no better place than here: social change in three Newfoundland communities* (Toronto, 1976).

42. James Overton and Lee Seymour, 'Towards an understanding of rural social change: a critique of *There's no better place than here*,' *Our Generation*, XII (1977), 58-64, and 'Unemployment in Newfoundland: a review of the report of the People's Commission on Unemployment, "Now that we've burned our boats," '*Our Generation*, XIII (1979), 50-60.

43. Harris, *Beliefs in society*, 83-84.

44. It is perhaps worth noting that Arensberg and Kimball, the originators of a whole tradition in the study of community and community development, were influenced in their original work on the west of Ireland in the 1930s by the writings of a group of people (mainly Dubliners) who were involved in the Irish Renaissance of the 1890s. Peter Gibbon argues that this led to a distinct tendency to romanticise and idalise the rural community by writers following this tradition; Peter Gibbon, 'Arensberg and Kimball revisited,' *Economy and Society*, II, no 4 (1973), 479-98.

45. Ralph Matthews, 'Ethical issues in policy research: the investigation of community resettlement in Newfoundland,' *Canadian Public Policy*, I (1975), 204-216; Parzival Copes, 'Ethical issues in policy research: a comment,' *Canadian Public Policy*, I (1975), 578-80.

46. Cabot Martin, 'Newfoundland's case on offshore minerals: a brief outline,' *Ottawa Law Review*, VII (1975), 34-61

47. P. O'Flaherty, 'Newfoundland writing, 1949-1974: a comment,' *Canadian Forum*, LIII (1974), 28-30.

48. Alexander, 'Development and dependence,' 27; and 'Newfoundland's traditional economy and development to 1934,' *Acadiensis*, V (1976), 76-77.

49. Canning, 'The illusion of progress,' 23.

50. *Ibid.*

51. L. Harris, 'The Atlantic region: an expedient fiction,' Memorial University of Newfoundland, *Gazette*, 18 November 1977, 4-5; Canning, 'The illusion of progress.'

52. *Evening Telegram*, 16 December 1978.

53. Harris, 'The Atlantic region,' 4.

54. Canning, 'The illusion of progress,' 23.

55. Harris, 'The Atlantic region,' 5.

56. *Financial Post*, 12 June 1976.

57. Martin, 'Newfoundland's case on offshore minerals;' Stratford Canning and Gordon Inglis, 'But will it make sope? Prospects for offshore petroleum development in Newfoundland,' a paper presented before the International Seminar on Marginal Regions, Plockton, Scotland, July 1977.

58. Newfoundland and Labrador, House of Assembly, *Budget*, 1978.

59. The April Fools, 'Why are we celebrating?' (St John's, April 1974).

60. Harrison, 'The Shetland's separate state.'

61. Clyde Rose in his foreword to Ted Russell, *The Holdin' Ground* (Toronto, 1974); O'Flaherty, 'Newfoundland writing;' Martin, 'Newfoundland's case on offshore minerals,' 54.

62. Martin, 'Newfoundland's case on offshore minerals,' 54.

63. M. Morgan, 'Excerpt from the president's report,' *The Morning Watch*, II, no 1 (1974), 3.

64. *Ibid.*

65. Nairn, *The break-up of Britain*, 340. See also Hobsbawm, *The age of capital*, 82-97, 277-302 and G. L. Mosse, *The culture of western Europe* (Chicago, 1974), 31-68.

66. Ernst Fischer, *The necessity of art* (Harmondsworth, 1967), 56.

67. Martin, 'Newfoundland's case on offshore minerals,' 54.

68. Gwyn, *Smallwood*, 62-63.

69. Neary, 'Democracy in Newfoundland,' 43.

70. Calhoun, 'The national identity of Newfoundlanders,' 49; Neary, 'Democracy in Newfoundland,' 43.

71. Neary, 'Democracy in Newfoundland,' 43.

72. Gwyn, *Smallwood*, 63, 181-98; Calhoun, 'Traditional identity of Newfoundlanders.'

73. Tom Nairn, 'Old nationalism and new nationalism,' *The red paper on Scotland*, ed. G. Brown (Edinburgh, 1975), 49.

74. *Intermediate adaptation in Newfoundland and the Arctic: a strategy of social and economic development*, ed. M. M. R. Freeman (St John's, 1969); Cato Wadel, *Marginal adaptations and modernization in Newfoundland* (St John's, 1969); Hugh Whalen, 'Public policy and regional disparity,' *Canadian Forum*, LV (1974), 19-21; Alexander, 'Newfoundland's traditional economy;' and T. H. Gorvin, *Papers relating to a long range reconstruction policy in Newfoundland* (St John's, 1938), 20-21, 40.

75. Matthews, *There's no better place than here*; and 'Canadian regional development strategy: a dependency theory perspective,' *Plan Canada*, XVII,no 2 (1977), 131-41.

76. Stratford Canning, 'Existence rationality and rural development policy in New-foundland,' *The Morning Watch*, II, no 4 (1975), 13-17; Matthews, *There's no better place than here*; F. D. McCracken and R. D. S. MacDonald, 'Science for Canada's Atlantic inshore seas fishery,' Fisheries Research Board of Canada, *Journal*, XXXIII, no 9 (1976), 2097-139; Overton and Seymour, 'Towards an understanding of rural social change;' James Overton, 'An evaluation of the "small is beautiful" model in rural/regional development,' a paper presented before the meetings of the Institute of British Geographers, Manchester, January 1979.

77. Martin, 'Newfoundland's case on offshore minerals;' Canning and Inglis, 'But will it make sope?'

78. James Overton, 'Economic romanticism in Newfoundland rural development strategies,' a paper presented before the Canadian Association of Geographers, Regina, June 1977; Overton and Seymour, 'Towards an understanding of rural social change.'

79. Angus Stewart, 'The social roots,' *Populism; its meanings and national characteristics*, ed. G. Ionescu and E. Gellner (London, 1969), 180-96; Frank Hearn, 'Remembrance and critique: the uses of the past for discrediting the present and anticipating the future,' *Politics and Society*, V, no 2 (1975), 201-227; Overton, 'Economic romanticism.'

80. Newfoundland and Labrador Federation of Labour, People's Commission on Unemployment, *Report*, (St John's, 1978); Overton and Seymour, 'Unemploument in Newfoundland.'

81. People's Commission on Unemployment, *Report*, 66.

82. *Ibid.*, 67.

83. *Ibid.*, 62.

84. Closely related to the dependency perspective are a number of other models of underdevelopment, including what is called metropolis-hinterland, or centre-periphery, theory and the theory of internal colonialism. Often integrated with this perspective is the dual economy model. According to the latter, Newfoundland's economy has two 'spheres' which are worlds apart; a modern one and a traditional one. For a detailed outline of this theory and some critical comments on it, see Overton, 'An evaluation of the "small if beautiful" model.'

85. Harris, 'The Atlantic region,' 5.

86. Colin Leys, 'Underdevelopment and dependency: critical notes,' *Journal of Contemporary Asia*, VII, no 1 (1977), 92-107.

87. H. Friedmann and J. Wayne, 'Dependency theory: a critique,' *Canadian Journal of Sociology*, II (1977), 399-416; Leys, 'Underdevelopment and dependency;' Henry Veltmeyer, 'Dependency and underdevelopment: some questions and problems,' *Canadian Journal of Political and Social Theory*, II no 2 (1978), 55-71.

88. Doreen Massey, 'Regionalism: some current issues,' *Capital and Class*, VI (1978), 106-125.

89. The extension service of Memorial University of Newfoundland has recently sponsored a seminar series with the title 'Dependency or development.' The implication is that underdevelopment is due to dependency and that more independence is a prerequisite for development.

90. *Evening Telegram*, 16 December 1978.

91. Canning and Inglis, 'But will it make sope?' Overton, 'An evaluation of the "small is beautiful" model.'

92. Calhoun, 'The national identity of Newfoundlanders;' Parzival Copes, *The resettlement of fishing communities in Newfoundland* (Ottawa, 1972); Alexander, 'Development and dependence.'

93. *Financial Post*, 29 April 1978, 40.

94. Newfoundland and Labrador, House of Assembly, *Budget*, 1978.

95. *Historical statistics of Newfoundland and Labrador*, Supplement (2v., St John's, 1978).

96. This discussion has developed in response to the writings of Poulantzas: *Political power and social classes* and *Classes in contemporary capitalism*. According to Clarke and Wright, Poulantzas' definition. of social class is *not* a Marxist one, but that of classical political economy as modified by bourgeois sociology. See Clarke, 'Marxism, sociology and Poulantzas' theory of the state' and 'Capital, fractions of capital and the state' and E. O. Wright, *Class, crisis and the state* (London, 1978).

97. A. D. Smith, 'Introduction: the formation of nationalist movements,' *Nationalist movements*, ed. A. D. Smith (London, 1976), 1-30; V. Kiernan, 'Nationalist movements and social classes,' *Nationalist movements*, Smith, 110-33.

98. Antonio Gramsci, *Selections from the prison notebooks*, ed. Quentin Hoare and G. Nowell Smith (New York, 1971), 3-33.

99. H. M. Enzenberger, 'On the irresistability of the petty bourgeoisie,' *Telos*, XXX (1976-77), 161-66.

100. Pierre Bourdieu and Luc Boltanski, 'Qualifications and jobs,' trans. Richard Nice (Birmingham, 1977); Eric Hobsbawm, 'The new dissent: the intellectuals, society and the left,' *New Scoiety*, 23 November 1978, 443-45. The important question of the origins of intellectuals in terms of which strata they are recruited from is not dealt with here. Do certain kinds of intellectuals come from certain strata? Are there rural-urban differences?

101. P. E. Willis, 'Human experience and material production: the culture of the shop floor' (Birmingham, 1975).

102. C. Offe and V. Ronge, 'Theses on the theory of the state,' *New German Critique*, VI (1975), 137-47.

103. H. Guidon, 'Social unrest, social class and Quebec's bureaucratic revolution,' *Queen's Quarterly*, LXXI (1964), 150-64; Bourque and Laurin-Frenette, 'Social classes and nationalist ideologies in Quebec, 1760-1970;' Milner, 'The decline and fall of the Quebec Liberal regime;' L. Pratt, 'The state and province-building: Alberta's development strategy,' *The Canadian state*, Panitch, 133-62.

104. Gramsci, *Selections from the prison notebooks*, 258.

105. Ralph Matthews, 'Perspectives on recent Newfoundland politics,' *Journal of Canadian Studies*, III (1974), 21.

106. Peter Neary, ' "Boots and all:" Newfoundland today,' *Canadian Forum*, LIII (1974), 14-16.

107. Newfoundland and Labrador Rural Development Council, 'Canada?' a brief presented before the Task Force on Canadian Unity, 27 October 1977, St John's.

108. *Ibid.*, 4.

109. *Ibid.*, 11.

110. Gramsci, *Selections from the prison notebooks*.

111. James Overton, ' "The real Newfoundland:" a case of mass deception?' a paper presented before the Second Canadian Congress on Leisure Research, Toronto, April 1978.

112. *Ibid.*

113. James Overton, 'Folk heroes, bleeding hearts and urban strangers: themes and issues in the seal hunt controversy,' in preparation.

114. Similar fears were mobilised by Smallwood in his fight to break the influence of the International Woodworkers of America in the late 1950s: Neary, 'Democracy in Newfoundland.'

115. Pratt, 'The state and province-building,' 134.

116. *Ibid.*, 158.

117. Bas Jamieson, 'Separatism is rearing up amongst Newfoundlanders,' *The Village Voice*, I, no 30 (1978), 6.

118. Hobsbawm, 'Some reflections on nationalism.'

119. Pratt, 'The state and province-building,' 155.

120. Overton, 'An evaluation of the "small is beautiful" model.'

121. Hobsbawm, 'Some reflections on *The break-up of Britain*.'

122. H. Lefebvre, *The survival of capitalism* (New York, 1976).

123. Norman Girvan, 'Economic nationalists v. multinational corporations: revolutionary or evolutionary change?' (n.p., n.d.).

124. Hobsbawm, 'Some reflections on *The break-up of Britain*.'

125. Christopher Lasch, *The world of nations* (New York, 1973), 182-202.

Notes about Contributors

STEVEN ANTLER was born in Chicago in 1945, and studied history and economics at the University of Wisconsin and the University of Connecticut. His research interests include economic development, British and Canadian economic history, and environmental economics; he has published a number of articles in these areas. He is currently assistant professor of economics at Memorial University of Newfoundland.

L. GENE BARRETT was born in Halifax in 1952. He studied sociology at King's College, Dalhousie University, and the University of Sussex, and now lectures in sociology at St Mary's University, Halifax. His research interests include dependency theory, regional development, the economy and society of the Maritimes, and all aspects of the fishing industry.

ROBERT BRYM was born in Saint John, New Brunswick, in 1951, and studied at Dalhousie University, the Hebrew University of Jerusalem, and the University of Toronto. Formerly on staff at Memorial University of Newfoundland, he is now assistant professor of sociology at the University of Toronto. He is interested mainly in the class, regional, and ethnic bases of politics in nineteenth and twentieth century Canada and Russia, and has published several books and articles on these subjects.

DAVID FRANK studied history at the University of Toronto and Dalhousie University. He is now a research associate at the College of Cape Breton, where he is working on the economic and social history of Cape Breton in the twentieth century.

BARBARA NEIS was born in North Bay, Ontario, in 1952, and studied sociology at Glendon College, York University, and Memorial University of Newfoundland. Her interests include the study of underdevelopment and social movements.

JAMES OVERTON was born in Lancashire, England, in 1943. He studied geography at the University of Hull, and after working as a planner trained as a teacher in further education. In 1968 he came to Canada and graduated from the University of Western Ontario with a PhD in geography. He taught geography and community and development studies at several Canadian universities, including Memorial University of Newfoundland, and is now assistant professor in the Department of Sociology and Anthropology, Acadia University, Wolfville, Nova Scotia. His current research is focused mainly on political, economic, and cultural aspects of uneven development, especially in Newfoundland.

NOLAN REILLY teaches Canadian social history at the University of Winnipeg. He is researching the working-class response in Amherst, Nova Scotia (1890-1925) to the effects of regional underdevelopment. He is also preparing a biography of Roscoe Fillmore, a prominent Maritime socialist.

R. JAMES SACOUMAN was born in Winnipeg in 1948 and studied sociology at the University of Guelph, Dalhousie University, and the University of Toronto. His research interests include Maritime political economy, uneven development, and social movements, and he has published several articles in these fields. He is currently assistant professor of sociology at Acadia University.

HENRY VELTMEYER was born in Haarlem, Netherlands, in 1944. Having grown up in Australia, he studied and worked for seven years in South America before moving to Canada in 1971. With a degree in history and a Licenciatura in linguistics from the Universidad de Guayaquil, Ecuador, he studied political science and sociology at McMaster University. His interests and publications are in political economy, Canadian society, and social theory. He is currently assistant professor of sociology at St Mary's University in Halifax.

RICK WILLIAMS was born in Windsor, Nova Scotia, in 1945. He did his BA in political science at Acadia University, spent three years doing rural development work in Tanzania, and did an MA in educational theory at the University of Toronto. He is currently a faculty member at the Maritime School of Social Work, where he teaches political economy and regional studies. He is actively involved as a research consultant with fishermen's organisations and other labour unions.

ABOUT THE TYPE

This book was set in Baskerville Roman and Italic, a typeface developed by John Baskerville (1706-75). Baskerville was an English calligrapher, engraver, and printer who worked in Birmingham. His roman is a face of excellent readability and rather broad design. In developing this face Baskerville ignored the tendency towards a more compact design, which at that time was making itself felt. By enhancing the contrast between the main and the connecting strokes Baskerville placed his work outside the province of the old faces, producing a prototype of a new group.